Travel Narratives
from the
Age of Discovery

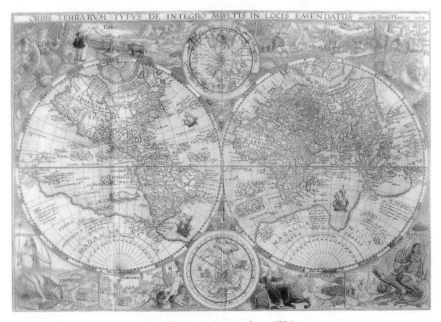

From Jan Huygen van Lischoten, *Itinerario*, Amsterdam, 1596

Travel Narratives
from the
Age of Discovery
An Anthology

Edited by

Peter C. Mancall

OXFORD
UNIVERSITY PRESS

2006

OXFORD
UNIVERSITY PRESS

Oxford University Press, Inc., publishes works that further
Oxford University's objective of excellence
in research, scholarship, and education.

Oxford New York
Auckland Cape Town Dar es Salaam Hong Kong Karachi
Kuala Lumpur Madrid Melbourne Mexico City Nairobi
New Delhi Shanghai Taipei Toronto

With offices in
Argentina Austria Brazil Chile Czech Republic France Greece
Guatemala Hungary Italy Japan Poland Portugal Singapore
South Korea Switzerland Thailand Turkey Ukraine Vietnam

Published by Oxford University Press, Inc.
198 Madison Avenue, New York, New York 10016

www.oup.com

Oxford is a registered trademark of Oxford University Press.

Library of Congress Cataloging-in-Publication Data
Travel narratives from the age of discovery: an anthology / edited by Peter C. Mancall.
p. cm.
Includes bibliographical references (p.).
ISBN-13 978-0-19-515596-9; 978-0-19-515597-6 (pbk.)
ISBN 0-19-515596-3; 0-19-515597-1 (pbk.)
1. Discoveries in geography.   2. Travel, Medieval.   3. Travelers' writings.   I. Mancall, Peter C.
G95.S59 2005   2005040643
910.4'09'031—dc22

1 3 5 7 9 8 6 4 2

Printed in the United States of America
on acid-free paper

For Sophie and Nicholas, world travelers

"In stead of a companion, let the Traveller have always with him some good Book in his pocket ..."

Fynes Moryson, *An Itinerary . . . Containing His ten Yeeres Travell* (London, 1617)

"Our visitors are here. Listen."

Ancient Ojibway prophecy anticipating the arrival of Europeans

Credits

Acknowledgments

I conducted most of the research for this volume in the collections of the Huntington Library in San Marino, California. For their constant support of my work there, I particularly thank the library staff (notably Mona Shulman); Roy Ritchie, the director of research; and David Zeidberg, the director of the library. In the course of preparing this anthology, I have benefited from the wise counsel of a number of individuals, who have helped both with the introduction as well as the selection of materials. In particular, I thank Daniela Bleichmar, Giancarlo Casale, Jennie Evenson, Alison Games, Carina Johnson, Lou Masur, Megan Reid, Alison Sandman, Ben Schmidt, Carole Shammas, Vanessa Schwartz, and Jack Wills, as well as the anonymous readers for the press. I especially want to thank Rolena Adorno for her extraordinary assistance and allowing me to include a long selection from her translation-in-progress of Guaman Poma. For helping this work find a perfect home I am indebted to my incomparable agent, Deirdre Mullane, and to my superb editor at Oxford, Susan Ferber, who arranged for careful external evaluations of earlier versions of the manuscript and offered sage advice throughout the editorial and production process. My production editor, Gwen Colvin, provided crucial assistance. As always, I am in thrall to Lisa Bitel, for her ongoing support for this project and all else.

Contents

Travel Narratives
from the
Age of Discovery

Introduction

"Every landscape appears first of all as a vast chaos, which
leaves one free to choose the meaning one wants to give it."

—Claude Lévi-Strauss, *Tristes Tropiques* (1955)

"Emperors and kings, dukes and marquises, counts, knights, and townsfolk, and all people who wish to know the various races of men and the peculiarities of the various regions of the world, take this book and have it read to you."[1] So began the account of Marco Polo, who traveled from Venice to East Asia in the late thirteenth century and subsequently left behind one of the most famous travel narratives ever written. Though he had spent twenty years away from Italy, his tales would have been lost to posterity had he not gone to war and ended up in a Genoese prison in 1298. That is where he probably met a writer named Rustichello of Pisa, who worked with Polo to write the Venetian's *Travels*. The partnership foretold the future: if news about distant places were to circulate, it would take efforts beyond the experience of travel itself. Traveler to chronicler to reader to listener: in this indirect way, knowledge of foreign places became common currency.

Polo's narrative appeared in Venice in the early fourteenth century, long before Johann Gutenberg had carved his first pieces of movable type and inaugurated (at least in Europe) a revolution in the circulation of ideas. Despite the fact that there was no printing press yet, Polo's ideas circulated across Europe in manuscript. As scribes and translators worked on subsequent editions, Polo's account changed. By the time the brilliant sixteenth-century Venetian chronicler Giovanni Battista Ramusio committed Polo's text to print, his version contained material not found in some of the manuscripts. There is, as a result, no single authoritative edition. As one of Polo's twentieth-century editors noted, though "there is so much diversity of opinion about the actual

1. Marco Polo, *The Travels of Marco Polo*, trans. Ronald Latham (Harmondsworth, Eng.: Penguin, 1958), 33.

3

words used by Polo or his chronicler," those differences "need not, however, shake our faith in the authenticity of the work as a whole." Rather, the discrepancies represent a stark reminder of the ways that texts were (and are) often unstable.[2]

When Ramusio set Polo's account into print in the 1550s in a vast compendium of information titled *Navigationi e Viaggi*, he was part of an intellectual trend that changed the way Europeans understood the world around them. Although Ramusio's efforts reached a primarily European audience, the desire to travel—and to keep accounts of it—was hardly a Western monopoly. At least since antiquity, when Greek poets memorized Homer's tale of the wanderings of Odysseus, peoples across the world had remembered expeditions. The Muslim traveler Abu 'Abdallah ibn Battuta first left his home in Morocco on a pilgrimage to Mecca in 1325, when he was twenty-one years old; by the time he finished his journeys thirty years later he had traveled perhaps 73,000 miles in lands now parts of forty-four nations.[3] Tales of journeys became part of the foundational myths told and retold over the generations. The Tupinambas of Brazil had well-developed rituals for greeting travelers, as the Huguenot writer Jean de Léry recognized.[4] In an age before printing presses could churn out hundreds of copies of a report with less effort than scribes writing by hand, hard-won knowledge about travels survived in manuscripts, some of them copied time and again, or in the memories of those capable of recalling precise details of events they never witnessed. Stories that escaped such refuges often faded away like the wake of a sailing ship cutting through an ocean's waves.

By the late fifteenth century, printing technology in Europe and China (where printing had developed even earlier) helped to preserve and spread more extensive records of travels. More important, travelers generated compelling stories that audiences wanted to read or have read to them. Illustrations of distant lands and peoples made many printed works even more valuable. Travelers also brought back souvenirs. Soon material objects from faraway places began to be displayed more publicly than before, often placed on the shelves, tucked into nooks, and even plastered onto the ceilings of

---

2. Polo, *Travels*, 24–26, quotation at 26. On the various versions of Polo's text, see especially the excellent discussion of this issue in John Larner, *Marco Polo and the Discovery of the World* (New Haven, Conn.: Yale University Press 1999), 68–87, 184–86.

3. Ross E. Dunn, *The Adventures of Ibn Battuta: A Muslim Traveler of the Fourteenth Century* (Berkeley: University of California Press, 1986), 1–3.

4. Jean de Léry, *History of a Voyage to the Land of Brazil, Otherwise called America*, trans. Janet Whatley (Berkeley: University of California Press, 1990), 164.

European private museums known as *wunderkammer* or cabinets of curiosity.[5] The Chinese were avid collectors, studying treatises about collecting and displaying newly acquired things (such as nonindigenous fruit trees) to mark their status.[6] By the mid-sixteenth century, European encyclopedists such as Sebastian Münster and the French royal cosmographer André Thevet produced vast compendia detailing life in distant locales.[7]

There is no doubt that printing technology spread news of distant places to ever larger audiences. But the printed word, however important, remained only one way that information reached from an observer to an audience. Visual images—whether painted on buffalo skins, carved into rocks, or printed—continued to have a substantial impact.[8] So did accounts preserved orally, which were especially crucial to peoples who relied on written languages less than did Europeans or Asians. Inkan *khipu* (or *quipu*), a series of knotted ropes, preserved information as well. As Ramusio informed his readers, "it is possible to find public houses full of those ropes, through which the person who is in charge of them can tell the past events, although they are far in the past, in the same way as we do with our letters."[9]

5. There has been extensive work on early modern collecting in recent years. For the development of cabinets, see, among others, Paula Findlen, *Possessing Nature: Museums, Collecting, and Scientific Culture in Early Modern Italy* (Berkeley: University of California Press, 1994); Marjorie Swann, *Curiosities and Texts: The Culture of Collecting in Early Modern England* (Philadelphia: University of Pennsylvania Press, 2001); and Anthony Alan Shelton, "Cabinets of Transgression: Renaissance Collections and the Incorporation of the New World," in *The Cultures of Collecting*, ed. Jas Elsner and Roger Cardinal (London: Reaktion Books, 1994), 177–203. For changes in the ways that Europeans coped with the transition from manuscripts to books and the need to store information in new ways, see Henry Petroski, *The Book on the Bookshelf* (New York: Alfred A. Knopf, 1999).

6. See Timothy Brook, *The Confusions of Pleasure: Commerce and Culture in Ming China* (Berkeley: University of California Press, 1998); and Craig Clunas, *Superfluous Things: Material Culture and Social Status in Early Modern China* (Urbana: University of Illinois Press, 1991).

7. Münster, *Cosmographia Lib. VI* (Basel, 1552); André Thevet, *Cosmographie Universelle*, 2 vols. (Paris, 1575).

8. See, e.g., Colin G. Calloway, *One Vast Winter Count: The Native American West before Lewis and Clark* (Lincoln: University of Nebraska Press, 2004), esp. 4–6; R. W. Scribner, *For the Sake of Simple Folk: Popular Propaganda for the German Reformation* (Cambridge: Cambridge University Press, 1981).

9. "Se ne trovano case publiche piene di dette corde, con le quai facilme[n]te da ad inte[n]der colui, che n'ha il carico, le cose passate, ben che elle siano di molta eta avanti di lui: si come noi facciamo con le nostre lettere" (Ramusio, *Terzo Volume Delle Navigationi et Viaggi* [Venice, 1556], 4ʳ). *Khipus* have attracted serious attention since the sixteenth century; for the earliest European views and modern analyses, see Jeffrey Quilter and Gary Urton, eds., *Narrative Threads: Accounting and Recounting in Andean Khipu* (Austin: University of Texas Press, 2002).

Ideas also continued to circulate in unpublished manuscripts, often copied and recopied in a process that scholars refer to as "scribal publication."[10] The phenomenon was not new in the sixteenth century. As the historian Anthony Grafton has noted, "communications networks" had "bound intellectuals together across Europe long before 1450."[11] Given the success of manuscripts in spreading information, it is no surprise to discover that handwritten work continued to be produced.[12] The most detailed travel accounts from the Ottoman Empire, Ming China, the Arabic world, and central and South Asia survived in manuscripts for centuries, thereby bearing silent witness to the fact that the printing press, however important to Europeans, was not the only way to preserve what travelers thought about distant places. Some of these texts, notably those describing Islamic travels in search of knowledge (*rihla*), became guides for later pilgrims.[13] Even within Europe, the "irreducible residue of oral culture" (to use the apt phrasing of the historian Carlo Ginzburg) continued to shape understandings of the world, even among those who were literate and had access to learned texts. While the spread of printed books promoted the retention of certain ideas, the transition from a world of oral to written to printed communication was often contested; information once preserved in the telling of stories—the gestures and expressions of the one giving the account, for example—could not survive the transition to the printed page.[14]

10. See Harold Love, *Scribal Publication in Seventeenth-Century England* (Oxford: Oxford University Press, 1993); and Marcel Thomas, "Manuscripts," in Lucien Febvre and Henri-Jean Martin, *The Coming of the Book: The Impact of Printing 1450–1800* (orig. pub. Paris, 1958), trans. David Gerard (London: NLB, 1976), 18–28.

11. Anthony T. Grafton, "The Importance of Being Printed," *Journal of Interdisciplinary History* 11 (1980): 285.

12. As David McKitterick recently observed about the coming of print and its relation to manuscripts, "it is more realistic to speak not of one superseding the other, but of the two working together." See McKitterick, *Print, Manuscript, and the Search for Order, 1450–1830* (Cambridge: Cambridge University Press, 2003), quotation at 21.

13. Suraiya Faroqhi, *Pilgrims and Sultans: The Hajj under the Ottomans, 1517–1683* (London: I. B. Tauris, 1994), 14; and Abderrahmane El Moudden, "The Ambivalence of *Rhila*: Community Integration and Self-Definition in Moroccan Travel Accounts, 1300–1800," in *Muslim Travellers: Pilgrimage, Migration, and the Religious Imagination*, ed. Dale E. Eickelman and James Piscatori (Berkeley: University of California Press, 1990), 75.

14. Carlo Ginzburg, *The Cheese and the Worms: The Cosmos of a Sixteenth-Century Miller* (Baltimore: Johns Hopkins University Press 1980), 59. The linguist Walter J. Ong argued for a more complete shift: "Oral cultures indeed produce powerful and beautiful verbal performances of high artistic and human worth, which are no longer even possible once writing has taken possession of the psyche. Nevertheless, without writing, human consciousness cannot achieve its fuller potentials, cannot produce other beautiful and powerful creations. In this sense, orality needs to produce and is destined to produce writing." See Ong, *Orality and Literacy: The Technologizing of the Word* (London: Methuen,1982), 14–15.

Further, though Europeans embraced the printing press, literacy was far from universal. As one literary critic recently observed, when Francisco Pizarro and the Incan emperor Atahualpa met in November 1532, "they had one thing in common: neither knew how to read."[15]

Still, though travelers' information circulated in these various media, the large volume of European printed accounts from the sixteenth century suggests an audience eager to learn from those who had ventured far from home. But the fact that many accounts appeared in print did not mean that they were accurate or objective. To modern eyes, the claims made on some pages of sixteenth-century printed books seem far-fetched. Rather than dismiss these texts, we must understand them within their own contexts. Sir John Mandeville's fourteenth-century tales of the East, for example, prompted one reader to note that "Mandeville's longest journey was to the nearest library." Yet there are hundreds of surviving accounts of Mandeville's journey, and among those who possessed copies were Leonardo da Vinci and Christopher Columbus.[16] Further, his claims were in many ways not that different from those of later observers, such as the English cleric and naturalist Edward Topsell, whose two enormous books on animals and serpents included creatures as fabulous as those Mandeville described, or the French anatomist Ambroise Paré, whose tetralogical studies described the monsters to be found in Europe.[17]

From a distance of four centuries, a reader today might be struck by the way that sixteenth-century travel accounts vacillated between admiration and disgust. The Mughal emperor Babur, for example, offered details about the landscape of Hindustan, a territory he had conquered in the 1520s, only to add that "Hindustan is a place of little charm. There is no beauty in its people, no graceful social intercourse, no poetic talent or understanding, no etiquette, nobility or manliness."[18] Yet by 1600, a few particularly sensitive observers had overcome such tendencies and wrote dispassionate ethnographic assessments of foreign societies. That move toward less overtly judgmental accounts represented a stark break with the ways that classical and medieval European

15. Julio Ortega, "Transatlantic Translations," *PMLA* 118 (2003): 25.
16. *The Travels of John Mandeville*, trans. C. W. R. D. Mosely (London: Penguin, 1983), 9–12, quotation at 12.
17. See Edward Topsell, *The Historie of Foure-Footed Beastes* (London, 1607), 12–19; and *Ambroise Paré on Monsters and Marvels*, trans. Janis L. Pallister (Chicago: University of Chicago Press, 1982). Such claims led Topsell's nineteenth-century biographer to note that his work "reflected the credulity of his age"; see *Dictionary of National Biography*, s.v. "Topsell."
18. Zahiruddin Muhammed Babur, *The Baburnama: Memoirs of Babur, Prince and Emperor*, trans. Wheeler M. Thackston (New York: Oxford University Press, 1996), 350.

authorities had described non-Western peoples primarily as savages. Still, the impact of these earlier scholars was enormous; as the anthropologist Margaret Hodgen put it, Europeans "lingered in this twilight of the mind" deep into the sixteenth century, evident in the reluctance even of the educated elite to cast off the prejudices that had built up for so long.[19] The historian Jacques Le Goff went so far as to suggest that Europeans understood the Indian Ocean as if in a trance since they possessed little actual knowledge to chase off the "dreams, myths, and legends" that medieval writers had spun.[20]

The sixteenth century marked a change in the spread of travel accounts. The shift is most evident in European sources, not because Europeans were fairer appraisers than others but because more evidence about their views has survived. Because printers had the technological ability to spread stories and sensed an audience for travel accounts, news about the larger world circulated faster and farther than ever before. What had once been information circulated in manuscript, such as religious texts and detailed historical annals, now became more widely available. This does not mean that earlier journeys had little impact or that travelers from the Mughal, Ottoman, or Ming empires played insignificant roles in the sixteenth century. Rather, with the advent of the printing press, the lessons to be learned from long-distance travel could now spread to a wider audience than the number of people who had access to manuscripts in the age before print. This moment was captured brilliantly by Hans Weigel, the compiler of a costume book printed in Nuremberg in 1577, who stationed emblematic representatives of Europe, Asia, Africa, and the Americas on the cover of his collection. There they stand, warily eyeing each other, a visual tableau of a world made smaller through acts of travel.

But as the peoples of the world looked at each other, they did not always like what they saw. Some of the narratives included here demonstrate that it was possible to be enthusiastic about others' cultures and architecture, most evident in accounts of European travels to East Asia. But the level of criticism

---

19. Margaret Hodgen, *Early Anthropology in the Sixteenth and Seventeenth Centuries* (Philadelphia: University of Pennsylvania Press, 1964), 71. This break with the past could be seen even earlier; as Hodgen argued, "One of the most arresting features of the Columbian account of the indigenous peoples of the New World is its friendliness, freshness, and modernity." For a review of classical and medieval authors, see Hodgen, *Early Anthropology,* 17–77; the quotation about Columbus can be found at 17.
20. Jacques Le Goff, "The Medieval West and the Indian Ocean: An Oneiric Horizon," in Le Goff, *Time, Work, and Culture in the Middle Ages* (Chicago: University of Chicago Press, 1980), 190.

Figure 1. Hans Weigel's *Peoples of the World* (1577)

aimed by travelers against the people they encountered—such as European views of Africans and Americans—suggests that something other than observation was also a subject of the printed reports. Though Europe remained a destination for travelers, many non-Europeans had little obvious motivation to go there. Europe possessed no holy sites for Muslims, and European ships were not known to be necessarily friendly to Muslim men or women, thereby diminishing both the appeal of the Continent and the ease of traveling there for those who wanted to pursue commercial opportunities. Europeans' hostility toward Muslims, evident in repeated aggression against targets in the Islamic world since at least the early fifteenth century, also created a climate of fear that made travel even less appealing.[21] Expelling Jews and Muslims, torturing the unlucky in Inquisitorial auto-da-fé, allowing countless thousands to eke out a marginal existence—Europe was hardly an inviting or civilized place in many instances, even by its own standards.

21. Nabil Matar, ed., *In the Lands of the Christians: Arabic Travel Writing in the Seventeenth Century* (New York: Routledge, 2003), xxv–xxvi.

In the past three decades, scholars have turned a fresh eye to early modern travel accounts, particularly those generated by Europeans.[22] In doing so, they have made one point obvious: it is impossible for modern readers to look at these texts in the same ways as the original audiences for them. As historians, literary critics, and anthropologists have argued, every author constructed his or her narrative according to certain cultural, economic, and ideological constraints. In the sixteenth century, many Europeans, whose accounts dominate the surviving texts because printers published so many of them, had specific political goals, notably the expansion of territories controlled by their nation. This aggressive agenda made itself felt in multiple ways. Some authors exaggerated what they saw, especially when they described customs such as cannibalism, which was more prevalent in Europeans' imaginations than in non-European places. Many emphasized what they believed was the primitive quality of non-Europeans' societies, evident (they thought) in styles of dress or a state of undress, rudimentary preparation of food, the practice of some form of paganism or devil worship, and simplistic architectural styles. Even observers who normally described places and peoples without overt condemnation could quickly mock those they encountered. By the eighteenth century, many of these early European accounts came to be linked together in the process that the literary critic Edward Said termed "Orientalism," a form of writing intended to exoticize the "other" in order to provide ideological justification for imperialistic expansion.[23] But it was not only western Europeans who took part in this process of defining others in an effort to establish power over them; the Ottomans, for example, engaged in similar acts.[24]

Every observer carried cultural baggage that shaped each observation.

22. Even the most recent comprehensive view of travel writing essentially ignored accounts by non-Europeans; see Peter Hulme and Tim Youngs, eds., *The Cambridge Companion to Travel Writing* (Cambridge: Cambridge University Press, 2002). For two excellent collections of European (mostly English) sixteenth- and early-seventeenth-century travel writings, see Andrew Hadfield, ed., *Amazons, Savages and Machiavels: Travel and Colonial Writing in English, 1550–1630: An Anthology* (Oxford: Oxford University Press, 2001); and Kenneth Parker, ed., *Early Modern Tales of the Orient: A Critical Anthology* (London: Routledge, 1999). For a superb collection that inverts this trend (of publishing European accounts), see Matar, *In the Lands of the Christians*. For an earlier assessment of travel within Europe and by Europeans, see E. S. Bates, *Touring in 1600: A Study in the Development of Travel as a Means of Education* (Boston, 1911).
23. "Taking the late eighteenth century as a very roughly defined starting point," Said wrote, "Orientalism can be discussed and analyzed as the corporate institution for dealing with the Orient—dealing with it by making statements about it, authorizing views of it, describing it, by teaching it, settling it, ruling over it: in short, Orientalism as a Western style for dominating, restructuring, and having authority over the Orient." Edward Said, *Orientalism* (New York: Pantheon, 1978), 3.
24. See Ussama Makdisi, "Ottoman Orientalism," *American Historical Review* 107 (2002): 768–796, esp. 773–78.

Politics invariably influenced perceptions, as did imperial rivalries and religious agendas. As two scholars of Islam have noted, "Muslim doctrine explicitly enjoins or encourages certain forms of travel," including *hajj* (pilgrimage to Mecca), *hijra* (obligatory migration to practice freely), *ziyaras* (travel to shrines), and *rihla* and *talab al-ʿilm* ("travel in search of knowledge"). These categories were not always distinct; Muslim travelers might journey for more than a single purpose.[25] Gender too determined the content of an account, though the fact that the vast majority of surviving texts from the period before 1600 were produced by men makes it difficult to know what alternative observations women travelers might have offered. Still, based on evidence from the modern era, it is likely that women's narratives, had they survived in greater number, would have portrayed very different scenarios. Given the centrality of gendered language in the surviving texts, the absence of a large number of female authors leaves the modern reader with little recourse to what are often particularly male representations of other places.[26]

The writing or recitation of travel accounts was part of the fabric of life in the sixteenth century, as at other times. But being common did not mean that these texts are wholly reliable. Travelers were famous for making exaggerations and distortions, and centuries later it is often impossible to tell exactly when their tales departed most seriously into a realm closer to fiction than nonfiction.[27]

25. Dale F. Eickelman and James Piscatori, "Social Theory in the Study of Muslim Societies," in *Muslim Travellers: Pilgrimage, Migration, and the Religious Imagination* (Berkeley: University of California Press, 1990), ed. Eickelman and Piscatori, 5. None of these concepts has been static over time. *Hijra*, for example, was the subject of debate, as the fourteenth-century scholar Ibn Khaldun recognized when he made a distinction between the obligation to migrate centuries earlier (during the lifetime of the Prophet Muhammad) and during his own time; see Muhammad Khalid Masud, "The Obligation to Migrate: The Doctrine of *hijra* in Islamic Law," in *Muslim Travellers*, 29–49, esp. 30–33. The search for knowledge in the concepts of *rihla* and *talab al-ʿilm* similarly shifted; see Sam I. Gellens, "The Search for Knowledge in Medieval Muslim Societies: A Comparative Approach," in *Muslim Travellers*, 50–65.

26. For one assessment of nineteenth- and twentieth-century travel accounts that pays particular attention to issues of gender, see Sara Mills, *Discourses of Difference: An Analysis of Women's Travel Writing and Colonialism* (London: Routledge, 1991). For an assessment of how the recognition of gender has shaped historical accounts in the Pacific, see Nicholas Thomas, "Partial Texts: Representation, Colonialism, and Agency in Pacific History," in *In Oceania: Visions, Artifacts, Histories*, ed. Nicholas Thomas (Durham, N.C.: Duke University Press, 1997), 40–42. For a review of issues related to gender in travel writing, see Susan Bassnett, "Travel Writing and Gender," in *Cambridge Companion to Travel Writing*, ed. Peter Hulme and Tim Youngs (Cambridge: Cambridge University Press, 2002), 225–41.

27. For an analysis of how travel shaped fiction and nonfiction in the eighteenth century in western Europe (primarily Britain and France), with a particular focus on "travel accounts that in the Age of Reason told untruths" and with authors who used deception "for the sake of money, pride, or a point of view," see Percy G. Adams, *Travelers and Travel Liars, 1660–1800* (Berkeley: University of California Press, 1962), quotation at vii.

The surviving texts themselves are, as the literary critic Philip Edwards put it, "flawed renderings of the perceptions—flawed by defect of language and failure of memory and self-protective falsehood." All readers of these tales now must recognize that each narrative is inherently partial, containing the details that the tale teller felt the audience would most likely appreciate, the bits of information that the traveler could remember and felt compelled to report. The noted anthropologist Claude Lévi-Strauss recognized that the stories travelers told reflected their transitory experiences. "Exploration is not so much a covering of surface distance as a study of depth," he wrote in *Tristes Tropiques* in the mid-twentieth century, "a fleeting episode, a fragment of landscape or a remark overheard may provide the only means of understanding and interpreting areas which would otherwise remain barren of meaning." For many travelers, the act of telling their story was as important to the journey as actual participation on it. The widespread availability of these tales, at least in Europe, suggests too that editors and printers stood ready to expend energy and money to spread these reports, often calling them "true" accounts to proclaim their accuracy.[28]

As will become evident in many of the texts contained in this anthology, all tale tellers arrived in distant places with viewpoints shaped by their home societies, mental maps that gave meaning to what they were seeing. None saw a scene *de novo* but, instead, looked upon peoples and landscapes through ideologies already well formed.[29] As the historian Anthony Pagden wrote about the earliest European encounters with the Western Hemisphere, "Observers in America, like observers of anything culturally unfamiliar for which there exist few readily available antecedents, had to be able to classify *before* they could properly see." They made their classifications through series of analogies—comparisons between what they observed and what they already knew.[30] That act appears repeatedly in the accounts here. Further, rather

28. Lévi-Strauss, *Tristes Tropiques* (1955), trans. John and Doreen Weightman (New York: Atheneum, 1974), 47–48. The information in this paragraph owes much to Philip Edwards's superb introduction to his *Last Voyages: Cavendish, Hudson, Ralegh: The Original Narratives* (Oxford: Oxford University Press, 1988), 1–17, quotation at 14. See also Chloe Chard, *Pleasure and Guilt on the Grand Tour: Travel Writing and Imaginative Geography, 1600–1830* (Manchester, UK: Manchester University Press, 1999), 9.
29. See Clifford Geertz, "Ideology As a Cultural System," in *The Interpretation of Cultures* (New York: Basic Books, 1973), 193–233, esp. 220.
30. Anthony Pagden, *The Fall of Natural Man: The American Indian and the Origins of Comparative Ethnology* (Cambridge: Cambridge University Press, 1982), 1–4, quotation at 2; and Donald F. Lach, *The Century of Discovery*, vol. 1 of *Asia in the Making of Europe* (Chicago: University of Chicago Press, 1965), 2: 686–87.

than being static categories, these same places became transformed in later accounts, and these changes reflected the observers' increased knowledge of what they saw on their travels—knowledge that was quite possibly gleaned from earlier travelers. When travel turned to settlement, observers' views became more detailed, though comparisons still appeared in their texts, sometimes quite explicitly.[31] The Jesuit Luis Fróis, for example, produced a lengthy work comparing Europeans to the Japanese after he had lived in Japan for more than two decades, perhaps as a guide to the missionaries who would arrive later.

Yet for all the problems modern readers have navigating these travel accounts, the texts that survive should not be dismissed as revealing more about the observer than the observed. Many of the travelers whose accounts can be found in this anthology strove to find ways to describe precisely what they saw. Though it is possible that these accounts helped Europeans in particular create an "other" seemingly awaiting the arrival of Christian colonizers, the travelers themselves did not necessarily write their accounts to promote such ventures. As the historian Joan-Pau Rubiés aptly put it, there "is much more to European accounts of non-Europeans than a justification of Empire." Read carefully, these accounts can be used to reveal foreigners struggling to understand new worlds. This is not to suggest that travelers left their political agendas behind. Rather, the ablest of these writers provided posterity with accounts that have proven to be fundamental for scholars trying to understand what particular societies were like. Since the arrival of visitors often transformed the places they landed, reading these early texts becomes one way, however flawed, to grasp what parts of the world looked like centuries ago.[32]

The early modern writers whose travel accounts appear in this collection did not invent the genre of writing about places they visited (or pretended to visit). The earliest account of an East Asian excursion to Europe, for example, dates from the thirteenth century.[33] Nor were the sixteenth-century travelers the first to feel the sensation of wonder about what seemed exotic to them.

31. For particularly well-documented interpretations of how views of natives and newcomers evolved in North America, see Karen Ordahl Kupperman, *Indians and English: Facing Off in Early America* (Ithaca, N.Y.: Cornell University Press, 2000); and Joyce Chaplin, *Subject Matter: Technology, the Body, and Science on the Anglo-American Frontier, 1500–1676* (Cambridge, Mass.: Harvard University Press, 2001).
32. Joan-Pau Rubiés, "New Worlds and Renaissance Ethnology," *History and Anthropology* 6 (1993): 157–97, quotation at 158.
33. Morris Rossabi, *Voyager from Xanadu: Rabban Sauma and the First Journey from China to the West* (Tokyo: Kodansha, 1992).

The Europeans engaged in the task of recounting their experience inhabited a society in which written travel literature had long existed. It constituted part of what the historian Caroline Walker Bynum has termed "the literature of entertainment"—a body of texts (including histories and collections of stories) that "drew on the encyclopedic tradition of the ancient world known as paradoxology—the collection of oddities (including monsters or hybrids, distant races, marvelous lands)—and on antique notions of portents or omens, that is, unusual events that foreshadowed the (usually catastrophic) future and were accompanied by a vague sense of dread." Within that world, travel could bring astonishment, as the Franciscan missionary William of Rubruck learned when he visited the Great Chan in the thirteenth century only to discover that the Chinese thought he was a monster because he did not wear shoes. Those he encountered interpreted his ascetic gesture as a sign that he must not need his feet "since they supposed we should lose them straightaway." William learned that the Chinese expressed wonder at him, thereby anticipating the kind of wonder that travelers frequently engendered among those they visited.[34] The sense of astonishment that medieval Europeans felt occurred time and again in the sixteenth century. Wonder was "not the sign of revulsion," as the literary critic Stephen Greenblatt put it in a commentary on Jean de Léry's account of his voyage to Brazil, "but of ravishment, an ecstatic joy that can be experienced" long after the end of the journey itself.[35] That sense of wonder can be found in most of the texts included here; it is inseparable from the other parts of any travel account.

Long before sailing ships could carry crews across open oceans, groups of people walked or paddled across vast distances. The ancestors of the native peoples of the Americas crossed the Bering Strait land bridge from Siberia between 40,000 and 10,000 years ago, and their descendants fanned out across the Western Hemisphere until some reached the southern tip of South

34. Caroline Walker Bynum, "Wonder," in her *Metamorphosis and Identity* (New York: Zone Books, 2001), 37–75, quotations at 53 and 56; Christopher Dawson, trans., *Mission to Asia* (1955; New York: Harper and Row, 1966), 150. William soon learned that the Chinese were right: shortly after dismissing the locals' questions about whether the Europeans were monsters, he wrote that "the tips of my toes froze so I could no longer go bare-foot" (p. 152). For the medieval context, see Mary B. Campbell, *The Witness and the Other World: Exotic European Travel Writing, 400–1600* (Ithaca, N.Y.: Cornell University Press, 1988).
35. Stephen Greenblatt, *Marvelous Possessions: The Wonder of the New World* (Chicago: University of Chicago Press, 1991), 16.

America. Perhaps more remarkably, Polynesian peoples used long canoes to cross the South Pacific, peopling islands that had previously had no human occupants. Groups of those migrants reached Aoteroa (modern New Zealand) around the turn of the first Christian millennium.[36] The fact of travel was common among the peoples of the Old World too. As one scholar recently noted, "one characteristic of the population [of France] at the end of the Middle Ages was mobility."[37] The same could be said for Muslims, who traveled in large caravans and by ship as well, in journeys that stretched across Europe, Africa, and much of Asia.[38]

Stories of epic journeys abound across Europe. Some told how Empress Helena, the mother of Constantine the Great, traveled from Britain to the Holy Land in the fourth century, a journey that took her from antiquity's periphery to its core. That expedition was well documented and plausible, especially compared to some of the more outrageous travel claims of the Middle Ages. Saint Brendan left Ireland for the "Blessed Isles" sometime in the sixth century, and his supporters have long maintained that he reached the Western Hemisphere. Six hundred years later an explorer named Madoc purportedly sailed from Wales to the West Indies. There is no material evidence that either of these travelers made it far from the western periphery of Europe. Yet their stories survived, and in the age of print they appeared again, nestled against more modern accounts of voyages to distant lands.[39]

Even before the age of large sailing ships it was possible to cross the Atlantic Ocean. Two ancient sagas tell what the Norse found when they began to sail westward from Scandinavia in the late ninth century. The oldest manuscript version of one, known as *Grœnlendinga's Saga*, dates to the late fourteenth century, when an Icelandic settler named Jon Hakonarson wrote it down. It remained in his family for more than 200 years until the king of

---

36. For an overview of the process, see Janet M. Davidson, "The Polynesian Foundation," in *The Oxford History of New Zealand*, ed. Geoffrey W. Rice, 2nd ed. (Auckland: Oxford University Press, 1992), 3–27.
37. "Une des caractéristiques de la population, à la fin du Moyen Age, est la mobilité des hommes": René Germain, "Déplacements temporaires et déplacements définitifs dans le centre de la France aux XIVe et XVe siècles," in *Voyages et Voyageurs au Moyen Age: XXVIe Congrès de la S.H.M.E.S.* (Paris: Publications de la Sarbonne, 1996), 53.
38. See Youssef Ragheb, "Les marchands itinerants du monde Musulman," in *Voyages et Voyageurs* , 177–215.
39. For Helena and Madoc, see Richard Hakluyt, ed., *The Principall Navigations, Voiages, and Discoveries of the English Nation* (London, 1589), 1–2, 506–07. Hakluyt did not include Brendan, though there were many manuscript editions extant by the sixteenth century; see James F. Kenney, *The Sources for the Early History of Ireland: Ecclesiastical* (Dublin: Pàdraic Ó Tàilliūir, 1979), 414–17.

Denmark received it as a gift from a loyal subject. The earliest surviving version of another tale, *Erik's Saga,* was not written down until the fourteenth century, also in Iceland, and it differs in places from another version which was written a century later. All of these sagas were written on vellum, the dried skin of sheep that had been used for centuries to record the most important texts in the West.[40]

According to the sagas, the Norse settled Iceland sometime around 870 A.D. and created the longest lasting colony of Europe. A century or so later they set off to the west again, eventually reaching Greenland, where they established another colony, and by the turn of the first Christian millennium they had reached lands they called Helluland, Markland, and Vinland. The keepers of Norse sagas told their listeners about the lands they found, the climate, the flora and fauna, and details about the people they labeled "skraelings," a term best translated as "wretches" and applied by these visitors to the Thule Inuit they met. *Erik's Saga* provided details about the trade that both natives and newcomers welcomed, but also about conflicts that set them against each other. The Inuit shouted at the Norse when they attacked, the saga recounted, and "when they clashed there was a fierce battle and a hail of missiles came flying over, for the Skraelings were using catapults." The Norse fled in fear, realizing "that although the land was excellent they could never live there in safety or freedom from fear, because of the native inhabitants." As they left they found five sleeping Inuit. Figuring that they were hostile, the Norse murdered them.[41]

The Norse sagas are among the earliest verifiable travel accounts that have survived. Though the authors of such tales left a fainter record than modern readers might want, they told enough about what they had seen to prove that at least some Norse men and women had in fact traveled to distant lands. Archaeological remains at L'Anse aux Meadows in modern Newfoundland confirm that the Norse had made it across the ocean.[42] Such finds give the sagas a kind of confirmation lacking for other ancient tales. The sagas also contained the sorts of details that became common in travel accounts in the

---

40. The manuscript of *Grœndlinga's Saga* can be found in the Royal Library in Copenhagen; the two early manuscripts of *Erik's Saga* are located in the Arnamagnæn Library in Copenhagen. For details about the manuscripts, see *The Vinland Sagas: The Norse Discovery of America,* trans. Magnus Magnusson and Hermann Pálsson (Harmondsworth, Eng.: Penguin, 1965), 29–35.
41. *Vinland Sagas,* 99–101.
42. Birgitta Linderoth Wallace, "The Viking Settlement at L'Anse Aux Meadows," in *Vikings: The North Atlantic Saga,* ed. William W. Fitzhugh and Elisabeth I. Ward (Washington, D.C.: Smithsonian Institution Press, 2000), 208–16.

sixteenth century, telling about conditions at sea, landing places, particular landscapes, animals and fish to be found, and indigenous peoples. Yet though these overseas settlements survived for a few centuries, ultimately the Norse abandoned such colonization ventures, in all likelihood because shifting economic and ecological circumstances made such journeys undesirable.[43]

The Norse expeditions through those frigid waters marked a decisive moment in the history of travel. Though the journeys were not the equal to the Polynesian migrations that had led to the peopling of the South Pacific, these northern voyages generated a body of literature that survived. Those texts became the precursors to the popular European travel accounts of the sixteenth century. In the period after the Norse abandoned their long-distance journeys, other Europeans realized the benefits of travel. Recognizing the potential audience for such tales, printers committed them to paper, thereby immortalizing journeys that might have passed from memory in earlier generations. This anthology brings together some of the most engaging and important accounts produced during that century. Each represents at least one extraordinary journey, and most document journeys to places far from the traveler's home. Virtually all of these accounts were written by Europeans in the century or so after Christopher Columbus's first historic voyage in 1492, and hence typically represent the views of Protestants and Catholics who often felt contempt for the non-Christians they encountered. This collection also includes portions of several vital non-European travel accounts, including excerpts from the fifteenth-century report of Ma Huan detailing Chinese travel to the Middle East, reports of fifteenth-century journeys to India (including parts of the Emperor Babur's account of territory that came under his control in the 1520s when he established the Mughal Empire), and the Peruvian Felipe Guaman Poma's return home after thirty years away.

As literary critics have demonstrated, no text is entirely stable. The words and ideas may change from one edition to the next, and crucial phrases may have been lost or altered in the act of translating accounts from the language of the traveler to that of the individual who spread the news in books, manuscripts, or orally. Before 1600, printers often stole material from authors' books, which meant that some texts circulated widely in pirated editions. To

43. See Alfred W. Crosby, *Ecological Imperialism: The Biological Expansion of Europe, 900–1900* (Cambridge: Cambridge University Press, 1986), 44–56.

this day scholars cannot be certain how many copies of a particular book were printed. In all likelihood publishers printed between 500 and 1,200 copies of any particular text. Some were reprinted often, others appeared only once. The records of the Stationers' Company in England list the titles of works that printers registered in an effort to establish their copyright. But some of those works no longer exist, including travel tales that might have provided yet more information about that age of discovery. There is, for example, no known copy of a book left by a companion of the English mariner Martin Frobisher; his printer claimed that the book included pictures of the peoples met by the sailors in the frozen lands of the North Atlantic.[44]

Still, despite the loss of possibly precious reports, hundreds of accounts have survived. How, then, to make sense of this extraordinary collection of information? One way is to group texts according to the parts of the world described in them, which is the method used here. The accounts in this volume describe voyages to Africa, Asia, the Americas, and Europe. Though there are similarities to be found in observations from one place to another, and similarities in the tone of the observers, the extant records of journeys through these parts of the world reveal startling differences.

Much has been written, and will continue to be written, about the exploits of Christopher Columbus and the significance of his journey of 1492. Yet it is important to see Columbus and the narratives he generated as a product of a particular time and place and to set his achievement into context. He was, for example, not the most successful captain of the fifteenth century, an honor that should be bestowed upon the Chinese mariners who piloted their junks far from home in the early years of the fifteenth century. Their fleet often hugged the coast of Southeast and South Asia, though it also sailed across the Indian Ocean to the Maldives and on to the east coast of Africa as well. Those journeys are well documented, unlike the improbable claim that the Chinese made it to the Americas in 1421.[45]

The largest of these junks measured 400 feet from stem to stern, almost

44. "A discription of the purtrayture and Shape of those strange kinde of people whiche the worthie master MARTIN FFOURBOSIER brought into England in Anno 1576 and 1577," listed in Edward Arber, ed., *A Transcript of the Stationers' Register, 1554–1640*, 5 vols. (London, 1875–1894), 2: 145.
45. For the argument that the Chinese did reach America, see Gavin Menzies, *1421: The Year the Chinese Discovered America* (New York: Bantam, 2002).

five times larger than Columbus's flagship, the *Santa Maria*. The Chinese termed them *bao chuan*—treasure ships—and to build them they harvested timber from deep in the nation's interior, floating the logs down the Min and Yangzi rivers to the ship-building docks. There were perhaps 28,000 sailors involved in the six expeditions that sailed outward from China from 1405 to 1421. They ventured westward toward what their eunuch admiral Zheng He (Cheng Ho) described as the "barbarian regions far away hidden in a blue transparency of light vapors." Yet though the Chinese under the Ming emperor Chéng-tsu managed to create what may have been the largest fleet in the world before the twentieth century, they abandoned their long-distance journeys when the emperor died in 1421. Zheng He led one last epic voyage, which departed from Nanking on January 19, 1431, again reaching the east coast of Africa on a journey ordered by the emperor Hsüan-te. He returned home in 1433, making a triumphal entry into Beijing on July 22, 1433, where the emperor received him. But after the celebration, the Chinese turned their attention inward.[46]

Yet while the Chinese came to ignore the lure of Africa, Europeans and Africans had remained in almost constant contact with each other at least since the fourteenth century. As early as 1150, Europeans had heard news of the legendary Christian king in Africa known as "Prester John" who lived somewhere on the eastern part of the continent near the Indian Ocean; eventually many would come to believe that he could be found in Ethiopia. During the centuries that followed this initial rumor, Africans traveled to Europe, and Europeans traveled to Africa. Over time, an increasing number of the African migrants were slaves, but from the fourteenth century through the sixteenth century—as the slave trade was emerging as one of the dominant institutions of the modern world—African elites sent embassies to European cities for political, military, and religious reasons. Some of these Africans, notably those from Ethiopia, were Christians. In 1306, thirty of these Ethiopian Christians paid a visit to Pope Clement V; he saw them at his palace at Avignon and then sent them to Rome so they could view the magnificent churches of the city. By the end of the fifteenth century, other Ethiopians had journeyed to parts of Europe—bringing leopards to the Venetian doge in 1402, and arriving in Florence in 1441 to seek an alliance with the church, in Naples in 1450 to seek

46. Ma Huan, *Ying-Yai Sheng-Lan: "The Overall Survey of Ocean's Shores,"* trans. J. V. G. Mills (Hakluyt Society, extra ser. 42 [Cambridge, 1970]): 1-18; and Louise Levathes, *When China Ruled the Seas: The Treasure Fleet of the Dragon Throne, 1405–1433* (New York: Simon and Schuster, 1994), 17–20, 75–85.

skilled European artisans, and in Milan in 1459 to buy books. Tasfa Seyon, whom Europeans called Peter the Ethiopian, spent fifteen years in the Vatican in the mid-sixteenth century translating a Missal and a New Testament into Ge'ez, the liturgical language of his homeland. Lisbon became a center for Africans in Europe, many of whom arrived there on Portuguese vessels. African embassies arrived in Portugal from the kingdom of Kongo in 1484, Benin in 1486, and the Jolof kingdom in 1487 and 1488. When another embassy from Kongo arrived in 1488, its members helped transform Lisbon's monastery of Saint Eloy into what one historian has called "a second center of African studies in Europe, where Kongolese learned European religious and secular knowledge and where Portuguese missionaries were trained in Kongolese culture." One of those who studied there was Henrique, the grandson of King João, who, along with his wife and son, had been baptized in 1491. After ten years in the monastery, Henrique became a priest; two years later Pope Leo X consecrated him a bishop. As the historian David Northrup has noted, he "was the first sub-Saharan African to become a Catholic bishop—and the last for over 250 years."[47]

Yet though many Africans visited Europe or even studied there, and many returned home, none left behind a travel account that was printed at the time. As a result, there is no exact way of knowing what those Ethiopians thought when they stared at the Basilica of St. Peter at the Vatican or gazed upon the hordes of Venetians on the piazza San Marco, no way to grasp what the monastery in Lisbon must have been like for visiting Kongolese. Though the history of these African embassies can be reconstructed, the record provides only the occasional glimpse into those who experienced it. Their journeys to Europe and then home again took weeks; some, like the prince Henrique, stayed for years. Others, sold into slavery, remained permanently. Most of their stories are gone, though some did survive in manuscript, including the account here of 'Abu-l-Hasan 'Ali al-Tamgruti, a Moroccan who traveled to Turkey in 1589 and wrote a vivid description of Constantinople's Hagia Sofia, the city's wondrous onetime Christian cathedral.

Europeans who went to Africa had better luck preserving their accounts. In the sixteenth century, none could match the impact of the Portuguese, who were at the time Europe's most skilled navigators and had the greatest willingness to travel to Africa. By the mid- to late fifteenth century, the Portu-

47. David Northrup, *Africa's Discovery of Europe, 1450–1850* (New York: Oxford University Press, 2002), 1–6, 34–35, quotations at 5–6 and 35. See also Adrian Hastings, *The Church in Africa, 1450–1950* (Oxford: Oxford University Press, 1994), 46–86.

guese had established colonies in the eastern Atlantic and began to extract wealth from Madeira and the Azores.[48] Though the legend that Prince Henry the Navigator established a center for navigators at Sagres dates from a later period and is quite probably more myth than history, he nonetheless played a crucial role in the ascendancy of the Portuguese as the master sailors of this age.[49] They recognized that travel by sea was quicker and thus cheaper than overland expeditions, such as medieval Crusaders' journeys to the Holy Land and the caravans that continued to trek across the ancient Silk Road. Those earlier travelers had demonstrated the benefits to be had from long-distance trade. The trick by the fifteenth century was how to make that commerce more efficient.

Bartholomeu Dias was only ten years old when Henry died, but he was one of the many who benefited from the Portuguese desire to learn about the patterns of winds and waves on the seas. When he was thirty-seven, Dias led an expedition around the Cape of Good Hope into the Indian Ocean and, in the process, helped the Portuguese create a maritime empire that would become the most important and profitable of its time. The mariner Vasco da Gama followed the route pioneered by Dias but went farther, reaching India and thereby providing the information the Portuguese would use to attempt to control the spice trade. He made observations of the places and peoples he encountered, including reflections on the Muslims he met in Mozambique in 1498. In his report he claims to have received news of Prester John. But while da Gama mused about the possibilities of Christianity spreading throughout the continent, tensions flared between his crew and local Muslims, a sign that religious hostility threatened European travelers to the region.

Wherever Europeans landed in Africa, they carried a three-part agenda.

48. Felipe Fernández-Armesto, *Before Columbus: Exploration and Colonization from the Mediterranean to the Atlantic, 1229–1492* (Philadelphia: University of Pennsylvania Press, 1987), 195–202. As Charles Verlinden pointed out a generation ago, the patterns for European colonization developed initially in the eastern Mediterranean and then moved westward; though there is now an enormous body of scholarship on the diversity of colonial experiences in the Atlantic world, Verlinden's essay remains worthwhile. See *The Beginnings of Modern Colonization: Eleven Essays with an Introduction*, trans. Yvonne Freccero (Ithaca, N.Y.: Cornell University Press, 1970), 3–32.
49. The Venetian traveler Alvise da Cà da Mosto took shelter there in 1454, taking advantage of the fact that Prince Henry had secured at least part of Cape Sagres to assist ships rounding Cape St. Vincent. See Peter Russell, *Prince Henry "the Navigator": A Life* (New Haven, Conn.: Yale University Press, 2000), 6–7, 291–292. The historian Donald F. Lach termed Henry "the guiding genius in the systematic and continuous exploration of the African west coast launched by the Portuguese in the early fifteenth century" (Lach, *Century of Discovery*, 1: 51).

First, they were eager to promote the spread of Christianity and thus welcomed any signs of Prester John's activities. Second, they assessed the peoples they met, typically seeing signs of savagery in what they described as Africans' nudity, idolatry, and cannibalism.[50] Third, they went looking to make a profit, which in Africa meant the purchase of human beings as well as rare commodities. When the English mariner John Lok led an expedition to Guinea in the mid-sixteenth century, those who traveled with him busily marked differences among Africans. According to the account of the journey by George Barne and others, some were "of high stature and black" and others "of browne or tawnie colour, and low stature." Some allegedly resembled the monsters inhabiting the pages of the ancient Greek writer Pliny and the fourteenth-century English knight Sir John Mandeville. The stories Europeans told mixed wonder with disgust. Cannibals and ichthyophagi—people who ate only fish—could be found in the interior of Ethiopia south of the equator, a land where moonbeams purportedly provided heat to counter the evening chill. Tales of nature's marvels blended seamlessly with mundane descriptions of domestic architecture and food preparation, including calculations of the value of the wheat grown in Ethiopia. It is almost impossible to classify this kind of report as anything more than a primitive ethnography, an attempt to render in a few pages an image of an entire continent and its diverse inhabitants.[51]

Most of the surviving sixteenth-century accounts of European travels to Africa were written by clerics, merchants, or ship captains, elite members of their own societies. If they survived their voyages, they returned home to share their knowledge and perhaps profit from their adventure. Some reports indicated how sophisticated Africans had become, especially those who had access to goods brought by a variety of Muslim traders who had long worked in disparate communities in the western Indian Ocean. By the time da Gama made it to the southeast coast of Africa at the end of the century, many locals may have deemed the Europeans' goods inferior to what they already pos-

---

50. As one scholar has noted, these three phenomena were so intertwined in Europeans' minds that "the presence of one could be adduced from the others." See Wyatt MacGaffey, "Dialogues of the Deaf: Europeans on the Atlantic Coast of Africa," in *Implicit Understandings: Observing, Reporting, and Reflecting on the Encounters between Europeans and Other Peoples in the Early Modern Era,* ed. Stuart B. Schwartz (Cambridge: Cambridge University Press, 1994), 261.

51. On the origins and development of the discipline of ethnography, see Hodgen, *Early Anthropology.*

sessed or could obtain.[52] A group of English merchants who arrived in Benin in 1588 left even fewer details about those they met; they were content to enumerate the goods to be found there, and especially eager to gather the pepper and elephants' tusks used in local trade. The English traveler Andrew Battel was less fortunate: taken prisoner by the Portuguese, he spent twenty years in captivity in Angola among the Imbangala, and returned home to describe what he claimed were the barbarous beliefs they held. But not all Europeans left such desperate views of Africa; the Portuguese writer Duarte Lopes offered a far more positive view of the kingdom of Kongo, including detailed accounts of the region's animals and royal city.

Of all the works that circulated about Africa, none had the significance of a history of the continent written by al-Hassan Ibn Muhammed al-Wazzan. Known to Europeans as Leo Africanus, this Muslim native of Granada composed the most important account of Africa in the sixteenth century. Leo Africanus knew North Africa best, and he described it in ways that humbled the achievements of other observers. While technically not a travel report—he wrote his history while he was living at the Vatican in the early 1520s—Leo Africanus's tale included the kinds of observations that travelers routinely made. His English language editor John Pory added material to the narrative after Leo Africanus was dead. Pory's account of the "manifold Religions professed in Africa" included details about Jews, Christians, Muslims, and people he termed "Gentiles," whom he described as the most primitive of the continent. There was little question where Pory's sympathies lay, especially when he told his readers about the ways that Moors and Turks kept Christians as slaves and forced them to suffer "beggerie, nakednes, hunger, famine, blowes, reproches, and tortures" for believing Christianity was the only true faith. The converts to Islam enjoyed all the comforts of the world while the Christians suffered for their beliefs.

Yet if his history was less a routine travel account than reports offered by individuals who sailed from one place to another and then returned to tell their tales, Leo Africanus's writings nonetheless reflected the fact that he had seen much. He had made the *hajj* to his holy land; he had studied in Morocco; he

---

52. As the historian Sanjay Subrahmanyam has noted, there was no single group that dominated trade in the region: "We are dealing with a political and commercial network that was poly-centric in its organization; and there was no single epicentre that generated a pulse to which the entire 'system' responded—even in the western Indian Ocean." See Subrahmanyam, *The Career and Legend of Vasco da Gama* (Cambridge: Cambridge University Press, 1997), 94–112, quotation at 95.

had lived at the Vatican. The breadth of his experience made him a particularly reliable authority, or so it seemed to those who encountered a man who could offer information about African life spans and could describe in detail the horrors that locusts visited upon their victims. In an age when an ever larger number of Africans left the continent as slaves—Leo Africanus was himself a captive until he was freed by Pope Leo X (who then baptized him)—there were not many whose testimony about the continent has survived.

To outsiders, Africa was often a forbidding place. Most Europeans who traveled there in the sixteenth century knew little beyond the shoreline. Few went far inland, and hence many accepted the outrageous claims told about dense jungles filled with the inexplicable, from peacocks guarding a grave to human-imitating monsters. Though some observers described how people lived, the descriptions that survive mostly tell of primitives, often locked in mortal conflict with each other or with visitors. Though there had long been similarities between Christianity and some African belief systems, the church could not forever sustain links. Ethiopians, who had been seeking alliances with Europeans since the fourteenth century, in part to turn back the spread of Islam, turned away from Christianity in the early decades of the seventeenth century.[53] By the eighteenth century only Angola, a Portuguese colony, and Kongo (where the reigning kingdom collapsed in the seventeenth century) had large numbers of Christians. The slave trade took hold too; by 1600 more than 27,000 Africans had been deported to the Americas, and the number escalated sharply in the next two centuries.[54] Yet despite an increasing frequency of travel, especially along the continent's shores, the sixteenth-century texts provide a sketch of a continent that seemed still to be beyond the intellectual grasp of most outsiders. Even those who knew the place well, like Andrew Battel, could offer little beyond caricatures of those he met. Leo Africanus did better, though only for northern Africa. The interior of sub-Saharan Africa remained largely unknown to outsiders.

Travelers to Asia, by contrast, often left more vivid and distinctive impressions, the mark of careful observation. What emerges from these accounts

53. Northrup, *Africa's Discovery of Europe*, 28–29, 41–45.
54. Herbert S. Klein, *The Atlantic Slave Trade* (Cambridge: Cambridge University Press, 1999), 210–211; see also Ronald Segal, *Islam's Black Slaves: The Other Black Diaspora* (New York: Farrar, Strauss and Giroux, 2001).

by western Europeans, Persians, and Russians—there are no known travel accounts to Asia left by Africans or Americans—stands in stark contrast to surviving European accounts of Africa despite the fact that Christianity, though
growing in places, remained a minor religion.

Most Europeans who traveled to Asia sailed along the west coast of Africa, around the southern tip of the continent, and into the Indian Ocean. The
Portuguese pioneered the route, following the course that da Gama had established. They had two principal motivations for these epic journeys, which
took months and led through territory where violent encounters with native peoples remained a constant threat. First, they went for the cinnamon,
cloves, and nutmeg from the Moluccas—the Spice Islands—off Southeast
Asia. Though spice merchants had arranged for the sale of their product long
before the sixteenth century, the Portuguese recognized that transporting
spices by ship instead of overland lowered costs by reducing the time and
effort it took to get the spices from producer to consumer. Second, many Europeans participated in the global effort to spread Christianity. In the age
of da Gama, all European missionaries shared the same faith. By the time
Ferdinand Magellan (Magalhães) departed on his epic journey to East Asia
by sailing west across the Atlantic in 1519, the church was in the early stages
of its deepest crisis and division. The theologian Martin Luther had made
his protests in Wittenberg two years before Magellan embarked. As a result,
most sixteenth-century Europeans who hoped to spread the word did so as
Catholics or as Protestants, competing not only against what they believed
were the demonic forces of heathenism but also against the aggressive heresy
of other Christians.

Our knowledge of what Magellan saw comes from the recollections of
his companion Antonio Pigafetta who, unlike the captain himself, survived
the circumnavigation. Pigafetta was not always the most discerning observer;
many of the islands he described in the Southwest Pacific bore uncanny re-
semblances to each other, a sign that the overwhelming strangeness of the
place left him unable to distinguish one land from another. Still, despite the
fact that the peoples encountered by the Portuguese would have shocked Europeans, Pigafetta managed to offer at least some guidelines to allow his readers to tell the residents of one paradisaical atoll from another. For instance, the
Portuguese chronicler realized the unique importance of Palawan, where the
sailors revived themselves after suffering at sea from a lack of fresh food. This
"Land of Promise," as he termed it, held many wonders for visitors, including
(for those fortunate enough to establish positive ties to the locals) a ride on

an elephant into the realm's sacred compound, an elaborate system for passing messages to a king who would listen to others only if their words were relayed to him through a small tube, and abundance of precious cloves that could be purchased with goods the travelers had brought with them. Palawan also lacked the cannibals or pygmies found on other islands.

The nature of reports about Asia depended both on local circumstances and, as always, on the particular perspective of the observer. The missionary Luís Fróis's long 1565 letter about Japan offered the kind of details that might naturally flow from the pen of a cleric who believed that the people he lived among were "blinded with many superstitions and ceremonies." Yet Fróis's hostility did not prevent him from offering a detailed description of Buddhist monasteries, nor did his aversion to local religious custom stop him from depicting elaborate funerary customs.

Fróis witnessed much in Japan, but he died too soon to learn about what happened to the spread of Christianity there. The Portuguese had introduced Christianity to Japan in the mid-sixteenth century, and by the early seventeenth century there were perhaps 100,000 converts to the new religion. But a change in local political sensibilities led to the revival of traditional religion in the mid-seventeenth century and the persecution of many converts. Some abandoned the church for ancestral ways. Others refused to do so, and their perseverance brought the death penalty. For their faith they were killed, some of them crucified.[55]

Surviving accounts suggest that all Europeans hoped that they would one day alter religious practice in Asia. But not all visitors held to such views in equal measure. Consider, for example, Duarte de Sande's account of late-sixteenth-century China. Sande was less avowedly evangelical than other travelers. Rather than scorn customs he found repellent, he instead celebrated some of China's most unique attributes, including the Great Wall and the locals' advanced printing abilities. He recognized too that there were different kinds of schools devoted to "the greater progress and increase of learning," similar to educational institutions in Europe. The Chinese attention to matters of moral philosophy, astronomy, herbs and medicines, and "martial affairs" all demanded attention, if not outright respect. The Chinese themselves celebrated their urbanity, piety, respect for contracts, and wisdom, all traits that impressed travelers. Though Europeans could bemoan the fact that the Chinese lacked Christianity and thus "lived in great errors and ignorance

55. John E. Wills, Jr., *1688: A Global History* (New York: W. W. Norton, 2001), 154.

of the truth," Sande's report reflected his obvious admiration for prevailing religious and moral codes.

Accounts about China circulated far in the late sixteenth century, especially in clerical circles. By the end of the century, the brilliant Jesuit Matteo Ricci had begun his twenty-seven-year residence in the country, living near Canton and then in Nanjing and Beijing, a stay that produced one of the most detailed accounts of China in the early modern age.[56] But no single work in the sixteenth century describing this part of the world had the impact within Europe of a book written by an Augustinian monk named Juan González de Mendoza, who traveled to East Asia in 1583 after Pope Gregory XIII asked him to write a history "of the things that are known about the kingdom of China." First published in Rome in 1585, the book quickly circulated around the Continent. Within a year it could be found in translation in Spanish and Italian. By the turn of the century, according to one estimate, it had been translated into seven languages and been printed forty-six times. Its popularity could be attributed to many things, including enormous demand for information about Asia from an audience that had heard about the arrival of Japanese visitors in Rome. Mendoza was also an able synthesizer whose work provided a seemingly comprehensive view of East Asia. His popularity, it should be noted, was not ascribable to his originality: Mendoza, like many writers in the sixteenth century, was more concerned with spreading information than with recognizing that much of his report derived from unacknowledged authorities.[57]

By the end of the sixteenth century, the two generations of western European scholars whose writings had offered insight into a distant world had produced enough work to stock a small library about East Asia. But China and Japan were not the only Asian destinations of travelers. The Mughal emperor Babur wrote about Hindustan. 'Abd al-Razz ās al Samarqāndī Herat in eastern Afghanistan, and the Russian Athanasius Nikitin from Twer also wrote about India during the fifteenth century. Each of these reports predated what became the most substantial travel account of India, produced by the Dutch writer Jan Huygen van Linschoten, who lived in India from the time of his departure from Lisbon in 1583 until his return to Holland in 1592. Linschoten's account was perhaps the most authoritative European appraisal of any place

---

56. Jonathan Spence, *The Chan's Great Continent: China in Western Minds* (New York: Norton, 1998), 31–35; see also Spence, *The Memory Palace of Matteo Ricci* (New York: Viking, 1984).
57. For details about Mendoza's use of sources and the context of his account, see Lach, *Century of Discovery*, 2: 742–751.

in Asia published in the sixteenth century, though in some ways it paled in comparison with the massive historical account by Mahomed Kasim Hindoo Shah Ferishta completed in 1612. Yet though Ferishta, who was born sometime around 1570 in Ahmadnagar and traveled to Bijapoor to immerse himself in manuscripts that could inform him about the rise of Islam in India, also lived there, his work (which he hoped to disseminate "far and wide over the regions of the earth") mostly consisted of detailed accounts of particular kingdoms. Though it contained more information than Linschoten's book, it is the Dutchman's account that stuck more closely to the genre of travel literature.[58]

Linschoten was a reader of travel accounts before he was a traveler himself. He started reading histories "and strange adventures" when he was young, and the words on the printed pages captured his attention. "I found my mind so much addicted to see & travel into strange Countries," he wrote, "that in the end to satisfy myself I determined, & was fully resolved" to leave home, family, and friends to pursue opportunities abroad. He left his parents behind in Enkhuizen and sailed for Seville, where he had contacts who, he presumed, would teach him Spanish. From there he went to Lisbon, where his older brother's contacts in the court of Philip II enabled the young man to join Vicente de Fonseca, who was on his way to Goa to become the new archbishop. Eventually Linschoten made his way, as da Gama had done almost a century earlier, around Africa to Goa, a thriving city midway between Bombay and Magladore on the western coast of India, an urban entrepot teeming with Muslims, Christians, Jews, and "heathens." By the time he left for home, he had gathered material for an illustrated account that remains one of the most important ethnographic works of the early modern age. Among his writings were a vivid portrait of Goa itself, descriptions of seasons and diseases in India, and religious worship at temples in various locales. He also described the sacrificial burning of a Brahmin widow (for which he included a picture), details about mangoes and coconuts, and the ways that local physicians used certain spices and drugs.[59]

58. Ferishta, *History of the Rise of the Mahomedan Power in India, till the year A.D. 1612*, trans. John Briggs, 4 vols. (London, 1829), quotation at I: xlix. As the historian Joan-Pau Rubiés has noted, Linschoten "produced an encyclopaedic regional account of Portuguese India—one which distinguished different ethnic groups and castes, and which was especially detailed and accurate when describing the society of Goa and its trade." See Rubiés, *Travel and Ethnology in the Renaissance: South India through European Eyes, 1250–1625* (Cambridge: Cambridge University Press, 2000), 380. For Nikitin, see "The Travels of Athanasius Nikitin, of Twer," in *India in the Fifteenth Century. Being a Collection of Narratives of Voyages to India*, ed. R. H. Major (Hakluyt Society, 1st ser., 22 [London, 1857]).
59. For a summary of Linschoten's work, see Lach, *Century of Discovery*, I: 480–490.

Linschoten did not applaud everything that he saw in India. But while he and other Europeans might have welcomed the day when the locals would abandon their religious practices, there was much about South Asia that deserved praise. His description suggests that by the end of the sixteenth century, European visitors to the region were eager to wrestle with the territory's complexity on its own terms. The Indians whom Linschoten met were inhabitants of a different world that could be seen and understood by those who had been captivated, as he had been, by the descriptions of foreign places found in travel accounts. Those who ventured there had to treat the Chinese, Japanese, and Indians as equals, not as subordinates. Europeans' presence in these locales depended on their abilities to sustain positive ties to the merchants or monarchs who had the authority to remove any unwanted visitors.

Many of the travelers who ventured on long-distance journeys during the sixteenth century were like Linschoten—young, typically male, able to make the kinds of mercantile or clerical connections that provided them space and food on a ship or an income-producing appointment upon their arrival. But not all were so fortunate. Among the travelers were captives taken from their homes and hauled far away. Many of them, such as the indigenous Americans taken to Europe by Columbus and Martin Frobisher, left no record of their impressions abroad.[60] Even large groups could voyage and leave scant trace, like the fifty Brazilians who staged a mock battle for King Henri II of France as part of his elaborate entry into Rouen in 1550.[61]

Yet while travelers came from varied lands, over the course of the century certain peoples came to dominate the seas. The most successful were the Portuguese and the Spanish, whose *reconquista* (reconquest) of the Iberian peninsula—forcibly taking it back from Moors who had held it since the eighth century—and near-simultaneous expulsion of Jews provided the epic

60. See Michael Harbsmeier, "Bodies and Voices from Ultima Thule: Inuit Explorations of the Kablunat from Christian IV to Knud Rasmussen," in *Narrating the Arctic: A Cultural History of Nordic Scientific Practices,* ed. Michael Bravo and Sverker Sörlin, (Canton, Mass.: Science History Publications, 2002), 37–39.
61. *Cest La Deduction du sumpeux ordre plaisantz spectacles et magnifiques theatres dresses, et exhibes parles citoiens de Rouen* (1551; facsimile titled *L'Entrée de Henri II à Rouen 1550* [Amsterdam, 1977]), sig. [Ki^v-Kii^r];]. For an analysis, see Michael Wintroub, "Civilizing the Savage and Making a King: The Royal Entry Festival of Henri II (Rouen, 1550)," *Sixteenth Century Journal* 29 (1998): 465–94; as Wintroub notes 250 Norman sailors dressed like Brazilians to participate in the mock battle between the Tupinambas and "Tabagarres."

backdrop for the most famous traveler of the age. When Columbus set sail on his history-making journey in the summer of 1492, he initiated a century of Spanish exploration that had permanent consequences for the peoples of the Atlantic basin. He also provided the first European account of one part of the Western Hemisphere, a place so varied in its peoples, resources, and landscapes that even scores of later visitors failed to master it in its entirety.

The narrative of Columbus's first journey testifies to the sense of wonder that he experienced. He knew that he had to describe in words a world that no European had yet seen. That meant capturing not only the sights but also the smells. It meant describing the actions of people whose language he could not speak. And it meant telling how to live in a place through frames of reference familiar to his readers but not designed for the West Indies. Yet amid these descriptions there is a persistent undercurrent. Columbus arrived in the Caribbean not merely as chronicler. He quickly became a conqueror as well. From that vantage point he argued that this new place should become the property of the monarchs who had sponsored his voyage. It was a fateful decision.

Columbus did not have a guide like Polo or Mandeville to counsel him when he left Palos on his journey, though he knew about Portuguese voyages and hoped to surpass their achievements. But he did have an idea about the probable size of the Atlantic. He based his knowledge on information that Europeans had gathered since antiquity. Prevailing theories taught him that the land masses of the Earth had to be in balance. There had to be, that is, as much land north of the Equator as south of it, and as much land to the east of the world's center (located at Jerusalem) as to the west. Using what he believed were the best estimates of the actual size of the Earth, Columbus argued that he could travel to Asia in a few weeks by sailing west. If he had been right, his sponsors would have precious knowledge of a sea route that promised to shorten the time it took to get from Europe to China and Japan.[62]

Columbus was surprised to discover that the Atlantic was much larger than he had anticipated. His journey across took weeks longer than he had planned, and the sailors grew restless. But on October 12, 1492, Columbus went ashore, possibly on modern-day San Salvador in the Bahamas. He and his shipmates labeled the people they met "Indians" in the mistaken belief that they had in fact reached the East Indies. Columbus proved himself ever

---

62. Columbus left a number of specific clues about what was in his mind when he planned his voyage; see Valerie Flint, *The Imaginative Landscape of Christopher Columbus* (Princeton, N.J.: Princeton University Press, 1992).

the opportunist. He claimed the land in the name of Ferdinand and Isabella, and he quickly set about renaming the islands.

The first report of Columbus's journey appeared in print soon after he arrived back in Spain in March 1493. The account, known now as the Barcelona Letter, quickly became perhaps the most widely disseminated travel narrative in history. By the end of 1493, ten versions had appeared in print, published in Barcelona, Rome, Antwerp, and Basel, where a printer added an illustration. That picture was the first visual depiction of any Native American population—a glimpse of naked Tainos huddled along a shore while Columbus and the other visitors arrive. That image became a poignant memorial to a people who quickly disappeared.

In the aftermath of Columbus's journey, Pope Alexander VI issued the Bull of the Donacion, which split the unchristianized portions of the world between the Spanish (who would own the western portion) and the Portuguese (who would own the eastern lands). The following year the monarchs of those imperial powers signed the Treaty of Tordesillas, establishing the boundary line somewhere west of the Azores and effectively granting to the Portuguese the territory of Brazil (which had not yet been seen by any Europeans). These twinned acts revealed much about European attitudes toward the larger world in this age. After 1494 Europeans who ventured westward presumed that they could lay claim to lands on the far side of the Atlantic. As a result, travel narratives relating to the Americas differed from those that described Africa or Asia. Linschoten, for example, could list the produce of India with a thought that merchants would want to acquire them for European consumers, but he knew that getting them would require negotiation. By contrast, Europeans who saw valuable goods in the Western Hemisphere enumerated nature's bounty with a sense that future colonists could own the land as well as draw on its resources.

Europeans' understanding of the Americas came in different forms. In some instances, observers who never left Europe might be able to see Native Americans who had been transported there, probably against their will. Though the documentary record of the Venetian explorer Sebastian Cabot's landfall in North America in 1497 remains scant, he brought back to his English sponsors three of the Americans he found. When they appeared in London, according to the records of the sixteenth-century English chronicler John Stowe, they were "clothed in Beastes Skinnes, and eate raw Flesh, but spake such a language, as no man could understand them." But only two years later they were dressed like Englishmen and walked the corridors of Westminster

Palace like other members of the royal court. They had become mobile spectacles and living proof of the fact that people, not monsters, inhabited the distant lands to which Europeans had recently found their way.[63]

But only the lucky European saw such natives on their side of the Atlantic. Most encountered America as readers. Although many authors tried to capture these societies in their texts or in pictures, few of them could have understood the significance of the European encounter with Native Americans. The mere arrival of these visitors had initiated changes that would eventually alter daily life from the Arctic reaches of modern-day Canada to Tierra del Fuego at the tip of South America.

Europeans who arrived in the Americas brought with them a variety of infectious diseases that devastated indigenous peoples who had never been exposed to them before and thus had acquired no immunities to ward off the contagions. The scale of death in the early modern age has never been paralleled and is beyond the human imagination. Smallpox, chicken pox, influenza, measles, and other ailments reduced American populations by perhaps 90 percent from 1492 to 1800. Some peoples, including populations described in the accounts in this volume, disappeared as distinct groups, though survivors invariably joined with the remnants of other afflicted nations. The fact of death was inescapable, and it made even the most sensitive of the surviving narratives incomplete accountings of what these societies had been like before 1492. In that sense the travel narratives that describe the Americas are different than those that describe Asia, Africa, or Europe, none of whose peoples experienced the so-called "virgin soil" epidemics and resulting demographic catastrophe. After 1492, no place in the Americas was ever stable again, at least not in the sense that its residents could experience life as they did before Europeans arrived with their deadly germs. Recent scholarship suggests that many of the indigenous peoples of the Americas might have survived despite the epidemiological assault, but the forces of colonization— notably the loss of land, declining supply of food, and often brutal treatment by the newcomers—made the infections even more lethal than they would otherwise have been.[64]

---

63. John Stowe, *The Chronicles of England* (London, 1580), 875.
64. Over the past generation scholars have paid extraordinary attention to the demographic catastrophe that unfolded in the Americas from 1492 to 1800. Among many works, see Noble David Cook, *Born to Die: Disease and New World Conquest, 1492–1650* (New York: Cambridge University Press 1998); Crosby, *Ecological Imperialism*; Elizabeth A. Fenn, *Pox Americana: The Great Smallpox Epidemic of 1775–82* (New York: Hill and Wang, 2001); David S. Jones, "Virgin Soils Revisited," *William and Mary Quarterly*, 3rd ser., 60 (2003):

The earliest accounts of the Americas mention the force of disease, though descriptions of epidemics did not fill the pages of these narratives. Instead, as with the case of the Spanish conquistador Hernán Cortés, epidemics became part of the story. When Cortés arrived in Mexico in 1519 he had plans to seize land for the Spanish. By the time he had completed his siege of Tenochtitlan (modern-day Mexico City), much of the city bore the marks of his soldiers' brutality. The crimes perpetrated by his men did not escape notice; local chroniclers, using Nahua and then Spanish, recorded how Cortés's soldiers engaged in acts of sadistic murder and deliberate attempts to eradicate local religious practice. The Dominican friar Bartolomé de Las Casas offered the most vivid portrayal of the violence deployed by Spaniards on the mainland and in the West Indies.[65]

Europeans who described American societies, especially in the first half century of contact, often wrote with contempt for the peoples they encountered. The Florentine explorer Amerigo Vespucci marveled at the physical beauty of native Brazilians, yet could not fathom why such handsome people would "nevertheless themselves destroy" with facial piercings so large that a single hole "was capable of holding a plum." The longer he remained, the more such behavior fit into a perceptible pattern. He believed that they were an irreligious people who participated in degrading sexual practices, waged war senselessly, and had a penchant for dismembering their enemies and salting down their flesh for a later meal. Each savage trait helped explain the others. This tone of condemnation of Tupinambas stands in stark contrast to Vespucci's description of the stars to be seen in Brazil or its wondrous landscape.

The consumption of human flesh was perhaps the aspect of American societies that Europeans found most horrifying. When the German captive Hans Stade spent weeks among the Tupinambas of eastern Brazil in 1557 he

703–42; Daniel T. Reff, *Disease, Depopulation, and Culture Change in Northwestern New Spain, 1518–1764* (Salt Lake City: University of Utah Press, 1991); Richard H. Steckel and Jerome C. Rose, eds., *The Backbone of History: Health and Nutrition in the Western Hemisphere* (Cambridge: Cambridge University Press, 2002); Russell Thornton, *American Indian Holocaust and Survival: A Population History since 1492* (Norman: University of Oklahoma Press, 1987); and John W. Verano and Douglas H. Ubelaker, eds., *Disease and Demography in the Americas* (Washington, D. C.: Smithsonian Institute Press, 1992).
65. For one indigenous account, see Bernardino de Sahagún, *Florentine Codex: The General History of the Things of New Spain*, trans. Arthur J. O. Anderson and Charles E. Dibble, 13 parts (Santa Fe, N.M.: School of American Research, 1950–1982), *Book 12: The Conquest of Mexico.* For an edition that brings together various indigenous authorities, see Miguel Leon-Portilla, *The Broken Spears: The Aztec Account of the Conquest of Mexico* (Boston: Beacon Press, 1962).

was traded from one group to another, constantly fearing for his life. At one point his captors even forced him to announce his arrival at a new place by shouting "*A junesche been ermi vramme*"—that is, "I, your food, have come." The fear of being eaten quite literally consumed his thoughts. Stade feared that the Tupinambas would kill him "*kawei pepicke*," meaning that they would drink ritually at a feast while they ate him. He expressed his anxieties so clearly and so repeatedly that the artists who added illustrations to the printed versions of his account felt compelled to depict such scenes in graphic detail. The Flemish engraver Theodor de Bry placed an image of a man and a woman on the frontispiece to his edition of the narratives of Stade and Jean de Léry, a Huguenot missionary who also sailed to Brazil in the mid-sixteenth century. Of the thirty-two pictures in that volume, six depict Tupinamba cannibalism. The images are hardly subtle: men and women chow down with glee on severed arms and legs, while others roast limbs over open flames.

Cannibalism, which was practiced among certain peoples in the Americas but was more limited than early modern European observers believed, disgusted visitors but did not deter them from traveling to the Western Hemisphere. The potential rewards far outweighed the possible dangers, especially given the fact that many of the early travelers found much to be admired. Even Vespucci himself marveled at the Brazilian landscape and speculated, as had Columbus, that "if the terrestrial paradise be in any part of this earth, I esteem that it is not far distant from those parts" that he had already seen. More common was astonishment at what visitors saw and even outright delight at the thought of harvesting American flora and fauna. Léry marveled at the aquatic wonders encountered during the voyage across the Atlantic from France to Brazil. He was even more amazed by the Tupinambas themselves, whom he described in far more complimentary terms than Vespucci or Stade had managed earlier in the century. They "are not taller, fatter, or smaller in stature than we Europeans are," he wrote, "their bodies are neither monstrous nor prodigious with respect to ours. In fact, they are stronger, more robust and well filled-out, more nimble, less subject to disease; there are almost none among them who are lame, one-eyed, deformed or disfigured."[66] His report, based on a year of living among them, reflected his obsessive attention to the natives' bodies and customs. In its details about men, women, and children, Léry's account conjured up precise images about what the Tupinambas looked like, and thus provided the kinds of information that allowed talented illustrators who re-

66. Jean de Léry, *History of a Voyage to the Land of Brazil*, trans. Janet Whatley (Berkeley: University of California Press, 1990), 56.

mained in Europe to craft similarly precise visual images. These pictures, like the accounts that artists used to make them, invariably reflected the cultural biases of their creators, especially since Léry was hardly an objective observer. Having arrived in Brazil as a missionary determined to spread the word of his gospel, he wanted to cure what he believed were the deficiencies in the Tupinambas' culture. Yet his evangelism could succeed only if he understood the potential converts. His report is the public face of his internal exploration.

Many of the Spaniards who went to the Western Hemisphere dwelled on aspects of the environment, what nature looked like, and how humans lived in these lands. Gonzalo Fernández de Oviedo y Valdés, a natural historian who became a Spanish imperial official in Hispaniola, was one of the more astute observers. Though Oviedo was directly involved in the maintenance of a growing colonial empire, he was more interested in indigenous species and customs ranging from the pearl divers harvesting their catch to the feathers of turtle doves and partridges in Cuba. Oviedo sensed that his words could convey what America looked like. In that way he had more confidence than the conquistador Francisco Vasquez de Coronado, who knew he needed help describing the Southwest of the modern-day United States, which he explored from 1539 to 1541. Coronado was so astonished by what he saw in the lands of the Pueblos that he ordered a native artist to paint a picture of the local birds, beasts, and fish onto cloth. The artist complied, but that did not prevent Coronado from later complaining that the pictures were "rudely done, because the painter spent but one day in drawing" them. Deep in the desert and far from navigable waterways, these Americans quickly realized what the Spanish were really looking for. They were right: Coronado had gone into the desert because he thought he would find Cíbola, a fabled city bedecked in precious metals and jewels.

Coronado failed to find the wealth he sought, but other Spaniards were more fortunate. In the decades after Cortés's conquest of the Aztec empire, emissaries of the Iberian monarchs traveled southward. The famed conquistador Francisco Pizarro and his fellow travelers were outnumbered by the Inkas they met on their way to Peru, but the invaders still managed to wrest control of the region and its vast resources from the natives. Their success hinged on the superiority of their weapons, the shock of their arrival to the natives, and the spread of infectious diseases that reduced the Inkas' ability to defend their homeland from invasion.[67]

67. Jared Diamond, *Guns, Germs, and Steel: The Fates of Human Societies* (New York: W. W. Norton, 1997), 67–81.

Yet if the conquest of Peru was notable for its rapidity and its command-er's brutality toward the Inkan emperor Atahualpa—whom Pizarro killed even after he received what may have been the largest ransom ever paid in human history—thousands of the region's conquered peoples survived the assault and diseases. Those survivors quickly became the subject of writers' speculation as information about Peru began to circulate across Europe by the middle of the century. Among those writers was Pedro de Cieza de León, whose work appeared widely in the sixteenth century, published first in Se-ville in 1553 and over the next two decades in Antwerp, Rome, and Venice. According to one twentieth-century commentator, the work "possesses the greatest objectivity of any history ever written about the Incas."[68]

Cieza de León claimed that he was moved to write his account after spending seventeen years in the West Indies. There "I saw the strange and wonderful things that exist in this New World of the Indies," he wrote, noting that "there came to me a great desire to write certain of them, those which I had seen with my own eyes, and also what I had heard from highly trust-worthy persons." In listing his reasons for writing his account, he added that "I had taken notice wherever I went that nobody concerned himself with writing aught of what was happening. And time so destroys the memory of things that only by clues and inference can the future ages know what really took place." Of course, he had a more explicit agenda as well: he wanted the world to know that since "these Indians all have our origin in our common parents," it was crucial "that the world should know how so great a multi-tude as these Indians were brought into the lap of the church by the efforts of the Spanish, an undertaking so great that no other nation of all the universe could have accomplished it." Telling his story would also bring glory to the crown of Castile, under whose guidance "the rich and widespread kingdoms of New Spain and Peru were settled and other islands and vast provinces discovered." But Cieza de León knew that the gain for the Spanish came at the expense of Americans. As he put it after providing a survey of the city of Tomebamba, "Today all is cast down and in ruins, but still it can be seen how great they were."[69]

Peru and its splendors beckoned the Spanish because the rewards were so obvious: abundance of silver to be mined, countless natives to be won over to Christ. Yet travelers headed for less promising destinations too. Perhaps no

68. Victor Wolfgang von Hagen, in *The Incas of Pedro Cieza de León*, trans. Harriet de Onis (Norman: University of Oklahoma Press, 1959), vii.
69. *Incas of Pedro Cieza de León*, 3, 73.

target of European explorers was less enticing than modern-day Canada, a place known by the late sixteenth century to be surrounded by frigid waters and populated by natives who often seemed incapable of even the most rudimentary kinds of civilized behavior. However forbidding Canada appeared, early modern European travelers had been going there since the age of the Cabots. Many of them went in search of the so-called Northwest Passage, a water route that they hoped would take them to Asia more quickly than the well-known but lengthy journey around Africa and India (or the even longer journey overland). Among the earliest European travelers to the region was Jacques Cartier, the most important French explorer of the sixteenth century, who maneuvered his ship far into the St. Lawrence River in the 1530s. By the time he reemerged he had gathered plentiful details about indigenous life there that would eventually find an audience across Europe when his work was published (by 1580) in French, Italian, and English. The *Narration* of his second voyage included his extended reflections on the settlement at Hochelaga and provided his readers with an assessment of the indigenous Canadians' belief in a sacred spirit called Cudruiagni who foretold the weather and punished misbehaving humans. Cartier told the Indians that this spirit was the devil and then wrote that many sought Christian baptism to escape the demon's cruel ways. His remarks reflected his views, not those of the natives. But rather than be dismissed as idle fantasy, Cartier's notions instead reflected the reality of demonic forces to early modern Europeans. Given the large number of surviving accounts about seemingly all variety of demonism across Europe, Cartier's assumptions made perfect sense. If the indigenous peoples he met did not understand the ubiquity of the Devil, that was but one more sign of their ignorance of how the world functioned.[70]

As the century wore on an ever larger number of European travelers explored North America, from the tepid waters of southern Florida to the frozen shores of the continent's northeastern coastline and nearby islands. Not surprisingly, visitors paid careful attention to the peoples who came to meet them. Traveling with Martin Frobisher on a search for the Northwest Passage in 1577, Dionyse Settle had little praise for the Inuit he saw. They subsisted on

---

70. One sign of the ubiquity of ideas about demonism was the widespread publication of books that dealt with the phenomenon; such thinking not only influenced thoughts about religion but also politics, science, history, and even the language that Europeans used in daily life. For a masterful survey of the subject, see Stuart Clark, *Thinking with Demons: The Idea of Witchcraft in Early Modern Europe* (Oxford: Oxford University Press, 1997).

raw flesh, a sign of their savagery. They lived in dwellings covered with the skins of animals and with doorways held open by whalebones. Still, however awful those people appeared, the English entertained hopes that these natives could use pen, ink, and paper to provide information about five men left behind on Frobisher's expedition a year earlier. They were wrong. The fate of those men remained a mystery to the English, who believed that the Inuit had killed them, until a nineteenth-century whaling captain met a local woman who knew the fate of those long-lost men. Ookijoxy Ninoo, sharing part of her people's history that had been maintained orally for almost four hundred years, told how the men had grown impatient and made their own small boat to sail back to England even before the chill of winter had left those waters. It was a fatal choice, something that Settle and others on Frobisher's voyages would have known.[71]

Yet if the northeast coast of North America was dangerous, the west coast held promise. That, at least, was the impression that readers of an account of Francis Drake's journey would have learned. When the English captain sailed northward up the Pacific coast of South America and into the waters off modern-day California, he found places that were anything but forbidding. During his successful circumnavigation, which began in 1577 and ended three years later, Drake had more problems with the Spanish who had already colonized portions of the west coast than he did with either native peoples or the environment. He found the local customs bizarre at times, but he seemed to appreciate a place where gender rules dictated the subordination of women. He also paid close attention to the welcoming rituals of the California natives. During one ceremony he even laid claim to the entire area, "wishing that the riches & treasure" of the region could be "transported to the inriching" of his queen's realm. Before he departed, Drake left a marker in place telling when he had arrived and the date on which, he claimed, the locals had voluntarily given up the region to Elizabeth I. Drake then sailed off to the west, seeking the Spanish treasure ships hauling American silver to the Philippines.

Although Europeans acquired much information about parts of the interior of South and North America over the course of the century, some travelers never saw what they claimed to have observed. Journeys might take weeks and still not get far inland. Walter Ralegh's search for Guiana, for ex-

---

71. The story can be found in Susan Rowley, "Frobisher Miksanut: Inuit Accounts of the Frobisher Voyages," in *Archaeology of the Frobisher Voyages,* ed. William W. Fitzhugh and Jacqueline S. Olin (Washington, D.C.: Smithsonian Institute Press, 1993), 30.

ample, took him no farther than the meandering tributaries of the Orinoco. Though what he claimed to see and hear there provided insight into unfamiliar environments, he had in fact barely penetrated the continent. The limited wanderings of many of those who wrote accounts meant that the surviving narratives about the Americas, as the selections in this volume demonstrate, often made only vague distinctions between different groups of Americans. Coronado saw different Pueblo settlements, but spent little time demarcating differences among them. Columbus and Ralegh encountered natives who seemed friendly, but each heard stories about the more savage and monstrous creatures who roamed just beyond the reach of European explorations. Cartier recognized differences among communities in the St. Lawrence Valley, but he never saw the Americans who lived in more temperate climes. Too often America's indigenous peoples existed in travel accounts as foils to superior Europeans—examples of primitive societies, idol-worshiping cults, and lustful individuals who sated their uncivilized passions by parading naked, swapping sexual partners, or eating their enemies.

Fortunately for later readers, America had its own version of India's Linschoten: two talented and perceptive men who traveled from England to the middle of the North Atlantic coast together in the 1580s, bound for the nascent colony at Roanoke. One was a young writer and mathematician named Thomas Harriot, the other a supremely talented painter named John White. Together they created an ethnographic masterpiece that described one particular North American population. Published first in unillustrated editions in London in 1588 and 1589, *The Briefe and True Report of the New Found Land of Virginia* had such promise that it appeared in 1590 in an illustrated edition, with Theodor de Bry's engravings of White's watercolors. The fact of its publication speaks volumes about its importance at the time. In an age when accounts of travel were sometimes kept secret and when even published versions typically appeared to serve a particular audience, the Harriot/White/de Bry collaboration appeared simultaneously in Latin, German, English, and French. It became the most famous book ever published about any specific American population, and it remains the most authoritative guide to the appearance, customs, architecture, beliefs, economy, and customs of a people who disappeared soon after the book's publication. The Carolina Algonquians described in those pages became victims of the forces that travel itself had unleashed: infectious diseases, missionaries bent on eradicating natives' cosmos, and land-hungry colonizers who used descriptions in travel accounts to plan their conquest of new territory.

Anyone who held the *Briefe and True Report* in his or her hands in the sixteenth century would have turned each page with anticipation. One short chapter after another detailed local plants and their uses, the extraordinary plenty to be found in nearby waterways, intricate religious beliefs and even mortuary practices. The thirty-four pages of text preceded twenty-three pictures, each with text describing what the image depicted. It is hard now to imagine the wonder that many readers must have felt as they ran their hands along those pages, perhaps touching the visual depiction of one marvel after another. But after the final image of the Algonquians, which depicted a local man with a tattoo on his back and explained the meaning of certain other forms of ritual scarification, the reader came face to face with images that had nothing to do with the Americas. Instead, he or she saw a naked man, himself heavily tattooed and holding a head still dripping blood (another head lies at his feet), and then another figure, and another, until the reader had seen five distinct images of the ancient inhabitants of Britain known as Picts. The verbal descriptions that appeared here were briefer than the text that had accompanied the images of Roanoke. Instead, the pictures themselves tell a story of humans in Europe in their savage state, before the redemptive power of civilization had brought out their innate potential. The Picts had dominated northern Britain when the Romans arrived fifteen centuries earlier, but now they were long gone. Located at the end of the most perceptive American travel account of the century, these pictures existed to make a single point: Western Europe had once been populated by individuals as savage as any to be found in the Americas. Over time they had become "reduced" to civilization, as early modern writers often referred to the process of eradicating indigenous culture and replacing it with Protestant or Catholic forms of Christianity, European gender roles, and the benefits of a market economy. The account of Roanoke became a tool for potential conquerors and colonists.

Before Columbus's arrival, the peoples of the Americas tended to live in discrete communities and shared only limited experiences. Like residents of settlements in other parts of the world, any individual's knowledge of what lay beyond the confines of his or her particular community was often a mystery. Travelers broached those boundaries, as did merchants, sailors, soldiers, and delegates of powerful polities. But most people lived and died in the region of their birth, and hence their mental worlds remained circumscribed by what they learned locally. Though many Native Americans traveled long distances during their lives, the hemisphere contained hundreds of distinct peoples, but no common culture, language, or set of shared experience. For them there was no concept of an "America."

But infectious diseases and imperial-minded conquerors broke through the boundaries that had made the experiences of one indigenous population different from another. Though knowledge of particular groups might not have traveled far—residents of an Iroquois community near the St. Lawrence River might not know anything of the Aztecs or the Inkas—the native peoples of the Americas came to share a common and often tragic fate. Neither Europeans nor the Old World diseases they inadvertently carried reached into every indigenous community in the Americas by 1600. But by the end of the sixteenth century, the course of events had become predictable. In the decades that followed, virtually all Americans came to know the tragedies that epidemics wrought, and many of them found their beliefs and everyday practices challenged by uninvited visitors.

The indigenous peoples of other continents did not face such challenges in the sixteenth century. To be sure, Europeans influenced other societies, either by persuading thousands to convert to Christianity (as occurred in parts of Asia and Africa) or by participating in a slave trade that transported men, women, and children far from their homes (as happened in Africa), or by establishing trade with non-Europeans that altered traditional economies. But the American situation was different because of the unprecedented devastations wrought by the combination of deadly pathogens and opportunistic conquerors.

The stories generated by European travelers to the Americas filled hundreds of thousands of printed pages in Europe by the end of the sixteenth century. Details about what or who could be found in particular places, and what happened when Europeans met America's native peoples, appeared in books, pamphlets, and broadsides. Printers produced this mountain of information because they knew there was a market for news of the Western Hemisphere, an audience of readers eager to make their own discoveries about what lay on the other side of the Atlantic Ocean. By 1600, European knowledge of the Americas gleaned through travel accounts had led to sustained speculation about the location of precious goods and even the route to the promised land. In the minds of the most capable and thoughtful writers, understanding America and its peoples came to be a way to understand Europe and Europeans too.

Among those who read travel accounts and ruminated on their meaning was the famed late sixteenth-century French courtier Michel de Montaigne, whose *Essais* (written mostly in the 1570s) analyze such phenomena as human emotions, war horses, and drunkenness. He never sailed across the Atlantic Ocean, yet one of his most famous essays treated the subject of cannibalism and made explicit reference to man-eaters found in the Americas. Humans who ate other humans had long been a fixture of the European imagination, but actual knowledge of such peoples had faded until Europeans who went to the Americas brought the fact of cannibalism back into common discourse, as the accounts of Stade and others had made so abundantly obvious. But unlike other writers, Montaigne wrote about American cannibalism not because it was so shocking to his sensibilities and not because he feared it. Instead, he used an account of cannibalism provided by "a simple and rough-hewn fellow," who was (Montaigne argued) too stupid to have made up what he reported, to contrast American primitiveness with European savagery, particularly the treatment of those accused or convicted of crimes. "I think there is more barbarism to eating men alive," he wrote, "then to feed up them being dead; to mangle by tortures and torments a body full of lively sense, to roast him in pieces," or to let dogs and swine gnaw on the body. Montaigne believed that the Americans he wrote about could use some improvement, but in his mind their existence had much to teach Europeans about the proper ways to live with each other.[72]

Readers of this volume may be disappointed to discover that virtually all of the travel narratives that appear here were written by Europeans and published in Europe. It is regrettable that there are few surviving sixteenth-century African travel accounts and no published accounts across South or East Asia that described sixteenth-century travels. To make up for this gap, this volume includes several fifteenth-century travel narratives. These include the extraordinary writing of the Ming chronicler Ma Huan, whose *Ying-Yai Sheng-Lan* (*The Overall Survey of the Ocean's Shores*), written in 1433 and published in 1451, included descriptions of Calicut, Ceylon, Mecca, and such places in the oceans as "the country of naked people" where residents had "naked bodies, all without a stitch of clothing, like the bodies of brute beasts."[73] There are also two accounts of early observers of India: 'Abd al-

---

72. Montaigne, "Of the Caniballes," in *The Essayes or Morall, Politike and Militarie Discourses,* trans. John Florio (London, 1603), 100–107, quotations at 101, 104.
73. Ma Huan, *Ying-Yai Sheng-Lan,* 124–25.

Razzāq al-Samarqandī, an emissary from Herat to Calicut; and the Emperor Babur to Hindustan, part of the territory that he conquered in the formation of the Mughal Empire.

Yet despite these texts, the silences in the historical record remain. Though Asians and Americans traveled to Europe, none left accounts that were printed in the sixteenth century. The gap is notable in part because no account was left by any members of a small group of Japanese travelers who came to Europe under the auspices of Pope Gregory XIII in 1585. Their visit produced an extraordinary number of reports about them—49 in 1585 alone—but not by them.[74] Nor did the journeys of scores of Native Americans to Europe leave much trace other than glimpses in the record.[75] Many Native American peoples preserved their own histories, of course, often in precise stories told from one generation to the next. Such indigenous sources should not be ignored. The details in some of the Mesoamerican chronicles provide crucial insights into the ways that Europeans took control of much of the Western Hemisphere. Like Las Casas's accounting of Spanish atrocities, they provide portraits of extraordinary human cruelty. But while they tell us much about the sixteenth century, they are in fact the opposite of travel accounts. They are depictions of peoples by themselves, not by outsiders. One notable exception was Felipe Guaman Poma de Ayala, a Peruvian; this anthology contains his account of his return home after an absence of thirty years.

This volume does include accounts left by Europeans who traveled to other parts of their own continent and such relatively nearby territory as the modern-day Middle East. Such ventures were, as some of the surviving writing reveals, just as replete with life's many mysteries. The English gentleman traveler Fynes Moryson first left his native land in 1591 and spent the next decade traveling through such well-known locales as Germany, Switzerland, and Poland. Part of his memorable journey took him through Venice and Jerusalem. His shipmates included his brother, a Greek crew, and some Italians, Persians, Turks, and Indians, all of them jostling together on the waves and coming on deck to recite their daily prayers when they heard the ship's bell. Moryson studied Jerusalem's architecture and spent enough time there to find out how most of the residents earned a living. But he did not like them

74. See Adriana Boscaro, *Sixteenth-Century European Printed Works on the First Japanese Mission to Europe: A Descriptive Bibliography* (Leiden: Brill, 1973).
75. According to the anthropologist Harald E. L. Prins, there were at least fifty-five journeys by perhaps 1,600 Native Americans to Europe by the early seventeenth century. See Prins, "To the Land of the Mistigoches: American Indians Traveling to Europe in the Age of Exploration," *American Indian Culture and Research Journal* 17, 1 (1993): 175–95.

very much. The city's inhabitants, he wrote, "are as wicked, as they were when they crucified our Lord, gladly taking all occasions to use Christians despitefully." He must have been happy to resume his journey, though his account bore witness to the kinds of routine troubles that hampered travelers—the need to provide for their own food, being held out of a port until the proper permissions had been received, sharing his cabin with the wares being hauled from one city to another, beating off would-be pirates and thieves. Moryson's is a curiously detailed sixteenth-century report. Although he himself prepared it for publication, he never hesitated to mix the mundane with the marvelous, which makes his book a particularly useful account since it merges the realities of travel together with the goals of the traveler.

As Europeans traveled from one nation to another, they often paid careful attention to formal elements of ritual. At times, Christian observers excoriated the practices of non-Christians, such as the people of Turkey whom the French geographer Nicholas Nicholay encountered in the 1550s. He described "the religious Hermites and Pilgrimes, both Turkes and Moores Mahometistes" as having a manner of living that was "so beastly and farre from the true religion under colour of their fained holinesse and vaine devotion, that by comparable reason it might better be called a life of brute beastes then of reasonable men."[76] But travelers within Europe did not always condemn those they met. When the German lawyer Paul Hentzner journeyed through Elizabethan England near the end of the century, he took note of the country's agricultural successes and even English sheep. Yet his account is most engaging when he turned his attention to the rituals of a state procession. He described the queen in language that would have been familiar to any reader of travel literature, emphasizing how she spoke to each ambassador in his own language, how she pulled off her glove to reveal a jewel-bedecked hand that needed to be kissed by the most fortunate, how her female assistants attended her, and how the royal court feasted. His keen eye for detail provides glimpses into a world that has slipped into oblivion.

The act of travel itself spawned more than a genre of literature. It also supported Europeans' obsessive desire to own and display fragments of the natural world. Thomas Platter's account of his journey to England in 1599 includes his enumeration of the contents of a cabinet of curiosity. There is no better way to measure the acquisitive impulses of this age of discovery

76. Nicholas Nicholay, *The Navigations, peregrinations and voyages, made into Turkie by Nicholas Nicholay Daulphinois, Lord of Arfeuile, Chamberlaine and Geographer ordinarie to the King of France*, trans. T. Washington the younger (London, 1585), f. 99ʳ.

than to imagine how an Arabian cloak, a necklace of teeth from Africa, the mummy of an infant, pitchers and boxes from China, and various parts of animals and insects came to lie together in the same room where its owner displayed them for invited visitors.

Yet as Europeans traveled far in their desire to acquire material goods—in addition to colonies and souls—they knew that they ran real risks. Ships often went down and countless numbers of men, women, and children drowned. Moryson's hope for a smooth voyage was not a casual part of his journey; he and the others on board knew the risks. Though tales of shipwrecks undoubtedly passed from mouth to mouth, especially in seaside communities where friends and relatives never returned from voyages, some sixteenth-century printers also realized there was a market for published accounts of disasters. The wreck of one Portuguese captain near the Azores resulted in an extraordinary narrative titled (in translation) *Shipwreck Suffered by Jorge D'Albuquerque Coelho*, published in Lisbon in 1601. The horrors experienced by those on board are almost beyond imagination. Even Afonso Luĩs, the author of the account, recognized that his words could not do justice to the primal fear that the men and women of that journey endured. The storm drove the ship hundreds of miles northward, from 43 degrees north latitude to 47 degrees. The terror escaped articulation. "One thing I can affirm," the author wrote after offering up some of the most harrowing details, "and that is that what little is written here is as different from what we actually endured as a painting is from real life."

This collection contains hundreds of pages of accounts as they appeared in the sixteenth century or soon after, most drawn from the sixteenth-century (or early-seventeenth-century) English printings (though there are a few modern translations). It also includes three groups of pictures that appeared in print then too—visual portfolios depicting the Brazil that Hans Stade and Jean de Léry saw, the India described by Jan Huygen van Linschoten, and Roanoke as it appeared to Thomas Harriot and John White. These pictures appeared in texts originally published in German, French, Dutch, Latin, and English, though images of distant lands also appeared in books printed in other languages, notably Spanish, Portuguese, and Italian. To understand the world that travelers described and their readers encountered, it is crucial to look at these images in context. Printers borrowed words from one another, and they also reprinted the same pictures. Sometimes an enterprising artist such as the

Flemish engraver Theodor de Bry would take old texts and pictures and create new versions of them, as is evident here in the pictures that accompany the texts of Stade and Léry. But more frequently printers would use old plates or commission artists to reprint old images without any changes.

Too often scholars have analyzed these sixteenth-century images as if they were unique. But just as readers considered the reliability of accounts in the context of other reports, so viewers of images saw them in context too. The selection that appears here represents a small fraction of the available visual material, just as the reports represent a tiny proportion of the surviving accounts. The pictures are not here to illustrate points made in the text. Instead, they provide clues to earlier mentalities by revealing how artists depicted what they saw or the images that appeared in their minds after reading evocative texts. Pictures, along with words, told stories. They too need to be read to understand how peoples 400 years ago shared information about the world they inhabited. These pictures cannot be taken to be any more accurate than the texts themselves. As one modern ethnographer has noted, European "engravers sat comfortably in their workshops" when they created pictures to fit the words that appeared in the accounts, and the results often "showed some consideration for the text, but just as often originated wholly in the imagination of the artist himself."[77]

Words and images together conveyed distant worlds to the individuals fortunate enough to acquire travel accounts. Scattered references in the surviving documents reveal that books often traveled far. One example will suffice. In the mid-1580s, the editor Richard Hakluyt's older cousin—who was also named Richard Hakluyt—suggested that the English explorers Arthur Pet and Charles Jackman take to China a copy of "the book of the attire of all nations." In all likelihood that book was the one that Hans Weigel produced in Germany in 1577. If the book made this journey, it would have been carried onto a ship that departed from London and sailed northward toward the hoped-for Northeast Passage. It would have been stowed under decks, probably in a packing crate, while the ship edged through the frozen seas that encrusted the northern edges of the Eurasian landmass. If the captain managed to steer his vessel through the ice and cold of those waters north of Russia without water flooding the cargo hold, the book would have made it to the Pacific. Having thus passed through the Northeast Passage, these images on paper would have remained secure, bound together inside a leather or wooden cover, as the ship hugged the east coast of Asia until it reached the kingdom of the great Chan.

77. Kaj Birket-Smith, "The Earliest Eskimo Portraits," *Folk* 1 (1959): 5.

Those who hauled the book through those hundreds of perilous miles would then have presented the book to the emperor since, as Hakluyt put it, "such a booke carried with you and bestowed in gift, would be much esteemed."[78] But that book never made it to its intended destination. Like countless travelers on the seas and on land, it disappeared without a trace.

Certain themes run through the accounts in this volume. Travelers routinely commented on religious practice, and almost invariably found the spiritual beliefs of others inferior to their own. They wrote about physical appearance and clothing. They described architecture. They rendered in words what places looked like, sounded like, even how they smelled. They also worried about what would happen next. Would a storm blow up and capsize their vessel? Would some unknown wild animal attack? Would the people they met decide to kill them? Such fears were reasonable. Yet the dominant tone of these accounts is not trepidation, but wonder at the marvels being witnessed and glee at the possibility of making a profit from new discoveries. What constituted profit differed from group to group, of course. American silver shipped to Spain or the Philippines made many Spaniards rich. But missionaries promoting Christianity also profited when they managed to persuade others to accept their views.

Less obvious in travelers' writings and pictures is another theme: the desire to record what the voyagers had experienced for posterity. Like the writers and painters of other generations, those of the sixteenth century battled oblivion. They all knew the risks of travel, and few if any embraced martyrdom for the sake of their discoveries. These intrepid travelers and others who left accounts found ways to preserve their observations. The printing press aided their struggle against the darkness of forgetting. It proved in the long run a more effective technology for the dissemination of information than oral history or *khipu*. Those who wrote the accounts printed here might not have "held up the sky," to borrow the indigenous American Rarámuris phrase for the preservation of culture through memory,[79] but

---

78. Hakluyt to Pet and Jackman, in *The Principall Navigations, Voiages, and Discoveries of the English Nation* (1589), 464.

79. Susan M. Deeds, "Legacies of Resistance, Adaptation, and Tenacity: History of the Native Peoples of Northwest Mexico, in *Mesoamerica*, vol. 2 of *The Cambridge History of the Native Peoples of the Americas*, ed. Richard E. W. Adams and Murdo J. Macleod (Cambridge: Cambridge University Press, 2000), 2: 44.

they handed down details of a world that would otherwise be invisible to us now.

When the English collector of travel accounts Samuel Purchas put together a large collection of narratives in the mid-1620s, he included an indigenous chronicle known as the "Codex Mendoza." Unlike the thousands of words that spilled across the pages of his four folio-sized volumes, this fifty-page section consisted mostly of images. It was, as Purchas called it, "The History of the Mexican Nation, described in pictures." He knew its value, terming the images "the choisest of my Jewels."[80] The indigenous Mexicans whose history was captured in the Codex suffered when uninvited visitors arrived on their shores in April 1519, though a series of prophecies had warned them that something ominous was on its way. In other parts of the Americas, indigenous groups heard rumors of newcomers. They too realized that the visitors would change their world.

Tragically, many non-Europeans' stories of this formative period of contact were lost in subsequent catastrophes. The travel narratives here will not revive or replace their accounts. But at least we can listen to the echoes of their stories in the tales that their visitors told.

80. Purchas, *Purchas His Pilgrimes*, 4 vols. (London, 1625), 3: 1065–1066.

A Note on Sources and Suggestions for Further Reading

This anthology contains excerpts from thirty-seven fifteenth- and sixteenth-century travel accounts. Yet despite this accumulation of evidence, these narratives represent a small fraction of the available travel literature for the early modern era. Given the enormous interest in travel writing, much of this literature, as well as scholarly studies that provide context and analysis, is now available. This note is intended to suggest avenues into this scholarship. Given the exciting work going on in this field, a moment of caution is in order: this note will provide an overview of the existing scholarship, but there is material beyond what is mentioned here. New research appears regularly in books and scholarly journals, including *Studies in Travel Literature*, an entire journal devoted to the subject.

Published collections of travel narratives have existed since the sixteenth century. Among the earliest and most important was Giovanni Battista Ramusio's *Navigationi e Viaggi*, published in three volumes in Venice from 1550 to 1559. There is a splendid modern Italian edition of Ramusio's work, edited by Marica Milanesi, published in six volumes in Torino by Giulio Einaudi (1978–1988). (Ramusio's volumes have never been translated in full into English, though many of the individual accounts have been translated into English and other modern languages.) Richard Hakluyt, who was inspired by Ramusio and whose efforts feature prominently in this volume, began his systematic collection of travel accounts with the first book to appear under his own name, *Divers Voyages touching the discoverie of America, and the Ilands adjacent* (London, 1582), and leading to his first grand effort, *The Principall Navigations, Voiages, and Discoveries of the English Nation*, first published in London in 1589; a facsimile edition of this work was published by Cambridge University Press for the Hakluyt Society in two volumes in 1965. Nine years after the *Principall Navigations* appeared, Hakluyt published the first of what became a three-volume work under the title *The Principal Navigations, Voyages, Traffiques, and Discoveries of the English Nation* (London, 1598–1600). Even before Hakluyt died in 1616, he passed his manuscripts on to a London preacher named Samuel Purchas, who began to produce his own version of travel accounts with the 1613 publication in London of *Purchas his pilgrimage* and culminating in 1625 in the publication of a massive four-volume work known as *Hakluytus Posthumous or purchase his pilgrimes*. Hakluyt and Purchas played such a conspicuous role in the history of travel narrative publication (among their other efforts) that each has attracted scholarly attention. The best start into this literature is through two publications of the Hakluyt Society: David Beers Quinn, ed., *Hakluyt Handbook*, published in two volumes in 1974 (2nd ser., 144–145); and L. E. Pennington, ed., *The Purchas Handbook: Studies of the Life, Times and Writings of Samuel Purchas, 1577–1626*, published in two volumes in 1997 (2nd ser., 185–186).

The modern printing of sixteenth-century (and earlier) travel narratives dates to the late eighteenth century, when William Mavor began the publication of what became a twenty-five-volume set of books titled *Historical Record of the Most Celebrated Voyages, Travels, and Discoveries, from the Time of Columbus to the Present Period* (London, 1796–1801). Over the course of the nineteenth century and into the beginning of the twentieth century, other editors offered multivolume collections or analyses as well. Among them were the 209 volumes of the *Nouvelles Annales de Voyages, de la Géographie et de l'Histoire* (Paris, 1819–1870); Robert Kerr, ed., *A General History and Collection of Voyages and Travels*, 18 vols. (Edinburgh and London, 1811–1824); Rueben G. Thwaites, *The Jesuit Relations and Allied Documents*, 77 vols. (Cleveland, Ohio, 1896–1901); and Emma H. Blair and James A. Robertson, ed., *The Philippine Islands, 1493–1803*, 55 vols. (Cleveland, Ohio, 1903–1909). In 1846 the Hakluyt Society began its ongoing efforts to publish travel accounts. An analysis of the society's efforts can be found in R. C. Bridges and P. E. H. Hair, eds., *Compassing the Vast Globe of the Earth: Studies in the History of the Hakluyt Society, 1846-1996* (Hakluyt Society, 2nd ser., 183 [London, 1996]); that volume includes (on pages 243 to 302) a listing of the society's books published from 1846 to 1996.

For those less interested in these older collections, one logical starting point into the field would be the extensive literature analyzing travel narratives, particularly those focused on the early modern era. Readers interested in analyses that primarily focus on European writers might want to start with Jas Elsner and Joan-Pau Rubiés, eds., *Voyages and Visions: Towards a Cultural*

History of Travel (London: Reaktion, 1999) and Peter Hulme and Tim Youngs, eds., *The Cambridge Companion to Travel Writing* (Cambridge: Cambridge University Press, 2002). A number of recent anthologies also include much of value beyond the reprinting of older texts. Among the best of these collections written in English are Andrew Hadfield, ed., *Amazons, Savages, and Machiavels: Travel and Colonial Writing in English, 1550–1630: An Anthology* (Oxford: Oxford University Press, 2001); Kenneth Parker, ed., *Early Modern Tales of the Orient: A Critical Anthology* (London: Routledge, 1999); and Louis B. Wright, ed., *The Elizabethans' America: A Collection of Early Reports by Englishmen on the New World* (Cambridge, Mass.: Harvard University Press, 1966). Those volumes can be profitably supplemented by Nabil Matar's valuable *In the Lands of the Christians: Arabic Travel Writing in the Seventeenth Century* (New York: Routledge, 2003). Insights into Europeans' views of others can also be found in works of the imagination, such as plays that depicted travel; for one excellent collection with a superb introduction, see Anthony Parr, ed., *Three Renaissance Travel Plays* (Manchester: Manchester University Press, 1995). The study of travel itself has evolved substantially, even in the modern period. One way to judge the changes is to compare two particularly well-known works: Boies Penrose, *Travel and Discovery in the Renaissance, 1420–1620* (Cambridge, Mass.: Harvard University Press, 1952); and Mary Louise Pratt, *Imperial Eyes: Travel Writing and Acculturation* (London: Routledge, 1992).

As various editors have made very clear, acts of travel did not begin in the sixteenth century, and some understanding of human movements in the era before 1500 can help to provide context for the period examined in this volume. Among the travelers whose explorations are most suggestive were the Norse. For their movements, see *The Sagas of the Icelanders* (New York: Viking Penguin, 2000), 626–674; Magnus Magnusson and Hermann Pálsson, trans., *The Vinland Sagas: The Norse Discovery of America* (Baltimore: Penguin Classics, 1965); Kirsten Seaver, *The Frozen Echo: Greenland and the Exploration of North America, ca. 1000–1500* (Stanford: Stanford University Press, 1996); and William W. Fitzhugh and Elisabeth I. Ward., eds., *Vikings: The North Atlantic Saga* (Washington, D.C.: Smithsonian Institution Press, 2000). For perhaps the most adventurous traveler in the world before 1600, see Ross E. Dunn, *The Adventures of Ibn Battuta: A Muslim Traveler of the Fourteenth Century* (Berkeley: University of California Press, 1986). For the medieval era, see *Voyages et Voyageurs au Moyen Age: XXVIe Congrès de la S.H.M.E.S.* (Publications de la Sarbonne: Paris, 1996); Mary B. Campbell, *The Witness and the Other World: Exotic European Travel Writing, 400–1600* (Ithaca, N.Y.: Cornell University Press,

1988); and Morris Rossabi, *Voyager from Xanadu: Rabban Sauma and the First Journey from China to the West* (Tokyo: Kodansha, 1992). For travel specifically to India, see R. H. Major, ed., *India in the Fifteenth Century, being a collection of Narratives of Voyages to India*, Hakluyt Society, 1st ser., 22 (London, 1857). Felipe Fernández-Armesto's *Before Columbus: Exploration and Colonization from the Mediterranean to the Atlantic, 1229–1492* (Philadelphia: University of Pennsylvania Press, 1987), provides the necessary context for understanding the westward travels of Europeans in the period after 1492.

Sixteenth-century travels have received extraordinary attention from early modern scholars of history, art history, literature, and (to a lesser extent) anthropology. Much recent scholarship has focused on the encounters of different peoples, especially (judging from the high number of works published on the area) on the interactions between Europeans and non-Europeans in the early modern and modern worlds. The best starting point for this scholarship is Stuart Schwartz, ed., *Implicit Understanding: Observing, Reporting, and Reflecting on the Encounters between Europeans and Other Peoples in the Early Modern Era* (Cambridge: Cambridge University Press, 1994). There is much about travelers' accounts as works of ethnography in Margaret Hodgen's classic *Early Anthropology in the Sixteenth and Seventeenth Centuries* (Philadelphia: University of Pennsylvania Press, 1964) and in Anthony Pagden's superb *The Fall of Natural Man: The American Indian and the Origins of Comparative Ethnology* (Cambridge: Cambridge University Press, 1982). Karen Ordahl Kupperman and Joyce Chaplin have each written vital works on how Europeans (primarily the English) based their opinions of Native Americans on what they read in travel accounts; see Kupperman, *Indians and English: Facing Off in Early America* (Ithaca, N.Y.: Cornell University Press, 2000), and Chaplin, *Subject Matter: Technology, the Body, and Science on the Anglo-American Frontier, 1500–1676* (Cambridge, Mass.: Harvard University Press, 2001). Joan-Pau Rubiés's study of South Asia pushes this kind of argument further, looking at travel accounts as fundamental documents in the development of the discipline of ethnology; see his *Travel and Ethnology in the Renaissance: South India through European Eyes, 1250–1625* (Cambridge: Cambridge University Press, 2000). For a sense of the material world that travelers saw, see the superb pictures and essays in Jay Levenson, ed., *Circa 1492: Art in the Age of Exploration* (Washington, D.C./New Haven, Conn.: National Gallery of Art/Yale University Press, 1991).

Given the centrality of travel in the shaping of the modern world, it is not surprising that some of the most exciting scholarship in the past generation has focused on particular travelers, not all of whom are represented in these pages. In the annals of modern scholarship there is little that can rival the extraordinary work of Rolena Adorno and Patrick Charles Pautz, whose three-volume *Álvar Núñez Cabeza de Vaca: His Account, His Life, and the Expedition of Pánfilo de Narváez* (Lincoln: University of Nebraska Press, 1999) has become a monument to close textual analysis of a travel account. [For the narrative alone see Adorno and Pautz, eds., *The Narrative of Cabeza de Vaca* (Lincoln: University of Nebraska Press, 2003).] For excellent studies and editions of the writers whose works can be found in this collection, see (in alphabetical order by author, editor, or translator) José de Acosta, *Natural and Moral History of the Indies,* ed. Jane E. Morgan (Durham, N.C.: Duke University Press, 2002); Rolena Adorno, *Guáman Pomo: Writing and Resistance in Colonial Peru,* 2nd ed. (Austin: Institute of Latin American Studies/University of Texas Press, 2000); Alexandra Parma Cook and Noble David Cook, eds., *Pedro de Cieza de León, The Discovery and Conquest of Peru: Chronicles of New World Encounter* (Durham, N.C.: Duke University Press, 1998); Ramsay Cook, ed., *The Voyages of Jacques Cartier* (Toronto: University of Toronto Press, 1993); Philip Edwards, ed., *Last Voyages: Cavendish, Hudson, Ralegh: The Original Narratives* (Oxford: Oxford University Press, 1988); Felipe Fernández-Armesto, *Columbus* (Oxford: Oxford University Press, 1991); Edward S. Forster, *The Turkish Letters of Ogier Ghiselin de Busbecq, Imperial Ambassador at Constantinople, 1554–1562* (Oxford: Oxford University Press, 1927); George P. Hammond and Agapito Rey, eds., *Narratives of the Coronado Expedition, 1540–1542* (Albuquerque: University of New Mexico Press, 1940); Harry Kelsey, *Sir Francis Drake: The Queen's Pirate* (New Haven, Conn.: Yale University Press, 1998); Jean de Léry, *History of a Voyage to the Land of Brazil,* trans. Janet Whatley (Berkeley: University of California Press, 1990); Frank Lestrigant's study of André Thevet and his milieu, titled *Mapping the Renaissance World: The Geographical Imagination in the Age of Discovery,* trans. David Fausett (Berkeley: University of California Press, 1994); Ma Huan, *Ying-Yai Sheng-Lan: "The Overall Survey of the Ocean's Shores,"* ed. J. V. G. Mills, Hakluyt Society, extra ser., 42 (1970); James McDermott, *Martin Frobisher: Elizabethan Privateer* (New Haven, Conn.: Yale University Press, 2001); Harriet de Onis, trans., *The Incas of Pedro de Cieza de León* (Norman: University of Oklahoma Press, 1959); Antonio Pigafetta, *Magellan's Voyage: A Narrative Account of the First Circumnavigation,* trans. R. A. Skelton (New Haven, Conn.: Yale University Press, 1969); Roger Schlesinger and Arthur P. Stabler, eds., *André Thevet's North America: A Sixteenth-Century View* (Kingston, Ontario: McGill-Queen's University Press, 1986); Jonathan Spence, *The Memory Palace of Matteo Ricci* (New York: Viking, 1984); Sterling A. Stoudemire, ed.,

Natural History of the West Indies by Gonzalo Fernández de Oviedo, University of North Carolina Studies in the Romance Languages and Literatures 32 (Chapel Hill: University of North Carolina Press, 1959); Sanjay Subrahmanyam, *The Career and Legend of Vasco da Gama* (Cambridge: Cambridge University Press, 1997); and Wheeler M. Thackston, ed., *The Baburnama* (Washington, D.C./New York/ Freer Gallery of Art: Oxford University Press, 1996; New York: Modern Library, with an introduction by Salmon Rushdie, 2002).

Readers interested in particular parts of the world can find much that puts place at the center of the analysis, with attention to issues of geography and travel to specific locales. Much of David Northrup's superb *Africa's Discovery of Europe, 1450–1850* (Oxford University Press, 2002) is based explicitly on travel accounts, as are portions of Adrian Hastings's major study of Christianity, *The Church in Africa, 1450–1950* (Oxford University Press, 1994). Those interested in Asia, and particularly how Europeans and Asians understood each other, can do no better than to start with the monumental labor of Donald Lach (and his later collaborator Edwin J. Van Kley). His (and their) *Asia in the Making of Europe* will long remain a fundamental overview of relations between these two continents. The work appeared in three multipart volumes: *The Century of Discovery* (2 books), *A Century of Wonder* (2 books), and *A Century of Admiration* (4 books), all published by the University of Chicago Press (1965–1993). For works that deal explicitly with China, see especially Louise Levathes, *When China Ruled the Seas: The Treasure Fleet of the Dragon Throne, 1405–1433* (New York: Simon and Schuster, 1994), and Jonathan Spence, *The Chan's Great Continent: China in Western Minds* (New York: Norton, 1998). Scholars have paid close attention to the various kinds of travel by Muslims. The best starting point is the excellent collection of essays in Dale F. Eickelman and James Piscatori, eds., *Muslim Travellers: Pilgrimage, Migration, and the Religious Imagination* (Berkeley: University of California Press, 1990); also of use are Suraiya Faroqhi, *Pilgrims and Sultans: The Hajj under the Ottomans, 1517–1683* (London: I. B. Tauris, 1994), and Ian R. Netton, ed., *Golden Roads: Migration, Pilgrimage, and Travel in Medieval and Modern Islam* (Richmond, Surrey: Curzon Press, 1993).

For the Americas, the literature is now so extensive that no brief summary can do justice to it. Still, among the many works produced in preparation for the 500th anniversary of Christopher Columbus's initial voyage to the West and in the years since, see (in alphabetical order by author) Emerson W. Baker et al., eds., *American Beginnings: Exploration, Culture, and Cartography in the Land of Norumbega* (Lincoln: University of Nebraska Press, 1994); J. H.

Elliott, *The Old World and the New, 1492–1650* (Cambridge: Cambridge University Press, 1970); Anthony Grafton, *New Worlds, Ancient Texts: The Power of Tradition and the Shock of Discovery* (Cambridge, Mass. Harvard University Press, 1992); Stephen Greenblatt, *Marvelous Possessions: The Wonder of the New World* (Chicago: University of Chicago Press, 1991); Anthony Pagden, *European Encounters with the New World: From Renaissance to Romanticism* (New Haven, Conn.: Yale University Press, 1993); and Benjamin Schmidt, *Innocence Abroad: The Dutch Imagination and the New World, 1570–1670* (New York: Cambridge University Press, 2001). For a view of the Americas as they existed before the arrival of European travelers (and later colonists), see Alvin M. Josephy, Jr., ed., *America in 1492: The World of the Indian Peoples before the Arrival of Columbus* (New York: Alfred Knopf, 1992).

This collection provides evidence about travel several centuries ago. But even the most descriptive text must be read with the sense that the traveler always needs to make sense of a new locale. The recent publication of the philosopher Alain de Botton's *The Art of Travel* (London: Penguin, 2003) contains perhaps the wittiest modern commentary on travel, including meditations on the importance of seemingly mundane events. Perhaps no one has investigated the meaning of travel as thoroughly as the structural anthropologist Claude Lévi-Strauss, whose *Tristes Tropiques* (Paris: Librarie Plon, 1955) is available in an excellent translation by John and Doreen Weightman (New York: Atheneum, 1974; New York: Penguin, 1992). Lévi-Strauss's writings demonstrate an extraordinary consciousness of the act of travel itself and the clearest reminder that narratives generated during and after expeditions always reflect both the insights of the observer and the world visited.

Note on the Text

Most of the texts in this anthology were taken from sixteenth- or early seventeenth-century English language editions of the accounts. Spelling and punctuation have been silently modernized in places. For background information on a number of English writers, I relied on the *Dictionary of National Biography*; more specific information about non-English writers can be found in the headnotes to the chapters. Information about editions of many texts in this volume can be found in John Alden, et al., eds., *European Americana: A Chronological Guide to Works Printed in Europe Relating to the Americas, 1493–1776*, 6 vols. (New York: Readex, 1980–1998).

All pictures are reproduced with the permission of the Henry E. Huntington Library in San Marino, California.

Part I
Africa

Document 1

A Journal of the First Voyage of Vasco da Gama
1497–1499

Trans. E. G. Ravenstein (London: Hakluyt Society, 1898), 22–31

*Born in Sines, Portugal, Vasco da Gama (1469?–1524) is best known today
for pioneering a sea route from the Iberian peninsula to India.[1] In July 1497,
he left Lisbon and arrived ten months later in Calicut. By doing so, he helped
the Portuguese establish control over the import of spices into Europe. The
timing of his journey was crucial. When he left, Europeans had known about
Columbus's expeditions, and many had come to realize that the Spanish were
on the verge of enriching themselves with their American possessions. For the
Portuguese, who already had experience establishing colonies in the Atlantic,
da Gama's journey made perfect sense for their maritime empire. Yet if his attempt to reach Asia by sail made sense for those who plotted such journeys on
maps, the outcome of the actual expedition was far from guaranteed. Da Gama
and his crew often faced hostile people during their first journey and on a subsequent expedition in 1502. The trail that later brought cinnamon, cloves,
and nutmeg from the Spice Islands to Europe ran along territory scarred
by skirmishes between travelers and local residents.*

*Much of da Gama's journey took him along the coast of Africa. The excerpt
here reveals one of the many encounters between religious traditions, in this
case the meeting of European Christians and African Muslims. Da Gama's account reminds us of the multiple religious differences that travelers confronted
when they landed far from their homes. This account is typical of the kind that
travelers recorded in journals during their expeditions. As a day-by-day record,
it emphasizes activities of the moment and indulges in more immediate, less
thoughtful observations than reports written after the fact, where memory can
merge with observation. This report of da Gama's journey reveals that even
momentous news, such as the potential discovery of the home of the legendary
African Christian prince Prester John, called for little more on-the-spot commentary than the more mundane details that often filled a traveler's days.*

---

1. Much about Da Gama's life remains a mystery, as Sanjay Subrahmanyam has noted;
even his birthplace is not known definitively; see Subrahmanyam, *The Career and Legend
of Vasco Da Gama* (Cambridge: Cambridge University Press, 1997), 18–23.

On Friday morning [March 2, 1498], Nicolau Coelho, when attempting to enter the bay, mistook the channel and came upon a bank. When putting about ship, toward the other ships which followed in his wake, Coelho perceived some sailing boats approaching from a village on this island, in order to welcome the captain-major and his brother. As for ourselves we continued in the direction of our proposed anchorage, these boats following us all the while, and making signs for us to stop. When we had cast anchor in the roadstead of the island from which these boats had come, there approached seven or eight of them, including *almadias*, the people in them playing upon *anafils*. They invited us to proceed further into the bay, offering to take us into port if we desired it. Those among them who boarded our ships ate and drank what we did, and went their way when they were satisfied.

The captain thought that we should enter this bay in order that we might find out what sort of people we had to deal with; that Nicolau Coelho should go first in his vessel, to take soundings at the entrance, and that, if found practicable, we should follow him. As Coelho prepared to enter he struck the point of the island and broke his helm, but he immediately disengaged himself and regained deep water. I was with him at the time. When we were again in deep water we struck our sails and cast anchor at a distance of two bowshots from the village.

The people of this country are of a ruddy complexion and well made. They are Mohameddans [Muslims], and their language is the same as that of the Moors. Their dresses are of fine linen or cotton stuffs, with variously colored stripes, and of rich and elaborate workmanship. They all wear *toucas* [hats] with borders of silk embroidered in gold. They are merchants, and have transactions with white Moors, four of whose vessels were at the time in port, laden with gold, silver, cloves, pepper, ginger, and silver rings, as also with quantities of pearls, jewels, and rubies, all of which articles are used by the people of this country. We understood them to say that all these things, with the exception of gold, were brought thither by these Moors; that further on, where we were going to, they abounded, and that precious stones, pearls and spices were so plentiful that there was no need to purchase them as they could be collected in baskets. All this we learned through a sailor the captain-major had with him, and who, having formerly been a prisoner among the Moors, understood their language.

These Moors, moreover, told us that along the route which we were about to follow we should met with numerous shoals; that there were many cities along the coast, and also an island, one half the population of which consisted of Moors and the other half of Christians, who were at war with each other. This island was said to be very wealthy.

We were told, moreover, that Prester John resided not far from this place; that he held many cities along the coast, and that the inhabitants of those cities were great merchants and owned big ships. The residence of Prester John was said to be far in the interior, and could be reached only on the back of camels. These Moors had also brought hither two Christian captives from India. This information, and many other things which we heard, rendered us so happy that we cried with joy, and prayed God to grant us health, so that we might behold what we so much desired.

In this place and island of Moncobiquy [Mozambique] there resided a chief who had the title of Sultan, and was like a viceroy. He often came aboard our ships attended by some of his people. The captain-major gave him many good things to eat, and made him a present of hats, *marlotas*, corals and many other articles. He was, however, so proud that he treated all we gave him with contempt, and asked for scarlet cloth, of which we had none. We gave him, however, of all the things we had.

One day the captain-major invited him to a repast, when there was an abundance of figs and comfits, and begged him for two pilots to go with us. He at once granted this request, subject to our coming to terms with them. The captain-major gave each of them thirty *mitkals* in gold and two *marlotas*, on condition that from the day on which they received this payment one of them should always remain on board if the other desired to go on land. With these terms they were well satisfied.

On Saturday, March 10, we set sail and anchored one league out at sea, close to an island [of S. Jorge], where mass was said on Sunday, when those who wished to do so confessed and joined in the communion.

One of our pilots lived on the island, and when we had anchored we armed two boats to go in search of him. The captain-major went in one boat and Nicolau Coelho in the other. They were met by five or six barcas [boats] coming from the island, and crowded with people armed with bows and long arrows and bucklers, who gave them to understand by signs that they were to return to the town. When the captain saw this he secured the pilot whom he had taken with him, and ordered the bombards to fire upon the boats. Paulo de Gama, who had remained with the ships, so as to be prepared to render succor in case of need, no sooner heard the reports of the bombards than he started in the *Berrio*. The Moors, who were already flying, fled still faster, and gained the land before the *Berrio* was able to come up with them. We then returned to our anchorage.

The vessels of this country are of good size and decked. There are no nails, and the planks are held together by cords, as are also those of their barcos. The sails are made of palm-matting. Their mariners have Genoese needles, by which they steer, quadrants, and navigating charts.

The palms of this country yield a fruit as large as a melon, of which the kernel is eaten. It has a nutty flavor. There also grow in abundance melons and cucumbers, which were brought to us for barter.

On the day in which Coelho entered the port, the Lord of the place came on board with a numerous suite. He was received well, and Coelho presented him with a red hood, in return for which the Lord handed him a black rosary, which he made use of when saying his prayers, to be held as a pledge. He then begged Nicolau Coelho for the use of his boat, to take him ashore. This was granted. And after he had landed he invited those who had accompanied him to his house, where he gave them to eat. He then dismissed them, giving them a jar of bruised dates made into a preserve with cloves and cumin, as a present for Nicolau Coelho. Subsequently he sent many things to the captain-major. All this happened at the time when he took us for Turks or for Moors from some foreign land, for in case we came from Turkey he begged to be shown the bows of our country and our books of the Law. But when they learnt that we were Christians they arranged to seize and kill us by treachery. The pilot, whom we took with us, subsequently revealed to us all they intended to do, if they were able.

On Sunday [March 11] we celebrated mass beneath a tall tree on the island [of S. Jorge]. We returned on board and at once set sail, taking with us many fowls, goats, pigeons, which had been given us in exchange for small glass-beads.

On Tuesday we saw high mountains rising on the other side of a cape. The coast near the cape was sparsely covered with trees, resembling elms. We were at that time over twenty leagues from our starting-place, and there we remained becalmed during Tuesday and Wednesday. During the following night we stood off shore with a light easterly wind, and in the morning found ourselves four leagues abast Mozambique, but we went again forward on that day until the evening, when we anchored once more close to the island [of S. Jorge] on which mass had been celebrated the preceding Sunday, and there we remained eight days waiting for a favorable wind.

During our stay here the King of Mozambique sent word that he wanted to make peace with us and to be our friend. His ambassador was a white Moor and sharif, that is priest, and at the same time a great drunkard.

Whilst at this place a Moor with his little son came on board one of our ships, and asked to be allowed to accompany us, as he was from near Mecca, and had come to Mozambique as pilot of a vessel from that country.

As the weather did not favor us it became necessary once more to enter the port of Mozambique, in order to procure the water of which we stood in need, for the watering place is on the mainland. This water is drunk by the inhabitants of the island, for all the water they have there is brackish.

On Thursday we entered the port, and when it grew dark we lowered our boats. At midnight the captain-major and Nicolau Coelho, accompanied by some of us, started in search of water. We took with us the Moorish pilot, whose object appeared to be to make his escape, rather than to guide us to a watering-place. As a matter of fact he either would not or could not find a watering-place, although we continued our search until morning. We then withdrew to our ships.

In the evening we returned to the main land, attended by the same pilot. On approaching the watering-place we saw about twenty men on the beach. They were armed with assegais [spears], and forbade our approach. The captain-major upon this ordered three bombards to be fired upon them, so that we might land. Having effected our landing, these men fled into the bush, and we took as much water as we wanted. When the sun was about to set we discovered that a negro belonging to João de Coimbra had effected his escape.

On Sunday morning, the 24th of March, being the eve of Lady Day, a Moor came abreast our ships, and told us that if we wanted water we might go in search of it, giving us to understand that we should meet with something which would make us turn back. The captain-major no sooner heard this than he resolved to go, in order to show that we were able to do them harm if we desired it. We forthwith armed our boats, placing bombards in their poops, and started for the village. The Moors had constructed palisades by lashing planks together, so that those behind them could not be seen. They were at the time walking along the beach, armed with assegais, swords, bows, and slings, with which they hurled stones at us. But our bombards soon made it so hot for them that they fled behind their palisades; but this turned out to their injury rather than their profit. During the three hours that we were occupied in this manner we saw two men killed, one on the beach and the other behind the palisades. When we were weary of this work we retired to our ships to dine. They at once began to fly, carrying their chattels in *almadias* to a village on the mainland.

After dinner we started in our boats, in the hope of being able to take a few prisoners, whom we might exchange for the two Indian Christians whom they held captive and the negro who had deserted. With this object in view we chased an *almadia*, which belonged to the sharif and was laden with his chattels, and another in which were four negroes. The latter was captured by Paulo da Gama, whilst the one laden with chattels was abandoned by the crew as soon as they reached the land. We took still another *almadia* which had likewise been abandoned. The negroes we took on board our ships. In the *almadias* we found fine cotton-stuffs, baskets made of palm-fronds, a glazed jar containing butter, glass phials with scented water, books of the Law, a box containing skeins of cotton, a cotton net, and many small baskets filled with millet. All these things, with the exception of the books, which were kept back to be shown to the king, were given by the captain-major to the sailors who were with him and with the other captains.

On Sunday we took in water, and on Monday we proceeded in our armed boats to the village, when the inhabitants spoke to us from their houses, they daring no longer to venture on the beach. Having discharged a few bombards at them we rejoined our ships.

On Tuesday we left the town and anchored close to the islets of São Jorge, where we remained for three days, in the hope that God would grant us a favorable wind.

Document 2

The Second Voyage to Guinea (1554)

"The second voyage to Guinea set out by Sir George Barne, Sir John Yorke, Thomas Lok, Anthonie Hickman and Edward Castelin, in the yere 1554," in Richard Hakluyt, ed., *The Principal Navigations, Voyages, Traffiques, and Discoveries of the English Nation*, 3 vols. (London, 1598–1600), 2:331–35

Europeans whose journeys took them to Africa in the sixteenth century tended to stay near the coastline. But they knew that there would be people at home who wanted to know about the interior. As a result, travelers tried to make distinctions between parts of the continent. Their depictions of what life was like might not fit a modern ethnographic account, and the details tend to be schematic. Still, the mixture of fiction (such as Europeans' continued belief in Prester John) and precise, detailed observations about what travelers did see could make for engaging reading. This account included much that would have enticed the curious, including mention of Blemmyae who lacked heads, Ganphantes who lived without clothes, satyrs who had the "shape" of humans but little else, and Ichthyophagi who lived on fish alone. To the unnamed author, such finds would have elicited little surprise since these monsters and other notable discoveries across Africa could be expected after references to them by learned authorities such as Pliny and Josephus centuries earlier.

In the account that follows, English explorers tried to gather information about what life was like in territory that they saw and in areas that they heard about. They also demonstrated the concern for travel itself, notably how long the journey took (especially the return, when the winds were less favorable). The travelers were fascinated by the African climate and its lack of winter, though they had obvious difficulty understanding how anyone could survive the blistering heat of the equatorial region. They were surprised by the agriculture of the Africans, noting that many of the crops grown there were impressive by European standards. Of course, some of the claims that they made might have seemed far-fetched when they got home. But given the exact description in so many places in the report, who would reasonably question any of the other claims in such an account? Not Richard Hakluyt, who came across this report decades later and found it sufficiently reliable to include in his collection of narratives.

Now therefore I will speak somewhat of the people and their manners, and manner of living, with another brief description of Africa also. It is to be understood, that the people which now inhabit the regions of the coast of Guinea, and the middle parts of Africa, as Libya the inner, and Nubia, with divers other great & large regions about the same, were in olden time called Æthiopes and Nigritæ, which we now call Moors, Moorens, or Negroes, a people of beastly living, without a God, law, religion, or common wealth, and so scorched and vexed with the heat of the sun, that in many places they curse it when it riseth. Of the regions and people about the inner Libya (called Libya interior) Gemma Phrysius writeth thus.

Libya interior is very large and desolate, in the which are many horrible wildernesses & mountains, replenished with divers kinds of wild and monstrous beasts and serpents. First from Mauritania or Barbary toward the South is Getulia, a rough and savage region, whose inhabitants are wild and wandering people. After these follow the people called Melanogetuli and Pharusij, which wander in the wilderness, carrying with them great gourds of water. The Ethiopians called Nigritæ occupy a great part of Africa, and are extended to the West Ocean. Southward also they reach to the river Nigritis, whose nature agreeth with the river of Nilus, forasmuch as it is increased and diminished at the same time, and bringeth forth the like beasts as the Crocodile. By reason whereof, I think this to be the same river which the Portuguese call Senega: For this river is also of the same nature. It is furthermore marvelous and very strange that is said of this river: And this is, that on the one side thereof, the inhabitants are of high stature and black, and on the other side, of brown or tawny color, and low stature, which thing also our men confirm to be true.

There are also other people of Libya called Garamantes, whose women are common: for they contract no matrimony, neither have respect to chastity. After these are the nations of the people called Pyrei, Sathiodaphnitæ, Odrangi, Mimaces, Lynxamate, Dolopes, Agangine, Leuci Ethiopes, Xilicei Ethiopes, Calcei Ethiopes, and Nubi. These have the same situation in Ptolemy that they now give to the kingdom of Nubia. Here are certain Christians under the dominion of the great Emperor of Ethiopia, called Prester John. From these toward the West is a great nation of people called Aphricerones, whose region (as far as may be gathered by conjecture) is the same that is now called Regnum Orguene, confining upon the East parts of Guinea. From hence Westward, and somewhat toward the north, are the kingdoms of Gambra and Budromel, not far from the river of Senega. And from hence toward the inland regions, and along by the sea coast, are the regions of Ginoie or Guinea, which we commonly call Ginnee. On the Westside of these regions toward the Ocean, is the cape or point called Cabo verde, or Caput viride, (that is) the green cape, to the which the Portuguese first direct their course when they sail to America, or the land of Brazil. Then departing from hence, they turn to the right hand toward the quarter of the wind called Garbino, which is between the West and the South. But to speak somewhat more of Ethiopia: although there are many nations of people so named, yet is Ethiopia chiefly divided into two parts, whereof the one is called Aethiopia under Egypt, a great & rich region. To this perteineth the Island Meroe, embraced round about with the streams of the river Nilus. In this Island women reigned in old time. Josephus writeth, that it was sometime called Sabea: and that the Queen of Saba came from thence to Jerusalem, to hear the wisdom of Salomon. From whence toward the East reigneth the said Christian Emperor Prester John, whom some call Papa Jonannes, & other say that he is called Pean Juan (that is) great John, whose Empire reacheth far beyond Nilus, and is extended to the coasts of the Red sea & Indian sea. The middle of the region is almost 66 degrees of longitude, and 12 degrees of latitude. About this region inhabit the people Clodi, Risophagi, Babylonij, Axiunitæ, Molili, and Molibæ. After these is the region called Troglodytica, whose inhabitants dwell in caves and dens: for these are their houses, & the flesh of serpents their meat, as writeth Pliny, and Diodorus Siculus. They have no speech, but rather a grinning and chattering. There are also people without heads, called Blemines, having their eyes and mouth in their breast. Likewise Strucophagi, and naked Ganphasantes: Satyrs also, which have nothing of men but only shape. Moreover Oripei, great hunters. Mennones also, and the region of Smyrnophora, which bringeth forth myrrh. After these is the region of Azania, in the which many Elephants are found. A great part of the other regions of Africa that are beyond the Aequinocitall line, are now ascribed to the kingdom of Melinde, whose inhabitants are accustomed to traffic with the nations of Arabia, and their king is joined in friendship with the king of Portugal, and payeth tribute to Prester John.

The other Ethiope, called Æthiopia interior (that is) the inner Ethiope, is not yet known for the greatness thereof, but only by the sea coasts: yet is it described in this manner. First from the Aequinoctiall toward ye South, is a great region of Aethiopians, which bringeth forth white Elephants, Tigers, and the beasts called Rhinoceroses. Also a region that bringeth forth plenty of cinnamon, lying between the branches of Nilus. Also the kingdom of Habech or Habasia, a region of Christian men, lying both on this side and beyond Nilus. Here are also the Aethiopians, called Ichthiophagi (that is) such as live only by fish, and were sometimes subdued by the wars of great Alexander. Furthermore the Aethiopians called Rhapsij, & Anthropophagi, who are accustomed to eat man's flesh, inhabit the regions near unto the mountains called Montes Lunæ (that is) the mountains of the Moon. Gazatia is under the Tropic of Capricorn. After this followeth the front of Africa, the Cape of Buena Speranza, or Caput Bonæ Spei, that is, the Cape of good hope, by the which they pass that sail from Lisbon to Calicut. But by what names the Capes and gulfs are called, forasmuch as the same are in every globe and card, it were here superfluous to rehearse them.

Some write that Africa was named by the Grecians, because it is without cold. For the Greek letter Alpha or A signifieth privation, void, or without: and Phrice signifieth cold. For in deed although in the stead of Winter they have a cloudy and tempestuous season, yet is it not cold, but rather smothering hot, with hot showers of rain also, and somewhere such scorching winds, that what by one means and other, they seem at certain times to live as it were in furnaces, and in manner already half way in Purgatory or hell. Gemma Phrisius writeth, that in certain parts of Africa, as in Atlas the greater, the air in the night season is seen shining, with many strange fires and flames rising in manner as high as the Moon: and that in the element are sometime heard as it were the sound of pipes, trumpets and drums: which noises may perhaps be caused by the vehement and sundry motions of such fiery exhalations in the air, as we see the like in many experiences wrought by fire, air and wind. The hollowness also, and divers reflexions and breaking of the clouds may be great causes hereof, beside the vehement cold of the middle region of the air, whereby the said fiery exhalations, ascending thither, are suddenly sticken back with great force: for even common and daily experience teacheth us, by the whissing of a burning torch, what noise fire maketh in the air, and much more where it striveth when it is enclosed with air, as appeareth in guns, and as the like is seen in only are enclosed, as in Organ pipes, and such other instruments that go by wind. For wind (as say the Philosophers) is none other than air vehemently moved, as we see in a pair of bellows, and such other.

Some of our men of good credit that were in this last voyage to Guinea, affirm earnestly that in the night season they felt a sensible heat to come from the beams of the moon. The which thing, although it be strange and insensible to us that inhabit cold regions, yet doth it stand with good reason that it may so be, forasmuch as the nature of stars and planets (as writeth Pliny) consisteth of fire, and conteineth in it a spirit of life, which cannot be without heat.

And, that the Moon giveth heat upon the earth the Prophet David seemeth to confirm in his 121 Psalm, where speaking of such men as are defended from evils by God's protection, he saith thus: Per diem Sol non exuret te, nec Luna per noctem. That is to say, In the day the Sun shall not burn thee, nor the Moon by night.

They say furthermore, that in certain places of the sea they saw certain streams of water, which they call spouts, falling out of the air into the sea, & that some of these are big as the great pillars of Churches: insomuch that sometimes they fall into ships, and put them in great danger of drowning. Some fain [are disposed to think] that these should be the Cataracts of heaven, which were all opened at Noah's flood. But I think them rather to be such fluxions and eruptions as Aristotle in his book de Mundo saith, to chance in the sea. For speaking of such strange things as are seen often times in the sea, he writeth thus. Oftentimes also even in the sea are seen evaporations of fire, and such eruptions and breaking forth of springs, that the mouths of rivers are opened, Whirlpools, and fluxions are caused of such other vehement motions, not only in the middest of the sea, but also in creeks & straights. At certain times also, a great quantity of water is suddenly lifted up and carried about with the Moon, &c. By which words of Aristotle it doth appear that such waters be lifted up in one place at one time, and suddenly fall down in an other place at another time. And hereunto perhaps perteineth it that Richard Chanceller told me that [he] heard Sebastian Cabot's report, that (as far as I remember) either about the coasts of Brazil or Rio de Plata, his ship or pinnace was suddenly lifted from the sea, and cast upon land, I wot [know] not how far. The which thing, and such other like wonderful and strange works of nature while I consider, and call to remembrance the narrowness of man's understanding and knowledge, in comparison of her mighty power, I can but cease to marvel and confess with Pliny, that nothing is to her impossible, the least part of whose power is not yet known to men. Many things more our men saw and considered in this voyage, worthy to be noted, whereof I have thought good to put some in memory, that the reader may as well take pleasure in the variety of things, as knowledge of the history. Among other things therefore, touching the manners and nature of the people, this may seem strange, that their princes & noble men use to pounce and raise their skins with pretty knots in divers forms, as it were branched damask, thinking that to be a decent ornament. And albeit they go in manner all naked, yet are many of them, & especially their women, in manner laden with collars, bracelets, hoops, and chains, either of gold, copper, or ivory. I myself have one of their bracelets of Ivory, weighing two pound and six ounces of Troy weight, which make eight and thirty ounces: this one of their women did wear upon her arm. It is made of one whole piece of the biggest part of the tooth, turned and somewhat carved, with a hole in the midst, wherein they put their hands to wear it on their arm. Some have on every arm one, and as many on their legs, wherewith some of them are so galled, that although they are in manner made lame thereby, yet will they by no means leave them off. Some wear also on their legs great shackles of bright copper, which they think to be no less comely. They wear also collars, bracelets, garlands, and girdles, of certain blue stones like beads. Likewise some of their women wear on their bare arms certain foresleeves made of the plates of beaten gold. On their fingers also they wear rings, made of golden wires, with a knot or wreath, like unto that which children make in a ring of a rush. Among other things of gold that our men bought of them for exchange of their wares, were certain dogs-chains and collars.

They are very wary people in their bargaining, and will not lose one spark of gold of any value. They use weights and measures, and are very circumspect in occupying the same. They that shall have to do with them, must use them gently: for they will not traffic or bring in any wares if they be evil used. At the first voyage that our men had into these parts, it so chanced that at their departure from the first place where they did traffic, one of them either stole a musk Cat, or took her away by force, not mistrusting that that should have hindered their bargaining in another place whither they intended to go. But for all the haste they could make with full sails, the same of their misusage so prevented him, that the people of that place also, offended thereby, would bring in no wares: insomuch that they were enforced either to restore the Cat, or pay for her at their price, before they could traffic there.

Their houses are made of four posts or trees, and covered with boughs.

Their common feeding is of roots, & such fishes as they take, whereof they have great plenty.

There are also such flying fishes as are seen in the sea of the West Indies. Our men salted of their fishes, hoping to provide store thereof: but they would take no salt, and must therefore be eaten forthwith as some say. Howbeit other affirm, that if they be salted immediately after they be taken, they will last uncorrupted ten or twelve days. But this is more strange, that part of such flesh as they carried with them out of England, which putrefied there, became sweet again at their return to the clime of temperate regions.

They use also strange making of bread, in this manner. They grind between two stones with their hands as much corn as they think may suffice their family, and when they have thus brought it to flour, they put thereto a certain quantity of water, and make thereof very thin dough, which they stick upon some post of their houses, where is it baked by the heat of the Sun: so that when the master of the house or any of his family will eat thereof, they take it down and eat it.

They have very fair wheat, the ear whereof is two handfuls in length, and as big as a great Bulrush, and almost four inches about where it is biggest. The stem or straw seemeth to be almost as big as the little finger of a man's hand, or little less. The grains of this wheat are as big as our peason, round also, and very white, and somewhat shining, like pearls that have lost their color. Almost all the substance of them turneth into flour, & maketh little bran or none. I told in one ear two hundred & threescore grains. The ear is enclosed in three blades longer then itself, & of two inches broad a piece. And by this fruitfulness the Sun seemeth partly to recompense such griefs and molestations as they otherwise receive by the fervent heat thereof. It is doubtless a worthy contemplation to consider the contrary effects of the sun: or rather the contrary passions of such things as receive the influence of his beams, either to their hurt or benefit. Their drink is either water, or the juice that droppeth from the cut branches of the barren Date trees, called Palmitos. For either they hang great gourds at the said branches every evening, and let them so hang all night, or else they set them on the ground under the trees, that the drops may fall therein. They say that this kind of drink is in taste much like unto whey, but somewhat sweeter, and more pleasant. They cut the branches every evening, because they are seared up in the day by the heat of the Sun. They have also great beans as big as chestnuts, and very hard, with a shell in the stead of a husk.

Many things more might be said of the manners of the people, and of the wonders and monstrous things that are engendered in Africa. But it shall suffice to have said thus much of such things as our men partly saw, and partly brought with them.

And whereas before speaking of the fruits of grains, I described the same to have holes by the side (as in deed it hath, as it is brought hither) yet was I afterward informed, that those holes were made to put strings through the fruit, thereby to hang them up to dry at the Sun. They grow not past a foot and a half, or two foot from the ground, and are as red as blood when they are gathered. The grains themselves are called of the Physitions Grana Paradisi.

At their coming home the keels of their ships were marvelously overgrown with certain shells of two inches length and more, as thick as they could stand, and of such bigness that a man might put his thumb in the mouths of them. They certainly affirm that in these there groweth a certain slimy substance, which at the length slipping out of the shell and falling in the sea, becommeth those fouls which we call barnacles. The like shells have been seen in ships returning from Iceland, but these shells were not past half an inch in length. Of the other that came from Guinea, I saw the Primrose lying in the dock, and in manner covered with the said shells, which in my judgment should greatly hinder her sailing. Their ships were also in many places eaten with the worms called Bromas or Bissas, whereof mention is made in the Decades. These creep between the planks, which they eat through in many places.

Among other things that chanced to them in this voyage, this is worthy to be noted, that whereas they sailed thither in seven weeks, they could return in no less space than twenty weeks. The cause whereof they say to be this: that about the coast of Cabo Verde the wind is ever at the East, by reason whereof they were enforced to sail far out of their course into the main Ocean, to find the wind at the West to bring them home. There died of our men at this last voyage about twenty and four, whereof many died at their return into the clime of the cold regions, as between the Islands of Azores and England. They brought with them certain black slaves, whereof some were tall and strong men, and could well agree with our meats and drinks. The cold and moist air somewhat offend them. Yet doubtless men that are born in hot Regions may better abide cold, then men that are born in cold Regions may abide heat, forasmuch as vehement heat resolveth the radical moisture of men's bodies, as cold constrainth and preserveth the same.

This is also to be considered as a secret work of nature, that throughout all Africa, under the Æquinoctial line, and near about the same on both sides, the regions are extreme hot, and the people very black. Whereas contrarily such regions of the West Indies as are under the same line are very temperate, and the people neither black, nor with curlde [curled] and short wool on their heads, as they of Africa have, but of the color of an Olive, with long and black hair on their heads: the cause of which variety is declared in divers places in the Decades.

It is also worthy to be noted that some of them that were at this voyage told me: That is, that they overtook the course of the Sun, so that they had it North from them at noon, the 14 day of March. And to have said thus much of these voyages, it may suffice.

Document 3

The Voyage Set Forth by M. John Newton and M. John Bird (1588)

By Anthony Ingram, "The voyage set forth by M. John Newton, and M. John Bird marchants of London to the Kingdom and City of Benin in Africa, in the year 1588," in Richard Hakluyt, ed., *The Principal Navigations, Voyages, Traffiques, and Discoveries of the English Nation*, 3 vols. (London, 1598–1600), 2: 331–35

When Richard Hakluyt published his Principall Navigations, Voyages, and Discoveries of the English Nation *in 1589 he had a number of goals for his project. By proving that the English had journeyed to distant parts of the world and profited from those excursions, he encouraged Queen Elizabeth and her advisors that colonizing the Atlantic coast of North America would be beneficial for the realm. But he was also keen to show how successful the English had been in other ventures too, from antiquity to the present.*

Despite the bulk of the materials that he gathered for his collection, Hakluyt continued to keep an eye out for additional tales or information that had escaped him in the late 1580s. Over the course of the 1590s, those in possession of certain crucial documents provided new information for him, no doubt hoping that their news would earn a coveted spot in any future collection of Hakluyt's travel accounts. Among those who approached Hakluyt were individuals who possessed knowledge of distant trading opportunities. When he organized a second collection for publication in three large volumes from 1598 to 1600, he changed the title to explicitly refer to the centrality of commerce. Titled the Principal Navigations, Voiages, Traffiques, and Discoveries of the English Nation, *the book provided readers with details about commercial as well as cultural discoveries.*

Anthony Ingram's account of the journey of two London merchants to Benin in 1588 was exactly the kind of document that Hakluyt wanted. This report went into great detail about the kinds of commodities to be found in certain locations, as well as the routes that merchants' ships had taken. Further, as Ingram and Hakluyt realized, alliances made for economic motivations could also serve to translate cultural or political details from one people to another. Yet as Ingram's account makes plain, the transmission of pathogens followed

these same routes, often devastating visitors who had no immunity to the
ravages of local diseases or any obvious cures for them.

Worshipful Sirs, the discourse of our whole proceeding in this voyage
will ask more time and a person in better health then I am at this present, so
that I trust you will pardon me, till my coming up to you: in the mean time let
this suffice. Whereas we departed in the month of December from the coast
of England with your good ship the Richard of Arundell and the pinnace, we
held on our direct course towards our appointed port, and the 14 day of February following we arrived in the haven of Benin, where we found not water
enough to carry the ship over the bar, so that we left her without in the road,
and with the pinnace & ship boat, into which we had put the chiefest of our
merchandise, we went up the river to a place called Goto, where we arrived
the 20 of February, the foresaid Goto being the nearest place that we could
come to by water, to go for Benin. From thence we presently sent Negroes to
the king, to certify him of our arrival, and of the cause of our coming thither:
who returned to us again the 22 day with a noble man in their company to
bring us up to the City, and with 200 Negroes to carry our commodities:
hereupon the 23 day we delivered our merchandize to the king's factor, & the
25 day we came to the great City of Benin, where we were well entertained:
The six & twenty day we went to the Court to have spoken with the king,
which (by reason of a solemn feast then kept amongst them) we could not do:
but yet we spoke with his Veadore, or chief man, that hath the dealing with
the Christians: and we conferred with him concerning our trading, who answered us, that we should have all things to our desire, both in pepper and
Elephants' teeth.

The first of March, we were admitted to the king's presence, and he made
us the like courteous answer for our traffic: the next day we went again to the
Court, where the foresaid Veadore showed us one basket of green pepper, and
another of dry in the stalks: we desired to have it plucked from the stalks and
made clean, who answered, that it would ask time, but yet [it] should be done:
and that against another year it should be in better readiness, & the reason
why we found it so unprepared was, because in this king's time no Christians
had ever resorted thither, to lade pepper. The next day there were sent us 12
baskets, and so a little every day until the 9 of March at which time we had
made upon 64 serons of pepper, and 28 Elephants' teeth. In this time of our

being at Benin (our natures at this first time not so well acquainted with that climate) we fell all of us into the disease of the fever, whereupon the Captain sent me down with those goods which we already had received, to the rest of our men at Goto: where being arrived, I found all the men of our pinnace sick also, and by reason of their weakness not able to convey the pinnace and any goods down to the place where our ship road: but by good hap within two hours after my coming to Goto, the boat came up from the ship, to see how all things stood with us, so that I put the goods into the boat, and went down towards the ship: but by that time I was come aboard, many of our men died: namely, Master Benson, the Cooper, the Carpenter, & 3 or 4 more, & my self was also in such a weak state that I was not able to return again to Benin. Whereupon I sent up Samuel Dunne, and the Surgeon with him to our men, that were about to let their blood, if it were thought needful: who at their coming to Benin, found the Captain and your son William Bird dead, and Thomas Hempsteede very weak, who also died within two days after their coming thither. This sorrowful accident caused them such pepper and teeth, as they could then find, speedily to return to the ship, as by the Cargason will appear: at their coming away the Veadore told them, that if they could or would stay any longer time, he would use all possible expedition to bring in more commodities: but the common sickness so increased and continued amongst us all, that by the time our men which remained were come aboard, we had so many sick and dead of our company, that we looked all for the same happe, and so though to loose both our ship, life, country and all. Very hardly and with much ado could we get up our anchors, but yet at the last by the mercy of God having gotten them up, but leaving our pinnace behind us, we got to sea, and set sail, which was upon the 13 of April. After which by little and little our men began to gather up their crumbs and to recover some better strength: and so sailing betwixt the Islands of Cape Verde, and the main we came to the Islands of the Azores upon the 25 of July, where our men began a fresh to grow ill, and divers died, among whom Samuel Dun[ne] was one, and as many as remained living were in a hard case: but in the midst of our distress, it fell so well out, by God's good providence, that we met with your ship the Barke Burre, on this side the North cape, which did not only keep us good company, but also sent us six fresh men aboard, without whose help, we should surely have tasted of many inconveniences. But by this good means we are now at the last arrived in Plymouth, this 9 day of September: and for want of better health at this time, I refer the further knowledge of more particularities, till my coming to London.

Document 4

The Adventures of Andrew Battel

"The Adventures of Andrew Battel of Leigh in Essex, sent by the Portuguese prisoner to Angola," in Samuel Purchas, *Hakluytus Posthumus, or Purchas His Pilgrimes,* 4 vols. (London, 1625), 2: 974–77

Andrew Battel, probably born in the small English town of Leigh in Essex, agreed to join the explorer Abraham Cocke's journey to Brazil in 1589. The journey across the Atlantic went well, and Battel and the other English travelers established themselves on the uninhabited island of Ile Grande off the coast. Getting low on supplies after one month on shore, Battel went along on a short voyage to the island of Saint Sebastian to find sustenance. There he and a few others were captured by natives, who apparently traded them to the Portuguese. Battel found himself a passenger on a vessel back across the Atlantic, this time bound for Angola.

As a captive Battel spent weeks at a time in different towns, often among the Imbangala (he called them "Gagas"). According to his account, they were cannibals and also engaged in infanticide routinely. They believed that all deaths could be attributed to witchcraft, a belief that would have made sense to his European readers. The Gagas inhabited a territory with an astonishing range of domesticated and wild animals, elephants whose tusks—which he routinely called "teeth"—were crucial in economic and spiritual matters.

Few details about Battel are known today. After his release from captivity, he returned to London in 1610, after having spent perhaps twenty years in Africa. He came home with an astonishing report that provided the English with a purported eyewitness account of human depravity. In the generations that followed, such reports contributed to the European notion that at least some Africans were savages and thus fit subjects for enslavement.

In our second Voyage turning up along the Coast, we came to the Morro, or Cliff of Benguele, which standeth in twelve degrees of Southerly latitude. Here we saw a mighty Cape of men on the Southside of the river Cova. And being desirous to know what they were, we went on shore with our Boat; & presently there came a troop of five hundred men to the water side. We asked them, Who they were? then they told us, that they were the Gagas, or Gindes; that came from Serra de Lion, and passed through the City of Congo; and so traveled to the East-ward of the great City of Angola, which is called Dongo. The great Gaga, which was their General, came down to the water's side to see us. For he had never seen white men before. He asked, wherefore we came? We told him, that we came to trade upon the Coast: then he bade us welcome, and called us on shore with our Commodities: we laded our ship with slaves in seven days, and bought them to good cheap, that many did not cost one Riall a piece, which were worth in the City twelve Millie-reys.

Being ready to depart the great Gaga stayed us, and desired our Boat to pass his men over the River Cova: for he determined to overrun the Realm of Benguele, which was on the North-side of the River Cova. So we went with him to his Camp, which was very orderly entrenched with piles of wood. We had Houses provided for us that night, and many burdens of Palm-wine, Cows, Goats, and Flour.

In the morning before day the General did strike his Gongo, which is an Instrument of War that soundeth like a Bell; and presently made an Oration with a loud voice, that all the Camp might hear, that he would destroy the Benguelas, with such courageous and vehement speeches, as were not to be looked for among the Heathen people: and presently they were all in arms, and marched to the River's side, where he had provided Gingados. And being ready with our Boat and Gingados, the General was fain [glad] to beat them back, because of the credit who should be first. We carried over eighty men at once; and with our Musket we beat the enemy off, and landed, but many of them were slain. By twelve of the clock all the Gagas were over.

Then the General commanded all his Drums, Tavales, Petes, Pongos, and all his Instruments of warlike Music to strike up, and gave the on-set, which was a bloody day to the Benguelas. These Benguelas presently broke and turned their backs, and a very great number of them were slain, and were taken Captives, man, woman, and child. The Prince Hombiangymbe was slain, which was Ruler of this Country, and more than one hundred of his chief Lords, and their heads presented, and thrown at the feet of the great Gaga. The men, women, and children, that were brought in captive alive, and the dead Corpses that were brought to be eaten, were strange to behold. For these Gagas are the greatest Cannibals and Man-eaters that be in the World, for they fed chiefly upon man's flesh, having all the Cattle of that Country.

They settled themselves in this Country, and took the spoil of it. We had great Trade with these Gagas five months, and gained greatly by them. These

Gagas were not contented to stay in this place of Benguela, although they lacked almost nothing. For they had great store of Cattle and Wheat, and many other Commodities, but they lacked Wine: for in these parts there are no Palm-trees.

After the five months were expired, they marched toward the Province of Bambala, to a great Lord, that is called Calicansamba, whose Country is five days journey into the Land. In these five months space we made three Voyages to the City of San Paul, and coming the fourth time we found them out.

Being loath to return without Trade, we determined to go up into the Land after them. So we went fifty on shore, and left our ship riding in the Bay of Benguela to stay for us: and marching two days up into the Country, we came to a great Lord, which is called Mofarigosat: and coming to his first Town, we found it burned to the ground, for the Gagas had passed and taken the spoil. To this Lord we sent a Negro, which we had bought of the Gagas, and lived with us, and bid him say, that he was one of the great Gaga's men, and that he was left to carry us to the Camp. This Lord bade us welcome for fear of the great Gaga: but he delayed the time, and would not let us pass, till the Gaga was gone out of his Country. This Lord Mofarigosat, seeing that the Gagas were clear of him, began to palter [haggle] with us, and would not let us go out of his Land, till we had gone to the wars with him; for he thought himself a mighty man having us with him. For in this place they never saw white men before, nor Guns. So we were forced to go with him, and destroyed all his Enemies, and returned to his Town again. Then we desired him, that he would let us depart: But he denied us, without we would promise him to come again, and leave a white man with him in pawn.

These Portuguese and Mulattos being desirous to get away from this place, determined to draw lots who should stay: but many of them would not agree to it. At last they consented together that it were fitter to leave me, because I was an Englishman, than any of themselves. Here I was fain to stay perforce. So they left me a Musket, Powder, and shot; promising this Lord Mofarigosat, that within two months they would come again, and bring an hundred men to help him in his Wars, and to trade with him: but all was to shift themselves away, for they feared that he would have taken us all Captives. Here I remained with this Lord till the two months were expired, and was hardly used, because the Portuguese came not according to promise.

The chief men of this Town would have put me to death, and stripped me naked, and were ready to cut off my head. But the Lord of the Town commanded them to stay longer, thinking that the Portuguese would come. And after that I was let loose again, I went from one Town to another, shifting for my self, within the liberties of this Lord. And being in fear of my life among them, I ran away, purposing to go to the Camp of the Gagas.

And having traveled all that night, the next day I came to a great Town, which was called, Cashil, which stood in a mighty over-grown thicket. Here I was carried into the Town to the Lord Cashil; and all the Town great and small came to wonder at me, for in this place there was never any white man seen. Here were some of the great Gaga's men, which I was glad to see, and went with these Gagas to Calicansamba, where the Camp was.

This Town of the Lord Cashil is very great, and is so over-grown with Olicondie Trees, Cedars, and Palms, that the streets are darkened with them. In the middle of the Town there is an Image, which is as big as a man, and standeth twelve foot high: and at the foot of the Image there is a Circle of El-ephants' Teeth, pitched into the ground. Upon these Teeth stand great store of dead men's skulls, which are killed in the wars, and offered to this Image. They use to pour Palm-wine at his feet, and kill Goats, and pour their blood at his feet. This Image is called Quesango, and the people have a great belief in him, and swear by him; and do believe when they are sick, that Quesango is offended with them. In many places of this Town were little Images, and over them great store of Elephants' Teeth piled.

The streets of this Town were paled [enclosed or fenced] with palm-canes very orderly. Their Houses were round like an Hive, and within hanged with fine mats very curiously wrought. On the South-east end of the Town was a Mokiso, which had more than three Tons of Elephants' Teeth piled over him.

From this Town of Cashil, I traveled up into the Country with the Gagas two days, and came to Calicansamba, where the great Gaga had his Camp, and was welcome to him. Among the Cannibal people, I determined to live, hoping in God, that they would travel so far to the West-ward, till we should see the Sea again; and so I might escape by some ship. These Gagas remained four months in this place, with great abundance and plenty of Cattle, Corn, Wine, and Oil, and great triumphing, drinking, dancing, and banqueting with man's flesh, which was an heavy spectacle to behold.

At the end of four months they marched toward the Serras, or Mountains of Cashindcabar, which are mighty high, and have great Copper-mines, and they took the spoil all the way as they went. From thence they went to the River Longa, and passed it, and settled themselves in the Town of Calango, and remained there five of six months. Then we arose, and entered into the

Province of Tondo, and came to the River Gonsa, and marched on the South-side of the River to a Lord that was called Makellacolonge, near to the great City of Dongo. Here we passed over mighty high Mountains, and found it very cold.

Having spent sixteen months among these Cannibals, they marched to the Westward again, and came along the River Gonsa, or Gunza, to a Lord that is called Shillambansa, Uncle to the King of Angola. We burned his chief Town, which was after their fashion very sumptuously built. This place is very pleasant and fruitful. Here we found great store of wild Peacocks, flying up and down the Trees, in as great abundance as other Birds. The old Lord Shillambansa was buried in the middle of the Town, and had an hundred tame Peacocks kept upon his Grave: which Peacocks he gave to his Mokeso, and they were called Angello Mokeso, that is, The Devils or Idols Birds, and were accounted as holy things. He had great store of Copper, Cloth, and many other things laid upon his Grave; which is the order of that Country.

From this place we marched to the Westward, along the River Coanza, and came right against the Serras, or Mountains of Cambanbe, or Serras de Prata. Here is the great fall of water, that falleth right down, and maketh a mighty noise, that is heard thirty miles. We entered into the Province of Casama, and came to one of the greatest Lords, which was called Langere. He obeyed the Great Gaga, and carried us to a Lord, called Casoch, which was a great Warrior; for he had some seven years before, overthrown the Portuguese side. This Lord did stoutly withstand the Gagas, and had the first day a mighty battle: but had not the victory that day. So we made a Sconse [small fort] of Trees after their fashion, and remained four months in the Wars with them. I was so highly esteemed with the Great Gaga, because I killed many Negroes with my Musket, that I had any thing that I desired of him. He would also, when they went out to the wars, give charge to his men over me. By this means I have been often carried away in their arms, and saved my life. Here we were within three days Journey of Massangano, before mentioned, where the Portuguese have a Fort: and I sought means, and got to the Portuguese again with Merchants Negroes, that came to the Camp to buy Slaves.

There were in the Camp of the Gagas, twelve Captains. The first, called Imbe Calandola, their General a man of great courage. He warreth all by enchantment, and taketh the Devil's counsel in all his exploits. He is always making of sacrifices to the Devil, and doth know many times what shall happen unto him. He believeth that he shall never die but in the Wars. There is no Image among them, but he useth certain ceremonies. He hath straight Laws

to his Soldiers: for, those that are faint-hearted, and turn their backs to the
Enemy, are presently condemned and killed for cowards, and their bodies
eaten. He useth every night to make a warlike Oration upon an high Scaffold,
which doth encourage his people.

It is the order of these people, wheresoever they pitch their Camp, although they stay but one night in a place, to build their Fort, with such wood
or trees as the place yieldeth: so that the one part of them cutteth down trees
and boughs, and the other part carrieth them, and buildeth a round Circle
with twelve Gates. So that every Captain keepeth his Gate. In the middle of
the Fort is the General's house, entrenched round about, and he hath many
Porters that keep the Door. They build their houses very close together, and
have their Bows, Arrows, and Darts, standing without their Doors: And when
they give alarm, they are suddenly all out of the Fort. Every company at their
Doors keep very good watch in the night, playing upon their Drums and
Tavales.

These Gagas told us of a River that is to the Southward of the Bay of
Vaccas, that hath great store of Gold: and that they gathered up great store
of grains of Gold upon the Sand, which the fresh water driveth down in the
time of rain. We found some of this Gold in the handles of their Hatchets,
which they use to engrave with Copper, and they called it Copper also, and
do not esteem it.

These Gagas delight in no Country, but where there is great store of Pal-
mares, or Groves of Palms. For they delight greatly in the Wine, and in the
Fruit of the Palm, which serveth to eat and to make Oil: and they draw their
Wine contrary to the Imbondos. These Palm-trees are six or seven fathoms
high, and have no leaves but in the top: and they have no leaves but in the top
of the Tree, and lay no bounds on it, and they draw the Wine in the top of the
tree in a Bottle.

But these Gagas cut the Palm-trees down by the root, which lie ten days
before they will give Wine. And then they make a square hole in the top and
heart of the Tree, and take out of the hole every morning a quart, and at night
a quart. So that every Tree giveth two quarts of Wine a day for the space of six
and twenty days, and then it drieth up.

When they settle themselves in any Country, they cut down as many
Palms as will serve them Wine for a month: and then as many more. So that
in a little time they spoil the Country. They stay no longer in a place, than it
will afford them maintenance. And then in Harvest time they arise, and settle
themselves in the fruitfullest place that they can find; and do reap their En-

emies' Corn, and take their Cattle. For they will not sow, nor plant, nor bring up any Cattle, more than they take by Wars. When they come into any Country that is strong, which they cannot the first day conquer, then their General buildeth his Fort, and remaineth sometimes a month or two quiet. For he saith, it is as great wars to the Inhabitants to see him settled in their Country, as though he fought with them every day. So that many times the Inhabitants come and assault him at his Fort: and these Gagas defend themselves and flesh them on for the space of two or three days. And when their General mindeth to give the on-set, he will in the night put out some one thousand men: which do emboske [shelter] themselves about a mile from their Fort. Then in the morning the great Gaga goeth with all his strength out of the Fort, as though he would take their Town. The Inhabitants coming near the Fort to defend their Country, being between them, the Gagas give the watch-word with their Drums, and then the embosked men arise, so that very few escape. And that day their General over-runneth the Country.

The great Gaga Calando hath his hair very long, embroidered with many knots full of Banba shells, which are very rich among them, and about his neck a Collar of Masoes, which are also shells, that are found upon that Coast, and are sold among them for the worth of twenty shillings a shell: and about his middle he weareth Lands, which are Beads made of the Ostrich's Eggs. He weareth a Palm cloth about his middle, as fine as Silk. His body is carved and cut with sundry works, and every day anointed with the fat of men. He weareth a piece of Copper across his nose, two inches long, and in his ears also. His body is always painted red and white. He hath twenty or thirty wives, which followed him when he goeth abroad; and one of them carrieth his Bow and Arrows, and four of them carry his Cups of drink after him. And when he drinketh, they all kneel down, and clap their hands and sing.

Their women wear their hair with high trompes, full of Bamba shells, and are anointed with Civet. They pull out four of their teeth; two above and two below for a bravery: And those that have not their teeth out, are loathsome to them, and shall neither eat nor drink with them. They wear great store of Beads about their necks, arms and legs; about their middles, Silk clothes.

The women are very fruitful, but they enjoy none of their children: For as soon as the woman is delivered of her Child, it is presently buried quick; So that there is not one Child brought up in all this Generation. But when they take any Town, they keep the Boys and Girls of thirteen or fourteen years of age, as their own children. But the men and women they kill and eat. These little Boys they train up in the wars, and hang a collar about their necks for a disgrace, which is never taken off till he proveth himself a man, and bring his enemies head to the General: And then it is taken off, and he is a Free-man and is called Gonso, or Soldier. This maketh them all desperate, and forward to be free, and counted men: and so they do increase. In all this Camp there were but twelve natural Gagas that were their Captains, and fourteen or fifteen women. For it is more than fifty years since they come from Serra de Lion, which was their native Country. But their Camp is sixteen thousand strong, and sometimes more.

When the great Gaga Calandola, undertaketh any great enterprise against the Inhabitants of any Country, he maketh a sacrifice to the Devil, in the morning before the Sun riseth. He sitteth upon a stool, having on each side of him a man Witch: then he hath forty or fifty women which stand round about him, holding in each hand a Zeveras, or wild horse's tail, where with they do flourish and sing. Behind them are great store of Petes, Ponges, and Drums, which always play. In the midst of them is a great fire; upon the fire an earthen pot with white powders, where-with the men Witches do paint him on the forehead, temples, thwart the breast and belly, with long ceremonies and enchanting terms. Thus he continueth till sun is down. Then the Witches bring his Casengala, which is a weapon like a hatchet, and put it into his hand, and bid him be strong against his enemies: for his Mokiso is with him. And presently there is a Man-child brought, which forthwith he killeth. Then are four men brought before him; two whereof, as it happeneth, he presently striketh and killeth; the other two he commandeth to be killed without the Fort.

Here I was by the men Witches commanded to go away, because I was a Christian. For then the Devil doth appear to them, as they say. And presently he commandeth five Cows to be killed in the Fort, and five without the Fort: And likewise as many Goats, and as many Dogs; and the blood of them is sprinkled in the fire, and their bodies are eaten with great feasting and triumph. And this is used many times by all the other Captains of their Army.

When they bury the dead, they make a vault in the ground, and a seat for him to sit. The dead hath his hair newly embroidered, his body washed, and anointed with sweet powders. He hath all his best robes put on, and is brought between two men to his grave, and set in his seat, as though he were alive. He hath two of his wives set with him, with their arms broken, and then they cover the vault on the top. The Inhabitants when they die, are buried after the same fashion, and have the most part of their goods buried with them. And every month there is a meeting of the kindred of the dead man, which mourn and sing doleful songs at his grave, for the space of three days; and kill many Goats, and pour their blood upon his grave, and Palm-Wine also; and use this ceremony as long as any of their kindred be alive. But those that have no kindred think themselves unhappy men, because they have none to mourn for them when they die. These people are very kind one to another in their health; but in their sickness they do abhor one another, and will shun their company. . . .

To the Eastward of Longeri is the Province of Bongo, and it bordereth upon Mocoke, the Great Angeca is King. In this place is great store of Iron, and Palm-cloth, and Elephants' teeth, and great store of Corn. To the North-east, is the Province of Cango, and it is fourteen days journey from the Town of Longo. This place is full of Mountains and rocky ground, and full of Woods, and hath great store of Copper. The Elephants in this place do excell. Here are so many, that the people of Longo fetch great store of Elephants' teeth, and bring them to the Port of Longo.

To the Northwards of Longo three leagues is the River Quell: and on the north side is, the Province of Calongo. This Country is always tilled, and full of Corn: and is all plain and champain ground, and hath great store of Honey. Here are two little Villages, that show at Sea like two homocks: which are the marks to know the Port of Longo. And fifteen miles Northward is the River Nombo: but it hath no depth for any Bark to go in. This Province, toward the East, bordereth upon Bongo; and toward the North, upon Mayombe, which is nineteen leagues from Longo, along the Coast.

This Province of Mayombe is all Woods and Groves; so overgrown, that a man may travel twenty days in the shadow without any Sun or heat. Here is no kind of Corn nor Grain: so that the people liveth only upon Plantains, and Roots of sundry sorts very good, and Nuts, nor any kind of tame Cattle, nor Hens. But they have great store of Elephants' flesh, which they greatly esteem; and many kind of wild Beasts; and great store of Fish. Here is a great Sandy Bay, two leagues to the Southward of Cape Negro, which is the Port of Mayombe. Sometimes the Portuguese lade Logwood in this Bay. Here is a great River, called Banna: in the Winter it hath no bar, because the general winds cause a great Sea. But when the Sun hath his South declination, then a Boat may go in: for then it is smooth because of the rain. This River is very great and hath many Islands, and people dwelling in them. The Woods are so covered with Baboons, Monkeys, Apes, and Parrots, that it will fear any man to travel in them alone. Here are also two kinds of Monsters, which are common in these Woods, and very dangerous.

The greatest of these two Monsters is called, Pongo, in their Language: and the lesser is called, Engeco. This Pongo is in all proportion like a man, but that he is more like a Giant in stature, than a man: for he is very tall, and hath a man's face, hollow eyed, with long hair upon his brows. His face and ears are without hair, and his hands also. His body is full of hair, but not very thick, and it is of a dunnish color. He differeth not from a man, but in his legs, for they have no calf. He goeth always upon his legs, and carrieth his hands clasped on the nape of his neck, when he goeth upon the ground. They sleep in the trees, and build shelters for the rain. They feed upon Fruit that they find in the Woods, and upon Nuts, for they eat no kind of flesh. They cannot speak, and have no understanding more than a beast. The People of the Country, when they travel in the Woods, make fires where they sleep in the night; and in the morning, when they are gone, the Pongos will come and sit about the fire, till it goeth out: for they have no understanding to lay the wood together. They go many together, and kill many Negroes that travel in the Woods. Many times they fall upon the Elephants, which come to feed where they be, and so beat them with their clubbed fists, and pieces of wood, that they will run roaring away from them. Those Pongo are never taken alive, because they are so strong, that ten men cannot hold one of them: but yet they take many of their young ones with poisoned Arrows. The young Pongo hangeth on his mother's belly, with his hands fast clasped about her: so that, when the Country people kill any of the females, they take the young one, which hangeth fast upon his mother. When they die among themselves, they cover the dead with great heaps of boughs and wood, which is commonly found in the Forests.

The Morombes use to hunt with their Country Dogs, and kill many kinds of little beasts, and great store of Pheasants. But their Dogs be dumb and cannot bark at all. They hang wooden clappers about their necks, and follow them by the rattling of the clappers. The Huntsmen have Petes, which they whistle their Dogs withal. These Dogs in all this Country are very little, with pricked ears, and are for the most part red and dun. The Portuguese mastie [mastiff?] Dog, or any other great Dog are greatly esteemed, because they do bark. I have seen a Dog sold up in the Country for thirty pounds.

In the Town of Mani Mayombe is a Fetisso, called Maramba: and it standeth in an high basket made like an Hive, and over it a great house. This is their house of Religion: for they believe only in him, and keep his laws, and carry his Relics always with them. They are for the most part Witches, and use their witchcraft for hunting and killing of Elephants, and fishing, and helping of sick and lame men: and to fore-cast journeys, whether they shall speed well or evil. By this Maramba are all thefts and murders tried: for in this Country they use sometimes to bewitch one another to death. And when any dieth, their neighbors are brought before Maramba: and if it be a great man that dieth, the whole Town commeth to swear. The order is, when they come before Maramba, to kneel and clasp Maramba in their arms, and to say; Emeno, eyge bembet Maramba: that is, I come to be tried, O Maramba. And if any of them be guilty, they fall down stark dead for ever. And if any of them that swear hath killed any man or child before, although it be twenty years past, he presently dieth. And so it is for any other matter. From this place as far as it is to Cape De lopo Gonsalves, they are all of this superstition. I was twelve months in this place, and saw many die after this sort.

These people be circumcised, as they be through all Angola, except the Kingdom of Congo, for they are Christians. And those that will be sworn, to Maramba, come to the chief Gangas, which are their Priests, or Men-witches; as Boys of twelve years of age, and men and women. Then the Gagas put them into a dark house, and there they remain certain days with very hard diet: after this they are let abroad, and commanded not to speak for certain days, what injury soever they be offered: so that they suffer great penury before they be sworn. Lastly, they are brought before Maramba, and have two marks cut upon both their shoulders before, like an half Moon; and are sworn by the blood that falleth from them, that they shall be true to him. They are forbidden some one kind of flesh, and some one kind of fish, with many other toys. And if they eat any of this forbidden meat, they presently sicken and never prosper. They all carry a relic of Maramba in a little box, and hang it about their necks, under their left arms. The Lord of this Province of Mayombe hath the Ensign or shape of Maramba carried before him, whithersoever he goeth; and when he sitteth down, it is set before him; and when he drinketh his Palm-wine, the first cup is poured at the foot of the Mokiso, or Idol; and when he eateth any thing whatsoever, the first piece he throweth toward his left hand, with enchanting words.

From Cape Negro Northward is a great Lord, called Mani Seat, which hath the greatest store of Elephants' teeth of any Lord in the Kingdom of Longo: for, his people practice nothing else but to kill Elephants. And two of those Negroes will easily kill an Elephant with their darts. And here is great store of Logwood.

There is another Lord to the Eastward, which is called Mani Kesocki, and he is eight days journey from Mayombe. Here I was with my two Negro Boys, to buy Elephants' hairs and tails; and in a month I bought twenty thousand, which I sold to the Portuguese for thirty Slaves, and all my charges borne.

From this place I sent one of my Negro Boys to Mani Seat with a Looking-glass: he did esteem it much, and sent me four Elephants' teeth (very great) by his own men; and desired me to cause the Portuguese, or any other ship, to come to the Northward of the Cape Negro, and he would make fires where his landing place is: For there was never yet any Portuguese, or other stranger in that place.

To the North-east of Mani Kesock, are a kind of little people, called Matimbas; which are no bigger then Boys of twelve years old, but are very thick, and live only upon flesh, which they kill in the Woods with their Bows and Darts. They pay tribute to Mani Kesock, and bring all their Elephants' teeth and tails to him. They will not enter into any of the Marombos houses, nor will suffer any to come where they dwell. And if by chance any Maramba, or people of Longo pass where they dwell, they will forsake that place, and go to another. The Women carry Bow and Arrows as well as the Men. And one of these will walk in the Woods alone, and kill the Pongos with their poisoned Arrows. I have asked the Marombos, whether the Elephant sheddeth his teeth or no? And they say no. But sometimes they find their teeth in the Woods, but they find their bones also.

When any man is suspected for any offence, he is carried before the King, or before Mani Bomma, which is as it were a Judge under the King. And if it be upon matter that he denyeth, and cannot be proved but by their oath; then the suspected person is thus sworn. They have a kind of root which they call Imbondo. This root is very strong, and is scraped into water. The virtue of this root is, that if they put too much of it into the water, the person that drinketh it cannot void urine: and so it striketh up into the brain, as though he were drunk, and he falleth down as though he were dead. And those that fall are counted as guilty, and are punished.

In this Country none of any account dyeth, but they kill another for him: for they believe they die not of their own natural death, but that some other hath bewitched them to death: And all those are brought in by the friends of the dead which they suspect, so that many times there come five hundred men and women to take the drink, made of the foresaid root, Imbonda. They are brought all to the High-street or Market-place, and there the master of the Imbonda sitteth with his water, and giveth every one a cup of water by one measure: and they are commanded to walk in a certain place till they make water, and then they be free: But he that cannot urine, presently falleth down, and all the people great and small fall upon him with their knives, and beat and cut him into pieces. But I think the Witch that giveth the water is partial, and giveth to him whom he will have to dye the strongest water, and by no man can perceive it that standeth by. And this is done in the Town of Longo, almost every week in the year.

Document 5

A Reporte of the Kingdom of Congo (1597)

By Duarte Lopes, A *Reporte of the Kingdom of Congo, a Region of Africa* (London, 1597), trans. Abraham Hartwell

In 1491, the future king of Kongo, Afonso I, was baptized. He remained committed to Christianity until his death in 1543, and his kingdom created a long-lasting edifice for Kongolese Catholicism. The cathedral build in São Salvador may have had a grass ceiling, as one modern historian has noted, but it became "the most striking edifice in all that part of Africa." Christianity spread from the ruler to the elites, with ongoing support from the Portuguese who lived in the region. Many of the members of this immigrant community participated actively in the slave trade, all the while supporting the Church and its ties to the state. For all that he did for his people, Afonso I was, according to the historian of the church in Africa, "the one African figure of the sixteenth century who continues to bestride his age as a colossus." By the latter decades of the century, relations between Portuguese missionaries and Kongo's rulers had degenerated. Yet despite the tensions that at times characterized the reign of Alvaro I, who ruled from 1568 to 1587, the region remained committed to Christianity. In 1571, the local bishop opened a seminary at São Tomé, and the dual processes of Christianization and "Portugalization" continued.[2]

In 1579 Duarte Lopes arrived in Mbanza Kongo. In 1583, he left Africa, bound for Rome as Alvaro's ambassador to the Vatican. Having established deep connections with the royal household in Kongo, including becoming a fidalgo *to signify his relationship, Alvaro apparently sent him to Europe to request the creation of a Kongolese bishopric. But Lopes's journey did not go well. Blown off course until his ship wrecked in the Caribbean, Lopes eventually made it to Rome. By the time he got there, his patron had died. Still, he had much to say about his time in Africa, and his account caught the atten-*

---

2. Adrian Hastings, *The Church in Africa, 1450–1950* (Oxford: Oxford University Press, 1994), 79–82, 84–86.

tion of a man named Philippo Pigafetta, who published Lopes's Relatione del reame di Congo *in 1591. Soon translated into Dutch, English, and Latin, the book gave many Europeans their first detailed knowledge of the Kongo, a region that had earlier been known only to the Portuguese. "From now on the rest of Europe was aware that there existed a strange Christian kingdom," the church historian Adrian Hastings has written, "commonly called Western Ethiopia, and that it was in the greatest need of priests."[3]*

Lopes filled his account with details about elephants and other African animals which caught his attention, but he paid just as much attention to the residents of the Kingdom of Kongo. At times, his two interests merged, as when he claimed that tigers in the region would eat only African men or women but not Europeans. Such comments suggest that his reporting blended observation with listening to local tales, perhaps favoring those told by other Portuguese visitors. That same sense of privileging Europeans came across in his assessment of the Kongolese themselves. Though he described the people that he saw and dwelled on the cities he visited in a neutral tone, he believed that the spread of Christianity had improved the lives of Africans who had accepted missionaries' teachings. In this sense the travel account resembled many others before and after. It became a testimonial not only to the vicissitudes experienced by the traveler but also a monument to the alleged virtues of Christianity.

When the Portuguese first arrived in the Kongo in the fifteenth century, those they met thought that they were, as one historian has noted, "voyagers from the world of the dead" whose strange languages, goods, and skin color all made the Kongolese suspicious of them.[4] But the territory that Lopes observed was very different, reflecting the interactions of Europeans and Africans. As the excerpt here makes clear, Christianity had taken root, and prompted changes that went beyond shifting religious views.

Of the Court of the King of Congo. Of the apparel of that people before they became Christians and after. Of the King's table, and manner of his Court.

Hitherto we have manifestly discovered the beginning of *Christian Religion* in *Congo,* & consequently the strange accidents that happened therein.

3. Hastings, *Church in Africa,* 86.
4. David Northrup, *Africa's Discovery of Europe, 1450–1850* (New York: Oxford University Press, 2002), 19–20.

And now it is time to discourse & lay open the manners and fashions of that Court, & other customs and conditions appertaining to that Realm. In ancient time this King and his Courtiers were appareled with certain cloth made of the *Palm-Tree*, (as we have told you before) wherewith they covered themselves from the girdlesteed downwards, and girded the same straight unto them with certain girdles made of the same stuff, very fair and like an apron, certain delicate and dainty skins, of little *Tigers*, of *Civet-Cats*, of *Sabelles*, of *Martens*, and of such like creatures for an ornament: and for a more glorious pomp and show, they did wear upon their shoulders a certain cape like a Whoode [hood]. Upon their bare skin they had a certain round garment like a *Rotchet* [Rochet, a cloak or mantle], which they call *Incutto*, reaching down to their knees, made after the manner of a net, but the stuff of it was very fine cloth of the said *Palm-Tree*, & at the skirts there hung a number of thread-tassels, that made a very gallant show. These *Rotchets* were turned up again, & tucked upon their right shoulder, that they might be the more at liberty on that hand. Upon that shoulder also they had the tail of a *Zebra*, fastened with a handle, which they used for a kind of bravery, according to the most ancient custom of those parts. On their heads they wore caps of yellow and red color, square above and very little, so that they scarcely covered the tops of their heads, and worn rather for a pomp and a vanity, than to keep them either from the air or from the Sun. The most part of them went unshod: but the King and some of the great *Lords* did wear certain shoes of the old fashion, such as are to be seen in the ancient *Images* of the *Romans*, and these were made also of the wood of the *Palm-Tree*. The poorer sort and the common people were appareled from their middle downwards, after the same manner, but the cloth was coarser: and the rest of their body all naked. The women used three kinds of traverses, or (as it were) aprons: beneath their girdlesteed. One was very long and reached to their heels: the second shorter than that, and the third shorter than both the other, with fringes about them, and every one of these three was fastened about their middle, and open before. From their breasts downwards, they had another garment, like a kind of doublet or jacket, that reached but to their girdle: and over their shoulders a certain cloak. All these several garments were made of the same cloth of the Palm-Tree. They were accustomed to go with their faces uncovered, and a little cap on the head, like a man's cap. The meaner sort of women were appareled after the same manner, but their cloth was coarser: Their Maid-servants and the basest kind of women were likewise attired from the girdle downward, and all the rest of the body naked.

But after that this kingdom had received the *Christian Faith*, the great *Lords* of the *Court* began to apparel themselves after the manner of the *Portuguese*, in wearing cloaks, *Spanish Capes*, and *Tabards* or wide Jackets of *Scarlet*, and cloth of *Silk*, every man according to his wealth and ability. Upon their heads they had hats, or caps, and upon their feet Moils [Mules or shoes] or Pantofles [slippers], of *Velvet* and of *Leather*, and buskins after the *Portuguese* fashion, and long *Rapiers* by their sides. The common people that are not able to make their apparel after that manner do keep their old custom. The women also go after the *Portuguese* fashion, saving that they wear no cloaks, but upon their heads they have certain veils, and upon their veils black velvet caps, garnished with jewels, and chains of gold about their necks. But the poorer sort keep the old fashion: for only the *Ladies* of the Court do bedeck themselves in such manner as we have told you.

After the King himself was converted to the *Christian Religion*, he conformed his Court in a certain sort after the manner of the King of *Portugal*. And first for his service at the table when he dineth of suppeth openly in public, there is a *Throne* of *Estate* erected with three steps, covered all over with *Indian Tapestry*, and thereupon is placed a Table, with a chair of *Crimson Velvet*, adorned with bosses and nails of Gold. He always feedeth alone by himself, neither doth any man ever sit at his table, but the Princes stand about him with their heads covered. He hath a *Cupboard* of Plate of *Gold* and *Silver*, and one that taketh assay of his meat and drink. He maintaineth a guard of the *Anzichi*, and of other nations, that keep about his palace, furnished with such weapons as are above mentioned: and when it pleaseth him to go abroad, they found their great instruments, which may be heard about five or six miles, and so signify that the King is going forth. All his Lords do accompany him, and likewise the *Portuguese*, in whom he reposeth a singular trust: but very seldom it is that he goeth out of his palace.

Twice in a week he giveth audience publicly, yet no man speaketh unto him but his *Lords*. And because there are none, that have any goods or lands of their own, but all belongeth to the *Crown*, there are but few suits or quarrels among them, saving peradventure about some words. They use no writing at all in the *Congo* tongue. In cases criminal they proceed but slenderly [unconvincingly], for they do very hardly and seldom condemn any man to death. If there be any riot or enormity committed against the *Portuguese* by the *Moci-Conghi*, (for so are the inhabitants of the Realm of *Congo* called in their own language,) they are judged by the laws of *Portugal*. And if any mischief be found in any of them, the king confineth the malefactor into some desert *Is-*

land: for he thinketh it to be a greater punishment to banish him in this sort, to the end he may do penance for his sins, then at one blow to execute him. And if it so happen that those which are thus chastised, do live ten or twelve years, the King useth to pardon them, if they be of any consideration at all, and doth employ them in the service of the State, as persons that have been tamed and well schooled, and accustomed to suffer any hardness. In Civil disagreements there is an order, that if a *Portuguese* have any suit against a *Moci-Congo*, he goeth to the Judge of *Congo*: but if a *Moci-Congo* do implead a *Portuguese*, he citeth him before the *Consul* or Judge of the *Portuguese*: for the King hath granted unto them one of their own nation to be Judge in that country. In their bargains between them and the *Portuguese*, they use no writings nor other instruments of bills or bonds, but dispatch their business only by word and witness.

They keep no histories of their ancient Kings nor any memorial of the ages past, because they cannot write. They measure their times generally by the Moons. They know not the hours of the day nor of the night: but they use to say, *In the time of such a man such a thing happened.* They reckon the distances of countries not by miles or by any such measure, but by the journeys and travel of men, that go from one place to another, either loaded or unloaded.

Touching their assembling together at feasts, or other meetings of joy, as for example, when they are married, they sing *Verses* and *Ballades* of *Love*, and play upon certain Lutes that are made after a strange fashion. For in the hollow part and in the neck they are somewhat like unto our *Lutes*, but for the flat side, (where we use to carve a *Rose*, or a *Rundell* to let the sound go inward) that is made not of wood, but of a skin, as thin as a bladder, and the strings are made of hairs, which they draw out of the *Elephant's* tail, and are very strong and bright: and of certain threads made of the wood of *Palm-Tree*, which from the bottom of the instrument do reach and ascend to the top of the handle, and are tied every one of them to his several rings. For towards the neck or handle of this *Lute*, there are certain rings placed some higher and some lower, whereat there hang divers plates of *Iron* and *Silver*, which are very thin, and in bigness different one from another, according to the proportion of the instrument. These rings do make a sound of sundry tunes, according to the striking of the strings. For the strings when they are struck, do cause the rings to shake, and then do the plates that hang at them, help them to utter a certain mingled and confused noise. Those that play upon this Instrument, do turn the stings in good proportion, and strike them with their fingers, like a *Harp*, but without any quill very cunningly: so that they make thereby

(I cannot tell whether I should call it a melody or no, but) such a sound as pleaseth and delighteth their senses well enough. Besides all this (which is a thing very admirable) by this instrument they do utter the conceits of their minds, and do understand one another so plainly, that every thing almost which may be explained with the tongue, they can declare with their hand in touching and striking this instrument. To the sound thereof they do dance in good measure with their feet, and follow the just time of that music with clapping the palms of their hands one against the other. They have also in the *Court, Flutes* and *Pipes*, which they sound very artificially, and according to the sound they dance and move their feet, as it were in a *Moresco*, with great gravity and sobriety. The common people do use little *Rattles*, and *Pipes*, & other instruments, that make a more harsh and rude sound, than the Court-instruments do.

In this kingdom, when they are sick, they take nothing but natural physic, as *Herbs*, and *Trees*, and the barks of *Trees*, and *Oils*, and *Waters* and *Stones*, such as *Mother Nature* hath taught them. The *Ague* is the most common disease that reigneth among them: and plagueth them in Winter by reason of the continual rain, that bringeth heat and moisture with it more than in Summer, and besides that the sickness which here we call the *French disease*, & *Chitangas* in the *Congo* tongue, is not there so dangerous and so hard to be cured, as it is in our Countries.

They heal the Ague with the poulder [powder] of a wood, called *Sandal*, or *Saunders*, whereof there is both red and gray, which is the wood of *Aguila*. This poulder being mingled with the oil of the *Palm-Tree*, and having anointed the body of the sick person two or three times withal from the head to the foot, the party recovereth. When their head acheth, they let blood in the temples, with certain little boxing horns [cupping]: first by cutting the skin a little, and then applying the *Cornets* [an instrument for bloodletting] thereunto, which with a suck of the mouth, will be filled with blood: and this manner of letting blood is used also in *Ægypt*. And so in any other part of a man's body, where there is any grief, they draw blood in this fashion and heal it. Likewise they cure the infirmity called *Chitangas*, with the same unction of *Saunders*: whereof there are two sorts, one red (as we told you) and that is called *Tavila*: the other gray, and is called *Chicongo*: and this is best esteemed, for they will not stick to give or sell a slave for a piece of it. They purge themselves with certain barks of trees, made into powder, and taken in some drink: and they will work mightily and strongly. When they take these purgations, they make no great account for going abroad into the air. Their wounds also they commonly cure with the juice of certain herbs, and with the herbs themselves. And the said *Signor Odo-ardo* hath affirmed unto me, that he saw a slave, which was stabbed through with seven mortal wounds of an Arrow, and was recovered whole and sound, only with the juice of certain herbs, well known unto them by experience. So that this people is not encumbered with a number of *Physicians*, for *Surgery*, for *Drugs*, for *Stirrups*, for *Electuaries*, for *Plasters*, and such like Medicines, but simply do heal and cure themselves with such natural Plants as grow in their own Country. Whereof they have no great need neither: for living (as they do) under a temperate climate, and not engorging themselves with much variety of meats to please their appetites, nor surcharging their stomachs with wine, they are not greatly troubled with those diseases, that commonly are engendered of meats and drinks that remain undigested.

Document 6

A Geographical Historie of Africa (1600)

By Leo Africanus, *A Geographical Historie of Africa*, trans. John Pory (London, 1600), 37–44, 377–78, 416–17

The man known to Europeans as Leo Africanus (fl. first half of the 16th century) was born in Granada as al-hassan Ibn Muhammad al-Wazzan. By the time he died, he had become the most important chronicler of Africa since the fourteenth-century writer Ibn Battuta. Educated in Fez, Morocco, Leo Africanus had traveled across the Sudan and to Mecca on a hajj *before he was captured near Tunis. From there he was taken to the Vatican to serve Pope Leo X, one of the most enlightened pontiffs of the early modern era who was famous (among other things) for keeping a well-stocked menagerie. Leo renamed him Johannis Leo de Medicis (he was also known as Giovanni Leone). He arrived at the Vatican in 1519. Seven years later he completed his report of Africa. The Venetian geographer Giovanni Battista Ramusio acquired the story, and published it in the first volume of his* Navigationi e Viaggi *in Venice in 1550. The text also appeared in Latin and French editions.*

The first half of the text here comes from the English translation done by an associate of Richard Hakluyt named John Pory (1572–1636).[5] The lat-

5. For information about Pory and his use of the text see William S. Powell, *John Pory, 1572–1636: The Life and Letters of a Man of Many Parts* (Chapel Hill: University of North Carolina Press, 1977), 9–19.

*ter portion contains other information about Africa drawn, so Pory wrote
in his book, from other unnamed Italian texts. Pory did not try to hide his
additions to the text. On the title page he informed his reader that he was
adding "a generall description of Africa, and also a particular treatise of all
the maine lands and Isles undescribed by John Leo." He also included "a
relation of the great Princes, and the manifold religions in that part of the
world" at the end of the volume. That latter section included the material
here on religion, European forts, Atlantic islands, and slaves, many of whom
were Christian captives.*

*Pory knew that he had a valuable text on his hands, a point confirmed by
Hakluyt. "I do hold and affirm it to be the very best, the most particular, and
methodicall, that ever was written, or at least that hath come to light, concerning the countries, peoples, and affairs of Africa," Hakluyt wrote. "For
which cause, and knowing well the sufficiencie of the translator, my self was
the first and only man that perswaded him to take it in hand. Wherein how
diligently and faithfully he hath done his part, and how he hath enlarged and
graced this Geographicall historie out of others, the best ancient and moderne
writers, by adding a description of all those African maine lands and isles,
and other matters very notable, which John Leo himself hath omitted: I re-
ferre to the consideration of all judiciall and indifferent Readers."*

The Geographical Historie of Africa *describes elements of African life
that frequently escaped the notice of foreign observers. Leo Africanus demonstrates here that he paid attention to life expectancy, local diseases, and
virtues and vices (as he perceived them). Pory's additions to the text suggest
the difference between a travel account, and the agenda of its author, and a
later translation. Pory's book, according to one modern biographer, shaped
views of Africa held by William Shakespeare, Ben Jonson, and Sir Walter
Ralegh, and it remained the most influential source on Africa available in
English until the nineteenth century.*

Of the length and shortness of the Africans' lives.

All the people of Barbary by us before mentioned live unto 65 or 70 years
of age, and few or none exceed that number. Howbeit in the foresaid mountains I saw some which had lived an hundred years, and others which af-

firmed themselves to be older, whose age was most healthful and lusty. Yea some you shall find here of fourscore years of age, who are sufficiently strong and able to exercise husbandry, to dress vines, and to serve in the wars; insomuch that young men are oftentimes inferior unto them. In Numidia, that is to say, in the land of dates, they live a long time: howbeit they lose their teeth very soon, and their eyes wax wonderfully dim. Which infirmities are likely to be incident unto them, first because they continually feed upon dates, the sweetness and natural quality whereof do by little and little pull out their teeth: and secondly the dust and sand, which is tossed up and down the air with eastern winds entering into their eyes, doth at last miserably weaken and spoil their eye sight. The inhabitants of Libya are of a shorter life; but those which are most strong and healthful among them live oftentimes till they come to threescore years; albeit they are slender and lean of body. The Negroes commonly live the shortest time of all the rest: howbeit they are always strong & lusty, having their teeth found even till their dying day: yet is there no nation under heaven more prone to venery; unto which vice also the Libyans and Numidians are too much addicted. To be short, the Barbarians are the weakest people of them all.

What kinds of diseases the Africans are subject unto.

The children, and sometimes the ancient women of this region are subject unto baldness or unnatural shedding of hair; which disease they can hardly be cured of. They are likewise oftentimes troubled with the head-ache, which usually afflicteth them without any ague joined therewith. Many of them are tormented with the tooth-ache, which (as some think) they are more subject unto, because immediately after hot pottage they drink cold water. They are oftentimes vexed with extreme pain of the stomach, which ignorantly they call the pain of the heart. They are likewise daily molested with inward gripings and infirmities over their whole body, which is thought to proceed of continual drinking of water. Yea they are much subject unto bone-aches and gouts, by reason that they sit commonly upon the bare ground, and never wear any shoes upon their feet. Their chief gentlemen and noblemen prove gouty oftentimes with immoderate drinking of wine and eating of dainty meats. Some with eating of olives, nuts, and such coarse fare, are for the most part infected with the scurvies. Those which are of a sanguine complexion are greatly troubled with the cough, because that in the spring-season they sit too much upon the ground. And upon Fridays I had no small sport and recreation to go and see them. For upon this day the people flock to church in great numbers to hear their Mahumetan sermons. Now if any one in the sermon-time falls a sneezing, all the whole multitude will sneeze with him for company, and so they make such a noise, that they never leave, till the sermon be quite done; so that a man shall reap but little knowledge by any of their sermons. If any of Barbary be infected with the disease commonly called the French pox, they die thereof for the most part, and are seldom cured. This disease beginneth with a kind of anguish and swelling, and at length breaketh out into sores. Over the mountains of Atlas, and throughout all Numidia and Libya they scarcely know this disease. Insomuch that oftentimes the parties infected travel forthwith into Numidia or the land of Negroes, in which places the air is so temperate, that only by remaining there they recover their perfect health, and return home sound into their own country: which I saw many do with mine own eyes; who without the help of any physician or medicine, except the foresaid wholesome air, were restored to their former health. Not so much as the name of this malady was ever known unto the Africans, before *Ferdinand* the king of Castile expelled all Jews out of Spain; after the return of which Jews into Africa, certain unhappy and lewd people lay with their wives; and so at length the disease spread from one to another, over the whole region: insomuch that scarce any one family was free of the same. Howbeit, this they were most certainly persuaded of, that the same disease came first from Spain; whereof they (for want of a better name) do call it, The Spanish pox. Notwithstanding at Tunis and over all Italy it is called the French disease. It is so likewise in Aegypt and Syria: for there it is used as a common proverb of cursing: The French pox take you. Amongst the Barbarians the disease in Latin *Hernia* is not so common; but in Aegypt the people are much troubled therewith. For some of the Aegyptians have their cods oftentimes so swollen, as it is incredible to report. Which infirmity is thought to be so common among them, because they eat so much gum, and salt cheese. Some of their children are subject unto the falling sickness; but when they grow to any stature, they are free from that disease. This falling sickness likewise possesseth the women of Barbary, and of the land of Negroes; who, to excuse it, say that they are taken with a spirit. In Barbary the plague is rife every tenth, fifteenth, or twentieth year, whereby great numbers of people are consumed; for they have no cure for the same, but only to rub the plague-sore with certain ointments made of Armenian earth. In Numidia they are infected with the plague scarce once in an hundred years. And in the land of Negroes they know not the name of this disease: because they never were subject thereunto. . . .

The commendable actions and virtues of the Africans.

Those Arabians which inhabit in Barbary or upon the coast of the Mediterranean sea are greatly addicted unto the study of good arts and sciences: and those things which concern their law and religion are esteemed by them in the first place. Moreover they have been heretofore most studious of the Mathematics, of Philosophy, and of Astrology: but these arts (as it is aforesaid) were four hundred years ago, utterly destroyed and taken away by the chief professors of their law. The inhabitants of cities do most religiously observe and reverence those things which appertain unto their religion: yea they honor those doctors and priests, of whom they learn their law, as if they were petty-gods. Their Churches they frequent very diligently, to the end they may repeat certain prescript and formal prayers; most superstitiously persuading themselves that the same day wherein they make their prayers, it is not lawful for them to wash certain of their members, when as at other times they will wash their whole bodies. Whereof we will (by God's help) discourse more at large in the second Book of this present treatise, when we shall fall into the mentioning of *Mahumet* and of his religion. Moreover those which inhabit Barbary are of great cunning & dexterity for building & for mathematical inventions, which a man may easily conjecture by their artificial works. Most honest people they are, and destitute of all fraud and guile; not only embracing all simplicity and truth, but also practicing the same throughout the whole course of their lives: albeit certain Latin authors, which have written of the same regions, are far otherwise of opinion. Likewise they are most strong and valiant people, especially those which dwell upon the mountains. They keep their covenant most faithfully; insomuch that they had rather die then break promise. No nation in the world is so subject unto jealousy; for they will rather lease [lose] their lives, than put up any disgrace in the behalf of their women. So desirous they are of riches and honor, that therein no other people can go beyond them. They travel in a manner over the whole world to exercise traffic. For they are continually to be seen in Aegypt, in Aethiopia, in Arabia, Persia, India, and Turkey: and whithersoever they go, they are most honorably esteemed of: for none of them will profess any art, unless he hath attained unto great exactness and perfection therein. They have always been much delighted with all kind of civility and modest behavior: and it is accounted heinous among them for any man to utter in company, any bawdy or unseemly word. They have always in mind this sentence of a grave author: Give place to thy superior. If any youth in presence of his father, his uncle, or any other of his kindred, doth sing or talk ought of love matters, he is deemed to be worthy of grievous punishment. Whatsoever lad or youth there lighteth by chance into any company which discourseth of love, no sooner heareth nor understandeth what their talk tendeth unto, but immediately he withdraweth himself from among them. These are the things which we thought most worthy of relation as concerning the civility, humanity, and upright dealing of the Barbarians. Let us now proceed unto the residue. Those Arabians which dwell in tents, that is to say, which bring up cattle, are of a more liberal and civil disposition: to wit, they are in their kind as devout, valiant, patient, courteous, hospitable, and as honest in life and conversation as any other people. They be most faithful observers of their word and promise: insomuch that the people, which before we said to dwell in the mountains, are greatly stirred up with emulation of their virtues. Howbeit the said mountains, both for learning, for virtue, and for religion, are thought much inferior to the Numidians; albeit they have little or no knowledge at all in natural philosophy. They are reported likewise to be most skillful warriors, to be valiant, and exceeding lovers and practisers of all humanity. Also, the Moors and Arabians inhabiting Libya are somewhat civil of behavior, being plain dealers, void of dissimulation, favorable to strangers, and lovers of simplicity. Those which we before named white, or tawny Moors, are most steadfast in friendship: as likewise they indifferently and favorable esteem of other nations: and wholly endeavor themselves in this one thing, namely, that they may lead a most pleasant and jocund life. Moreover they maintain most learned professors of liberal arts, and such men as are most devout in their religion. Neither is there any people in all Africa that lead a more happy and honorable life. . . .

What vices the foresaid Africans are subject unto.

Never was there any people or nation so perfectly endued [endowed] with virtue, but that they had their contrary faults and blemishes: now therefore let us consider, whether the vices of the Africa[n]s do surpass their virtues & good parts. Those which we named the inhabitants of the cities of Barbary are somewhat needy and covetous, being also very proud and high-minded, and wonderfully addicted unto wrath; insomuch that (according to the proverb) they will deeply engrave in marble any injury be it never so small, & will in no wise blot it out of their remembrance. So rusticall they are & void of good manners, that scarcely can any stranger obtain their familiarity and friendship. Their wits are but mean, and they are so credulous, that they will believe matters impossible, which are told them. So ignorant are they of natural philosophy, that they imagine all the effects and operations of nature to be extraordinary and divine. They observe no certain order of living nor of laws. Abounding exceedingly with choler, they speak always with an angry and loud voice. Neither shall you walk in the day time in any of their streets, but you shall see commonly two or three of them together by the ears. By nature they are a vile and base people, being no better accounted of by their governors than if they were dogs. They have neither judges nor lawyers, by whose wisdom and counsel they ought to be directed. They are utterly unskillful in trades of merchandize, being destitute of bankers and money-changers: wherefore a merchant can do nothing among them in his absence, but is himself constrained to go in person, whithersoever his wares are carried. No people under heaven are more addicted to covetise [covetousness?] than this nation: neither is there (I think) to be found among them one of an hundred, who for courtesy, humanity, or devotion's sake, will vouchsafe any entertainment upon a stranger. Mindful they have always been of injuries, but most forgetful of benefits. Their minds are perpetually possessed with vexation and strife, so that they will seldom or never show themselves tractable to any man; the cause whereof is supposed to be; for that they are so greedily addicted unto their filthy lucre, that they never could attain unto any kind of civility or good behavior. The shepherds of that region live a miserable, toilsome, wretched and beggarly life: they are a rude people, and (as a many may say) born and bred to theft, deceit, and brutish manners. Their young men may go a wooing to divers maids, till such time as they have sped of a wife. Yea, the father of the maid most friendly welcommeth her suitor; so that I think scarce any noble or gentleman among them can choose a virgin for his spouse: albeit so soon as any woman is married, she is quite forsaken of all her suitors; who then seek out other new paramours for their liking. Concerning their religion, the greater part of these people are neither Mahumetans, Jews, nor Christians; and hardly shall you find so much as a spark of piety in any of them. They have no churches at all, nor any kind of prayers, but being utterly estranged from all godly devotion, they lead a savage and beastly life: and if any man chanceth to be of a better disposition (because they have no law-givers nor teachers among them) he is constrained to follow the example of other men's lives & manners. All the Numidians being most ignorant of natural, domesticall, & commonwealth-matters, are principally addicted unto treason, treachery, further, theft, and robbery. This nation, because it is most slavish, will right gladly accept of any service among the Barbarians, be it never so vile or contemptible. For some will take upon them to be dung-farmers, others to be scullions [servants], some others to be hostlers [stablemen], and such like servile occupations. Likewise the inhabitants of Libya live a brutish kind of life; who neglecting all kinds of good arts and sciences, do wholly apply their minds unto theft and violence. Never as yet had they any religion, any laws, or any good form of living; but always had, and ever will have a most miserable and distressed life. There cannot any treachery or villainy be invented so damnable, which for lucre's sake they dare not attempt. They spend all their days either in most lewd practices, or in hunting, or else in warfare; neither wear they any shoes nor garments. The Negroes likewise lead a beastly kind of life, being utterly destitute of the use of reason, of dexterity of wit, and of all arts. Yea they so behave themselves, as if they had continually lived in a forest among wild beasts. They have great swarms of harlots among them; whereupon a man may easily conjecture their manner of living; except their conversation perhaps be somewhat more tolerable, who dwell in the principal towns and cities: for it is like that they are somewhat more addicted to civility.

Neither am I ignorant, how much mine own credit is impeached, when I my self write so homely of Africa, unto which country I stand adebted [indebted?] both for my birth, and also for the best part of my education: Howbeit in this regard I seek not to excuse my self, but only to appeal unto the duty of an historiographer, who is to set down the plain truth in all places, and is blame-worthy for flattering or favoring of any person. And this is the cause that hath moved me to describe all things so plainly without glossing or dissimulation: wherefore here I am to request the gentle Reader friendly to accept of this my most true discourse, (albeit not adorned with fine words, and artificial eloquence) as of certain unknown strange matters. Wherein how indifferent and sincere I have showed my self, it may in few words appear by that which followeth. It is reported of a lewd countryman of ours, that being convicted of some heinous crime, he was adjudged to be severely beaten for it. Howbeit the day following, when the executioner came to do his business, the malefactor remembered that certain years before, he had some acquaintance and familiarity with him: which made him to presume, that he should find more favor at his hands, than a mere stranger. But he was foully deceived; for the executioner used him no better, than if he had never known him. Wherefore this caitiff [prisoner] at the first exclaiming upon his executioner, or (saith he) my good friend, what maketh you so stern, as not to acknowledge our old acquaintance? Hereupon the executioner beating him more cruelly than before: friend (quoth he) in such business as this I use to be mindful of my duty, and to show no favor at all: and so continually laying on, he ceased not, till the judicial sentence was fulfilled. It was (doubtless) a great argument or impartial dealing, when as respect of former friendship could take no place.

Wherefore I thought good to record all the particulars aforesaid; least that describing vices only I should seem to flatter them, with whom I am now presently conversant; or extolling only the virtues of the Africans, I might hereafter be said to sue for their favor (which I have of purpose eschewed) to the end that I might have more free access to them. Moreover, may it please you for this purpose to hear another resemblance or similitude. There was upon a time a most wily bird, so endued by nature, that she could live as well with the fishes of the sea, as with the fowls of the air; wherefore she was rightly called Amphibian. This bird being summoned before the king of birds to pay her yearly tribute, determined forthwith to change her element, and to delude the king; and so flying out of the air, she drenched herself in the Ocean sea. Which strange accident the fishes wondering at, came flocking about Amphibian, saluting her, and asking her the cause of her coming. Good fishes (quoth the bird) know you not, that all things are turned so upside down, that we wot [know] not how to live securely in the air? Our tyrannical king (what fury haunts him, I know not) commanded me to be cruelly put to death, whereas no silly bird respected ever his commodity as I have done. Which most unjust edict I no sooner heard of, but presently (gentle fishes) I came to you for refuge. Wherefore vouchsafe me (I beseech you) some odd corner or other to hide my head in; and then I may justly say, that I have found more friendship among strangers, than ever I did in mine own native country. With this speech the fishes were so persuaded, that Amphibian stayed a whole year amongst them, not paying one penny or halfpenny. At the year's end the king of fishes began to demand his tribute, insomuch that at last the bird was sessed [assessed] to pay. Great reason it is (saith the bird) that each man should have his due, and for my part I am contented to do the duty of a loyal subject. These words were no sooner spoken, but she suddenly spread her wings, and up she mounted into the air. And so this bird, to avoid yearly exactions and tributes, would eftsoons change her element. Out of this fable I will infer no other moral, but that all men do most affect that place, where they find least damage and inconvenience. For mine own part, when I hear the Africans evil spoken of, I will affirm my self to be one of Granada: and when I perceive the nation of Granada to be discommended, then I will profess myself to be an African. But herein the Africans shall be the more beholding unto me; for that I will only record their principal and notorious vices, omitting their smaller and more tolerable faults. . . .

Pory's addition to the text starts here.

A summary discourse of the manifold Religions professed in Africa: and first of the Gentiles.

Africa containeth four sorts of people different in religion: that is to say, Gentiles, Jews, Mahumetans [Muslims], and Christians. The Gentiles extend themselves along the shore of the Ocean, in a manner from Cabo Blanco, or the white Cape, even to the northern borders or Congo; as likewise, from the southerly bounds of the same kingdom, even to Capo de buena Esperança; & from thence, to that De los Corrientes: and within the land they spread out from the Ethiopick Ocean, even unto Nilus, and beyond Nilus also from the Ethiopick, to the Arabian sea. These Gentiles are of divers sorts, for some of them have no light of God, or religion, neither they are governed by any rule or law. Whereupon the Arabians call them Cafri, that is to say, lawless, or without law. They have but few habitations, and they live for the most part in caves of mountains, or in woods, wherein they find some harbor from wind and rain. The civilest among them, who have some understanding and light of divinity and religion, obey the Monomotapa, whose dominion extendeth with a great circuit, from the confines of Matama, to the river Cuama: but the noblest part thereof is comprehended between the mighty river of magnice or Spirito Sancto, and that of Cuama, for the space of six hundred leagues. They have no idols, and believe in one only God, called by the Mozimo. Little differing from these we may esteem the subjects of Mohenemugi. But among all the Cafri, the people called Agag or Giacchi, are reputed most brutish, inhabiting in woods and dens, and being devourers of man's flesh. They dwell upon the left bank of Nilus, between the first and second lake. The Anzichi also have a shambles of man's flesh, as we have of the flesh of oxen. They eat their enemies whom they take in war; they sell their slaves to butchers, if they can light on no greater prize: and they inhabit from the river Zaire, even to the deserts of Nubia. Some others of them are rather addicted to witchcraft, than to idolatry: considering that in a man, the fear of a superior power is so natural, that though he adore nothing under the name and title of a God, yet doth he reverence and fear some superiority, although he know not what it is. Such are the Biafresi, and their neighbors, all of them being addicted in such sort to witchcraft, as that they vaunt, that by force of enchantment, they can not only charm, and make men die, much more molest and bring them to hard point: but further, raise winds and rain, and make the sky to thunder and lighten, and that they can destroy all herbs and plants, and make the flocks and herds of cattle to fall down dead. Whereupon they reverence more the devil than any thing else: sacrificing unto him of their beasts and fruits of the earth, yea their own blood also, and their children. Such are likewise the priests of Angola, whom they call Ganghe. These make profession that they have in their hands dearth and abundance; fair weather and foul; life and death. For which cause it can not be expressed, in what veneration they are held amongst these Barbarians. In the year 1587 a Portuguese captain being in part of Angola with his soldiers, a Ganga was requested by the people, to refresh the fields, which were dry and withered, with some quantity of water. He needed no great entreaty, but going forth with divers little bells, in presence of the Portuguese, he spent an half hour in fetching sundry gambols & skips, & uttering divers superstitious murmurings: and behold, a cloud arose in the air, with lightning and thunder. The Portuguese grew amazed; but all the Barbarians with great joy admired and extolled unto heaven, their Ganga, who now gave out intolerable brags, not knowing what hung over his head: For the winds outrageously blowing, the sky thundering after a dreadful manner, instead of the rain by him promised, there fell a thunderbolt, which like a sword cut his head clean from his shoulders. Some other idolaters not looking much aloft, worship earthly things: such were the people of Congo before their conversion, and are at this day those that have not yet received the Gospel. For these men worship certain dragons with wings, and they foolishly nourish them in their houses, with the delicatest meats that they have. They worship also serpents of horrible shape, goats, tigers, and other creatures, and the more they fear and reverence them, by how much the more deformed and monstrous they are. Amongst the number of their gods also, they reckon bats, owls, owlets, trees, and herbs, with their figures in wood and stone: and they do not only worship these beasts living, but even their very skins when they are dead, being filled with straw, or some other matter: and the manner of their idolatry is, to bow down before the foresaid things, to cast themselves groveling upon the earth, to cover their faces with dust, and to offer unto them of their best substance. Some lifting up their minds a little higher, worship stars, such be the people of Guinea, and their neighbors, who are inclined to the worship of the sun, the greatest part of them: and they hold opinion, that the souls of those dead that lived well, mount up into heaven, and there dwell perpetually near unto the sun. Neither want there amongst these, certain others so superstitious, as they worship for God the first thing they mete withal, coming out of their houses. They also hold their kings in the account & estimation of gods, whom they suppose to be descended from heaven, & their kings, to maintain themselves in such high reputation, are served with wonderful ceremonies, neither will they be seen but very seldom. . . .

Of the fortresses and colonies maintained by the Spaniards and Portuguese upon the main of Africa: by means whereof the Christian religion hath there some small footing. Which albeit in other respects they have been mentioned before, yet here also in this one regard, it seemeth not from our purpose briefly to remember them.

To the propagation of Christianity, those fortresses & colonies wonderfully help, which the Castilians, but much more the Portuguese, have planted on the coast of Africa. For they serve very fitly either to convert infidels upon divers occasions, or by getting an habit of their languages and customs, to make a more easy way to their conversion. For those who are not sufficient to preach, serve for interpreters to the preachers. And thus God hath oftentimes been well served, and with excellent fruit and effect, by the endeavor of some soldiers. On the coast of Africa upon the Mediterranean sea, the Spaniards have Oran, Mersalchibir, Melilla, & c. and the Portuguese, Tanger, and Çueta, and without the straights of Gibraltar, Arzilla, and Mazagan; and in Ethiopia, Saint George de la mina. They have also a settled habitation in the city of Saint Salvador, the Metropolitan of the kingdom of Congo, and in Cumbiba, a country of Angola. Beyond the cap de Buena esperança, they hold the fortresses, and colonies of Sena, Cefala, and Mozambiche. Here besides their secular clergy, is a convent of Dominicans, who endeavor themselves to instruct the Portuguese, and the Pagans also which there inhabit, and do traffic thither. . . .

Of the Islands of the Atlantic Ocean, where the Spaniards and Portuguese have planted religion.

The Christian name is also augmented, and doth still increase in the Atlantic Ocean, by means of the colonies conducted thither, partly by the Spaniards and partly by the Portuguese. The Spaniards undertook the enterprise of the Canaries, in the year of our Lord 1405 using there in the assistance of *John Betancort*, a French gentleman, who subdued Lançarota, & Fuerteuentura.

They were taken again certain years after, and were first subdued by force of arms, & afterwards by the establishment of religion: so that at this present, all the inhabitants are Christians. Also the Portuguese have assayed to inhabit certain other islands of that Ocean, & especially Madeira, which was discovered in the year 1420. This at the first was all over a thick and mighty wood: but now it is one of the best manured [cultivated] islands that is known. There is in the same, the city of Funcial, being the seat of a bishop. Puerto Santo, which is forty miles distant from Madeira, was found out in the year 1428 and this also began presently to be inhabited. The isles of Arguin, being six or seven, and all but little ones, came to the knowledge of the Portuguese in the year 1443. Here the king hath a fortress for the traffic of those countries. The islands of Cabo Verde were discovered in the year 1440 by *Antonino di Nolli* a Genoway, or (as others affirm) in the year 1455 by *Aloizius Cadamosto*. These be nine in number: the principal of them is Sant Iago, being seventy miles in length: where the Portuguese have a town situate upon a most pleasant river, called Ribera Grande, which consisteth at the least of five hundred families. The isle of Saint Thomas being somewhat greater than Madeira, was the last island discovered by the Portuguese, before they doubled the cape De Buena Esperança. They have here a colony called Pouasaon [Povasaon?], with a bishop, who is also the bishop of Congo, and it containeth seven hundred families. Under the government of Saint Thomas are the neighbor islands of Fernando Pó, and that del Principe, which are as it were boroughs belonging to the same. The island Loanda, though it be under the king of Congo, yet is a great part thereof inhabited by the Portuguese. For here is the famous port of Mazagan, wither the ships of Portugal and Brazil do resort. Here the fleets are harbored, and the soldiers refreshed, and here they have their hospital. As also here the Portugal priests (who endeavor the conversion of the natural inhabitants) have a place of residence.

Of the Negroes.

Most of the Islands inhabited by the Portuguese, especially those of Saint Thomas and Madeira, besides the Portuguese themselves, contain a great multitude of Negro-slaves, brought thither out of Congo and Angola, who till the earth, water the sugar-canes, and serve both in the cities, and in the country. These are for the most part gentiles, but they are daily converted rather through continual conversation, than any other help that they have;

and it is a matter likely, that in process of some few years, they will all become Christians. There is no greater hindrance to their conversion, than the avarice of their masters, who, to hold them in the more subjection, are not willing that they should become Christians.

Of those poor distressed European Christians in Africa, who are holden as slaves unto the Turks and Moors.

But the best and most sincere Christianity in all Africa, is that of those poor Christians, who are fettered by the feet with chains, being slaves to the Arabians & Turks. For besides them that have remained there ever since the days of Barbarossa and other Turkish captains (which were brought into the Mediterranean seas by the French) as also since the great loss at Gerbi, and the battle of Alcazar wherein *Don Sebastian* the king of Portugal was overthrown: there passeth not a year, but the rovers and pirates of those parts, without granting any league or respite to the Northern shores of the Mediterranean Sea, take great numbers of Christians from off the coasts of Spain, Sardinia, Corsica, Sicilia, yea even from the very mouth of Tiber. It is generally thought, that the number of slaves, which are in Alger amount to eighteen thousand. In Tunis, Bona, and Biserta there are great multitudes: but many more in Fez, and Maroca; as likewise in Mequenez and Tarodant, and in divers other cities of those kingdoms. The estate surely of these distressed people is most worthy of compassion, not so much for the misery wherein they lead their lives, as for the danger whereto their souls are subject. They pass the day in continual travel, and the greatest part of the night without repose or quiet, under insupportable burdens, and cruel stripes. Beasts among us labor not more, nor are more slavishly entreated. Yea, albeit under those brutish Barbarians, they endure all that toil, which beasts do here with us: yet are they neither so well fed, nor so carefully looked unto, as our beasts commonly are. They were out the whole day in the sun, rain, and wind, in continual labor, sometimes carrying burdens, sometimes digging or ploughing the fields, and otherwhiles in turning of hand-mills, feeding of beasts, or in performance or other labors: being bound to bring in so much every day to their masters, and they themselves to live of the rest, which many times is nothing at all, or (if it were possible) less than nothing. They have always the chain at their necks and feet, being naked winter and summer, and therefore are sometimes scorched with heat, and otherwhiles frozen with cold. They must not fail in any iota of their duties, and yet though they do not, it can not be expressed with what cruelties they are tormented. They use for the chastising & torture of their bodies, chains or iron, dried sinews of oxen, but-hoops steeped in water, boiling oil, melted tallow, & scalding hot lard. The houses of those Barbarians resound again, with the blows that are given these miserable men, on the feet and belly: and the prisons are filled with hideous lamentations and yellings. Their companions' hair at this noise stands an end, and their very blood freezeth within them, by considering how near themselves are to the like outrages. They pass the nights in prisons, or in some caves of the earth, being hampered and yoked together like brute beasts. Here the vapor and damp choaketh them, and the uncleanness and filth of their lodging con-sumeth them (as rust doth iron) even alive. But though the labors of their bodies be so grievous, yet those of their minds are much more intolerable, for (besides that they want such as might feed them with the word of God, & with the sacraments, and might teach them how to live and die well, so as they remain like plants without moisture) it can not be expressed, with what forc-ible temptations their faith is continually assailed. For not only the desire to come forth of these unspeakable miseries, doth tempt them; but the com-modities and delights also wherein they see others to live, that have damnably renounced their Christianity. The persecutors of the primitive church, to in-duce the Martyrs to deny Christ and to sacrifice to their idols, tried them first with torments, and then with ease and delights, which they propounded unto them, if they would become as themselves. For to those, who in the middest of winter were thrown into frozen lakes, there were contrariwise appointed soft and delicate beds, with a fire kindled hard by, and a thousand other re-storatives and comforts; to the end they might be doubly tempted, both by the rigor of the cold which benumbed them, and by the sweetness of things com-fortable and nourishing, which allured them. The Christian slaves are at this day no less tormented; for on the one side, they are afflicted with beggary, nakedness, hunger, famine, blows, reproaches, and tortures, without any hope in a manner ever to come out thereof: and on the other side they see them that have reneged our holy faith for Mahumets' superstition, to live in all worldly prosperity and delight, to abound with wealth, to flourish in honor, to govern cities, to conduct armies, and to enjoy most ample liberty. But amidst all these so great miseries, they have a double comfort. The one is of priests, who to-gether with themselves were taken captive. These men sometimes adminis-tering the sacraments, & other whiles delivering the word of God in the best manner that they can, are some help and assistance to others, being for this greatly reverenced and respected amongst them. The other is of the religious in general, who contend and labor for their freedom. Wherein Spain deserveth most high commendation. For there be two most honorable orders, whose exercise it is, to move and solicit for the freedom of captives. The one is called La Orden de la Merced, and it flourisheth most in Aragon; and the other (which is far greater) is named Del Resgate or of ransom or redemption, the which although it largely extendeth over all France, yet at this day above all other places, it is most rife in Castilia. From whence some of them have gone into Sicily, to the kingdom of Naples, and to Rome: and have there begun to lay foundations of their convents. These two religious orders gather every year mighty sums of money, wherewith they make speedy redemption first all the religious, and priests, and after them those of the younger sort, first the king of Spain's subjects, and then others. They always leave one religious man in Alger, and another in Fez, who inform themselves of the state & quality of the slaves, with their necessity, to make the better way for their liberty the year following[.] The king of Spain (whom it most concerneth) furthereth this so charitable a work, with a bountiful and liberal hand. For ordinarily he giveth as much more, as the foresaid orders have gathered and collected by way of alms. For this is so good an enterprise, that by the ancient canons no other is so much favor and allowed of. Yea S. *Ambrose* and other holy men have pawned, for the delivery of Christian captives, the chalices and silver vessels of their churches. And Saint *Paulinus* for the same end and purpose, sold his own self. For all other actions of charity are some spiritual, and others corporal, but this in a very eminent degree is both spiritual and corporal together. For among corporal miseries the servitude of infidels is most grievous, & among spiritual calamities the danger of apostasy is of all others the greatest: but those slaves so redeemed, are set free both from the one and from the other. Whereupon there are very few borne in Spain, who dying, leave not some alms behind them, for the ransoming of slaves. The fathers of redemption have gone also many times to Constantinople: where in the year 1583 by the order of Pope *Gregory* the thirteenth, they redeemed five hundred persons. The brotherhood also of the Consalone in Rome, labor very diligently in this point, who in *Sixtus Quintus* time, redeemed a great number of captives. Of whom many also, urged partly by the hardness of servitude, & partly by the sweetness of liberty, free themselves, either by that which they gain over & above their master's due, or by their good demeanor, or else by flight. And they fly away, sometimes by repairing speedily to such fortresses as the king of Spain hath in Africa and in Barbary: and otherwhiles they seize on some shipping, or on the self same galleries wherein they are chained. Many also retire themselves to the Princes of Brisch, &c. who willingly receive and arm them, using their assistance in the war which they continually make with the Turks of Alger.

Part II
Asia

Ying-Yai Sheng-Lan—The Overall Survey of the Ocean's Shores (1433)

*Ma Huan, Ying-Yai Sheng-Lam: The Overall Survey of the Ocean's
Shores,* trans. J. V. G. Mills (Cambridge, England: Hakluyt Society
Extra Series no. 42, 1970), 77–85, 137–46, 173–78

*Ma Huan was probably born around 1380 in a family from Kuei chi, about
seven miles from Hang chou bay. Scholars know little about his life. He
was in all likelihood of humble origin, but he gained sufficient education to
be appointed to join some, but not all, of the voyages led by Cheng Ho (c.
1371–1435), the Ming admiral who led perhaps the most substantial fleet
in the world at the time from China to the east coast of Africa. He returned
from his final voyage in 1433. Eighteen years later he published* Ying-Yai
Sheng-Lan—The Overall Survey of the Ocean's Shores.

*The excerpts here testify to the range of Ming travel expertise and to Ma
Huan's ability, often in a very few pages, to render telling portraits of the
peoples whom he met and the places that he saw. The material here comes
from his encounters with three very different places: Champa (in central
Vietnam), Calicut, and Mecca. In each of these places he described the economy, especially local agricultural practices, and dominant religious patterns.
His eye for detail is especially apparent in his description of keeping track
of time in Champa or the architecture of the central mosque in Mecca. His
writing tended to be less overtly judgmental than that of other travelers of
this age. He was also a very precise writer, repeatedly providing the values
of goods and the distances from one place to another. Though his text occasionally erred in statements of fact, as his modern editor J. V. G. Mills has
pointed out in a superb series of gloss notes to the translation used here, such
occasional inaccuracy does not detract from the obvious effort to provide a
guide to others who would presumably follow in the future. Cheng Ho led
seven expeditions from his initial departure in 1405 to his final return in
1433; Ma Huan accompanied him on three of them.*

There are no known surviving copies of the original 1451 printing of the
Overall Survey. *For the text that follows, Mills used three variant editions,
relying on one published around 1617 (known as "Version C"), but also referring frequently to an edition published in 1824 (known as "Version S"),*

and on occasion to a third (and rarer) version composed sometime between 1451 and 1644 (known as "Version K"; the text here removes many of the brackets Mills used when creating a singular text with material from these variant editions). Ma Huan died around 1460. As Mills has noted, "His book was never widely read, he never achieved fame, and he had been forgotten before 1773, when the imperial library of the Ch'ien-lung emperor was being formed." It is a tragedy that the text was not better known for so many generations because its contents, as the excerpts here reveal, provide a necessary corrective to European and American notions about much of the world that was, for Ma Huan and Cheng Ho, the "West," not the "East."[1]

The Country of Chan City [Champa, Central Vietnam]

This is the country called Wang she ch'eng in the Buddhist records. It lies in the south of the great sea which is south of the sea of Kuang tung. Starting from Wu hu strait in Ch'ang lo district of Fu chou prefecture in Fu chien province and traveling south-west, the ship can reach this place in ten days with a fair wind. On the south the country adjoins Chen la [Cambodia]; on the west it connects with the boundary of Chiao chih [Tonking]; and on both east and north it comes down to the great sea.

At a distance of one hundred *li* to the north-east from the capital, there is a port named New Department Haven. On the shore they have a stone tower which constitutes a land-mark. Ships from all places come here for the purpose of mooring and going ashore. On the shore there is a fort, named by the foreigners She pi-nai; they have two headmen in charge of it; and inside the fort live fifty or sixty families of foreigners, to guard the harbour.

Going south-west for one hundred *li* you come to the city where the king resides; its foreign name is Chan city. The city has a city-wall of stone, with openings at four gates, which men are ordered to guard. The king of the country is a So-li man, and a firm believer in the Buddhist religion. On his head he wears a three-tiered elegantly-decorated crown of gold filigree, resembling that worn by the assistants of the *ching* actors in the Central Country. On his body he wears a long robe of foreign cloth with small designs worked in

1. Ma Huan, *Ying-Yai Sheng-Lan: "The Overall Survey of the Ocean's Shores"* [1433], trans. J. V. G. Mills (Hakluyt Society, extra ser., 42 [Cambridge, 1970]), 34–41, quotation at 36.

threads of the five colours, and round the lower part of his body a kerchief or coloured silk; and he has bare feet. When he goes about, he mounts an elephant, or else he travels riding in a small carriage with two yellow oxen pulling in front.

The hat worn by the chiefs is made of *chiao-chang* leaves, and resembles that worn by the king, but has gold and coloured ornamentation; and differences in the hats denote the gradations of rank. The coloured robes which they wear are not more than knee-length, and round the lower part of the body the wear a multi-coloured kerchief of foreign cloth.

The house in which the king resides is tall and large. It has a roof of small oblong tiles on it. The four surrounding walls are ornately constructed of bricks and mortar, and look very neat. The doors are made of hard wood, and decorated with engraved figures of wild beasts and domestic animals.

The houses in which the people live have a covering made of thatch; the height of the eaves from the ground cannot exceed three ch'ih; people go in and out with bent bodies and lowered heads; and to have a greater height is an offence.

As to the colour of their clothing: white clothes are forbidden, and only the king can wear them; for the populace, black, yellow, and purple coloured clothes are all allowed to be worn; but to wear white clothing is a capital offence.

The men of the country have unkempt heads; the women dress the hair in a chignon at the back of the head. Their bodies are quite black. On the upper part of the body they wear a short sleeveless shirt, and round the lower part a coloured silk kerchief. All go bare-footed.

The climate is pleasantly hot, without frost or snow, always like the season in the fourth or fifth moon. The plants and trees are always green.

The mountains produce ebony, *ch'ieh-lan* incense, Kuan yin bamboo, and laka-wood. The ebony is a very glossy black, and decidedly superior to the produce of other countries. The *ch'ieh-lan* incense is produced only on one large mountain in this country, and comes from no other place in the world; it is very expensive, being exchanged for its own weight in silver.

The Kuan yin bamboo resembles a small rattan stick; it is one *chang* seven or eight *ch'ih* in length, and iron black in colour; it has two or three joints to every one inch; it is not produced elsewhere.

Rhinoceros' and elephants' teeth are very abundant. The rhinoceros resembles a water-buffalo in shape; a large one weighs seven or eight hundred *chin*; the whole body is hairless, black in colour, and all covered with scale;

the skin is lined, mangy, and thick; the hoof has three digits; and the head has one horn which grows in the middle of the bridge of the nose, a long horn being one *ch'ih* four or five *ts'un* [in height]. It does not eat grass, but it eats prickly trees and prickly leaves; it also eats large pieces of dry wood. It drops excrement which resembles the sumach-refuse of a dyer's shop.

Their horses are short and small, like donkeys. Water-buffaloes, yellow oxen, pigs and goats—all these they have. Geese and ducks are scarce. The fowls are small; the largest ones do not exceed two *chin* [in weight]; and their legs are one and a half *ts'un* and at the most two *ts'un*, in height. The cock birds have red crowns and white ears, with small waists and high tails; they crow, too, when people tame them up in their hands; they are very likeable.

For fruits they have such kinds as the plum, orange, water-melon, sugar-cane, coconut, jack-fruit and banana. The jack-fruit resembles the gourd-melon; the outside skin is like that of the litchi from Ch'uan [Szechuan]; inside the skin there are lumps of yellow flesh as big as a hen's egg, which taste like honey; inside these lumps there is a seed resembling a chicken's kidney; and when roasted and eaten, it tastes like a chestnut.

For vegetables, they have the gourd-melon, cucumber, bottle-gourd, mustard plant, onion and ginger, and that is all; other fruits and vegetables are entirely lacking.

Most of the men take up fishing for a livelihood; they seldom go in for agriculture, and therefore rice and cereals are not abundant. In the local varieties of rice the kernel is small, long, and reddish. Barley and wheat are both wanting. The people ceaselessly chew areca-nut and betel-leaf.

When men and women marry, the only requirement is that the man should first go to the woman's house, and consummate the marriage. Ten days or half a moon later, the man's father and mother, with their relatives and friends, to the accompaniment of drums and music escort husband and wife back to the paternal home; then they prepare wine and play music.

As to their wine: they take some rice and mix it with medicinal herbs, seal the mixture in a jar, and wait till it has matured. When they wish to drink it, they take a long-joined small bamboo tube three or four *ch'ih* in length, insert it into the wine-jar, and sit around; then they put in some water according to the number of persons, and take it in turns to suck up the wine and drink it; when the jar is sucked dry, they again add water and drink; this they do until there is no more taste of wine; and then they stop.

As to their writing: they have no paper or pen; they use either goat-skin beaten thin or tree-bark smoked black; and they fold it into the form of a classical book, in which, with white chalk, they write characters which serve for records.

As to the punishable offences in this country: for light offences, they employ thrashing on the back with a rattan stick; for serious offences, they cut off the nose; for robbery, they sever a hand; for the offence of adultery, the man and the woman are branded on the face so as to make a scar; for the most heinous offences, they take a hard wood stick, cut a sharp point to it, and set it up on a log of wood which resembles a small boat; this they put in the water; and they make the offender sit on the wood spike; the wood [stick] protrudes from his mouth and he dies; and then the corpse is left on the water as a warning to the public.

In the determination of time they have no intercalary moon, but twelve moons make one year. One day and night are divided into ten watches, which they signal by beat of a drum. As to the four seasons: they take the opening of the flowers as spring, and the falling of the leaves as autumn.

On the day of the New Year holiday the king takes the gall of living persons, mixes it with water, and bathes in it; the chiefs of every locality collect this gall and offer it to him as a ceremonial presentation of tribute.

When the king of the country has reigned for thirty years, he abdicates and becomes a priest, directing his brothers, sons, and nephews to administer the affairs of the country. The king goes into the depths of the mountains, and fasts and does penance, or else he merely eats a vegetarian diet. He lives alone for one year. He takes an oath by Heaven and says "When formerly I was the king, if I transgressed while on the throne, I wish wolves or tigers to devour me, or sickness to destroy me." If, after the completion of one whole year, he is not dead, he ascends the throne once more and administers the affairs of the country again. The people of the country acclaim him, saying "His-li Ma-ha-la-cha," this is the most venerable and most holy designation.

The so-called "corpse-head barbarian" is really a woman belonging to a human family, her only peculiarity being that her eyes have no pupils; at night, when she is sleeping, her head flies away and eats the tapering faeces of human infants; this infant, affected by the evil influence which invades its abdomen, inevitably dies; and the flying head returns and unites with its body, just as it was before. If people know of this and wait till the moment when the head flies away, and then remove the body to another place, the returning head cannot unite with the body, and then the woman dies. If the existence of such a woman in a household is not reported to the authorities, in addition to the killer the whole family become parties to an offence.

Again, there is a large pool connected with the sea, called "the crocodile pool"; if in litigation between persons there is a matter which is difficult to elucidate and the officials cannot reach a decision, they make the two litigants ride on water-buffaloes and cross through this pool; the crocodiles come out and devour the man whose cause is unrighteous; but the man whose cause is righteous is not devoured, even if he crosses ten times; this is most remarkable.

In all the mountains beside the sea there are wild water-buffaloes, very fierce; originally they were domestic plough-oxen which ran away into the mountains; there they lived and grew up by themselves, and in the course of long years they developed into herds; but if they see a strange man wearing blue clothes, they will certainly pursue him and gore him to death; they are most vicious.

The foreigners are very particular about their heads; and if anyone touches them on the head, they feel the same hatred against him as we in the Central Country feel against a murderer.

In their trading transactions they currently use pale gold which is seventy per cent pure, or else they use silver.

They very much like the dishes, bowls, and other kinds of blue porcelain articles, the hemp-silk, silk-gauze, beads, and other such things from the Central Country, and so they bring their pale gold and give it in exchange. They constantly bring rhinoceros' horns, elephants' teeth, *ch'ieh-lan* incense, and other such things, and present them as tribute to the Central Country.

The Country of Ku-Li [Calicut]

This is the great country of the Western Ocean.

Setting sail from the anchorage in the country of Ko-chih, you travel north-west, and arrive here after three days. The country lies beside the sea. Traveling east from the mountains for five hundred, or seven hundred, *li,* you make a long journey through to the country of K'an-pa-li. On the west [the country of Ku-li] abuts on the great sea; on the south it joins the boundary of the country of Ko-chih; and on the north side it adjoins the territory of the country of Hen-nu-erh.

"The great country of the Western Ocean" is precisely this country.

In the fifth year of the Yung-lo [period] the court ordered the principal envoy the grand eunuch Cheng Ho and others to deliver an imperial mandate to the king of this country and to bestow on him a patent conferring a title of honour, and the grant of a silver seal, also to promote all the chiefs and award them hats and girdles of various grades.

So Cheng Ho went there in command of a large fleet of treasure-ships, and he erected a table with a pavilion over it and set up a stone which said "Though the journey from this country to the Central Country is more than a hundred thousand *li*, yet the people are very similar, happy and prosperous, with identical customs. We have here engraved a stone, a perpetual declaration for ten thousand ages."

The king of the country is a Nan-k'un man [Brahman or Kshatriya?]; he is a firm believer in the Buddhist religion [N.B., Ma Huan's mistake; the king was a Hindu]; and he venerates the elephant and the ox.

The population of the country includes five classes, the Muslim people, the Nan-k'un people, the Che-ti people, the Ko-ling people, and the Mu-kua people.

The king of the country and the people of the country all refrain from eating the flesh of the ox. The great chiefs are Muslim people; and they all refrain from eating the flesh of the pig. Formerly there was a king who made a sworn compact with the Muslim people, saying "You do not eat the ox; I do not eat the pig; we will reciprocally respect the taboo"; and this compact has been honoured right down to the present day.

The king has cast an image of a Buddha in brass; it is named Nai-na-erh; he has erected a temple of Buddha and has cast tiles of brass and covered the dais of Buddha with them; and beside the dais a well has been dug. Every day at dawn the king goes to the well, draws water, and washes the image of Buddha; after worshipping, he orders men to collect the pure dung of yellow oxen; this is stirred with water in a brass basin until it is like paste; then it is smeared all over the surface of the ground and walls inside the temple. Moreover, he has given orders that the chiefs and wealthy personages shall also smear and scour themselves with ox-dung every morning.

He also takes ox-dung, burns it till it is reduced to a white ash, and grinds it to a fine powder; using a fair cloth as a small bag, he fills it with the ash, and regularly carried it on his person. Every day at dawn, after he has finished washing his face, he takes the ox-dung ash, stirs it up with water, and smears it on his forehead and between his two thighs—thrice in each place. This denotes his sincerity in venerating Buddha and in venerating the ox.

There is a traditional story that in olden times there was a holy man named Mou-hsieh [Moses], who established a religious cult; the people knew that he was a true man of Heaven, and all men revered and followed him. Later the holy man went away with others to another place, and ordered his younger brother named Sa-mo-li [the Samaritan] to govern and teach the people.

But his younger brother the holy man returned; he saw that the multitude, misled by his younger brother Sa-mo-li, were corrupting the holy way; thereupon he destroyed the ox and wished to punish his younger brother; and his younger brother mounted a large elephant and vanished.

Afterwards, the people thought of him and hoped anxiously for his return. Moreover, if it was the beginning of the moon, they would say "In the middle of the moon he will certainly come," and when the middle of the moon arrived, they would say once more "At the end of the moon he will certainly come"; right down to the present day they have never ceased to hope for his return.

This is the reason why the Nan-k'un people venerate the elephant and the ox.

The king has two great chiefs who administer the affairs of the country; both are Muslims.

The majority of the people in the country all profess the Muslim religion. There are twenty or thirty temples of worship, and once in seven days they go to worship. When the day arrives, the whole family fast and bathe, and attend to nothing else. In the *ssu* [9 to 11 A.M.] and *wu* [11 A.M. to 1 P.M.] periods, the menfolk, old and young, go to the temple to worship. When the *wei* [1 to 3 P.M.] period arrives, they disperse and return home; thereupon they carry on with their trading, and transact their household affairs.

The people are very honest and trustworthy. Their appearance is smart, fine, and distinguished.

Their two great chiefs received promotion and awards from the court of the Central Country.

If a treasure-ship goes there, it is left entirely to the two men to superintend the buying and selling; the king sends a chief and a Che-ti Wei-no-chi [chetty broker?] to examine the account books in the official bureau; a broker comes and joins them; and a high officer who commands the ships discusses the choice of a certain date for fixing prices. When the day arrives, they first of all take the silk embroideries and the open-work silks, and other such goods which have been brought there, and discuss the price of them one by one; and when the price has been fixed, they write out an agreement stating the amount of the price; this agreement is retained by these persons.

The chief and the Che-ti, with his excellency the eunuch, all join hands together, and the broker then says, "In such and such a moon on such and such a day, we have all joined hands and sealed our agreement with a hand-clasp; whether the price be dear or cheap, we will never repudiate it or change it."

After that, the Che-ti and the men of wealth then come bringing precious stones, pearls, corals, and other such things, so that they may be examined and the price discussed; this cannot be settled in a day; if done quickly, it takes one moon; if done slowly, it takes two or three moons.

Once the money-price has been fixed after examination and discussion, if a pearl or other such article is purchased, the price which must be paid for it is calculated by the chief and the Wei-no-chi who carried out the original transaction; and as to the quantity of the hemp-silk or other such article which must be given in exchange for it, goods are given in exchange according to the price fixed by the original hand-clasp—there is not the slightest deviation.

In their method of calculation, they do not use a calculating-plate abacus; for calculating, they use only the two hands and two feet and twenty digits on them; and they do not make the slightest mistake; this is very extraordinary.

The king uses gold of sixty per cent purity to cast a coin for current use; it is named a *pa-nan*; the diameter of the face of each coin is three *fen* eight *li* in terms of our official *ts'un*; it has lines characters on the face and on the reverse; and it weighs one *fen* on our official steelyard. He also makes a coin of silver; it is named a *ta-erh*; each coin weighs about three *li*; and this coin is used for petty transactions.

In their system of weights, each one *ch'ien* on their foreign steelyard equals eight *fen* on our official steelyard; and each one *liang* on their foreign steelyard, being calculated at sixteen *ch'ien*, equals one *liang* two *ch'ien* eight *fen* on our official steelyard. On their foreign steelyard twenty *liang* make one *chin*, equal to one *chin* nine *liang* six *ch'ien* on our official steelyard. Their foreign weight is names a *fan-la-shih*.

The fulcrum of their steelyard is fixed at the end of the beam, and the weight is moved along to the middle of the beam; when the beam is raised to the level, that is the zero position; when you weigh a thing, you move the weight forward; and according as the thing is light or heavy, so you move the weight forward or backward. You can weigh only ten *chin*, which is equivalent to sixteen *chin* on our official steelyard.

In weighing such things as aromatic goods, two hundred *chin* on their foreign steelyard make one *po-ho*, which is equivalent to three hundred and twenty *chin* on our official steelyard. If they weigh pepper, two hundred and fifty chin make one *po-ho*, which is equivalent to four hundred *chin* on our official steelyard.

Whenever they weigh goods, large and small alike, they mostly use a pair of scales for testing comparative weights. As to their system of measurement: the authorities make a brass casting, which constitutes a *sheng*, for current use; the foreign name for it *tang-chia-li*; and each *sheng* equals one *sheng* six *ko* in terms of our official *sheng*. "Western Ocean" cloth, named *ch'e li* cloth in this country, comes from the neighboring districts of K'an-pa-í and other such places; each roll is four *ch'ih* five *ts'un* broad, and two *chang* five *ch'ih* long; and it is sold for eight or ten of their local gold coins.

The people of the country also take the silk of the silk-worm, soften it by boiling, dye it all colors, and weave it into kerchiefs with decorative stripes at intervals; the breadth is four or five *ch'ih*, and the length one *chang* two or three *ch'ih*; and each length is sold for one hundred gold coins.

As to the pepper: the inhabitants of the mountainous countryside have established gardens, and it is extensively cultivated. When the period of the tenth moon arrives, the pepper ripens; and it is collected, dried in the sun, and sold. Of course, big pepper-collectors come and collect it, and take it up to the official storehouse to be stored; if there is a buyer, an official gives permission for the sale; the duty is calculated according to the amount of the purchase price and is paid in to the authorities. Each one *po-ho* of pepper is sold for two hundred gold coins.

The Che-ti mostly purchase all kinds of precious stones and pearls, and they manufacture coral beads and other such things.

Foreign ships from every place come there; and the king of the country also sends a chief and a writer and others to watch the sales; thereupon they collect the duty and pay it to the authorities.

The wealthy people mostly cultivate coconut trees—sometimes a thousand trees, sometimes two thousand or three thousand—;this constitutes their property.

The coconut has ten different uses. The young tree has a syrup, very sweet, and good to drink; and it can be made into wine by fermentation. The old coconut has flesh, from which they express oil, and make sugar, and make a foodstuff for eating. From the fiber which envelops the outside of the nut they make ropes for ship-building. The shell of the coconut makes bowls and makes cups; it is also good for burning to ash for the delicate operation of inlaying gold or silver. The trees are good for building houses, and the leaves are good for roofing houses.

For vegetables they have mustard plants, green ginger, turnips, caraway seeds, onions, garlic, bottle-gourds, egg-plants, cucumbers, and gourd-melons—

all these they have in all the four seasons of the year. They also have a kind of small gourd which is as large as one's finger, about two *ts'un* long, and tastes like a green cucumber. Their onions have a purple skin; they resemble garlic; they have a large head and small leaves; and they are sold by the *chin* weight.

The *mu-pieh-tzu* tree is more than ten *chang* high; it forms a fruit which resembles a green persimmon and contains thirty or forty seeds; it falls of its own accord when ripe; and the bats, as large as hawks, all hang upside down and rest on this tree.

They have both read and white rice, but barley and wheat are both absent; and their wheat-flour all comes from other places as merchandise for sale here.

Fowls and ducks exist in profusion, but there are no geese. Their goats have tall legs and an ashen hue; they resemble donkey-foals. The water-buffaloes are not very large. Some of the yellow oxen weigh three or four hundred *chin*; the people do not eat their flesh; but consume only the milk and cream. The people never eat rice without butter. Their oxen are cared for until they are old; and when they die, they are buried. The price of all kinds of sea-fish is very cheap. Deer and hares from up in the mountains are also for sale.

Many of the people rear peafowl. As to their other birds: they have crows, green hawks, egrets, and swallows; but of other kinds of birds besides these they have not a single one, great or small. The people of the country can also play and sing; they use the shell of a calabash to make a musical instrument, and copper wires to make the strings; and they play this instrument to accompany the singing of their foreign songs; the melodies are worth hearing.

As to the popular customs and marriage- and funeral-rites, the So-li people and the Muslim people each follow the ritual forms of their own class, and these are different.

The king's throne does not descend to his son, but descends to his sister's son; descent is to the sister's son because they consider that the offspring of the woman's body alone constitutes the legal family. If the king has no elder or younger sister, the throne is yielded up to some man of merit. Such is the succession from one generation to another.

The king's laws do not include the punishment of flogging with the bamboo. If the offence is slight, they cut off a hand or sever a foot; if it is serious, they impose a money-fine or put the offender to death; and if it is very heinous, they confiscate his property and exterminate his family. A person who offends against the law is taken under arrest to an official, whereupon he accepts his punishment.

If there is perhaps something unjust about the circumstances and he does not admit the sentence, then he is taken before the king or before a great chief; there they set up an iron cooking-pot, fill it with four or five *chin* of oil and cook it to the boil; first they throw in some tree-leaves to test whether they make a crackling noise; then they make the man take two fingers of his right hand and scald them in the oil for a short time; he waits till they are burnt and then takes them out; they are wrapped in a cloth on which a seal is affixed; and he is kept in prison at the office.

Two or three days later, before the assembled crowd, they break open the seal and examine him; if the hand has a burst abscess, then there is nothing unjust about the matter and a punishment is imposed; but if the hand is un-damaged, just as it had been before, then he is released.

The chief and other men, with drums and music, ceremonially escort this man back to his family; all his relations, neighbors, and friends give him presents and there are mutual congratulations; and they drink wine and play music by way of mutual felicitation. This is a very extraordinary matter.

On the day when the envoy returned, the king of the country wished to send tribute; so he took fifty *liang* of fine red gold and ordered the foreign craftsmen to draw it out into gold threads as fine as hair; these were strung together to form a ribbon, which was made into a jeweled girdle with incrus-tations of all kinds of precious stones and large pearls; and the king sent a chief, Nai-peng, to present it as tribute to the Central Country.

The Country of the Heavenly Square [Mecca]

This country is the country of Mo-ch'ieh. Setting sail from the country of Ku-li [Calicut], you proceed towards the south-west—the point *shen* on the compass; the ship travels for three moons, and then reaches the jetty of this country. The foreign name for it is Chih-ta [Jidda]; and there is a great chief who controls it. From Chih-ta you go west, and after traveling for one day you reach the city where the king resides; it is named the capital city of Mo-ch'ieh.

They profess the Muslim religion. A holy man first expounded and spread the doctrine of his teaching in this country, and right down to the present day the people of the country all observe the regulations of the doctrine in their actions, not daring to commit the slightest transgression.

The people of this country are stalwart and fine-looking, and their limbs and faces are of a very dark purple color.

The menfolk bind up their heads; they wear long garments; on their feet they put leather shoes. The women all wear a covering over their heads, and you cannot see their faces.

The speak the A-la-pi [Arabic] language. The law of the country prohibits wine-drinking. The customs of the people are pacific and admirable. There are no poverty-stricken families. They all observe the precepts of their religion, and law-breakers are few. It is in truth a most happy country.

As to the marriage- and funeral-rites: they all conduct themselves in accordance with the regulations of their religions.

If you travel on from here for a journey of more than half a day, you reach the Heavenly Hall mosque; the foreign name for this Hall is K'ai-a-pai.

All round it on the outside is a wall; this wall has four hundred and sixty-six openings; on both sides of the openings are pillars all made of white jade-stone; of these pillars there are altogether four hundred and sixty-seven—along the front ninety-nine, along the back one hundred and one, along the left-hand side one hundred and thirty-two, and along the right-hand side one hundred and thirty-five.

This Hall is built with layers of five colored stones; in shape it is square and flat-topped. Inside, there are pillars formed of five great beams of sinking incense wood, and a shelf made of yellow gold. Throughout the interior of the Hall, the walls are all formed of clay mixed with rosewater and ambergris, exhaling a perpetual fragrance. Over the Hall is a covering of black hemp-silk. They keep two black lions to guard the door.

Every year on the tenth day of the twelfth moon all the foreign Muslims—in extreme cases making a long journey of one or two years—come to worship inside the Hall. Everyone cuts off a piece of the hemp-silk covering as a memento before he goes away. When it has been completely cut away, the king covers over the Hall again with another covering woven in advance; this happens again and again, year after year, without intermission.

On the left of the Hall is the burial-place of Ssu-ma-i, a holy man; his tomb is all made with green *sa-pu-ni* gem-stones; the length is one *chang* or two *ch'ih*, the height three *ch'ih*, and the breadth five *ch'ih*; the wall which surrounds the tomb is built with layers of purple topaz, and is more than five *ch'ih* high.

Inside the wall of the mosque, at the four corners, are built four towers; at every service of worship they ascend these towers, to call the company, and chant the ceremonial. On both sides, left and right, are the halls where all the patriarchs have preached the doctrine; these, too, are built with layers of stone, and are decorated most beautifully.

As to the climate of this place: during all the four seasons it is always hot, like summer, and there is no rain, lightning, frost, or snow. At night the dew is very heavy; plants and trees all depend on the dew-water for nourishment; and if at night you put out an empty bowl to receive it until day-break, the dew-water will be three *fen* [0.3 inches deep] in the bowl.

As to the products of the land: rice and grain are scarce; [and] they all cultivate such things as unhusked rice, wheat, black millet, gourds, and vegetables. They also have water-melons and sweet melons; and in some cases it takes two men to carry each single fruit. Then again they have a kind of tree with twisted flowers, like the large mulberry-tree of the Central Country; it is one or two *chang* approximately ten to twenty feet in height; the flowers blossom twice a year; and it lives to a great age without withering. For fruits, they have turnips, Persian dates, pomegranates, apples, large pears, and peaches, some of which weigh four or five *chin* [approximately five to six pounds].

Their camels, horses, donkeys, mules, oxen, goats, cats, dogs, fowls, geese, ducks, and pigeons are also abundant. Some of the fowls and duck weigh over ten *chin* [approximately 13 pounds].

The land produces rose-water, *an-pa-erh* [ambergris] incense, *ch'i-lin* [giraffe], lions, the "camel-fowl" [ostrich], the antelope, the "fly-o'er-the-grass" [lynx], all kinds of precious stones, pearls, corals, amber, and other such things.

The king uses gold to cast a coin named a *t'ang-chia*, which is in current use; each has a diameter of seven *fen* [approximately .8 inches], and weighs one *ch'ien* [approximately 3.73 grams] on our official steelyard; compared with the gold of the Central Country it is twenty per cent purer.

If you go west again and travel for one day, you reach a city named Mo-ti-na [Medina]; the tomb of their holy man Ma-ha-ma [Muhammad] is situated exactly in the city; and right down to the present day a bright light rises day and night from the top of the grave and penetrates into the clouds. Behind the grave is a well, a spring of pure and sweet water, named A-pi San-san; men who go to foreign parts take this water and store it at the sides of their ships; if they meet with a typhoon at sea, they take this water and scatter it; and the wind and waves are lulled.

In the fifth year of the Hsüan-te [period: 1430] an order was respectfully received from our imperial court that the principal envoy the grand eunuch Cheng Ho and others should go to all the foreign countries to read out the imperial commands and to bestow rewards.

When a division of the fleet reached the country of Ku-li, the grand eunuch Hung [probably Hung Pao] saw that this country was sending men to travel there; whereupon he selected an interpreter and others, seven men in all, and sent them with a load of musk, porcelain articles, and other such things; and they joined a ship of this country and went there. It took them one year to go and return.

They bought all kinds of unusual commodities, and rare valuables, *ch'i-lin*, lions, "lion-fowls," and other such things; in addition they painted an accurate representation of the "Heavenly Hall" and they returned to the capital [Beijing].

The king of the country of Mo-ch'ieh also sent envoys who brought some local articles, accompanied the seven men—the interpreter and others—who had originally gone there, and presented the articles to the court.

Document 8

Narrative of a Journey to Hindustan (1442–1444)

By 'Abd al-Razzāq al-Samarqandī, "Narrative of a Journey to Hindustan," in *India in the Fifteenth Century,* trans. R. H. Major (London: Hakluyt Society, 1857)

In June 1442, the Timurid leader Shahrukh sent 'Abd al-Razzāq al-Samarqandī to be an ambassador to Vijayanagara. Born in Herat in 1413, he left a detailed record of his journey to the Asian subcontinent and his return to Herat in 1445. His account shared similarities with European accounts of India. As the historian Joan-Pau Rubiés has noted, "While the Europeans established comparisons with Paris or Milan, 'Abd al-Razzāq referred to Herat, the Khorasani capital." Like European observers, Abdul-Razzaq took careful note of the structure of politics, the local economy, and the army's use of elephants. Much of the narrative focuses on the politics of the court at Vijayanagara, a reflection of the ambassador's interests in affairs at home.[2]

In 1462, 'Abd al-Razzāq was elected sheikh of the monastery of Mirza Shahrukh. He died there two decades later, having left behind a travel account that included details of his journey from Herat to Calicut, Magalore, Beloor, and Vijayanagara, and back home again. That return journey did not go

---

2. Joan-Pau Rubiés, *Travel and Ethnology in the Renaissance: South India through European Eyes, 1250–1625* (Cambridge: Cambridge University Press, 2000), 23–25.

well for 'Abd al-Razzāq and his shipmates. "All of a sudden from adverse winds, like those who quaff the boat of wine, a change took place in the ship,"
he wrote, "and the planks, which had been joined together like the letters in a musalsal *script, flew apart like cut-out letters." Hoping to find security by lightening their load, the passengers "cast away much of their belongings into the sea and disencumbered themselves of possessions like Sufis." 'Abd al-Razzāq initially gave up hope. "I myself, seeing the state the sea was in, washed my hands of my life with the tears of my eyes and stood, dry of lip and wet of lash, transfixed in awe at the sea. I inscribed the words, 'We submit to God's destiny,' on the tablet of my mind." With passages from the Koran in his mind—"despair not the mercy of God" (Koran 12:87)—'Abd al-Razzāq learned that the storm ended. "The cold, adverse wind changed into a favorable breeze," he noted, "and the tyranny of the storm ended. The sea turned as calm as the heart could have wished." He had passed the ordeal and would soon make it to Herat.³*

The account first appeared in print in Collection portative de Voyages, *published in Paris (1798 to 1820), and first appeared in an English-language translation in one of the early volumes published by the Hakluyt Society, the learned society named for the sixteenth-century editor of travel accounts.⁴ The selection here focuses on the city of Calicut and includes details of the local ways of catching elephants, a subject that fascinated 'Abd al-Razzāq.*

Calicut is a perfectly secure harbour, which, like that of Ormuz, brings together merchants from every city and from every country; in it are to be found abundance of precious articles brought thither from maritime countries, and especially from Abyssinia, Zirbad, and Zanzibar; from time to time ships arrive there from the shores of the House of God [Mecca] and other parts of the Hejaz, and abide at will, for a greater or longer space, in this harbour; the town is inhabited by Infidels, and situated on a hostile shore. It

3. Kamaluddin Abdul-Razzaq Samarqandi, "Mission to Calicut and Vijayanagar," in *A Century of Princes: Sources on Timurid History and Art*, ed. W. M. Thackston (Cambridge, Mass: Aga Khan Program for Islamic Architecture, 1989), 317–18.
4. The text here follows Major's nineteenth-century translation, except for silent shifting of that text's occasional third person to first person. In addition, I have modernized the names of places, peoples, and titles following Thackston's recent translation of this account in *A Century of Princes*, 299–321.

contains a considerable number of Muslims, who are constant residents, and have built two mosques, in which they meet every Friday to offer up prayer. They have one Kadi [*cadi*], a priest, and for the most part they belong to the sect of Shafi í. Security and justice are so firmly established in this city, that the most wealthy merchants bring thither from maritime countries considerable cargoes, which they unload, and unhesitatingly send into the markets and the bazaars, without thinking in the meantime of any necessity of checking the account or of keeping watch over the goods. The officers of the custom-house take upon themselves the charge of looking after the merchandise, over which they keep watch day and night. When a sale is effected, they levy a duty on the goods of one-fortieth part; if they are not sold, they make no charge on them whatsoever.

In other ports a strange practice is adopted. When a vessel sets sail for a certain point, and suddenly is driven by a decree of Divine Providence into another roadstead, the inhabitants, under the pretext that the wind has driven it there, plunder the ship. But at Calicut, every ship, whatever place it may come from, or wherever it may be bound, when it puts into this port is treated like other vessels, and has no trouble of any kind to put up with. . . .

As soon as I landed at Calicut I saw beings such as my imagination had never depicted the like of.

> *Extraordinary beings, who are neither men nor devils,*
> *At sight of whom the mind takes alarm;*
> *If I were to see such in my dreams*
> *My heart would be in a tremble for many years.*
> *I have had love passages with a beauty, whose face was like the moon;*
> > *but I could never fall in love with a negress.*

The blacks of this country have the body nearly naked; they wear only bandages round the middle, called *lankoutah*, which descend from the navel to above the knee. In one hand they hold an Indian poignard, which has the brilliance of a drop of water, and in the other a buckler of ox-hide, which might be taken for a piece of mist. This costume is common to the king and to the beggar. As to the Muslims, they dress themselves in magnificent apparel after the manner of the Arabs, and manifest luxury in every particular. After I had had an opportunity of seeing a considerable number of Muslims and Infidels, I had a comfortable lodging assigned to me, and after the lapse of three days was conducted to an audience with the king. I saw a man with his body naked, like the rest of the Hindus. The sovereign of this city bears the title of samuri. When he dies it is his sister's son who succeeds him, and his inheritance does not belong to his son, or his brother, or any other of his relations. No one reaches the throne by means of the strong hand.

The Infidels are divided into a great number of classes, such as the Brahmins, the yogins, and others. Although they are all agreed upon the fundamental principles of polytheism and idolatry, each sect has its peculiar customs. Amongst them there is a class of men, with whom it is the practice for one woman to have a great number of husbands, each of whom undertakes a special duty and fulfils it. The hours of the day and of the night are divided between them; each of them for a certain period takes up his abode in the house, and while he remains there no other is allowed to enter. The samuri belongs to this sect.

When I obtained my audience of this prince, the hall was filled with two or three thousand Hindus, who wore the costume above described; the principal personages amongst the Muslims were also present. After they had made me take a seat, the letter of his majesty, the happy [*Khaqan*], was read, and they caused to pass in procession before the throne, the horse, the pelisse, the garment of cloth of gold, and the cap to be worn at the ceremony of Nauruz. The samuri showed me but little consideration. On leaving the audience I returned to my house. Several individuals, who brought with them a certain number of horses, and all sorts of things beside, had been shipped on board another vessel by order of the king of Hormuz; but being captured on the road by some cruel pirates, they were plundered of all their wealth, and narrowly escaped with their lives. Meeting them at Calicut, we had the honor to see some distinguished friends. . . .

The humble author of this narrative having received his audience of dismissal, departed from Calicut by sea. After having passed the port of Panderani, situated on the coast of Malibar, I reached the port of Mangalore, which forms the frontier of the kingdom of Vijayanagar. After staying there two or three days he continued his route by land. At a distance of three parasangs [leagues] from Mangalore I saw a temple of idols, which has not its equal in the universe. It is an equilateral square, of about ten *gaz* [yards] in length, ten in breadth, and five in height. It is entirely formed of cast bronze. It has four *estrades*. Upon that in the front stands a human figure, of great size, made of gold; its eyes are formed of two rubies, placed so artistically that the statue seems to look at you. The whole is worked with wonderful delicacy and perfection. After passing this temple, I came each day to some city or populous town. At length I came to a mountain whose summit reached the skies, and the foot of which was covered with so great a quantity of trees and thorny underwood, that the rays of the sun could never penetrate the obscurity, nor could the beneficial rains at any time reach the soil to moisten it. Having left this mountain and this forest behind me, I reached a town called Pednur the houses of which were like palaces, and its women reminded one of the beauty of the Houris. In it there is a temple of idols, so lofty as to be visible at a distance of many parasangs. It would be impossible to describe such a building without being suspected of exaggeration. I can only give a general idea of it. In the middle of the town is an open space, of about ten *gaz* in extent, and which, if one may use a comparison, rivals the garden of Irem. The roses of all kinds are as numerous as the leaves of the trees, on the borders of the streams rise a great number of cypresses, whose towering height is reflected in the waters, plaintain trees shoot out their tufted branches, and it would seem as if heaven itself looks down upon this beautiful spot with pleasure and admiration. All the ground of this parterre, all the environs of this place of delight, are paved with polished stones, joined together with so much delicacy and skill, that they seem to form but one single slab of stone, and look like a fragment of the sky which might be supposed to have been brought down to the earth. In the middle of this platform rises a building composed of a cupola formed of blue stones, and terminating in a point. The stone presents three rows of figures.

What can I say of this cupola, which, as regards the delicacy of the work, offered the world an idea of paradise?

Its vault, rounded and lofty, resembled a new moon; its elevation vied with that of the heavens.

So great a number of pictures and figures had been drawn by the pen and the pencil, that it would be impossible, in the space of a month, to sketch it all upon damask or taffeta. From the bottom of the building to the top there is not a hand's breadth to be found uncovered with paintings, after the manner of the Franks and the people of Khata [China].[5] The temple consists of a structure of four estrades; this structure is thirty *gaz* in length, twenty in breadth, fifty in height.

Since that its head shot up towards the skies, that vault, previously without stones in it, now seems formed of them.

5. Thackston renders this passage as "From top to bottom of that structure there was not the space of a hand free of *firangi* and *khatai* designs" (*A Century of Princes*, 307).

Since that its stones have rubbed themselves against the sun, the gold of that orb has taken a purer alloy.

All the other buildings, great and small, are covered with paintings and sculptures of extreme delicacy. In this temple morning and evening, after devotional exercises, which have nothing in them which can be agreeable to God, they play on musical instruments, perform concerts, and give feasts. All the inhabitants of the town have rents and pensions assigned to them on this temple. The most distant cities send hither their alms. In the opinion of these men without religion, this place is the kaba of the guebres.

After having sojourned in this town for the space of two or three days we continued our route, and at the end of the month of Dhu 'l-Hijja [April] we arrived at the city of Vijayanagara. The king sent a numerous cortège to meet us, and appointed us a very handsome house for our residence.

The preceding details, forming a close narrative of events, have shown to readers and writers that the chances of a maritime voyage had led 'Abd al-Razzāq , the author of this work, to the city of Vijayanagar. I saw a place extremely large and thickly peopled, and a king possessing greatness and sovereignty to the highest degree, whose dominion extends from the frontier of Serendip to the extremities of the country of Galbarga. From the frontiers of Bengal to the environs of Belinar [Malibar], the distance is more than a thousand parasangs [leagues]. The country is for the most part well culti-vated, very fertile, and contains about three hundred harbors. One sees there more than a thousand elephants, in their size resembling mountains, and in their forms resembling devils. The troops amount in number to eleven lacs.

One might seek in vain throughout the whole of Hindustan to find a more absolute *ray* (raja or king); for the monarchs of this country bear the title of *ray*. Next to him the Brahmins hold a rank superior to that of all other men. The book of *Kalila u Dimna*, the most beautiful work existing in the Persian language, and which presents us with the stories of a *raï* and a Brahmin, is probably a production of the talent of the literati of this country.

The city of Vijayanagar is such that the pupil of the eye has never seen a place like it, and the ear of intelligence has never been informed that there existed anything to equal it in the world. It is built in such a manner that seven citadels and the same number of walls enclose each other. Around the first citadel are stones of the height of a man, one half of which is sunk in the ground while the other rises above it. These are fixed one beside the other, in such a manner that no horse or foot soldier could boldly or with ease ap-proach the citadel. If any one would wish to find what point of resemblance this fortress and rampart present with that which exists in the city of Herat, let him picture to himself that the first citadel corresponds with that which extends from the mountain of Mukhtar and Dara-i Du baradaran (the Valley of the Two Brothers) as far as the banks of the river and the bridge of Malan, situated east of the town of Ghizan, and west of the village of Saynan.

It is a fortress of a round shape, built on the summit of a mountain, and constructed of stones and lime. It has very solid gates, the guards of which are constantly at their post, and examine everything with a severe inspection.

The second fortress represents the space which extends from the Juy-i Naw bridge in Herat of the new river, to the bridge of the Darqarah, lying to the east of the bridge of Rikina and Chakan, and to the west of the garden of Zubayda and of the village of Hasân.

The third citadel comprises as much space as lies between the mausoleum of the Imam Fakhruddin Razi and the dome-shaped monument of Mohammed Sultanshah.

The fourth corresponds to the space which separates the bridge Injil from the bridge of Kard.

The fifth comprises a space equal to that which extends from the garden of Zaghan to the bridge of Ab-i Chakan.

The sixth is equivalent to the space contained between the King's gate and the gate of Firozabad.

The seventh fortress, which is placed in the centre of the others, occupies an area ten times larger than the marketplace of the city of Herat. It is the palace which is used as the residence of the king. The distance from the gate of the first fortress, which lies on the north, to the first gate, which is situated in the south, is calculated to be two parasangs. It is the same distance from the east to the west. The space which separates the first fortress from the second, and up to the third fortress, is filled with cultivated fields, and with houses and gardens. In the space from the third to the seventh one meets a numberless crowd of people, many shops, and a bazaar. At the gate of the king's palace are four bazaars, placed opposite each other. On the north is the portico of the palace of the *ray*. Above each bazaar is a lofty arcade with a magnificent gallery, but the audience hall of the king's palace is elevated above all the rest. The bazaars are extremely long and broad. The rose merchants place before their shops high *estrades*, on each side of which they expose their flowers for sale. In this place one sees a constant succession of sweet smelling and fresh looking roses. These people could not live without roses, and they look upon them as quite as necessary as food.

Each class of men belonging to each profession has shops contiguous the one to the other; the jewelers sell publicly in the bazaar pearls, rubies, emeralds, and diamonds. In this agreeable locality, as well as in the king's palace, one sees numerous running streams and canals formed of chiseled stone, polished and smooth. On the left of the Sultan's portico rises the *diwankhana* (the council-house), which is extremely large and looks like a palace. In front of it is a hall, the height of which is above the stature of a man, its length thirty gaz, and its breadth ten. In it is placed the archives, and here sit the scribes. The writing of this people is of two kinds: in one they write their letters with a kalam [reed] of iron upon a leaf of the Indian nut (the cocoa-nut tree), which is two gaz in length and two fingers in breadth. These characters have no color, and the writing lasts but a short time. In the second kind of writing they blacken a white surface, they then take a soft stone, which they cut like a kalam, and which they use to form the letters; this stone leaves on the black surface a white color, which lasts a very long time, and this kind of writing is held in high estimation.

In the middle of this palace, upon a high estrade, is seated an eunuch, called the *dhannâyak*, who alone presides over the divan. At the end of the hall stand hussars drawn up in line. Every man who comes upon any business, passes between the hussars, offers a small present, prostrates himself with his face to the ground, then rising up explains the business which brought him there, and the *dhannâyak* pronounces his opinion, according to the principles of justice adopted in this kingdom, and no one thereafter is allowed to make any appeal.

When the *dhannâyak* leaves the divan they carry before him several parasols of different colors, and sound a trumpet. On each side of him walk panegyrists, who pronounce complimentary expressions in his honor. Before reaching the king's apartment there are seven doors to be passed, each of which is guarded by a janitor. When the *dhannâyak* arrives at each door a parasol is unfolded. He passes through the seventh door alone, gives the prince an account of what matters are going on, and after the lapse of a few minutes retires. Behind the king's palace are the house and hall allotted to the *dhannâyak*. To the left of the said palace is the mint. . . .

This empire contains so great a population that it would be impossible to give an idea of it without entering into the most extensive details. In the king's palace are several cells, like basins, filled with bullion, forming one mass. All the inhabitants of this country, both those of exalted rank and of an inferior class, down to the artisans of the bazaar, wear pearls, or rings adorned with precious stones, in their ears, on their necks, on their arms, on the upper part of the hand, and on the fingers. Opposite the mint is the house of the elephants.

Although the king possesses a considerable number of elephants in his dominions, the largest of these animals are kept near the palace, in the interior of the first and second fortress, between the north and the west. These elephants copulate, and bring forth young. The king possesses one white elephant of an extremely great size, on whose body is scattered here and there grey spots like freckles. Every morning this animal is led out before the monarch, and the sight of him seems to act as a happy omen. The elephants of the palace are fed upon *kitchri* [kedgeree]. This substance is cooked, and it is taken out of the copper in the elephant's presence; salt is thrown on it, and fresh sugar is sprinkled over it, and the whole is then mixed well together. They then make balls of it, weighing about two *man,* and, after steeping them in butter, they put them in the elephant's mouth. If one of these ingredients has been forgotten, the elephant attacks his keeper, and the king punishes this negligence severely. These animals take this food twice a day.

Each elephant has a separate compartment, the walls of which are extremely solid, and the roof composed of strong pieces of wood. The neck and the back of these animals are bound with chains, the end of which is strongly fastened to the top of the roof. If they were fixed otherwise, the elephant would easily undo them: the fore feet also are held by chains.

The mode of catching the elephant is as follows. On the road which the animal takes when he goes to drink, they dig a trench, and cover the mouth of it over, but very lightly. When an elephant falls into it, two or three days are allowed to elapse before any one goes near him. At the end of that time a man comes and strikes the animal with several blows of a stick well applied: upon this another man shows himself, and violently drives away the man who struck the blows, and, seizing his stick, hurls it a great way off; after which he throws some food to the elephant, and goes away. For several days the first of these men comes to beat the elephant, and the second prevents him from continuing to do so. Before long the animal becomes very friendly with this latter individual, who by degrees approaches the elephant, and offers him fruits, for which this animal is known to have a liking. He then scratches him and rubs him, and the elephant, won over by this maneuver, submits without resistance, and allows a chain to be passed around his neck.

The story goes, that an elephant having escaped, fled into the desert and into the jungles. His keeper, who went in pursuit of him, dug a trench on his road. The animal, who dreaded the contrivances of this man (like a gazelle which has escaped from the net of the hunter), took up with his trunk a block of wood like a beam, placed it before him at short distances, on the surface of the ground, as he proceeded; and thus testing the road, he reached the watering place. The keepers of the elephant had lost all hope of retaking him, and yet the king had a very strong desire to gain possession of this animal again. One of the keepers hid himself in the branches of a tree under which the elephant had to pass. At the moment when the elephant came up, this man threw himself upon the back of the animal, who still had about his body and chest one of the thick cords with which the elephants are bound. This cord he laid strong hold of. Do what the elephant would to shake himself and twist about, and to strike blows with his trunk both right and left, he could not get free. He rolled himself on his side, but every time he did so the man leapt cleverly to the opposite side, and at the same time gave him some heavy blows upon his head. At length the animal, worn out, gave up the contest, and surrendered his body to the chains and his neck to the fetters. The keeper led the elephant into the presence of the king, who rewarded him with a noble generosity.

Even the sovereigns of Hindustan take part in hunting the elephant. They remain a whole month, or even more, in the desert or in the jungles, and when they have taken any of these animals they are very proud of it. Sometimes they cause criminals to be cast under the feet of an elephant, that the animal may crush them to pieces with his knees, his trunk, and his tusks. The merchants who trade in elephants go to seek them in the island of Ceylon, and export them to different countries, where they sell them according to the tariff, which varies by the *gaz*.

Document 9

Magellan's Voyage

By Antonio Pigafetta, *Magellan's Voyage*, trans. R. A. Skelton (New Haven, Conn.: Yale University Press, 1969), 97–101, 136–141

On September 20, 1519, Ferdinand Magalhães (Magellan; 1480?–1521) led five ships out of the Portuguese port at San Lucar de Barrameda near Seville on a journey across the Atlantic toward the Spice Islands, territory that the Portuguese already knew from earlier voyages. Magellan passed near the Brazilian region of Pernambuco in late November of that year on his way around the southern tip of South America and through the straits that now bear his name. He reached the Philippines in March 1521. Three years after the journey began, the *Victoria*, the only surviving vessel, sailed into the port where the expedition had begun. Among the eighteen Europeans on board was Antonio Pigafetta (1491?–1534?), who had kept careful notes of the journey. Magellan himself did not survive; he had been killed in a skirmish in the Philippines on April 27, 1521. Residents of the island of Mattan "rushed upon him with lances of iron and of bamboo," Pigafetta wrote, "and with these javelins, so that they slew our mirror, our light, our comfort, and our true guide." Though he never made it back to Europe, Magellan still got credit for arranging perhaps the most important journey in the sixteenth century—the first circumnavigation of the earth. The event, the English translator of travel narratives Richard Eden wrote a generation later, "is one of the greatest and moste marveylous thynges that hath bynne knowen to owre tyme."[6]

Soon after his return Pigafetta began to prepare the report of the journey. He had gone on the expedition, he wrote in the prologue, after "reading of divers books and from the report of many clerks and learned men" about "the great terrible things of the Ocean Sea." The journey would be difficult, he knew, but he wanted it told that he had "made the voyage and saw with my eyes the things hereafter written, and I might win a famous name with posterity." There are four surviving manuscripts, including a beautifully rendered work in the Beinecke Library at Yale University. Unlike some of the other travel accounts of the age, the first printed versions came out more slowly, appearing in French, Italian, and English between 1526 and 1555.[7]

Pigafetta's report was somewhat vague on details of exact locations, but the survival of several derroteros (pilots' logs) have made it possible for modern scholars to identify the locales where the ships landed. This reconstruction is particularly important for the islands of the South-West Pacific, many of which blended together in Pigafetta's telling. In the passages here, Pigafetta offers details about what he saw in the Spice Islands. By the time he made these observations, Magellan was already dead.

6. Richard Eden, *The Decades of the newe worlde or west India* (London, 1555), 214ᵛ.
7. For details about the manuscripts and the location of places mentioned in the text, see the superb scholarly apparatus in Antonio Pigafetta, *Magellan's Voyage: A Narrative Account of the First Circumnavigation*, trans. R. A. Skelton (New Haven, Conn.: Yale University Press 1969).

Chapter 30: Arrival at Pulaoan

Leaving that place on a course between west and southwest, we came to an island, not very large and almost uninhabited, whose people are Moors, and they were banished from an island called Burne [Borneo]. They go naked like the others. They have bows with quivers at their side full of arrows poisoned with herbs. They have daggers with hafts enriched with gold and precious stones, lances, bucklers. And they called us holy bodies. In that island little food is found, but plenty of large trees. And it is in latitude seven and a half degrees toward the Arctic Pole, and distant from Chippit forty-three leagues. And it is called Caghaian [Cayagan Island]

About twenty-five leagues from that island, between west and northwest, we discovered a large island, where grow rice, ginger, swine, goats, poultry, figs half a cubit long and as thick as the arm, which are good, and some others much smaller, which are better than all the others. There are also coconuts, sweet potato, sugarcanes, roots like turnips, and rice cooked under the fire in bamboos or wood, which lasts longer than that cooked in pots. We could well call that land the Land of Promise, because before finding it we suffered very great hunger, so that many times we were ready perforce to abandon our ships and go ashore that we might not starve to death. The king of that island made peace with us, making a small cut in his chest with one of our knives, and with his finger marked with blood his tongue and his brow as a sign of truest peace. And we did likewise. That island is in latitude toward the Arctic Pole nine and a third degrees, and in longitude from the line of demarcation one hundred and sixty and a third. And it is named Pulaoan [Palawan].

Chapter 31: On Pulaoan

The people of Pulaoan go naked like the others, and they all work their fields. They have bows with wooden and tipped arrows longer than a palm, some having long and sharp fishbones poisoned with venomous herbs, and others tipped with poisoned points of bamboo. They have at the head a piece of soft wood fixed instead of feathers. To the end of their bows they fasten a piece of iron like a mace, with which they fight after shooting all their arrows. They prize brass rings and chains, knives, and even more copper wire for binding their fishhooks. They have very large domestic cocks, which they do not eat for a certain veneration they have for them. Sometimes they make them joust and fight against one another, and each man takes a wager on his own; then he whose cock is victorious takes the other man's cock and wager. They have wine distilled from rice, stronger and better than that of the palm.

Ten leagues thence to the southwest, we came to an island, and as we coasted it, it seemed to me that we went upward. And after we entered the port, the holy body appeared to us in very dark weather. And from the beginning of that island to the port are fifty leagues. The following day, the ninth of July, the king of that island sent us a very fair ship, having the prow and the poop worked in gold, and at the prow was a white and blue banner with peacock's feathers at the point. Some men played instruments like drums. And with this ship came to *Almadies*, which are their fishing boats. And this ship was called *Prao*, which is like a foist. Then eight old men, among the chief of them, entered the ships, and seated themselves on a carpet in the stern, and they presented to us a painted wooden jar full of betel and areca, which are the fruits that they always chew, with orange flowers. The said jar was covered with a cloth of yellow silk. Also they gave us two cages full of poultry, a pair of goats, three jars full of distilled rice wine, and some bundles of sugarcane. And they did likewise for the other ship. Then they embraced us, and we took leave. The said rice is clear as water, but so strong that some of our men became intoxicated, and they call it *Arach*.

Six days later, the king sent again three ships in great pomp, playing instruments and tambourines, and they came about our ships, and saluted us with their cloth caps, which cover only the top of their head. And we greeted them with our artillery without shot. Then they gave us a present of divers viands of rice, some wrapped in leaves and made into fairly long pieces, others like sugar loaves, and others made after the manner of tarts with eggs and honey. And they told us that the king was content that we should take water and wood, and should do as we wished. Hearing that, seven of us went aboard the ship and took a present to the king, which was a green velvet robe after the Turkish fashion, a chair of violet velvet, five cubits of red cloth, a red cap, a covered cup, three quires of paper, and a gilt writing case. We gave to the queen three cubits of yellow cloth, a pair of silver shoes, and a silver needle case full of needles. To the governor, three cubits of red cloth, a cap, and a gilt cup. To the herald who had come to the ship we gave a robe of red and green cloth after the Turkish fashion, a cap, and a quire of paper. And to the seven other chief men, to one a piece of cloth, to others caps, and to each a quire of paper. Then forthwith we departed.

When we arrived at the city, we remained about two hours in the ship until two elephants covered with silk came, and twelve men, each with a porcelain jar covered with silk, to carry our gifts. Then we mounted the elephants, and the twelve men marched ahead with the jars and gifts. And so we went to the governor's house, where we were given a supper of divers viands, and at night we slept on cotton mattresses. Next day we remained in the house until noon. Then we went to the king's palace on the said elephants, with the gifts ahead, as on the previous day.

Between the house and the king's palace all the streets were full of people with swords, spears, and targets, for the king had willed it thus. And we entered the palace courtyard on the elephants. Then we mounted by steps, accompanied by the governor and other notables. And we entered a large hall full of barons and lords, where we were seated on a carpet with the gifts and vessels with us. At the head and end of this hall was another one, higher but not so large, and all hung with silk drapery, and from it two windows with crimson curtains opened, by which light entered the hall. Three hundred naked men were standing there, with swords and sharp stakes posed at their thigh to guard the king. And at the end of this hall was a window, and when a crimson curtain was drawn, we perceived within the king seated at a table, with one of his little sons, and they were chewing betel. Behind him were only many ladies. Then one of the chief men told us that we could not speak to the king, but that if we desired anything we should tell him, and he would tell a more notable man, who would communicate it to one of the governor's brothers, who was in the smaller hall, and he would speak through a speaking tube by a hole in the wall to the one who was inside with the king. And he instructed us that we were to make three obeisances to the king with hands clasped above our head, raising our feet one after the other, since we had to kiss them.

All this was done, after the manner of their royal obeisance. And we told him that we were servants of the King of Spain, who desired peace with him and required no more than to do trade. The king caused us to be told that, since the King of Spain was his friend, he was very willing to be his, and he ordered that we should be allowed to take water and wood and merchandise at our will. This done, we gave him presents, to which at each thing we made a little bow with his head. Then on his behalf were given to each of us cloths of crimson and gold and silk, which they put on our left shoulders. And they forthwith gave us a collation of cloves and cinnamon. Then the curtains were quickly drawn and the windows closed.

All the men in the palace had cloth of gold and of silk round their shameful parts, daggers with gold handles, adorned with pearls and precious stones, and many rings on their fingers. After this we returned on the elephants to the governor's house, whither seven men carried the king's gift ahead. And when we arrived there, they gave to each of us his gift, and they put it on our left shoulders, in return for which we gave each of them for their trouble a pair of knives.

While we were at the governor's house, nine men came from the king with as many very large wooden trays, and in each tray were ten or twelve porcelain plats filled with flesh of calf, capons, chickens, peacocks, and other animals, with fish. And we supped there on the ground (on a palm mat) from thirty-two kinds of meat, besides the fish and other things, and at each mouthful we drank from a porcelain cup as big as an egg the aforesaid distilled wine. We ate rice and other sweetmeats with golden spoons, after our fashion. Where we slept two nights, there were two torches of white wax burning in two rather tall silver candlesticks, and two large lamps filled with oil, each having four wicks, and two men were continually snuffing them. After that we went on the elephants to the seashore, where two of their boats were ready and took us to our ships.

That city [Brunei] is all built in salt water, except the king's house, and the houses of certain chief men. And it was twenty or twenty-five thousand hearths. All their houses are of wood, and built on great beams raised from the ground. And when the tide is high, the women go ashore in boats to sell and buy the things necessary for their food. In front of the king's houses is a thick wall of brick, with towers in the manner of a fortress, and in it were fifty-six large brass cannon, and six of iron. And in the two days that we were there they discharged many of them. That king is a Moor, and he is named Raia Siripada, and aged forty years. He was fat, and no one rules him except the ladies and daughters of the chief men. He never leaves his palace save when he goes hunting. And one cannot speak to him but through a speaking tube. He keeps two scribes who write down all his state and business on very thin tree bark. And they are called *Xiritoles*. . . .

Chapter 44: In the Sunda Islands

Departing from that island of Buru, on a course southwest by west over about eight degrees of longitude, we came to three islands close to one another, called Zolot, Nocemanor, and Galiau [Solor, Nobokemor Rus, Lomblen]. And as we sailed through the midst of them, a great storm assailed and struck us, wherefore we made a pilgrimage to Our Lady of Guidance. And with the gale on our poop we anchored at a high island, but before reaching it we were in great travail for the very strong winds and currents of water which came down from their mountains. The men of this island are savage and bestial. They eat human flesh, and have no king. And they go naked, with that bark like the others; but when they go to war, they wear certain pieces of oxhide before, behind, and at the sides, decorated with small shells and swine's teeth, and with tails of goatskins fastened before and behind. They wear their hair high, with some pins of bamboo which pass through it from side to side, and so keep it high. They wear their beards wrapped in leaves and thrust into small bamboos, which is a thing ridiculous to see. And they are the ugliest people who are in those Indies. Their bows and arrows are of bamboo, and they have certain sacks of leaves of trees, in which they carry their food and drink. And when their women saw us, they came to meet us with their bows. But after we had given them some presents, we were immediately their friends. And we remained there fifteen days to refit our ships. In this island are poultry, goats, coconuts, and wax. There is found also long pepper, the tree of which is like ivy, which twists itself and clings like it to trees. But the leaves are like those of the mulberry, and they call it *Luli*. Round pepper grows like it, but in ears like Indian corn, from which it is shelled off; and they call it *Lada*. And in those countries the fields are all full of this pepper. There we took a man to guide us to some island where there would be provisions. The said island is in the latitude of eight and a half degrees toward the Antarctic Pole, and in the longitude of one hundred and sixty-nine and two-thirds degrees from the line of partition; and it is named Mallua [Alor].

Chapter 45: On Timor

Our old pilot of Molucca told us that nearby was an island named Aruchete, where the men and women are no taller than a cubit and have ears so large that of one they make their bed, and with the other they cover themselves. They are shaven and quite naked, and run swiftly, and have shrill and thin voices. They live in caves underground. They eat fish and a thing which grows between the barks of trees, which is white and round like a sugarplum and which they call *Ambulon*. We could not go thither by reason of the strong currents and many reefs which are there.

On Saturday the twenty-fifth of January, one thousand five hundred and twenty-two, we departed from the island of Mallua. And on the Sunday following we came to a large island [Timor] five leagues distant from the other, between south and southwest. And I went ashore alone to speak to the chief man of a town named Amabau, that he might give us provisions. He answered that he would give us oxen, pigs, and goats; but we could not agree together, because he desired, for an ox, too many things of which we had little. Wherefore, since hunger constrained us, we retained in our ships one of their principal men with a son of his, who was from another town called Balibo. And, fearing lest we kill them, they gave us six oxen, five goats, and two pigs, and to complete the number of ten pigs and ten goats they gave us an ox, for we had set them to this ransom. Then we sent them ashore very well pleased, for we gave them linen, cloths of silk and of cotton, knives, scissors, mirrors, and other things.

This lord of Amabau, to whom I spoke, had only women to serve him. They go all naked like the others, and wear in their ears little gold rings hanging from silk threads, and on their arms, up to the elbow, they have many bracelets of gold and of cotton. And the men go like the women, but that they have and wear on their neck certain gold rings as large and round as a trencher, and set in their hair bamboo combs garnished with gold. And some of them wear other gold ornaments. In this island, and nowhere else, is found white sandalwood, besides ginger, oxen, swine, goats, poultry, rice, figs, sugarcanes, oranges, lemons, wax, almonds, and other things, and parrots of divers sorts and colors.

On the other side of this island are four brothers, its kings. And where we were there are only towns, and some chiefs and lords of them. The names of the habitations of the four kings are: Oibich, Lichsana, Suai, and Cabanazza. Oibich is the largest town. In Cabanazza (as we were told) a quantity of gold is found in a mountain, and they purchase all their things with certain small gold pieces which they have. All the sandalwood and the wax which is traded by the people of Java and Malacca comes from this place, where we found a junk of Lozzon [Luzon] which has come to trade for sandalwood.

Document 10

The Baburnama

By Zahiruddin Muhammed Babur, *The Baburnama*, trans.
Wheeler M. Thackston (New York: Oxford University Press, 1996)

Zahiruddin Muhammad Babur, a native of Transoxiana (present-day Ta-jikistan and Uzbekistan), was not a typical early modern traveler. Born as a prince of Fergana in 1483, he left his homeland and eventually moved west-ward, conquering territory and founding the Mughal Empire, which lasted in India from 1526 to 1858. His conquest was at times ruthless, yet he pos-sessed extraordinary literary skills. Centuries later he remains a controver-sial figure. "Who, then, was Babur," the novelist Salman Rushdie recently asked, "scholar or barbarian, nature-loving poet or terror-inspiring warlord? The answer is to be found in the Baburnama, *and it's an uncomfortable one: he was both."[8] In crafting his memoirs, the earliest Islamic autobiogra-phy, Babur described scenes with remarkable precision—even in Hindustan, which he detested.*

In many ways, the Baburnama *is an unusual text. Babur chose not to write his memoirs in Persian, "the universal language of culture and literature of his time and place," as his modern translator Wheeler Thackston has noted, but in Chaghatay Turkish, the spoken language of the Timurids which was widely used across the Turco-Mongolian realm. Though his decision to use Chaghatay limited those who could read it, the manuscript still attracted adherents, including many who by the end of the sixteenth century produced illustrated versions. Yet because the language was difficult for them, and because the memoirs contained place-names that were often unfamiliar to the copyists, errors crept into the text. Further, some of the places that Babur named no longer survive, making it even more difficult to link some of his observations with modern-day sites.[9]*

The excerpt here comes from the section of the Baburnama *dealing with Hin-dustan. Though Babur transformed the territory—and in the process engen-dered hostilities that still linger—he never came to love it. "A Timurid prince*

8. Salmon Rushdie, introduction to Zahiruddin Muhammed Babur, *The Baburnama: Mem-oirs of Babur, Prince and Emperor*, trans. Wheeler M. Thackston (New York: Modern Li-brary, 2002), x–xii.
9. Babur, *Baburnama*, xvii–xviii, xxv, xviii–xxix.

accustomed to the society of Transoxiana and the beautiful landscape and climate of Kabul," Thackston noted, "he disapproved of almost everything he saw in Hindustan and longed to return to his beloved Kabul, a trip he made only posthumously." Babur, for his part, thought that he was describing things as he saw them. "I have not written all this to complain," he wrote at one point. "I have simply written the truth. I do not intend by what I have written to compliment myself: I have simply set down exactly what happened."[10] Modern critics might disagree with Babur's (or anyone's) ability to tell an unvarnished story; there is much in his description of Hindustan that reflects his negative opinions of India. But though his position as an emperor differentiated him from virtually all other travelers of his era, his goal in his own writing was similar to many: to produce a written description of a place that was new to him. His talents emerge clearly here in his description of Hindustan's climate, topography, and even its flowers; his obsession with detail can be found in his account of local ways of measuring time.

Hindustan is a vast and populous kingdom and a productive realm. To the east and south, in fact to the west too, it ends at the ocean. To the north is a mountain range that connects the mountains of the Hindu Kush, Kafiristan, and Kashmir. To the northwest are Kabul, Ghazni, and Kandahar. The capital of all Hindustan is Delhi. After Sultan Shihabuddin Ghurri's reign until the end of Sultan Firozshah's, most of Hindustan was under the control of the Delhi sultans. Up to the time that I conquered Hindustan, five Muslim padishahs and two infidels had ruled there. Although the mountains and jungles are held by many petty rays and rajahs, the important and independent rulers were the following five.

One was the Afghans, who took the capital Delhi and held in their grasp from Bhera to Bihar. Before the Afghans, Jaunpur was held by Sultan Husayn Sharqi, and the dynasty was called Purabi. The Purabi ancestors were cupbearers for Sultan Firozshah and those sultans; after Firozshah, they gained control over the kingdom of Jaunpu. Delhi was in Sultan Alauddin's hands, and the dynasty was the Sayyids. When Temür Beg took Delhi, he gave the governorship of Delhi to their ancestors and left. Sultan Bahlul Lodi the Afghan and his son Sultan Iskandar seized Delhi and Jaunpur, and the two capitals formed one kingdom.

10. Babur, *Baburnama*, xxix, 241.

The second was Sultan Muzaffar in Gujurat, who passed away several days before the defeat of Sultan Ibrahim. He was a religiously observant ruler and a student of the religious sciences, he read hadith, and he always copied Korans. His dynasty was called the Tang. Their fathers also were cup-bearers for Sultan Firozshah and those sultans. After Firozshah, they gained control of the province of Gujarat.

Third were the Bahmanids in the Deccan, but as of this date the sultans of the Deccan have no power of their own left—the great begs have gained control of all the provinces. If the sultan needs anything, he has to ask the begs for it.

Fourth was Sultan Mahmud in the province of Malwa, which is also called Mandu. The dynasty was called the Khalji. Rana Sanga the Infidel defeated him and seized most of the province, but he had grown weak. The ancestors of the dynasty were patronized by Firozshah. Afterward they seized the province of Malwa.

Fifth was Nusrat Shah in Bengal. His father became padishah in Bengal and was a sayyid known as Sultan Alauddin.

Nusrat Shah ruled by hereditary succession. There is an amazing custom in Bengal: rule is seldom achieved by hereditary succession. Instead, there is a specific royal throne, and each of the amirs, viziers, or officeholders has an established place. It is that throne that is of importance to the people of Bengal. For every place, a group of obedient servants is established. When the ruler desires to dismiss anyone, all the obedient servants then belong to whomever he puts in that person's place. The royal throne, however, has a peculiarity: anyone who succeeds in killing the king and sitting on the throne becomes king. Amirs, viziers, soldiers, and civilians all submit to him, and he becomes the padishah and ruler like the former ruler. The people of Bengal say, "We are the legal property of the throne, and we obey anyone who is on it." For instance, before Nusrat Shah's father, Sultan Alauddin, an Abyssinian killed the king, took the throne, and reigned for a time. The Abyssinian was killed by Sultan Alauddin, who then became king. Sultan Alauddin's son has now become king by hereditary succession. Another custom in Bengal is that it is considered disgraceful for anyone who becomes king to spend the treasuries of former kings. Whoever becomes king must accumulate a new treasury, which is a source of pride for the people. In addition, the salaries and stipends of all the institutions of the rulers, treasury, military, and civilian are absolutely fixed from long ago and cannot be spent anywhere else.

The five great Muslim padishahs with vast realms and huge armies are the five who have been mentioned.

Of the infidels, the greater in domain and army is the rajah of Vijayanagar. The other is Rana Sanga, who had recently grown so great by his audacity and sword. His original province was Chitor. When the sultans of Mandu grew weak, he seized many provinces belonging to Mandu, such as Ranthambhor, Sarangpur, Bhilsan, and Chanderi. Chanderi had been in the *daru'l-harb* ["abode of war," an Islamic phrase referring to non-Islam states] for some years and held by Sanga's highest ranking-officer, Medini Rao, with four or five thousand infidels, but in 934 [1528], through the grace of God, I took it by force within a ghari or two, massacred the infidels, and brought it into the bosom of Islam, as will be mentioned.

All around Hindustan are many rays and rajahs. Some are obedient to Islam, while others, because they are so far away and their place impregnable, do not render obedience to Muslim rulers.

Hindustan lies in the first, second, and third climes, with none of it in the fourth clime. It is a strange country. Compared to ours, it is another world. Its mountains, rivers, forests, and wildernesses, its villages and provinces, animals and plants, peoples and languages, even its rain and winds are altogether different. Even if the Kabul dependencies that have warm climates bear a resemblance to Hindustan in some aspects, in others they do not. Once you cross the Indus, the land, water, trees, stones, people, tribes, manners, and customs are all of the Hindustani fashion. The mountain range in the north that has been mentioned—as soon as the Indus is crossed these mountains are dependent provinces to Kashmir. Although as of this date the provinces in this range, like Pakhli and Shahmang, mostly are not obedient to Kashmir, nonetheless they used to be inside Kashmir. Once past Kashmir, there are innumerable peoples, tribes, districts, and provinces in this range. There are people continuously in these mountains all the way to Bengal, even to the ocean. This much has been ascertained and confirmed by the people of Hindustan, but of these groups no one can give any real information. All they say is that the people of the mountains are called Khas. It has occurred to me that since Hindustanis pronounce the sound *sh* as *s*, since the principal city in the mountains is Kashmir, which means "mountain of the Khasis," since *mir* means mountain and the people of this mountain are called Khasia, and since aside from Kashmir no other city has ever been heard of in these mountains, this may be why they call it Kashmir. The products of the people are musk, yak-tails, saffron, lead, and copper. The people of India call the range Sivalik Parbat. In the language of India *sava* means a quarter, *lak* means a hundred thousand, and *parbat* means mountain—therefore Siwalik Parbat means "a quarter lac plus a hundred thousand mountains," that is, 125,000 mountains. The snow never melts on these mountains, and the snow-covered caps can be seen from some of the provinces of Hindustan, such as Lahore, Sirhind, and Sambhal. In Kabul this mountain range is called the Hindu Kush. From Kabul the range runs to the east and slightly to the south. South of it is all Hindustan. To the north of the range and the unknown tribes who are called Khas is the province of Tibet. Many large rivers rise in this range and flow though Hindustan. Six large rivers to the north of Sirhind—the Indus, the Bahat [modern-day Jhelum], the Chenab, the Ravi, the Beas, and the Sutlej—all join at one place in the vicinity of Multan. After they all join it is called the Indus. It flows to the west, passes through the province of Tatta, and joins the Indian Ocean. Aside from these six, there are other great rivers like the Jumna, the Ganges, the Rapti, the Gomati, the Gagra, the Sarju, the Gandak, as well as many other large ones, all of which join the Ganges. Flowing to the east, the Ganges passes through Bengal and spills into the ocean. The source of all these is the Sivalik Range.

There are still other large rivers that rise in the mountains of Hindustan, like the Chambhal, Banas, and Betwa, but there is never any snow on these mountains. These rivers also join the Ganges.

Hindustan has other mountain ranges too. Among them is a range that runs from north to south beginning in the province of Delhi at a building made by Firozshah called the Jahannuma, which is situated on a rocky little mountain. Running from there are patches of rocky little mountains in the vicinity of Delhi. When they reach the province of Mewat, the mountains become larger. Passing through Mewat they go to the province of Bayana. The mountains of Sikri, Bari, and Dholpur are of this same range. Although it is not contiguous, Gwalior, which is also called Galior, is a spur of the range. The mountains of Ranthambhor, Chitor, Mandu, and Chanderi are also of this range. In some places there are breaks of seven or eight leagues. They are low, rugged, rocky, and forested and never have any snow on them. Some rivers in Hindustan have their sources in these mountains.

Most of the provinces of Hindustan are located on flat terrain. So many cities and so many provinces—yet there is no running water anywhere. The only running water is in the large rivers. There are still waters in some places, and even in cities that have the capability of digging channels for running water they do not do so. This may be for one of several reasons. One is that the agriculture and orchards have absolutely no need for water. Fall crops are watered by the monsoon rains, and strangely the spring crops come even if there is no rain. For a year or two sapling trees are watered either by waterwheel or by bucket, but after that they have no need of irrigation. Some vegetables are watered. In Lahore, Dipalpur, Sirhind, and those regions a waterwheel is used. Two long pieces of rope are looped the size of the well. Wooden stakes are fastened across the two pieces of rope, and jars are fastened to the wooden stakes. The ropes to which the jars are fastened are thrown around a wheel that is over the well. Another wheel is put on the other end of the axle of this wheel. Next to this wheel yet another wheel like the first one is put. As an ox turns this wheel, the spokes enter the spokes of the second wheel and turn the wheel with the jars. A trough is put at the place where the water spills out, and by means of the trough the water is taken wherever it is needed.

In Agra, Chandwar, Bayana, and those regions they irrigate by means of the bucket. This is a laborious and filthy method. A forked stick is raised next to a well, and across the fork a pulley is fastened. A large bucket is fastened to a long rope, which is thrown over the pulley. One end of the rope is tied to an ox. It takes one person to lead the ox and another to empty the water from the bucket. Every time the ox is led out to pull up the bucket and then led back, the rope is dragged through the ox's path, which is sullied with ox urine and dung, as it falls back into the well. For some types of agriculture that need irrigation, water is carried in jars by men and women.

The cities and provinces of Hindustan are all unpleasant. All cities, all locales are alike. The gardens have no walls, and most places are flat as boards.

On the banks of some large rivers and riverbeds, due to the monsoon rains, are gullies that prevent passage. In some places in the plains are forests of thorny trees in which the people of those districts hole up and obstinately refuse to pay tribute. In Hindustan there is little running water aside from the great rivers. Occasionally in some places there are still waters. All the cities and provinces live from well or pond water, which is collected from the monsoon rains. In Hindustan the destruction and building of villages and hamlets, even of cities, can be accomplished in an instant. Such large cities in which people have lived for years, if they are going to be abandoned, can be left in a day, even half a day, so that no sign or trace remains. If they have a mind to build a city, there is no necessity for digging irrigation canals or building dams. Their crops are all unirrigated. There is no limit to the people.

A group gets together, makes a pond, or digs a well. There is no making of houses or raising of walls. They simply make huts from the plentiful straw and innumerable trees, and instantly a village or city is born. . . .

[There follows a long description of the flora and fauna of Hindustan. After that discussion, Babur provides details about local flowers, conceptions of time, weights and measures, and more general comments about the area.]

There are some marvelous flowers in Hindustan. One is the hibiscus, which some Hindustanis call *gudhal.* It is not a shrub but a tree with stems. It is somewhat taller than the red rose, and its color is deeper than the pomegranate flower. It is as large as a red rose. The red rose blossoms all at once after budding, but when the hibiscus blossoms, from the middle of the petals yet another slender stalk is formed, as long as a finger, from which still more hibiscus petals open. The result is a double, fairly amazing flower. The flowers look beautiful in color on the tree but do not last long. They blossom and fade within a day. They bloom well and plentifully during the four months of monsoon and often throughout most of the year. Despite their profusion they have no odor.

Another flower is the oleander, which occurs in both white and red. It has five petals like the peach blossom. The red oleander bears a resemblance to the peach blossom, but the oleander blooms with fourteen or fifteen flowers in one place, so that from a distance it looks like one big flower. The bush is larger than the red rose. The red oleander has a faint but agreeable smell. It too blooms beautifully and abundantly during the monsoon and can be found throughout most of the year.

The screw pine is another. It has a delicate scent. Whereas musk has the disadvantage of being dry, this could be called "wet musk." In addition to the plant's having a strange appearance, the flowers can be from one-and-a-half to two spans long. The long leaves are like those of the reed and have spines. When compressed like a bud, the outer leaves are spiny and greenish and the inner leaves soft and white. Nestled among the inner leaves are things like in the middle of a flower, and the good scent comes from there. When it first comes up, before it develops a stalk, it resembles the male reed bush. The leaves are flattish and spiny. The stalk is extremely unharmonious. The roots are always exposed.

Then there is the jasmine. The white variety is called champa. It is larger and has a more pronounced fragrance than the jasmine in our country. . . .

In our country are four seasons, but in Hindustan there are three: four months of summer, four of monsoon, and four of winter. The months begin with the crescent moon in opposition. Every three years one month is added to the monsoon months, then three years later a month is added to the winter months, then three years later a month is added to the summer months. This is their intercalation.

The summer months are Chait, Baisakh, Jeth, and Asarh, corresponding to Pisces, Aries, Taurus, and Gemini. Those of the monsoon are Sanwan, Bhadon, Kuar, and Katik, corresponding to Cancer, Leo, Virgo, and Libra. The winter months are Aghan, Pus, Magh, and Phagun, corresponding to Scorpio, Sagittarius, Capricorn, and Aquarius.

Having assigned four months each to the seasons, they take two months of each season to be the hottest, the rainiest, or the coldest. Of the summer months the last two, Jeth and Asarh, are the ones of extreme heat. Of the monsoon months the first two, Sanwan and Bhadon, are the height of the rains. Of the winter months the middle two, Pus and Magh, are the months of extreme cold. By this reckoning they have six seasons.

They also have names for the days of the week: Sanichar, Etwar, Somwar, Mangal, Budh, Brihaspati, Sukrawar.

In our country a day and night is conventionally divided into twenty-four parts, each of which is called an hour, and every hour is divided into sixty parts, each of which is called a minute, so there are 1,440 minutes in a day and night. The duration of a minute is about what it takes to say the Fatiha with the Basmala six times, so that during a day and night the Fatiha and Basmala could be recited 8,640 times.

The people of India divide the day and night into sixty parts, each of which is called a ghari. Moreover, the night and the day are each divided into four parts, each of which is called a *pahar*, or what in Persian is called a *pas*. In Transoxiana, I had heard the expressions *pas* [watch] and *pasban* [watchman], but I did not know what they denoted. For keeping time, in all the important towns of Hindustan a group of men called *ghariyalis* is appointed and assigned. They cast a disc of brass as large as a tray and two fingers thick. This brass object, called a *ghariyal* is hung in a high place. Another vessel has a hole in the bottom, like an hourglass, that fills up once every ghari. The ghariyalis take turns putting the vessel in water and waiting for it to fill up. For example, when the vessel that they put in water at daybreak fills up once, they strike the ghariyal with a mallet. When it fills up twice, they strike it twice, and so on until a watch is completed. The close of each watch is announced by the striking of the ghariyal many times in rapid succession. When the first watch of the day is finished, after repeated striking, the ghariyalis pause and strike once. When the second watch is finished, they strike many times and then strike twice. For the third, thrice; for the fourth, four times. When the four watches of the day have ended and the night watches have begun, the night watches are introduced in the same way. They used to announce the new watches by striking only when the previous ones were finished, but people who woke up during the night and heard the sound of three or four gharis being struck did not know whether it was for the second or the third watch. I therefore ordered them to herald the watches of the night and cloudy days by striking only after they had struck the ghari first. For example, after striking the third ghari of the first watch of the night, they would pause and announce the watch by striking once more, so it was obvious that it was the third ghari of the first watch. After striking the fourth ghari of the third watch of the night, they would pause before striking three times. It was a great idea. Whenever people woke up at night and heard the sound of the ghariyal, they knew which watch and which ghari it was.

Every ghari is divided into sixty parts, each of which is called a *pal*, so that a day and night consist of 3,600 pals. They say that a pal lasts the time it takes to shut and open the eyes sixty times, so during a day and a night you could shut your eyes and open them 216,000 times. By experiment it has been determined that a pal is approximately the length of time it takes to say *qul huwa'llah* and *bismillah* eight times, so during a day and a night you could say *qul huwa'llah* and *bismillah* 28,800 times.

The people of India also have wonderful weights and measures. Eight *rattis* equal 1 *masha*; 4 *mashas* equal 1 *tank*, or 32 *rattis*; 5 *mashas* equal 1 *mithcal* or 40 *rattis*; 12 *mashas* equal 1 *tola*, or 96 *rattis*; 14 *tolas* equal 1 *seer*. It is set everywhere that 40 *seers* equal 1 *maund*. 12 *maunds* equal 1 *mani*; 100 *manis* is called a *manyasa*. Jewels and pearls are weighed by the tank.

The people of India have also an excellent system of numbering. One hundred thousand equal 1 lac; 100 lacs equal 1 crore; 100 crores equal 1 *arb*; 100 *arbs* equal 1 *kharb*; 100 *kharbs* equal 1 *nil*; 100 *nils* equal 1 *padam*; 100 *padams* equal 1 *sankya*. The creation of these numbers indicates the vast wealth of Hindustan.

Most of the people of Hindustan are infidels, whom the people of India call Hindu. Most Hindus believe in reincarnation. Tax collectors, artisans, and craftsmen are all Hindus. In our country the people who move about the countryside have clan names, but in India even those who dwell in towns and villages have clan names. Every craft and trade is passed down from father to son.

Hindustan is a place of little charm. There is no beauty in its people, no graceful social intercourse, no poetic talent or understanding, no etiquette, nobility or manliness. The arts and crafts have no harmony or symmetry. There are no good horses, meat, grapes, melons, or other fruit. There is no ice, cold water, good food or bread in the markets. There are no baths and no madrasas. There are no candles, torches, or candlesticks.

Instead of candles and torches they have a numerous group of filthy people called *deotis* who carry the lamps. In their left hands the deotis hold a small wooden tripod; on the end of one of its legs an iron piece like the top of a candlestick is fastened to the wood of the tripod. Next to it they fasten a wick as thick as a thumb. In their right hands the deotis carry a gourd with a narrow slit from which oil can be trickled. Whenever the wick needs oil, they pour it from the gourd. Great men keep deotis by the hundred and use them in place of candles or torches. When kings and noblemen have business at night that requires lighting, the filthy deotis bring this sort of lamp and hold it nearby.

Aside from the streams and still waters that flow in ravines and hollows, there is no running water in their gardens or palaces, and in their buildings no pleasing harmony or regularity.

The peasantry and common people parade around stark naked with something like a loincloth tied around themselves and hanging down two spans below their navels. Under this rag is another piece of cloth, which they pass between their legs and fasten to the loincloth string. Women fasten around themselves one long piece of cloth, half of which they tie to their waists and the other half of which they throw over their heads.

The one nice aspect of Hindustan is that it is a large country with lots of gold and money. The weather turns very nice during the monsoon. Sometimes it rains ten, fifteen, or twenty times a day; torrents are formed in an instant, and water flows in places that normally have no water. During the rainy season, the weather is unusually good when the rain ceases, so good in fact that it could not be more temperate or pleasant. The one drawback is that the air is too humid. During the monsoon, bows from that country cannot be used to shoot or they are ruined. Armor, books, bedding, and textiles are also affected. Buildings do not last long either. Aside from the monsoon, there are periods of good weather during both winter and summer, but the constant north wind always stirs up a lot of dust. Near the monsoon it gets so strong at least four or five times and creates so much dust that people cannot see each other. The wind is called *andhi*. In the summer during Taurus and Gemini it gets hot, but the heat is not so intense, nothing like the heat of Balkh and Kandahar, and it lasts only half as long.

Another nice thing is the unlimited numbers of craftsmen and practitioners of every trade. For every labor and every product there is an established group who have been practicing that craft or professing that trade for generations. For instance, in the *Zafarnama*, Mulla Sharaf writes eloquently that during Temür Beg's building of the stone mosque two hundred stonemasons from Azerbaijan, Fars, Hindustan, and other places were employed on it daily. In Agra alone there were 680 Agra stonemasons at work on my building every day. Aside from that, in Agra, Sikri, Bayana, Dholpur, Gwalior, and Koil, 1,491 stonemasons were laboring on my buildings. There are similar vast numbers of every type of craftsmen and laborers of every description in Hindustan.

The regions from Bhera to Bihar that are currently under my control are worth 52 crores, as can be seen in the following table. Of these, eight to nine crores' worth are districts of rays and rajahs who are in obedience and have been awarded these districts for their maintenance as of old. . . .

As much of the characteristics and peculiarities of the peoples and places of Hindustan as has been ascertained has been written. Hereafter, whenever anything worth writing about is noticed or anything worth telling is heard I will write it down.

Document 11

Of the Ilande of Giapan, 1565

By Luīs Fróis, "Of the Ilande of Giapan, 1565" in Richard Willes, *The History of Travayle in the West and East Indies* (London, 1577), 253–58

Richard Willes never saw Japan with his own eyes. Like other editors of travel accounts, he relied on reports generated by others and then translated them for a local audience. But like his predecessor Richard Eden, the first English translator of the Italian humanist Pietro Martire D'Anghiera, Willes performed a valuable service by gathering travel accounts together and publicizing their contents. Among the works that crowded his 1577 History of Travayle in the West and East Indies *were accounts of Ferdinand Magellan and Martin Frobisher. Willes had a keen interest in the East, and he took the time to synthesize various accounts and put some of the highlights in his own words. He also presented his readers with a long letter from the mission-*

ary Luĩs Fróis (1532–1597), whose religious work had taken him to Japan. This letter was written from Meaco (modern Kyoto) on February 19, 1565.

Fróis was among the first wave of missionaries to bring Christianity to Japan. No European had set foot in Japan before the Portuguese merchants Francisco Zeimoto, António Peixoto, and António da Mota arrived there on a Chinese junk that had left the Siamese capital of Ayuthia, encountered a typhoon, and landed near Tanegashima in late September 1543. They stayed a short time while the locals fixed their boat, and then they proceeded on their way. Six years later the famous theologian Francis Xavier sailed to Japan. "The people whom we have met so far, are the best who have yet been discovered," he later wrote, "and it seems to me that we shall never find among heathens another race equal to the Japanese."[11] Xavier's enthusiasm reflected the Church's fervent hopes that at last Europeans had found a place where the truths of their religion would find fertile ground. In Japan, those hopes proved realistic, at least for a time. Within a century of the first missionaries' arrival, 300,000 Japanese had converted to Christianity.

Although information about Japan was often unreliable by the time it reached European readers, Fróis's epistle offered descriptions that modern scholars have accepted as more reliable than the fabrications and exaggerations of others, including Richard Willes, who added unsubstantiated details about Japan to accompany the missionary's letter. As the historian Donald Lach noted, Fróis's ability to learn Japanese made his writings particularly valuable because of his "avid concern for concrete data and detail."[12] When the Jesuits themselves wanted a history of their efforts in Christianity, they turned to Fróis himself, "the chronicler par excellence of the Japanese mission" as one scholar recently noted. But the history he wrote did not appeal to authorities in Rome, who looked instead for another chronicler.[13] Fróis's long history remained unpublished for almost two hundred years, though at least some of his writings circulated in the sixteenth century. Soon after the missionary died in Japan, the younger Hakluyt used three of his letters in the expanded edition of his Principal Navigations, Voyages, Traffiques,

11. Quoted in Derek Massarella, *A World Elsewhere: Europe's Encounter with Japan in the Sixteenth and Seventeenth Centuries* (New Haven, Conn.: Yale University Press, 1990), 24.
12. Lach, *The Century of Discovery,* Vol. 1 of *Asia in the Making of Europe* (Chicago: University of Chicago Press, 1965), 683–84.
13. *João Rodrigues's Account of Sixteenth-Century Japan,* ed. Michael Cooper (Hakluyt Society, 3rd ser., 7 [London, 2001]), xxiii–xxiv.

and Discoveries of the English Nation *published in London from 1598 to 1600, including the letter that Willes had printed earlier.*

Alosius Froes, to his companions in Jesus Christ that remain in China and Indie:

The last year, dear brethren, I wrote unto you from *Firando,* how *Cosmus Turrianus* had appointed me to travel to *Meaco,* to help *Gaspar Vilela,* for that there the harvest was great, the laborers few, and that I should have for my companion in that journey Aloisus *Almeida.* It seemeth now my part, having by the help of God ended so long a voyage, to signify unto you by letter such things specially as I might think you would most delight to know. And because at the beginning *Almedia* and I so parted the whole labor of writing letters betwixt us, that he should speak of our voyage, and such things as happened therein, I should make relation of the *Meachians* estate, and write what I could well learn of the *Japanese* manners and conditions: setting aside all discourses of our voyage, that which standeth me upon I will discharge in this Epistle, that you considering how artificially, how cunningly, under the pretext of religion that crafty adversary of mankind, leadeth and draweth unto perdition the *Japanese* minds, blinded with many superstitions and ceremonies, may the more pity this nation.

The inhabitants of Japan, as men that never had greatly to do with other nations, in their Geography divided the whole world into three parts, *Japan, Siam,* and *China.* And albeit the *Japanese* received out of *Siam,* and *China,* their superstitions and ceremonies, yet do they nevertheless condemn all other nations in comparison of themselves, & standing in their own conceit do far prefer themselves before all other sorts of people in wisdom and policy.

Touching the situation of the country, & nature of the soil, unto the things afterwards first written, this one thing will I add: in the Islands the summer to be more hot, the winter extreme cold. In the kingdom of Cana, as we call it, falleth so much snow, that the houses being buried in it, the inhabitants keep within doors certain months of the year, having no way to come forth except they break up the tiles. Whirlwinds most vehement, earthquakes so common, that the Japanese dread such kind of fears little or nothing at all. The country is full of silver mines, otherwise barren, not so much by fault of nature, as through the slothfulness of the inhabitants: how being Oxen they keep, & that for tillage sake only. The air is wholesome, the waters good, the people very fair & well bodied: bare headed commonly they go, procuring baldness with sorrow & tears, afterwards rooting up with pinsars all the hair of their heads as it groweth, except it be a little behind, the which they know and keep with all diligence. Even from their childhood they wear daggers and swords, which they use to lay under their pillows when they go to bed: in show courteous and affable: in deed haughty and proud. They delight most in warlike affairs, and their greatest study is arms. Men's apparel diversely colored, is worn down half the legs, and to the elbows: women's attire made handsomely, like unto a veil, is somewhat longer: all manner of dicing and theft they do eschew. The merchant, although he be wealthy, is not accounted of. Gentlemen, be they never so poor, retained their place: most precisely they stand upon their honor and worthiness, ceremoniously striving among themselves in courtesies and fair speeches. Wherein if any one happily be less careful than he should be, even for a trifle many times he getteth evil will. Want, though it trouble most of them, so much they do detest, that poor men cruelly taking piety [pity?] of their infants newly born, especially girls, do many times with their own feet strangle them. Noble men, and other likewise of meaner calling, generally have but one wife apiece, by whom although they have issue, yet for a trifle they divorce themselves from their wives, and the wives also sometimes from their husbands, to marry with others. After the second degree, cousins may there lawfully marry. Adoption of other men's children is much used among them. In great towns most men and women can write and read.

This nation feedeth sparsely, their usual meat is rice and salattes [salads], and near the sea side fish. They feast on an other many times, wherein they use great diligence, especially in drinking one to an other, insomuch that the better sort, least they might rudely commit some fault therein, do use to read certain books written of duties and ceremonies appertaining unto bankettes. To be delicate and fine, they put their meat into there mouths with little forks, accounting it great rudeness to touch it with their fingers: winter and summer they drink water hot as they may possible abide it. Their houses are in danger of fire, but finely made, and clean, laid all over with straw palettes, whereupon they do both sit in stead of stools, and lie in their clothes, with billets under their heads. For fear of defiling these palettes, they go either barefoot within doors, or wear straw pantofles on their buskins when they come abroad, the which they lay aside at their return home again. Gentlemen for the most part do pass the night in banketting [banqueting], music, and vain discourses, they sleep the day time. In *Meaco* and *Sacaio* [Sekai] there is good store of beds, but they be very little, and may be compared unto our pews.

In bringing up their children they use words only to rebuke them, admonishing as diligently and advisedly boys of six or seven years age, as though they were old men. They are given very much to entertain strangers, of whom most curiously they love to ask even in trifle what foreign nations do, and their fashions. Such arguments and reasons as be manifest, and are made plain with examples, do greatly persuade them. They detest all kind of theft, whosoever is taken in that fault may be slain freely of any body. No public prisons, no common jails, no ordinary Justicers: privately each householder hath the hearing of greater crimes that deserve death without delay. Thus usually the people is kept in awe and fear. . . .

I come now to other superstitions and ceremonies, that you may see, dear brethren, that which I said in the beginning, how subtle the devil hath deceived the *Japanese* nation, and how diligent and ready they be to obey and worship him. And first, all remembrance and knowledge not only of Christ our redeemer, but also of that one God the maker of all things, is clean extinguished, & utterly abolished out of the *Japanese* hearts. Moreover their superstitious sects are many, whereas it is lawful for each one to follow that which liketh him best; but the principal sects are two, namely the *Amidans* and *Xacaians*. Wherefore in this country shall you see many monasteries, not only of *Bonzii* men, but also of *Bonziæ* women diversely attired, for some do wear white under, and black upper garments, other go appareled in ash color, & their Idol hath name *Denichi*: from these the *Amidanes* differ very much. Again the men *Bonzii* for the most part dwell in sumptuous houses, and have great revenues. These fellows are chaste by commandment, marry they may not under pain of death. In the midst of their Temple is erected an Altar, whereon standeth a wooden idol of *Amida*, naked from the girdle upward, with holes in his ears, after the manner of Italian Gentlewomen, sitting on a wooden rose, goodly to behold. They have great libraries, and halls for them all to dine and sup together, and bells wherewith they are certain hours called to prayers. In the evening the Superintendent giveth each one a theme for meditation. After midnight before the Altar in their Temple they do say Matins as it were out of *Xaca* his last book, one quier [quire? choir?] one verse, the other quier another. Early in the morning each one giveth himself to meditation one hour: they shave their heads and beards. Their Cloisters be very large, and within the precinct thereof, Chapels of the Fotoquiens, for by that name some of the *Japanese* Saints are called: their holidays yearly be very many. Most of these *Bonzii* be Gentlemen, for that the *Japanese* nobility, charged with many children, use to make most of them *Bonzii*, not being able to leave for each one a patrimony good enough. The *Bonzii* most covetously bent, know all the ways how to come by money. They sell unto the people many scrolls of paper, by the help whereof the common people thinketh itself warranted from all power of the devils. They borrow likewise money to be repaid with great usury in another world, giving by obligation unto the lender an assurance thereof, to which departing out of this life he may carry with him to hell.

There is another great company of such as are called Inambuxu, with curled and staring heare [hair?]. They make profession to find out again things either lost or stolen, after this sort. They set before them a child, whom the devil invadeth, called up thither by charms: of that child then do they ask that which they are desirous to know.

These men's prayers both good and bad are thought greatly to prevail, insomuch that both their blessings and their curses they sell unto the people. The Novices of this order, before they be admitted, go together two or three thousand in a company. Up a certain high mountain to do penance there, threescore days voluntarily punishing themselves. In this time the devil sheweth himself unto them in sundry shapes: and they, like young graduates, admitted as it were fellows into some certain company, are set forth with white tassels hanging about their necks, and black Bonnets that scarcely cover any more than the crown of their heads. Thus attired they range abroad in all *Japan*, to set out themselves and their cunning to sale, each one beating his basin he carryeth always about with him, to give notice of their coming in all towns where they pass.

There is also an other sort called Genguis, that make profession to show by soothsaying where stolen things are, and who were the thieves. These dwell in the top of an high mountain, black in face for the continual heat of the sun, for the cold, winds, and rains they do continually endure. They marry but in their own tribe and line: the report goeth that be horned beasts. They climb up most high rocks and hills, and go over very great rivers by the only art of the devil, who to bring those wretches the more into error, biddeth them to go up a certain high mountain, where they stand miserably gazing and earnestly looking for him as long as the devil appointeth them. At the length at noontide, or in the evening, commeth that devil, whom they call *Amida*, among them to show himself unto them: this show breedeth in the brains and hearts of men such a kind of superstition, that it can by no means be rooted out of them afterward. . . .

North from *Japan*, three hundred leagues out of *Meaco*, lyeth a great country of savage men, clothed in beasts skins, rough bodied, with huge beards, and monstrous mustaches, the which they hold up with little forks as they drink. These people are great drinkers of wine, fierce in wars, and much feared of the *Japanese*: being hurt in fight, they wash their wounds with salt water, other surgery they have none. In their breasts they are said to carry looking glasses: their swords they tie to their heads, in such wise, that the handle do rest upon their shoulders. Service and ceremonies have they none at all, only they are wont to worship heaven. To *Aquita*, a great town in that *Japanese* kingdom, we call Gevano, they much resort for merchandise, and the *Aquitanes* likewise do travel into their country, howbeit not often, for that there many of them are slain by the inhabitants.

Much more concerning this matter I had to write, but to avoid tediousness, I will come to speak of the Japanese madness again, who most desirous of vain glory, do think that specially to get immortal fame, when they procure themselves to be most sumptuously and solemnly buried. Their burials and obsequies in the city of *Meaco*, are done after this manner. About one hour before the dead body be brought forth, a great multitude of his friends, appareled in their best array, to before unto the fire, with them goes their kinswomen, and such as be of their acquaintance, clothed in white (for that is the mourning color there) with a changeable colored veil on their heads. Each woman hath with her also, according to her abilities, all her family trimmed up in white like maccado: the better sort and wealthier women go in litters of *Cedar*, artificially wrought, and richly dressed. In the second place marcheth a great company of footmen sumptuously appareled. Then a far of commeth one of these *Bonzii*, master of the ceremonies for that superstition, bravely clad in silks & gold, in a large & high litter excellently well wrought, accompanied with 30 other *Bonzii*, or thereabout, wearing hats, linen albs [tunics], and fine black upper garments. Then attired in ash color (for this color also is mourning) with a long torch of pineapple, sheweth the dead body the way unto the fire, least it either stumble, or ignorantly go out of the way. Well near 200 *Bonzii* follow him singing the name of that devil the which the party deceased chiefly did worship by his lifetime, and therewithal a very great basin is beaten, even to the place of fire, instead of a bell. Then follow two great paper baskets hanged open at staves ends, full of paper roses diversely colored: such as bear them, do march but slowly, shaking ever now & than their staves, that the aforesaid flowers may fall down by little & little, as it were drops of rain, and be whirled about with the wind. This shower say they is an argument that the soul of the dead man is gone to Paradise. After all this, eight beardless *Bonzii* orderly two and two draft after them on the ground long spears, the points backward, with stages of one cubit a piece, wherein the name also of that Idol is written. Then be there carried ten Lanterns trimmed with the former inscription, overcast with a fine veil, and candles burning in them. Besides this, two young men clothed in ash color, bear pineapple torches, not lighted, of three foot length, the which torches serve to kindle the fire wherein the dead corpses is to be burnt. In the same color follow many other that wear on the crowns of their heads fair, little, three square, black leather caps, tied fat under their chins (for ye is honorable amongst them) with papers on their heads, wherein the name of the devil, I speak of, is written. And to make it the more solemn, after commeth a man with a table one cubit long, one foot broad, covered with a very fine white veil, in both sides whereof is written in golden letters the aforesaid name. At the length by four men is brought forth the corpses sitting in a gorgeous litter, clothed in white, hanging down his head, and holding his hands together like one that prayed: to the rest of his apparel may you add an upper gown of paper, written full of that book the which his God is said to have made, when he lived in the world, by whose help and merits commonly they do think to be saved. The dead man his children come next after him most gallantly set forth, the youngest whereof carrieth likewise a pineapple torch to kindle the fire. Last of all followeth a great number of people in such caps as I erst spoke of.

When they are all come to the place appointed for the obsequies, all the *Bonzii* with the whole multitude, for the space of one hour, beating pans & basins with great clamors, call upon the name of that devil, the which being ended, the obsequy is done in this manner. In the midst of a great quadrangle, tailed about, hanged with coarse linen, and agreeably unto the four parts of the world, made with four gates to go in and out at, is digged a hole: in the hole is laid good store of wood, whereon is raised gallantly a waved roof, before that stand two tables furnished with divers kinds of meats, especially dry figs, pomegranates, and tarts good store, but neither fish nor flesh: upon one of them standeth also a chaffer with coals, and in it sweet wood to make perfumes. When all this is ready, the cord wherewith the litter was carried, is thrown by a long rope into the fire: as many as are present strive to take the rope in their hands, using their aforesaid clamors, which done, they go in procession as it were round about the quadrangle thrice. Then setting the litter on the wood built up ready for the fire, that *Bonziis* who then is master of the ceremonies, sayeth a verse that nobody there understandeth, whirling thrice about over his head a torch lighted, to signify thereby that the soul of the dead man had neither any beginning, he shall have at any time an end, and throweth away the torch. Two of the dead man his children, or of his near kin, take it up again, and standing one at the East side of the litter, the other at the West, do for honor and reverence, reach it to each other thrice over the dead corpses, and so cast it into the pile of wood: by and by they throw in oil, sweet wood, and other performs, accordingly as they have plenty, and so with a great flame bring the corpses to ashes: his children in the meanwhile putting sweet wood into the Chaffer at the table, with odors, do solemnly and religiously worship their father as a Saint: which being done, the *Bonzii* are paid each one in his degree. The master of the ceremonies hath for his part five ducats, sometimes ten, sometimes xx, the rest have ten Julies a piece, or else a certain number of other presents called *Caxa*. The meat that was ordained, as soon as the dead corpse's friends and all the *Bonzii* are gone, is left for such as served at the obsequy, for the poor, and impotent lazars [poor and diseased].

The next day return to the place of obsequy the dead man his children, his kindred, and friends, who gathering up his ashes, bones, and teeth, do put them in a gilded pot, and so carry them home, to be set up in the same pot covered with cloth in the midst of their houses. Many *Bonzii* return likewise to these private funerals, and so do they again the seventh day. Then carry they out the ashes to be buried in a place appointed, laying thereupon a foursquare stone, where is written in great letters, drawn all the length of the stone over, his life time. Every day afterward his children resort unto that grave, with roses and warm water, that the dead corpse thirst not. Nor the seventh day only, but the seventh month, and year, within their own houses they renew this obsequy, to no small commodities and gain of the *Bonzii*: great rich men do spend in these their funerals 3000 ducats, or there about, the meaner sort two or three hundred. Such as for poverty be not able to go to that charges, are in the night time, dark long without all pomp & ceremonies, buried in a dunghill.

Document 12

An Excellent Treatise of the Kingdom of China (1590)

By Duarte de Sande, "An excellent treatise of the kingdom of China," in Richard Hakluyt, ed., *The Principal Navigations, Voyages, Traffiques, and Discoveries of the English Nation*, 3 vols. (London, 1598–1600), 2: 88–98

In September 1592, English privateers who had captured a Portuguese car-rack called the Madre de Deus, *a ship used in the trade between the Spice Islands and Europe, brought back what the editor of travel accounts Richard Hakluyt claimed was "the most exact" report of Japan and northern China to ever "come to light." Originally printed in Latin in Macao in 1590, the book arrived "inclosed in a case of sweete Cedar wood, and lapped up almost an hundred fold in fine calicut-cloth, as though it had beene some incompa-rable jewell."[14] Once unwrapped, this account revealed precise details about sixteenth-century Chinese society.*

Sande's account included information that had been gathered by the Jesuits who had been living in Macao. As a result, his account at times drew on the writings of other Jesuits, including Matteo Ricci whose journeys had taken him to the interior of the nation. Sande knew Ricci personally; in his mid-fifties he met Ricci at Chao-Ch'ing in 1585, where a small group of Jesuits discussed possibilities for spreading their faith farther. Unlike Ricci, Sande tended to believe that more could be done elsewhere, so he returned to Macao three years later. There he wrote a report to his superiors in Rome about the prospects for Christianity in China. Though his report appeared in print in Rome in 1591, it arrived at a time of such crisis for the Vatican—including the deaths of four popes within two years—that it drew little attention from those who might have paid heed to Sande's concerns about the difficulty of spreading Christianity in China.[15]

This excerpt from Sande's writing was first published in English by Hakluyt, who retained the dialogue form of the original.

---

14. Richard Hakluyt, ed., *The Principal Navigations, Voyages, Traffiques, and Discoveries of the English Nation*, 3 vols. (London, 1598–1600), II: sig *4ʳ.
15. Lach, *Century of Discovery*, I: 214, 302; 2: 809–12.

Leo: I have heard, amongst those munitions, a certain strange and admirable wall reported of, wherewith the people of China do repress and drive back the Tartars attempting to invade wherewith their territories.

Michael: Certes [Assuredly] that wall which you have heard tell of is most worthy of admiration; for it runneth alongst the borders of three Northerly provinces, Xiensi, Xansi, and Paquin, and is said to contain almost three hundred leagues in length, and in such sort to be built, that it hindereth not the courses and streams of any river, their channels being overthwarted and fortified with wonderful bridges and other defenses. Yet it is not unlikely, that the said wall is built in such sort, that only low and easy passages be therewith stopped and environed; but the mountains running between those low passages are, by their own natural strength, and inaccessible height, a sufficient fortification against the enemy.

Linus: Tell us (Michael) whether the kingdom of China be so frequented with inhabitants, as we have often been informed, or no.

Michael: It is (Linus) in very deed a most populous kingdom, as I have been certified from the fathers of the society: who having seen sundry provinces of Europe renowned for the multitude of their inhabitants, do notwithstanding greatly admire the infinite swarms of people in China. Howbeit these multitudes are not pell-mell and confusively dispersed over the land, but most conveniently and orderly distributed in their towns and famous cities: of which assemblies there are divers kinds among the Chinians. For they have certain principal cities called by the name of Fu: other inferior cities called Cheu: and of a third kind also named Hien, which be indeed walled towns, but are not privileged with the dignities and prerogatives of cities. To these may be added two other kinds of lesser towns, which are partly villages, and partly garrisons of soldiers. Of the first and principal kinds is that most noble city standing near unto the port of Macao, called by the Chinians Coanchefu, but by the Portuguese commonly termed Cantam, which is rather the common name of the province, than a word of their proper imposition. Unto the third kind appertaineth a town, which is yet nigher unto the port of Macao, called by the Portuguese Ansam, but by the Chinese Hiansanhien. At the foresaid provinces therefore have their greater cities named Fu, & their lesser cities called Cheu, unto both of which the other towns may be added. Moreover, in every province there is a certain principal city which is called the Metropolitan [Metropolis?] thereof, wherein the chief magistrates have their place of residence, as the principal city by me last mentioned, which is the head of the whole province called Coantum. The number of the greater cities throughout the whole kingdom is more than 150, and there is the same or rather a greater multitude of inferior cities. Of walled towns not endued with the privileges of cities there are mo[re] than 1120: the villages & garrisons can scarce be numbered: over & besides the which convents it is incredible what a number of country farms or granges there be: for it is not easy to find any place desert or void of inhabitants in all that land. Now in the sea, in rivers, & in barks there are such abundance of people, and of whole families inhabiting, that even the Europeans themselves do greatly wonder thereat: insomuch that some (albeit beyond measure) have been persuaded that there are as many people dwelling upon the water as upon the land. Neither were they induced so to think altogether without probability: for whereas the kingdom of China is in all parts thereof interfused with commodious rivers, & in many places consisteth of waters, barges & boats being everywhere very common, it might easily be supposed, that the number of water-men was equal unto the land inhabitants. Howbeit, that is to be understood by amplification, whereas the cities do swarm to full with citizens & the country with peasants.

Leo: The abundance of people which you tell us of seemeth very strange: whereupon I conjecture the soil to be fertile, the air to be wholesome, and the whole kingdom to be at peace.

Michael: You have (friend Leo) full judicially conjectured those three: for they do all excel, the which of the three in this kingdom be more excellent, it is not easy to discern. And hence it is that this common opinion hath been rife among the Portuguese, namely, that the kingdom of China was never visited with those three most heavy & sharp scourges of mankind, war, famine, & pestilence. But that opinion is more common than true: sithens [continuously] there have been most terrible intestine [domestic] and civil wars, as in many and most authentical histories it is recorded: sithens also that some provinces of the said kingdom, even in these our days, have been afflicted with the pestilence and contagious diseases, and with famine. Howbeit, that the foresaid three benefits do mightily flourish and bound in China, it cannot be denied. For (that I may first speak of the salubrity of the air) the fathers of the society themselves are witnesses, that scarcely in any other realm there are so many found that live unto decrepit and extreme old age: so great a multitude is there of ancient and grave personages: neither do they use so many confections and medicines, nor so manifold and sundry ways of curing diseases, as we saw accustomed in Europe. For amongst them they have no Phlebotomy or letting of blood: but all their cures, as ours also in Japan, are achieved by fasting, decoctions of herbs, & light or gentle potions. But in this behalf let every nation please themselves with their own customs. Now, in fruitfulness of soil this kingdom certes [assuredly] doth excel, far surpassing all other kingdoms of the East: yet is it nothing comparable unto the plenty and abundance of Europe, as I have declared at large in the former treatises. But the kingdom of China is, in this regard, so highly extolled, because there is not any region in the East parts that aboundeth so with merchandise, and from whence so much traffic is sent abroad. For whereas this kingdom is most large & full of navigable rivers, so that commodities may easily be conveyed out of one province into another: the Portuguese do find such abundance of wares within one and the same City, (which perhaps is the greatest Mart throughout the whole kingdom) that they are verily persuaded, that the same region, of all others, most aboundeth with merchandise: which notwithstanding is to be understood of the Oriental regions: albeit there are some kinds of merchandise, wherewith the land of China is better stored than any other kingdom. This region affordeth especially many sundry kinds of metals, of which the chief, both in excellency & in abundance, is gold, whereof so many Pezoes are brought from China to India, and to our country of Japan, that I heard say, that in one and the same ship, this present year, 2000 such pieces consisting of massie gold, as the Portuguese commonly call golden loaves, were brought unto us for merchandise: and one of these loaves is worth almost 100 ducats. Hence it is that in the kingdom of China so many things are adorned with gold, as for example, beds, tables, pictures, images, litters wherein nice and dainty dames are carried upon their servants' backs. Neither are these golden loaves only brought by the Portuguese, but also great plenty of gold-twine and leaves of gold: for the Chinese can very cunningly heat and extenuate gold into places and leaves. There is also great store of silver, whereof (that I may omit other arguments) it is no small demonstration, that every year there are brought in to the city commonly called Cantam by the Portugal merchants to buy wares, at the least 400 Sestertium thereof, and yet nothing in a manner is conveyed out of the Chinese kingdom: because the people of China abounding with all necessaries, are not greatly inquisitive or desirous of any merchandise from other kingdoms. I do here omit the Silver mines whereof there are great numbers in China, albeit there is much circumspection used in digging the silver thereout: for the king standeth much in fear least it may be an occasion to stir up the covetous and greedy humor of many. Now their silver, which they put to uses, is for the most part passing fine, and purified from all dross, and therefore in trying it they use great diligence. What should I speak of their iron, copper, lead, tin, and other metals, and also of their quick-silver: Of all which in the realm of China there is great abundance, and from thence they are transported into divers countries. Hereunto may be added the wonderful store of pearls, which, at the Isle of Hainan, are found in shell-fishes taken very cunningly by certain Divers, and do much enlarge the king's revenues. But now let us proceed unto the Silk or Bombycine [silken] fleece, whereof there is great plenty in China: so that even as the husbandmen labor in manuring the earth, and in sowing of Rice; so likewise the women do employ a great part of their time in preserving of silk-worms, and in keeming [combing] and weaving of Silk. Hence it is that every year the King and Queen with great solemnity come forth in to a public place, the one of them touching a plough, and the other a Mulberry tree, with the leaves whereof Silk-worms are nourished: and both of them by this ceremony encouraging both men and women unto their vocation and labor: whereas otherwise, all the whole year throughout, no man besides the principal magistrates, may once attain to the sight of the king. Of this Silk or Bombycine fleece there is such abundance, that three ships for the most part coming out of India to the port of Macao, & at the least one every year coming unto us, are laden especially with this freight, and it is used not only in India, but carried even unto Portugal. Neither is the Fleet it self only transported thence, but also divers & sundry stuffs woven thereof, for the Chinese do greatly excel in the Art of weaving, and do very much resemble our weavers of Europe. Moreover the kingdom of China aboundeth with most costly spices & odors, and especially with cinnamon [albeit not comparable to the cinnamon of Zeilan [Ceylon?] with camfer also & musk, which is very principal & good. Musk deriveth his name fro[m] a beast of the same name (which beast resembleth a Beaver) fro[m] the parts whereof bruised & putrefied proceedeth a most delicate & fragrant smell which the Portuguese highly esteem, co[m]monly calling those parts of the foresaid beasts (because they are like unto the gorges of fouls) Papos, & convey great plenty of them into India, & to us of Japan. But who would believe, that there were so much gossipine or cotton-wool in China; whereof such variety of clothes are made like unto linen; which we ourselves do so often use, & which also is conveyed by sea into so many regions: Let us now entreat of that earthen or pliable matter commonly called porcelain, which is pure white, & is to be esteemed the best stuff of that kind in the whole world: whereof vessels of all kinds are very curiously framed. I say, it is the best earthen matter in all the world, for three qualities; namely, the cleanness, the beauty, & the strength thereof. There is indeed other matter to be found more glorious, and more costly, but none so free from uncleanness, and so durable: this I add, in regard of glass, which indeed is immaculate and clean, but may easily be broken in pieces. This matter is digged, not throughout the whole region of China, but only in one of the fifteen provinces called Quiansi, wherein continually very many artificers are employed about the same matter: neither do they only frame thereof smaller vessels, as dishes, platters, salt-sellers, ewers, and such like, but also certain huge tunnes and vessels of great quantity, being very finely and cunningly wrought, which, by reason of the danger and difficulty of carriage, are not transported out of the realm, but are used only within it, and especially in the king's court. The beauty of this matter is much augmented by variety of picture, which is laid in certain colors upon it, while it is yet new, gold also being added thereunto, which maketh the foresaid vessels to appear more beautiful. It is wonderful how highly the Portuguese do esteem thereof, seeing they do, with great difficulty, transport the same, not only to us of Japan and into India, but also into sundry provinces of Europe. Unto the merchandise above-mentioned may be added divers and sundry plants, the roots whereof be right wholesome for men's bodies, and very medicinal, which are brought unto our Isles of Japan, and unto many other Islands, amongst the which that wood may be reckoned, which (by a synecdoche) is called the wood of China, being of notable force to expel out of men's bodies those humors, which would breed contagious diseases. To these you may add sugar-canes (for in the realm of China there is great store of excellent sugar) which is conveyed by the Portuguese very plentifully, both into our country, and also into India. My speeches uttered immediately before concerned merchandize only, in regard whereof this kingdom is beneficial not to itself alone, but most profitable to many other nations also. As for those fruits which pertain to yearly sustenance and common food, they can scarce be numbered: albeit, of those three commodities which they of Europe so greatly account of; namely of corns, vines, and olives the land of China is not very capable: for the Chinese know not so much the name of an Olive tree (out of the fruit whereof oil is expressed) neither yet the name of a vine. The province of Paquin is not altogether destitute of wine, but whether it be brought from other places, or there made, I am not able to say: although it aboundeth with many other, and those not unpleasant liquors, which may serve in the stead of wine itself. Now, as touching corn, there is indeed wheat sown in all the provinces, howbeit rice is in far more use and request than it: and so in regard of these two commodities profitable for man's life; namely, wine and corn; the kingdom of China and our country of Japan may be compared together. . . .

Linus: Tell us now (Michael) of the industry of that people, whereof we have heard great reports.

Michael: Their industry is especially to be discerned in manual arts and occupations, and therein the Chinese do surpass most of these Easterly nations. For there are such a number of artificers ingeniously and cunningly framing sundry devices out of gold, silver, and other metals, as likewise of stone, wood, and other matters convenient for man's use, that the streets of cities being replenished with their shops and fine workmanship, are very wonderful to behold. Besides whom also there are very many Painters, using either the pencil or needle (of which the last sort are called Embrotherers [embroiderers?]) and others of all kinds are diligently conveyed by the Portuguese into India. Their industry doth no less appear in founding of guns and in making of gun-powder, whereof are made many rare and artificial fire-works. To these may be added the art of Printing, albeit their letters be in manner infinite and most difficult, the portraitures whereof they cut in wood or in brass, and with marvelous facility they daily publish huge multitudes of books. Unto these mechanical & liberal crafts you may add two more; that is to say, navigation and discipline of war; both of which have been in ancient times most diligently practiced by the inhabitants of China: for (as we have before signified in the third dialogue) the Chinese sailing even as far as India, subdued some of their realm by dispersing them into many provinces, altering their counsel, they determined to contain themselves within their own limits: within which limits (as I have said) there were in olden time vehement and cruel wars, both between the people of China themselves, and also against the Tartarian king, who invaded their kingdom and by himself and his successors, for a long season, usurped the government thereof. Howbeit the kings of the Tartarian race being worn out, and their stock and family being utterly abolished, the Chinese began to lift up their heads, and to advance themselves, enjoying for these 200 years last past exceeding peace and tranquility, and at this day the posterity of the same king that expelled the Tartars, with great dignity weareth the crown, and wieldeth the royal scepter. Albeit therefore the people of China (especially they that inhabit Southerly from the province of Paquin) are, for the most part, by reason of continual ease and quiet, grown effeminate, and their courage is abated, notwithstanding they would prove notable and brave soldiers, if they joined use and exercise wars against the most barbarous and cruel Tartars. Howbeit in this kingdom of China there is so great regard of military discipline, that no city nor town there is destitute of a garrison, the captains and governors keeping each man his order; which all of them, in every province, are subject unto the king's lieutenant general for the wars, whom they call Chumpin, and yet he himself is subject unto the Tutan or viceroy. Let us now come unto that art, which the Chinese do most all profess, and which we may, not unfitly, call literature or learning. For although it be commonly reported, that many liberal sciences, and especially natural and moral arts are delivered and taught, yet, for the most part, this opinion is to be esteemed more popular than true: but I will declare, upon what occasion this conceit first grew. The people of China do, above all things, profess the art of literature; and learning it most diligently, they employ themselves a long time and the better part of their age therein. For this cause, in all cities and towns, yea, and in petty villages also, there are certain school-masters hired for stipends to instruct children: and their literature being (as ours in Japan is also) in manner infinite, there children are put to school even from their infancy and tender years, from whence not withstanding such are taken away, as are judged to be unfit for the same purpose, and are trained up to merchandise or to manual sciences: but the residue do so dedicate themselves to the study of learning, that (a strange thing it is to consider) being conversant in the principal books, they will easily tell you, if they be asked the question, how many letters be contained in every page, and where each letter is placed. Now, for the greater progress and increase of learning, they (as the manner is in Europe) do appoint three degrees to the attaining of noble sciences; that is to say, the lowest, the middle degree, and the highest. Graduates of the first degree are called Siusai, of the second Quiugan, and of the third Chinzu. And in each city or walled town there is a public house called the School, and unto that all they do resort from all private and petty-schools that are minded to obtain the first degree; where they do amplify a sentence or theme propounded unto them by some magistrate: and they, whose style is more elegant and refined, are, in each city, graced with the first degree. Of such as aspire unto the second degree trial is made only in the metropolitan or principal city of the province, whereunto, they of the first degree, every third year, have recourse, and, in one public house or place of assembly, do, the second time, make an oration of another sentence obscurer then the former, and do undergo a more severe examination. Now, there is commonly such an huge multitude of people, that this last year, in the foresaid famous city of Cantam, by reason of the incredible assembly of persons flocking to that public act or commencement, at the first entrance of the doors, there were many trodden under foot, and quelled to death, as we have been most certainly informed. Moreover they that sue for the highest degree are subject unto a more severe and exact censure, whereby they are to be examined at the King's Court only, and that also every third year next ensuing the said year wherein graduates of the second degree are elected in each province, and, a certain number being prescribed unto every particular province, they do ascend unto that highest pitch of dignity, which is in so great regard with the king himself, that the three principal graduates do, for honors sake, drink off a cup filled even with the King's own hand, and are graced with other solemnities. Out of this order the chief magistrates are chosen: for after that they have attained unto this third degree, being a while trained up in the laws of the realm, and in the precepts of urbanity, they are admitted unto divers functions. Neither are we to think that the Chinese be altogether destitute of other arts. For, as touching moral philosophy, all those books are fraught with the precepts thereof, which, for their instructions sake, are always conversant in the hands of the foresaid students, wherein such grave and pithy sentences are set down, that, in men void of the light of the Gospel, more can not be desired. They have books also that entreat of things and causes natural, but herein it is to be supposed, that as well their books as ours do abound with errors. There be other books among them, that discourse of herbs and medicines, and others of chivalry and martial affairs. Neither can I here omit, that certain men of China (albeit they be but few, and rare to be found) are excellent in the knowledge of astronomy, by which knowledge of theirs the days of the new moon incident to every month are truly disposed and digested, and are committed to writing and published: besides, they do most infallibly foretell the eclipses of the Sun and Moon: and whatsoever knowledge in this art we of Japan have, it is derived from them. . . .

Linus: I perceive (Michael) that drawing to an end of these dialogues, and being weary of your long race, you begin to affect brevity: yet let it not seem troublesome unto you to speak somewhat of the religion of China, which only thing seems to be wanting in this present dialogue.

Michael: I confess indeed that I endeavor to be brief, not so much in regard to wearisomnesse, as for fear least I have been over tedious to you: howbeit I will not fail but accomplish that which I have undertaken, and (according to your request) add somewhat more concerning religion. Whereas therefore the kingdom of China hath hitherto been destitute of true religion, and now the first beginnings thereof are included in most narrow bounds, that nation being otherwise a people most ingenious, and of an extraordinary and high capacity, hath always lived in great errors and ignorance of the truth, being distracted into sundry opinions, and following manifold sects. And among these sects there are more three more famous than the rest: the first is of them that profess the doctrine of one Confucius a notable philosopher. This man (as it is reported in the history of his life) was one of most upright and incorrupt manners, whereof he wrote sundry treatises very pithily and largely, which above all other books, are seriously read and perused by the Chinese. The same doctrine do all Magistrates embrace, and others also that give their minds to the study of letters, a great part whereof Confucius is said to have invented: and he is had in so great honor, that all his followers and clients, upon the days of the new and full Moon, do assemble themselves at the common School, which I have above mentioned, and before his image, which is worshipped with burning of incense and with tapers, they do thrice bend their knees, and bow their heads down to the ground; which not only the common scholars, but the chief Magistrates do perform. The sum of the foresaid doctrine is, that men should follow the light of nature as their guide, and that they should diligently endeavor to attain unto the virtues by me before mentioned: and lastly, that they should employ their labor about the orderly government of their families and of the Common-wealth. All these things are in very deed praise-worthy, if Confucius had made any mention of almighty God and of the life to come, and had not ascribed so much unto the heavens, and unto fatal necessity, nor yet had to curiously entreated of worshipping the images of their forefathers. In which regard he can very hardly or not at all be excused from the crime of idolatry: notwithstanding it is to be granted, that none other doctrine among the Chinese approacheth so near unto the truth as this doeth. The second sect is of them which follow the instructions of Xaquam, or as the Chinese call him Xequiam, whose opinions, because they are well known amongst us, it were bootless to repeat; especially sithens in the Catechism composed by our grave visitor, they are notably refuted. This doctrine do all they embrace, which are in China called *Cen*, but with us at Japan are named *Bonzi*. For this I do briefly and by the way give you to understand, that all words of the Chinese language are of one syllable only, so that if there be any word that consisteth of more syllables than one, it consisteth also of more words than one. These sectaries called *Cen* do shave their beards and their heads, and do for the most part, together with divers of their associates, inhabit the temples of Xaquam, or of others which in regard of the same profession have in their Calendars been canonized for Saints, and do rehearse certain prayers after their manner, either upon books or beads, using other ceremonies after the manner of our *Bonzi*. These men have some inkling of the life to come, and of the rewards of good men, and the punishments of the wicked: howbeit all their assertions are fraught with errors. The third sect is of them which are called *Tauzu*: and those do imitate a certain other man, to be adored, as they think, for his holiness. These also are Priests after their kind, howbeit they let their hair grow, and do in other observations differ from the former. Now, because the sect of Confucius is the most famous of all the three, and the two other sects called *Cen* and *Tauzu* are not much addicted unto learning, their religion prevailing only among the common sort, the Priests of both the said sects do lead a most base and servile life amongst the Chinese, insomuch that they kneel down before the Magistrates, and are not permitted to sit beside them, and sometimes, if the Magistrate please, are abased unto the punishment of bastinado: whereas in our Isles of Japan it is far otherwise, Priests, even of false religion, being had in so great honor among us.

Leo: I heard also (Michael) that the Saracens' superstition takes place in China: now, whether it doth or no, you can resolve us.

Michael: That foreign superstition was brought into China what time the Tartars invaded the kingdom, and usurped the government thereof. All the Saracens therefore in China are originally descended of the Tartars, who, because they were an infinite number, could not utterly be expelled and rooted out of the kingdom, but remaining still there, have propagated their posterity, though not their religion. These therefore are soldiers for the greater part of them, and sometimes do obtain martial dignities: and except a few ceremonies of their superstition which is now become stale and almost worn out, they do live altogether after the Chinese fashion, their predecessors being brought into the same kingdom about four hundred years ago.

Document 13

A Discourse of the Kingdome of China

By Matteo Ricci, "A Discourse of the Kingdome of China" in Samuel
Purchas, *Hakluytus Posthumus, or Purchas His Pilgrimes*, 4 vols.
(London, 1625)

*"It not infrequently happens that the beginnings of vast expeditions and mighty
undertakings which have matured in the course of ages are all but a closed book
to those who live long after these events."[16] So wrote the Jesuit Matteo Ricci, one
of the most remarkable European observers of China in the sixteenth century.
Though Ricci was not the first Westerner to arrive in China, he left behind the
most thorough description of the peoples he encountered as well as a detailed account of the Jesuit mission there. Ricci's insights were first published in Rome in
1615, and there was such a demand for them that printers offered Latin editions in
1616, 1617, 1623, and 1648. But such news could not be confined to the educated
elite who read Latin, and so printers across Europe began to issue translations.
Publishers offered French editions in 1616, 1617, and 1618, German in 1617, and
Italian and Spanish in 1621. Its first appearance in English was in Samuel Purchas's monumental collection of travel accounts published in London in 1625.*

*That Ricci's words attracted notice comes as no great surprise. As his seven-
teenth-century promoter Trigault noted then, Ricci was a well-trained Jesuit
who had moved from his native Macerata (where he was born in 1552) to
Rome to study theology and law. He became a member of the Society of Jesus
on August 15, 1571, the date of the feast of the Assumption. In 1577 he decided to join the Jesuit mission to India. After a stay in Coimbra (where his
traveling party had to remain since they had missed the sailing of the Portuguese fleets to the East), they finally left Lisbon for the journey to India.
On September 13, 1578, when Ricci was one month shy of his twenty-sixth
birthday, his ship docked in Goa. Four years later he joined the Society of
Jesus mission to China. He remained there for twenty-seven years, and his
writings offered European readers, in the words of the historian Jonathan
Spence, "a new level of insight into the realities of Chinese society, even if
one tinged with exaggeration and nostalgia."[17]*

16. Matthew Ricci, *China in the Sixteenth Century: The Journals of Matthew Ricci, 1583–1610*,
   trans. Louis J. Gallagher (New York: Random House, 1953), 3.
17. Jonathan Spence, *The Chan's Great Continent: China in Western Minds* (New York: Norton,
   1998), 32.

When Trigault offered Ricci's description of Chinese society and his history of the church in the East to readers in 1615, he noted that up to that time there had been "two kinds of authors who had written about China; those who have imagined much, and those who have heard much and have published the same without due consideration." Few Europeans at the time had much firsthand knowledge about China. Ricci, who had spent years traveling across China "learning to speak the native language and to read their books," had an immediate impact. Those years of devotion allowed Ricci to describe China in an accurate and meaningful way. His observations of everyday life, especially the kinds of celebrations and rituals described in the excerpt here, reveal the kind of deep knowledge of others that could be gained only by living among the subjects of the account.

Their manifold rites in Salutations, Entertainments, and other Civility: to the King and Magistrates: Of Burials and Marriages, Birthdays; their Men, Women, Names, and Games, Habits

Courtesy or Civility, is reckoned one of their five Cardinal virtues, much commended in their Books. (Their common Rites ye have had largely in Pantoia.) When greater respect is used, as after long absence, or on a Solemn day, after the common bowing, both fall on their knees with the forehead to the ground, and then rise and down again in like sort three or four times. When they do this reverence to a Superior, he stands at the head of the Hall, or sits, and at all those prostrations joining his hands, bows a little and sometime for greater modesty he goeth to the side of the Hall, whose head is Northwards as the door is Southwards. The same rites they perform to their Idols; and sometimes as the Servants to their Master, or the meanest of the people to honorable persons, which is presently to kneel and knock the ground thrice with their forehead: they stand at his side when their Master speaks, and kneel at every answer. When one speaks to another, they use not the second person, nor the first person when they mention themselves, except to their inferiors, and have as many forms of depressing themselves, as of exalting others, the lowliest of which is to call a man's self by his proper name, instead of I. When they speak any thing of another man's, they use a more honorable form; of their own, or theirs, a more modest: which a man must learn both for manners sake, and to understand their meaning.

The Visitors send their Libels or papers of visitation, so many that the Porter is fain [glad] to keep a note of their names, and where they dwell, lest we should forget; and if the party to be visited be not at home or at leisure, that libel is left with the Porter for a testimony. The more honorable the Visitor, the larger he writes his name. In sending Presents they use like libeling; setting down also each gift in a line by it self, part of which may be sent back without offence, which is done with a like libel of thanks. They often send money or pieces of Gold for presents. They have Garments proper for visitations. The chief place in both Royal Courts is given to Strangers, most remote especially, which made us commonly to be preferred. The servant, when they are set, brings as many little Cups of Cia [tea] as are Guests. When they part, near the Hall door, they reiterate their bowings, then at the Door, and at the passing out, and after they are in their Chair or on Horseback, again without doors; and lastly, a Servant is sent after in his Master's name, to salute them, and they send their servants likewise to resalute.

Their Banquets are not so much comessations [feasts] as Compotations [drinking bouts]; for although their Cups be as little as Nut-shells, yet they drink often. Their Civil and Religious affairs are therein handled, besides the demonstration of kindness. In eating they have neither Forks, nor Spoons, nor Knives; but use small smooth sticks, a palm and a half long, wherewith they put all meats to their mouths, without touching them with their fingers. They bring all things to the Table cut in little pieces, except it be of softer condition, as Eggs, Fish, and such things as their sticks will divide. They use to drink hot, even in hottest weather, whether their Cia-decoction, or Wine, or Water: which it seemeth is profitable to the Stomach; for they live long, and are strong at seventy or eighty years: Neither is any of them troubled with the Stone, which I suppose is occasioned by our cold drink. When any is Invited, a Libel is sent a day or more days (if it be to a solemn Banquet) before, signifying, that the Inviter hath prepared a Banquet of Herbs, and hath washed his Cups, that at such a day and hour (which commonly is near night) he may hear and learn somewhat of him: At the day they send another like Libel (on the out-side of these Libels, there is a red paper added with the more honorable Name of the invited, which the Chinese use besides their proper name) in the morning to each Guest, and a third at the hour. Their furniture is not Hangings (whereof they have no use) but Pictures, Flowers, Vessels; to each Guest his Table, and sometimes two to one, the one before the other. These Tables are some Cubits long and broad, but more in length, and covered with a cloth as our Altars. The Seats shine with their Varnish, adorned also with Pictures and Gold. The first entertainment is with Cia in the Hall: and thence they go to the Feasting-room. Before they sit down, the Inviter salutes the principal Guest with a low courtesy, and holding a cup of Wine: then goeth to the door or porch, and first making a low courtesy, turning his face to the South, pours out that cup on the ground, offering it to the Lord of Heaven, and bowing down again, returneth, and filling another cup goeth to that principal Guest, and bowing salutes him in the place in which the rites of salutation are used: and then they go together to the Table where the chief Guest may sit. The midst of it is the chief place; there with both his hands he sets a dish with great veneration, and taking the two sticks (which usually are of Ebony, or Ivory tipped with Gold or Silver, where they touch the meat) lays them by, and taking a sea, brusheth it with his sleeves lightly, and sets it in the middest; after which both go back and bow themselves in the middest of the Room. Thus he doth to every one, placing the second on the left hand, the third on the right. Lastly, he which shall have the chief room receiveth of his servant then Inviter's Dish and Cup, and bids Wine to be filled, and together with other Guests and the Inviter's, boweth down and placeth the Dish on his Table (which is placed in the lower part of the Hall, with his back to the South, and face to the chief Table) with the sticks and seat, as he had done before to him; and then all go again to their place, with great ceremony, to fit them better with both hands, he to whom the rite is done, standing by the side of the door with his hands in his sleeves, and modestly bowing with thanks. They wash neither before nor after. After all this, they perform the last rite of inclination to the Inviter together, and then each to other, and then sit down. When they drink, the Inviter with both hands takes the Cup in the Dish, and lightly lifting it up, and then letting it down invites them to drink, all turning to him at the same time, and beginning to drink, or to sip rather, four or five times setting it to his mouth, not as we use with one continued draught. After the first Cup the Dishes are brought in, of which the Inviter beginning, all with their sticks apply a bit or two to their mouths, diligently observing, not to lay down their sticks before the principal Guest hath laid down his: and then the servants fill his, and after every man's Cup, with hot Wine: and the same rite is again and again repeated, but more sipping then eating. Mean-while some discourse, or Comedy, or Music continue. The grace of their Feast is variety, a little of each, Flesh also and Fish mixed, taking off nothing, but setting one Dish on another like Castles and Towers. Bread, and Rice (which there supplies our Bread) comes not in solemn Banquets. They have games also, in which the loser is fined to drink, with others disport.

None is compelled to drink above his strength. Their drink is tipsy, boiled like our Beer. Their solemn Banquets last all night, the remainders given to the Guest's servants. Near the end of the Feast they change Cups. In eating they are more moderate.

The King is observed with more Rites than any other in the World. None speaks to him but his Eunuchs, and those which live in his Palace, Sons and daughters. None of the Magistrates without the Palace (the Eunuchs also have their degrees) speak to the King but by Petition, and those with so many forms of veneration that none can make them, which is not well exercised, though he be learned. Every new year which begins with that New Moon which next precedeth or followeth the Nones [ninth day] of February, out of every Province a Legate is sent to visit the King, which is done more solemnly every third year. Also in every City on every Change day, all the Magistrates assemble to one place in their City, where the King's Throne and Dragon-ensigns are carved and gilded, often bowing and kneeling before it with peculiar composition of the body to veneration, and wish ten thousand years of life to the King. The like is done on his Birth-day yearly, the Pequin Magistrates and Provincial Legates, and the King's kindred make their appearance there and presents. All also which are named to any Office by the King go to give thanks to the Throne (for the King is not there) with rites prescribed with habit peculiar to that purpose, with an Ivory Table covering their mouth as oft as they speak before the King: the King was wont to come forth to a window, with such a Table in his hand, and another on his head, over his Crown hanged about with threads of gems, his face hidden in presence from the beholders.

The King's color is yellow (forbidden to others) of which his garment is wrought with many golden Dragons, which are carved or painted in all the Palace, and Vessel, and furniture; in the roof also; whence some have thought to be of Gold or Brass, being of a yellow Earth, each nailed to the Timber: with Nails gilded on the heads, that all may appear yellow. It were treason for another to arrogate that color or Arms, except he be of the Royal lineage. . . .

The mourning color is white, and all their habit from the Shoes to the Cap of a strange and miserable fashion. The cause of three years mourning for Parents, is because so long they carried them in arms with so much labor of education: for others as they please, a year, or three months, as they are in nearness: For the King they mourn three years through all the Kingdom, and for the Lawful Queen. Their funeral Rites are written in a Book which they consult on that occasion, all the parcels of the habit there pictured. When a man of rank is dead, the Son or next Kinsman sends Libels to the friends within three or four days: all the Room is white, with an Altar in the midst, on which they place the Coffin and Image of the dead. Thither all the friends come in mourning one after another, & offer Odors and two Wax-candles on the Altar: whiles they burn, making four bendings and kneelings, having first censed against the Image. The Sons stand at the side, and the women behind, covered with a Curtain, mourning the while: the Priests also burn Papers and Silks, with certain rites to minister Clothes to the deceased. They abstain from wonted [familiar] Beds (sleeping on Straw-beds on the ground near the Corps) from flesh and other daintier food, Wine, Baths, company with their Wives, Bankets [Banquets], not going out for certain months, remitting by degrees as the three years expire. On the funeral day the friends are by another Libel invited, to which they go in Procession form, in mourning; many Statues of Men, Women, Elephants, Tigers, Lions, or Paper all going before, diversified in color and gilding, which are all burnt before the Grave: a long rank of Idol Priests, Prayers, and Players on divers Instruments observing divers rites in the way; huge Bell-censers also carried on men's shoulders; after which follows the Hearse under a huge carved Canopy adorned with Silks, carried with forty or fifty men. Next the children on foot with staves, and then the women enclosed within a white gustatory Curtain, that they may not be seen: followed by women of the kindred in mourning Seats. The Graves are all in the Suburbs. If the Sons be absent, the Funeral pomp is deferred till their coming. They bring (if it may be) the deceased in another Country to lie by his friends. The Graves are adorned with Epitaphs in Marble magnificently. Thither on certain days yearly the kindred resort to cense and offer, and make a funeral banquet.

Their Marriages and Espousals are with many rites, done in their youth; the Contracts compounded by the Parents without their [the youths?] consent; they observe equality in years and degree in the lawful Wife. In their Concubines, lust, beauty, price bear sway. The poorer also buy their Wives, and when they list sell them. The King and his kindred respect only beauty, Magistrates appointed to make the choice. One is his lawful Wife; the King and his Heir having nine other Wives a little inferior, and after them six and thirty, which are also called Wives: his Concubines are more. Those which bring forth Sons are more gracious, especially the Mother of the eldest. This is also familiar to other families through the Kingdom. Their first Wife sits at Table; others (except in the Royal families) are as Hand-maids, and may not sit, but stand in presence of either of them: their Children also calling that lawful Wife their Mother, and for her (though not the true Parent) observe triennial mourning. In Marriages they are curious not to take any of the same sur-name, of which sur-names there are not a thousand in all that vast Kingdom. Nor may any man frame a new sur-name, but must have one ancient of the Father's side, except he be adopted into another family. They respect no affinity or consanguinity in a differing sur-name, and so marry with the Mother's kindred almost in any degree. The Wife brings no portion, and although when she first goeth to her Husband's house the street full of household attends her, yet is all provided by his costs which sends money some months before as a gift to her for that purpose.

Every man's Birth-day is festively celebrated with Presents, Banquets and jollity: especially after the fiftieth year explete [is completed] (at which time they are reckoned amongst old men) and then every tenth year. The Children then procure Emblems of their friends, and Epigrams, and some write Books. That day is also festival in which they are of age to take the Man's cap, which is about twenty years, till that time wearing their hair loose. But the first New and Full Moon of the year is most generally festival; each man then having ingeniously devised Lights or Lamps made of Paper, Glass, or other matter, the house seeming by the diversified Lights to be on a light fire. They run up and down also with great stirs in the night with Dragon-fashioned Lights, and make great shows of Powder-fire-works.

The Chinese are white (but nearer the South more brown) with thin beards (some having none) with staring [bristling] hairs, and late growing; their hair wholly black; eyes narrow, of Egg form, black and standing out: the nose very little, and scarcely standing forth; ears mean; in some Provinces they are square faced. Many of Canton and Quamsi Provinces on their little toes have two nails, as they have generally in Cachin-china [Cochin China]. Their women are all low, and account great beauty in little feet, for which from their infancy they bind them straight with clothes, that one would judge them stump-footed: this, as is thought, devised to make them house-wives. The men and women both alike let their hair grow without cutting: but Boys and Girls till they are fifteen year old, are cut round, leaving a lock only on the crown: after which they let it grow loose over their shoulders till twenty. The most of the Priests shave head and beard every eighth day. When they are men they bind up their hair in a Cap or Coif made of horse or man's hair, or in a silken Cowl; and in Winter of woolen: on the top it hath a hole, where the hair comes forth, and is tied in a neat knot. The women wear not this Cap, but bind up their hair in a knot, and make it up with a dress of Gold, Silver, Stones, and Flowers. They wear Rings on their ears, but not on their fingers.

The men and women wear long garments. The men double them on their breast, and fasten them under both the arm-holes; the women on the midst of the breast. They wear wide long sleeves; but the women's wider, the man's straighter, at the wrists. Their Caps are artificially wrought. Their Shoes are much differing from ours; the men wear them of Silk with divers works and flowers, exceeding the elegance of our Matrons. Shoes of Leather none but the meaner sort wear; and scarcely they admit they Leather soles, but of Cloth. The Caps of their Learned are square, of others, round. Every one spends half an hour at least in combing and trimming his hair. They wind also long clouts about their feet and legs, and therefore wear their Breeches loose. They wear no Shirts, but a white Coat next the skin, and wash often. They have a servant to carry a Shadow or great Sombrero over their heads against the rain and Sun; the poor carry one for themselves. . . .

Some Cities are in the midst or Rivers and Lakes, in which they have very neat Boats to pass the streets. And because they go more by water than ours, therefore their Shipping is more convenient and elegant. But the Magistrate's, built by public cost are as commodious as Houses, with divers Lodgings, a Hall, Kitchen, Cells, so neat as seeming Great men's houses, rather than Ships; and therefore they make their solemn Banquets a Ship-board, passing along the Rivers and Lakes for further pleasure. All within shines with Ciaram or shining Varnish in diver colors, and the Carved works gilded in places, with combined sweets to the Eyes and Nose. They honor their Masters more than with us, so that if a man have been another's Scholar but one day in any Art, he calls him Master ever after, and never sits in any meeting but at his side, and doth him all honor.

Dice-play and Cards are common with them: Chess also with the graver persons, not altogether unlike ours: but their King never removes but to the four next rooms, and the Bishops have their Queens. They have also which they call Poulder pawns, which go before the Knights and follow the Pawns. They have a grave Game in a table of three hundred rooms with two hundred men white and black, in which Magistrates spend much time, and the cunning skill whereof gets much credit to a man, although he can do nothing else: and some choose such their Masters with wonted rites. Theft is not punished with Death: the second fault therein, is branded with an hot Iron and Ink in the Arm, with two Characters, the third time in the Face, after their terrible Whipping or condemning to the Galleys, for a time limited: so that there are abundance of Thieves. Every night in Cities, many Watchmen at certain times beat Basins as they walk the streets, the streets are also enclosed and shut, yet many thefts are committed, the Fox being the Gooseherd, and the Watch partners with the Thief. The Cities in greatest Peace in the midst of the Kingdom, are shut every Night, and the Keys carried to the Governor.

Of their Superstitions, Cruelties, fears of Magistrates, of the King's kindred, of Strangers and Soldiers . . .

No superstition is so general in the Kingdom, as the observation of lucky and unlucky Days and Hours, for which purpose yearly is Printed a two-fold Table of days by the King's Astrologers, in such plenty that every house is full of them. In them is written on every day, what may be done or not, or to what hour ye must forbear business, which may in that year happen. There are other more dangerous Masters, which make a living by this Wizardly profession of selling lies, or prescribing fit hours: whereby many differ the beginning of Building, or Journeying till their appointed day or hour come: & then how unfitting soever that prooveth with cross weather, they set on nevertheless, though it be but a little onset, that the work might thence appear to take beginning. The like superstitious observation they have of the moment of the Nativity, which they precisely set down, divers professing by Astrology, or by superstitious numbers or by Physiognomy, or Palmistry, or Dreams, or words in Speech, or posture of the body & by innumerable other ways to foretell future Fortunes; many Gypsie-jugglings used to such impostures, as by a stalking Knave which shall by learning out of printed Books which describe every City, Street and Family, what hath happened as an argument of the truth of that which they say shall happen. Yea, their credulity breeds such strong imagination, that some being foretold of a Sickness such a day, will then fall sick of conceit.

Many also consult with Devils and familiar Spirits, and receive Oracles from the mouth of Infants, or of Beasts, not without fraud. They are superstitious in choosing a plot of ground, to erect a dwelling House, or Sepulcher, conferring it with the head, tail and feet of divers Dragons, which live (forsooth) under our earth, whence depends all good or bad Fortune. Divers Learned men busy their wits in this abstruse Science, and are consulted when any public Buildings are raised. And as Astrologers by the Stars, so these Geologers by inspection of Rivers, Fields, Mountains and site of Regions, foretell Destinies; dreaming by setting a Door or Window this or that way, conveying the rain to the right or left hand, by a higher or lower roof, honor and wealth shall accrue to the House. Of these Impostors the Streets, Cities, Courts, Shops, Markets are full, which sell that which themselves want, good Fortune to all Fool-fortunate buyers: yea, Women and blind folks profess it, and some find such Chapmen of the Learned, Noble, King, and all, that they grow to great riches by others little wits. All disasters public or private are attributed to Fate, and ill site of some City, House or Palace. The noise of Birds, the first meeting in the Morning, Shadows caused by the Sun in the house, are their Fortune-guides.

For other vices, some will make themselves Servants to rich men, to have one of the hand-maids become his Wife, so multiplying issue to bondage. Others buy a Wife, but finding their family become too numerous sell their Sons and Daughters as Beasts, for two or three pieces of Gold (although no dearth provoke him) to everlasting separation and bondage, some to the Portuguese. Hence is the Kingdom full of Slaves, not captive in war, but of their own free-borne. Yet is service there more tolerable than else-where; for every man may redeem himself at the price paid for him, when he is able; and there are many poor which with hard labor sustain themselves. A worse evil in some Provinces is theirs, which finding themselves poor, smother their new-born Babes, specially Females, by an impious piety and pitiless pity preventing that sale to Slavery, by taking away that life which even now they had given. They pretend hereunto also their Metempsychosis, dreaming that the Soul of that Infant shall the sooner pass into some more fortunate body: and are not therefore ashamed to do this in other's presence, yea not the meanest of the communalty [community]. Many more inhumanely kill themselves, either weary of a miserable life, or willing after death to be revenged of some enemy, whiles to the Enemy of mankind many thousands yearly Sacrifice themselves, by Halter, Drowning, and Poison. Another immanitie [monstrous cruelty] in the Northern Provinces is used upon Male Infants, whom for hope of Palace preferments their Parents make Eunuchs; of which in the King's house are ten thousand, a dull and blockish kind of unkind unmanly men. Their Whippings also take away more lives, than the executions of sentences to Death; their Reeds slit two ells long, a finger thick and four broad, at the first blow breaking the skin and flesh on the hinder part of the thighs: to prevent which many bribe the Magistrates, of whose domineering fullness of power they live in perpetual fear, where calumnies and lies are so rife: which China perfidiousness made the Kings come so guarded abroad and unknown, and now not to come forth at all.

The King's kindred are now grown to sixty thousand, and daily increasing become a burthen to the public, and daily increase in idleness, impotence, numbers, the King being very jealous of them, and setting Guards, besides their perpetual exile from Pequin and Nanquin. No marvel if Strangers be no better trusted in China, where the Natives and Blood are suspected: out of whose Books they scorn to learn, and repute them little better than Beasts: and the Characters whereby they express them are taken from Beasts. How Legates are held as prisoners in public houses is else-where delivered. Commanders of Soldiers, which guard places are guarded and watched, and not trusted with the pay of their Companies: neither is there any more base than the Soldiery, most Slaves or condemned persons, for their own or their Ancestors' evils: and when they are free from exercises of war, they become Muletters, Porters, and of other base Offices. The Captains only have some authority. Their arms are worthless for offence or defense, and only make a show, the Captains being also subject to the Magistrate's whippings. Their Alchemistical vanity, and study of long Life, with precepts and huge books of both, I omit. The founders forsooth of these Sciences have gone body and soul to Heaven. The making of Silver hath made many spend their silver, wits and credit, cheated by professing Artists; and the great Magistrates (few in Pequin free) are taken up with the other Study; some shortening their life to make it longer. They write of one of their Kings which had procured such a potion of immortality, whom a friend of his was not able to dissuade from that conceit, enraged, by his sudden snatching & drinking his prepared potion: which he seeking by death to revenge, the other answered, how can I be killed, if this draught cause immortality? and if I may, then have I freed thee of this error.

Discourse of Voyages into ye Easte and West Indies (1598)

By Jan Huygen [John Huighen] van Linschoten, *Discourse of Voyages into ye Easte and West Indies* (London, 1598), 64–66, 88–83

Ever since the start of the sixteenth century, Europeans had been journeying to India. But over the course of the century, no traveler left a particularly detailed account of what he or she saw. Not, that is, until a young Dutchman named Jan Huygen van Linschoten (1563–1611) decided to leave his native Haarlem in Utrecht to go find his fortune. He was sixteen years old when he left for Spain. He eventually made his way to Lisbon, though he never severed his ties to his home. In 1583 he agreed to go on a Dutch mission to India. He soon started to work for the new archbishop of Goa named Vincente de Fonseca. He adored India, though he decided to go home after Fonseca's death in 1588. In September 1592, he arrived back in Holland.

The account that Linschoten produced after his return became one of the most thorough travel narratives of the sixteenth century. Published originally in Dutch in 1596, it attracted sufficient attention to be translated into English and published in London two years later. The text includes details about India that reflect Linschoten's vast knowledge of the locale. His decision to include 36 illustrations and six large maps made his account all the more valuable. The pictures depicted elephants, local plants, unique boats, and pagodas with sculptures carved out of hillsides. A sample of these pictures is located after the end of the excerpts from Linschoten's book.

The heart of Linschoten's account of India can be found in his elaborate description of Goa. He paid attention to the city's many peoples—not only its indigenous inhabitants but also the Arabs, Ethiopians, Kaffirs from Mozambique, Jesuits, Jews, and Armenian Christians who lived there too. Modern scholars have praised Linschoten's description of the city. As the historian Donald Lach put it, Linschoten's account of Goa "provides therein what is probably the best geographical description of the island city, the neighboring islands and peninsulas, and the relationships of one to the other and to the mainland to appear in print before 1600."[18]

18. Lach, *The Century of Discovery I,* 482; see also Rubiés, *Travel and Ethnology in the Renaissance,* 380.

Upon his return, Linschoten produced a massive account, in the spirit of Ramusio and Hakluyt. Unlike his predecessors, Linschoten offered eye-witness testimony about the world far beyond Europe's borders. His account of India included details about the customs of the people he met, how individuals in various castes behaved, their religious and marital practices (including suttee, the burning of Brahmin widows), their foodways, and the nature of the region's flora (including peppers, coconuts, and poppy) and what could be made from them. What follows here is a brief excerpt from one of the greatest ethnographic works produced in the sixteenth century. Precise illustrations enhanced the texts, in much the same way as the engravings by Theodor de Bry (from watercolors done on the spot by John White) illuminated aspects of Thomas Harriot's Briefe and True Report of the New Found Land of Virginia, *a book that had been published only a few years before Linschoten's account began to roll off presses in Amsterdam, the Hague, Frankfurt-Am-Main, and London from 1596 to 1599.*

The excerpt here begins with Linschoten's own opening: his telling of his desire to see the world. That was an idea common to many, perhaps all, of the travelers whose accounts fill these pages, but few articulated it so succinctly in their narratives. Fewer still left such precise descriptions of worlds so far from their homes.

The Voyage and travels of *Iohn Hugen van Linschoten* into the East or *Portingales* Indies: setting down a brief discourse of the said Lands, and sea coasts, with the principal Havens, Rivers, Creeks, and other places of the same, as yet not known nor discovered by the Portuguese: Describing withal not only the manner of apparel of the Portuguese inhabiting therein, but also of the natural born Indians, their Temples, Idols houses, trees, Fruits, Herbs, Spices, and such like: Together with the customs of those countries, as well for their manner of Idolatrous religion and worshipping of Images, as also for their policy and government of their houses, their trade, and traffic in Merchandise, how and from whence their wares are sold, & brought thither: With a collection of the most memorable and worthiest things happened in the time of his being in the same countries, very profitable and pleasant to all such as are welwillers, or desirous to hear and read of strange things.

Being young, and living idly in my native Country, sometimes applying my self to the reading of histories, and strange adventures, wherein I took no small delight, I found my mind so much addicted to see & travel into strange Countries, thereby to seek some adventure, that in the end to satisfy my self I determined, & was fully resolved, for a time to leave my Native Country, and my friends (although it grieved me) yet the hope I had to accomplish my desire, together with the resolution, taken in the end overcame my affection and put me in good comfort, to take the matter upon me, trusting in God that he would further my intent. Which done, being resolved, thereupon I took leave of my Parents, who as then dwelt at Enckhuysen, and being ready to embark myself, I went to a fleet of ships that as then lay before Tassell, staying the wind to sail for Spain, and Portugal, where I imbarked [embarked; enclosed] myself in a ship that was found for S. Lucas de Barameda, being determined to travel into Seville, where as then I had two brethren that had continued there certain years before: so to help my self the better, & by their means to know the manner and custom of those Countries, as also to learn the Spanish tongue. . . .

Of the heathens, Indians and other strangers dwelling in Goa

In the town and Island of Goa, are resident many Heathens, Moors (which are Mahometans [Muslims]), Jews, and all strange nations bordering thereabout, every one of them using several customs, and superstitions in Religion. The Moors hold Mahomet's [Muhammad's] law, and the Jews Moses's law. There are also many Persians, Arabians, and Abexijns, some of them Christians, and some of them Moors. There is in Goa many Armenians that are Christians, and others that go and come to traffic there, as Persians, Arabians, Banianes, of Cambaia, Gusarates, and Decanijns &c. The Moors eat all things except Swine's flesh, and dying are buried like the Jews, by the Heathens, as Decanijns, Gusarates, and Canaras, and other Indians being dead, are burnt to ashes, and some women being alive are burned with them, that is such as are Gentlemen or Noblemen, and the wives of the Brahmins, which are their Idolatrous Priests. Also for the Merchants some of them eat all things, except Cow's or Buffalo's flesh, which they esteem to be holy. Others eat not any thing whatsoever, that hath either life or blood in it, as those of Gusarata, and the Banianes of Cambaia, which observe Pythagoras law: most of them pray unto the Sun and Moon, yet they do all acknowledge a God that made, created and ruleth all things, and that after this life there is an other, wherein men shall be rewarded according to their works. But they have Idols and Images, which they call Pagodas, cut and formed most ugly, and like monstrous Devils, to whom daily they offer, and say, that those holy men have been living among them, whereof they tell so many miracles, as it is wonderful, and say that they are intercessors between them and God. The Devil often times answereth them out of those Images, whom they likewise know, and do him great honour by offering unto him, to keep friendship with him, and that he should not hurt them. They have a custom when any maid is to be married, and that they will honour their Pagoda, for the more credited to the Bridegroom, they bring the Bride with great triumph and Music before their Pagoda, which is made with a Pin of Ivory bone, to whom the nearest friends and kinswomen of the Bride, together with the Bride do go, and by force make the Image to take the Bride's maidenhead, so that the blood remaineth still upon the Image, for a remembrance thereof, and then after other devilish superstitions and ceremonies, having made their offerings, they bring the Bride home, where she is delivered to the Bridegroom, he being very joyful and proud, that their Pagoda hath honoured him so much and eased him of so much labour. They have for the most part a custom to pray unto the first thing they meet withal in the morning, and all that day after they pray unto it, be it Hog, or any other thing. And if in the morning when they go out, they chance at the first sight to see a Crow (whereof there are great numbers in India) they will not go forth of their doors all that day, no not for all the goods in the world, for they esteem it an evil sign, and an unlucky day. They pray likewise to the new Moon, and when she first appeareth, they fall upon their knees, and salute her with great devotion, there are among them certain people called Iogos, which are such as we call Hermits, and those they esteem for holy men, these men live a very strict life with great abstinence, and make the common people believe many strange things. They have likewise many Soothsayers and Witches, which use Juggling [trickery], and travel throughout the country, having about them many live Snakes, which they know how to bewitch, and being shut up in little baskets, they pull them out and make them dance, turn, and wind at the sound of a certain Instrument, whereon they play, and speak unto them. They wind them about their necks, arms, and legs, killing them, with a thousand other devises, only to get money. They are all for the most part very skilful in preparing of poisons, wherewith they do many strange things, and easily poison each other, their dwellings and houses are very little and low, covered with straw, without windows, and very low and narrow doors, so that a man must almost creep upon his knees to go in, their household stuff is mats of straw, both to sit and lie upon, their Tables, Tableclothes, and Napkins, are made of the great Indian fig leaves, they serve them not only for Tables, Sheets, and other linen, but also for Dishes, wherein they put their meat, which you shall likewise see in the Grocers', and Apothecaries' shops, to put and wrap in all things whatsoever they have within their shops (as we do in paper.) They likewise join them together in such sort, that they can put both butter, oil, & such liquid stuffs therein, and also whatsoever cometh to hand. To dress their meat they have certain earthen pots wherein they seed Rice, and make holes in the ground, wherein they stamp it, or beat it with a wooden pestle made for the purpose, and they are so miserable, that they buy the Rice in the Husks, as it groweth on the ground, and some of them have Rice sown behind their house to serve their necessary use. They use to drink out of a copper Can with a spout, whereby they let the water fall down into their mouths, and never touch the pot with their lips. Their houses are commonly strawed with Cow dung, which (they say) killeth fleas. They are very clean on their bodies, for every day they wash themselves all their body over, as often as they ease themselves or make water, both men and women, like the Moors or Mahometans. They wash themselves with the left hand, because they eat with the right hand, and use no spoons. They do keep and observe their ceremonies and superstitions, with great devotion, for they never go forth without praying, when they travel by the way. They have on every hill, cliff, hole, or den their Pagodas and Idols in most devilish and deformed shapes, cut and hewed out of the stones and rocks, with their furnaces hard by them, and a cistern not far from them, which is always full of water, and every one that passeth by, washeth their feet therein, and so fall down before their Idol, some setting before him for an offering fruits, Rice, Eggs, Hens, &c. as their devotions serve, & then commeth the Brahmins their priest and taketh it away and eateth it, making the common people believe that the Pagoda hath eaten it.

When they will make a voyage to Sea, they use at the least fourteen days before they enter into their ships, to make so great a noise with sounding of Trumpets, and to make fires, that it may be heard and seen both by night and day, the ship being hanged about with flags, wherewith (they say) they feast their Pagoda, that they may have a good Voyage, the like do they at their return for a thanksgiving fourteen days long, and thus they use to do in all their feasts, affairs, marriages, childbirths, and at other times of the year, as sowing, and mowing, &c.

The heathenish Indians that dwell in Goa are very rich Merchants, and traffic much. There is one street within the town, that is full of shops kept by those Heathenish Indians, that not only sell all kinds of Silks, Satins, Damasks, and curious works of Porcelain from China and other places, but all manner of wares of velvet, Silken, Satin and such like, brought out of Portugal, which by means of their Brokers they buy by the great, and sell them again by the piece or ells, wherein they are very cunning, and naturally subtle. There are in the same street on the other side, that have all kinds of linen, and shirts, with other clothes ready made for all sorts of persons, as well slaves as Portuguese, and of all other linen work that may be desired. There are Heathens that sell all kinds of women's clothes, and such like wares, with a thousand sorts of cloths and cottons, which are like Canvas for sails and sacks. There is also another street where the Benianes of Cambaia dwell, that have all kinds of wares out of Cambaia, and all sorts of precious stones, and are very subtle and cunning to bore and make holes in all kinds of stones, pearls, and corals, on the other side of the same street dwell other heathens, which sell all sorts of bedsteads, stools and such like stuff, very cunningly covered over with Lacquer, most pleasant to behold, and they can turn the Lacquer into any colour that you will desire. There is also a street full of gold and Silver Smiths that are Heathens, which make all kind of works, also divers other handicrafts men, as Coppersmiths, Carpenters, and such like occupations, which are all heathens, and every one a street by themselves. There are likewise other Merchants that deal all by great, with Corn, Rice, and other Indian wares and Merchandise, as wood and such like. Some of them farm the king's rents and revenues, so that they are skilful every way to make their profits. There are also many Heathen Brokers, very cunning and subtle in buying and selling, and with their tongues to plead on both sides.

The Heathens have likewise their shops with all kind of spices, which they sell by retail, both by weight and measure, as Grocers and Apothecaries do with us, and this is only used among them. They have likewise all sorts of wares whatsoever, but yet with less curiosity then with us, for it is mingled with dust and garbage. These are commonly the Brahmins, which serve likewise for priests and Idolatrous Ministers, & have their ships throughout the City. In every place and corner, and under pentises [sleeping rooms], whereby every man may have to serve him at his need.

There are likewise many barbers, which in every end of the streets do call to those that have cause to use them. They keep no shops, but for a small piece of money come to men's houses to cut their hair, and make clean their nails, as well of their feet as of their hands, as also their ears, & their teeth, and to rub their legs and their bodies. They are so importunate to work, that a man can hardly get them out of his house, so that you have much service of them for a small reward, & sometimes they have blows of the Portuguese for their labors, and dare not do any thing against them, but shrink in their shoulders, and be quiet. There are in Goa many Heathen physicians which observe their gravities with hats carried over them for the sun, like the Portuguese, which no other heathens do, but only Ambassadors, or some rich Merchants. These heathen physicians do not only cure their own nations and countrymen, but the Portuguese also, for the Viceroy himself, the Archbishop, and all the Monks and Friars do put more trust in them, than in their own countrymen, whereby they get great store of money, and are much honoured and esteemed. The countrymen in the village round about Goa, and such as labor and fill the land, are most Christians: but there is not much difference among them from the other heathens, for that they can hardly leave their heathenish superstitions, which in part are permitted them, and is done to draw the other heathens to be christened, as also that otherwise they would hardly be persuaded to continue in the Christian faith. There is in every place of the street exchangers of money, by them called *Xaraffos*, which are all Christian Jews. They are very ready and expert in all manner of accounts, and in knowledge of all sorts of money, without whose help men dare not receive any money, because there is much counterfeit money abroad, which is hard to be known from the good, were it not for these *Xaraffos*, which can discern it with half an eye. The Indian heathens have a custom, that no man may change nor alter trade or occupation, but must use his father's trade, and marry men's daughters of the same occupation, trade or dealing, which is so nearly looked unto, that they are divided and set apart, each occupation by itself, as Countries and Nations are, and so they call one another: for if they speak to a man, they ask him of what trade he is, whether he be a Goldsmith, Barber, Merchant, Grocer, Fisherman, or such like. They give no household stuff with their daughters, but only Jewels, and pay the charges of the wedding. The Sons inherit all their goods. This shall suffice to show the manners, customs, and common kind of life of the Heathens, and Indian Moors in Goa. . . .

Of the Pagodas and Indian Idols forming, keeping ceremonies and superstitions in general, briefly described

The Pagodas and Images are many and innumerable throughout the Oriental countries, whereof some are holden in great reverence & estimation, more than the common sort, and from all places are sought unto, and visited both by Indians & Heathens, in manner of pilgrimages to purchase pardons, which above all others, are very costly made and richly set forth: of those only do I mean to speak as need requireth, that you may know them from the rest. By the town of Bassaym, which lyeth northwards from Goa, upo[n] the coast of India, and is inhabited by Portuguese, there lyeth an Island called Salsette. There are two of the most renowned Pagodas, or temples, or rather holes wherein the Pagodas stand in all India: whereof one of their holes is cut out from under a hill of hard stone, and is of compass within about the bigness of a village of 400 houses: when you come to the foot of the hill; there is a Pagodas house, with Images therein cut out of the very rocks of the same hill, with most horrible and fearful forms and shapes, whereat this day the Gray Fryers have made a Cloister called S. Michaels: and as you go in under the hill, in the first circle you may see many Pagodas, and stepping somewhat higher it hath an other circle or Gallery of Chambers and Pagodas, & yet higher it hath such an other Gallery of Chambers and Pagodas, all cut out of the hard rocks: and by these chambers standeth a great cistern with water, and hath certain holes above, whereby the rain water falleth into it: above that it hath an other Gallery with Chambers and Pagodas, so that to be brief, all the chambers and houses within this compass or four Galleries, are 300 and are all full of carved Pagodas, of so fearful, horrible and devilish forms and shapes, that it is wonderful to behold. The other temple or hole of Pagodas in this Island, is in another place, hewed also out of hard rocks, and very great, all full of Pagodas, cut out likewise of the same stones, with so evil favoured and ugly shapes, that to enter therein it would make a man's hair stand upright. There is yet another Pagoda, which they hold & esteem for the highest & chiefest Pagoda of all the rest, which standeth in a little Island called Pory: this Pagoda by the Portuguese is called the Pagoda of the Elephant. In that island standeth an high hill, & on the top thereof there is a hole, that goeth down into the hill, digged & carved out of the hard rock, or stones as big as a great cloister: within it hath both places and cisterns for water, very curiously made, and round about the walls are cut & formed, the shapes of Elephants, Lions, tigers, and a thousand other such like wild and cruel beasts: also some Amazons and many other deformed things of divers sorts, which are all so well and workmanlike cut, that it is strange to behold. It is thought that the Chinos (which are very ingenious workmen) did make it, when they used to traffic in the Country of India. These Pagodas and buildings are now wholly left, overgrown, and spoiled, since the Portuguese had it under their subjections. By these places may it be conjectured, that their Pagodas are still within the land, even till this day, specially where the Kings and governors are all of that Religion, and keep their Courts and Palaces.

In the Island of Ceylon, whereof I have already spoken, there is a high hill called Pico d'Adam, or Adams Hill, upon the top whereof standeth a great house, as big as a Cloister: wherein standeth a Pagoda of great account. In this place in time past there was a Tooth of an Ape, shrined in Gold and precious stones, and therein was kept this Tooth, which for costliness and worthiness was esteemed the holiest thing in all India, and had the greatest resort unto it from all the countries round about it: so that it passed both S. James in Galisia, and S. Michaels Mount in France, by reason of the great indulgences & pardons that were there daily to be had: for which cause it was sought unto with great devotion by all the Indians within 4 or 500 miles round about it in great multitudes: but it happened an 1554 when the Portuguese made a road out of India, and entered the Island of Ceylon, they went by upon the hill, where they thought to find great treasure, because of the fame that was spread abroad of the great resort and offering in that place, where they sought the Cloister and turned up every stone thereof, and found nothing but a little Coffer, made fast with many costly precious stones, wherein lay the Ape's tooth. This booty or relique they took with them unto Goa, which when the Kings of Pegu, Sion, Bengala, Bisnagar, and others heard of, they were much grieved that their so costly Jewel was in that manner taken from them, whereupon by common consent they sent their Ambassadors unto the Viceroy of India, desiring him of all friendship, to send them their Ape's tooth again, offering him for a ransom (besides other presents, which as then they sent unto him) 700 thousand Ducats in Gold, which the Viceroy for covetousness of the money was minded to do. But the Archbishop of Goa called Con Gaspar, my Lord's predecessor, dissuaded him from it, saying, that they being Christians, ought not to give it them again, being a thing whereby Idolatry might be furthered, and the Devil worshipped, but rather were bound by their profession, to root out and abolish all Idolatry and superstition, as much as in them lay. By which means the Viceroy was persuaded to change his mind, and flatly denied the Ambassador's request: having in their presence first burnt the Ape's tooth, the Ashes whereof he caused to be thrown into the Sea. Whereupon the Ambassadors fearing some further mischief, took their leave and departed, being much astonished that he refused so great a sum of money, for a thing which he so little esteemed that he burnt it, and threw the Ashes into the Sea. Not long after there was a Beniane (as the Benianes are full of subtlety) that had gotten another Ape's tooth, and made the Indians and Heathens believe, that he had miraculously found the same Ape's tooth, that the Viceroy had, and that it was revealed unto him by a Pagoda in a vision, that assured him it was the same, which he said the Portuguese thought they had burned, but that he had beene there invisible and taken it away, laying another in the place. Which the Heathens presently believed, so that it came unto the King of Bisnagar's ears, who thereupon desired the Beniane to send it to him, and with great joy received it, giving the Beniane a great summer of Gold for it, where it was again holden and kept in the same honour and estimation, as the other that was burnt, had been.

In the kingdom of Narsina, or the coast called Choramandel, there standeth a Pagoda, that is very great, exceeding rich, and holden in great estimation, having many Pilgrimages and visitations made unto it from all the countries bordering about it, where every year they have many fairs, feasts, and processions, and there they have a Wagon or a Cart, which is so great and heavy, that three or four Elephants can hardly draw it, and this is brought forth at fairs, feasts, and processions. At this Cart hang likewise many Cables or Ropes, whereat also the country people, both men and women of pure devotion do pull and hale [haul]. In the upper part of this Cart standeth a Tabernacle or seat, wherein fitteth the Idol, and under it sit the King's wives, which after their manner play on all instruments, making a most sweet melody, and in that sort is the Cart drawn forth, with great devotion and processions: there are some of them, that of great zeal and pure devotion do cut pieces of flesh out of their bodies, and throw them down before the Pagoda: others lay themselves under the wheels of the Cart, and let the Cart run over them, whereby they are crushed to pieces, and pressed to death, and they that thus die are accounted for holy and devout Martyrs, and from that time forwards are kept and preserved for great and holy Reliques, besides a thousand other such like beastly superstitions, which they use, as one of my Chamber fellows, that had seen it, showed me, and it is also well known throughout all India.

Upon a time I and certain Portuguese my friends, having licence from the Viceroy were at a banket [banquet] and meeting, about five or six miles within the firm land, and with us we had certain Decanijns, and natural born Indians, that were acquainted with the country, the chief cause of our going, was to see their manner of burning the dead Brahmin, and his wife with him, being alive because we had been advertised, that such a thing was to be done. And there among other strange devices that we saw, we came into some Villages, and places inhabited by the Indians, where in the way, and at every hill, stony Rock or hole, almost within a Pater noster length, we found a Carved

Pagoda, or rather Devils, and monsters in hellish shapes. At the last we came into a Village, where stood a great Church of stone, wherein we entered, and found nothing in it but a great Table that hung in the middle of the Church, with the Image of a Pagoda, painted therein so misshaped and deformed, that more monstrous was never seen, for it had many horns, and long teeth that hung out of his mouth down to the knees, and beneath his navel and belly, it had an other such like face, with many horns and tusks. Upon the head thereof stood a triple Crowned Mitre, not much unlike the Pope's triple crown, so that in effect it seemed to be a monster, such as are described in the Apocalypse. It hung before a Wall, which made a partition front another Chamber, in manner of a Quier, yet was it close made up without windows, or any place for light, in the middle whereof was a little narrow close door, and on both sides of the door, stood a small Furnace made within the wall, wherein were certain holes or Lattices, thereby to let the smoke or savour of the fire to enter into that place, where any offering should be made. Whereof we found some there, as Rice, Corn, Fruits, Hens, and such like things, which the Indians daily offered, but there came so filthy a smoke and stink out of the place, that whosoever went near it, was almost ready to choke, the said place being all black, smelly and foul therewith. Before this door being shut, in the middle of the Church, there stood a Calf of stone, whereon one of our company leaped, and laughing, began to cry out, which the Brahmin that kept the Church, perceiving, began to call and cry for help, so that presently many of the neighbours ran thither, to see what the cause might be, but before the throng of people came, we dealt so well with the Brahmin (acknowledging our fault, & saying it was unadvisedly done) that he was well content, & the people went home again. Then we desired the Brahmin to open us the door that stood shut, which after much entreaty, he yielded unto, offering first to throw certain Ashes upon our foreheads, which we refused, so that before he would open us the door, we were forced to promise him that we would not enter further in, tha[n] to the door. The door of their Sancta Sanctorum, or rather Diaboloru[m], being opened, it showed within like a Lime kill [kiln], being close vaulted round about, over the head without either hole or window to cast in light, but only at the door, neither was there any light in all the Church, but that which came in at the door we entered by. Within the said cell or vault, there hung at the least 100 burning Lamps, in the middle whereof stood a little Altar and covered over with cloth made of cotton wool, & over that with pure gold, under the which (as the Brahmin had told us) sat the Pagoda being of clean gold, of the bigness of a Puppet or a Baby sold in fairs: hard by the Church without the great door, stood within the Earth a great four cornered or square Cistern, hewed out of free stone, with stairs on each side to go down into it, full of green, filthy and stinking water, wherein they wash themselves when they mean to enter into the Church to pray. From thence we went further, and still as we went, in every place we found Pagodas hewed out of hard stones, & standing in their holes, of such lively shapes and figures as we told you before. These stand in the ways under certain cover-tures, without the Churches, and have hard by each of them a small Cistern of water, cut out of the stone to wash their feet, with half an Indian Nut, that hath a handle and hangeth there to take up water withal. And this is ordained for the travelers, that pass by, who commonly at every one of those Pagodas do fall down and make their prayers, and wash their feet in those Cisterns. By the said Pagodas, commonly do stand [two] little furnaces with a Calf or Cow of stone, before the which they set their offerings, which are of such things, as are to be eaten, every man as his devotion serveth, which they think the Pa-goda eateth in the night, but is taken away by the Brahmin. We found in every place such offerings standing, but we had little desire once to taste thereof, it looked so filthily, and as we had sufficiently beholden their misshapen fig-ures and monstrous Images, we returned again into the village, wherein we saw the stone Church, because the Brahmin had advertised us, that the same day about Evening, the Pagoda should be carried in procession to sport itself in the fields, and to fetch a circuit, which we desired to see. And about the time which he appointed, they rung a little Bell, which they had gotten of the Christians, wherewith all the people began to assemble, and took the Pagoda out of his diabolical Cell, which with great reverence, they set in a Palamkin [Palanquin; a covered litter carried on poles] borne by the chief men of the town, all the rest with great devotion following after, with their usual noise and sounds of Trumpets and other instruments, wherewith they went a rea-sonable way round about a field, & then brought him very clean (although he were very filthy stinking) they carried him again into his Cell, leaving him shut herein withal his Lamps. To make good cheer, and having made a foul smoke and stink about him, and every man left his offering behind him, they went home to their houses, leaving the Brahmin alone, who in steed of the Pagoda, made good cheer at their costs, with his wife and family.

This is the manner of their ceremonies and daily superstitions, worship-ings of false gods, wherein the Devil hath so blinded them, that thereby they are without all doubt persuaded to obtain eternal life, and tell many miracles of their Idols, whereby we are moved and put in mind, to call to remembrance how much herein we are bound to God, and to give him thanks, that it hath pleased him to illuminate us, with the truth of his holy Gospel, and that we are not born or brought up among those Heathens, and devilish Idolaters, and to desire God that it would please him of his gracious goodness, to open their eyes, and to give both them and us that which is most necessary for our souls, Amen. The better to understand the manner of their devilish shapes and figures of Pagodas, I have hereunto annexed the picture thereof, even as they openly stand in the high ways or hills, with a Cow or Calf of stone up them, also their Church called *Meskita*, belonging to the Mahometans and Moors, dwelling in Malabar, with the Cistern of water wherein they wash themselves.

Figure 2. Shrines of India

Travelers almost always described the religious practices of those they encountered. Linschoten was no exception. His book included this dual picture of a "Pagode" and a "Mesquita" or Muslim shrine. The first caption refers to the effigies of idols before which the natives give offerings; the second describes the temple of the Indian Muslims. In his text he described what he had seen at one shrine on the Coromandel coast where "there stands a Pagode, that is very great, exceeding rich, and held in great estimation, having many Pilgrimages and visitations made unto it from all the countries bordering about it, where every year they have many fairs, feasts, and processions, and there they have a Wagon or a Cart, which is so great and heavy, that three or four Elephants can hardly draw it, and this is brought forth at fairs, feasts, and processions. At this Cart hang likewise many Cables or Ropes, whereat also the country people, both men and women of pure devotion do pull and hale. In the upper part of this Cart stands a Tabernacle or seat, wherein sits the Idol, and under it sit the King's wives, which after their manner play on all instruments, making a most sweet melody, and in that sort is the Cart drawn forth, with great devotion and processions: there are some of them, that of great zeal and pure devotion do cut pieces of flesh out of their bodies, and throw them down before the Pagode: others lay themselves under the wheels of the Cart, and let the Cart run over them, whereby they are crushed to pieces, and pressed to death, and they that thus die, are accounted for holy and devout Martyrs, and from that time forwards are kept and preserved for great and holy Relics, besides a thousand other such like beastly superstitions, which they use, as one of my Chamber fellows, that had seen it, showed me, and it is also well known throughout all India" (Linschoten, Discourse, 82).

Linschoten was no fan of what he observed at such shrines. "This is the manner of their ceremonies and daily superstitions," he concluded, "worshipings of false gods, wherein the Devil hath so blinded them, that thereby they are without all doubt persuaded to obtain eternal life, and tell many miracles of their Idols." Like other travelers, his views of what he saw confirmed his own religious beliefs. Seeing the pagodas, he insisted, "we are moved and put in mind, to call to remembrance how much herein we are bound to God, and to give him thanks, that it hath pleased him to illuminate us, with the truth of his holy Gospel, and that we are not born or brought up among those Heathens, and devilish Idolaters, and to desire God that it would please him of his gracious goodness, to open their eyes, and to give them the truth of his holy word among them, as he is our only trust, for they are in all things like us, made after God's own Image" (Linschoten, Discourse, 83).

Though Linschoten went on at great length about pagodas, he made very little comment about Muslim houses of worship. About the picture here, he wrote only that he was presenting a picture of "their Church called Meskita, belonging to the Mahometans and Moors, dwelling in Malabar, with the Cistern of water wherein they wash themselves" (Linschoten, Discourse, 83).

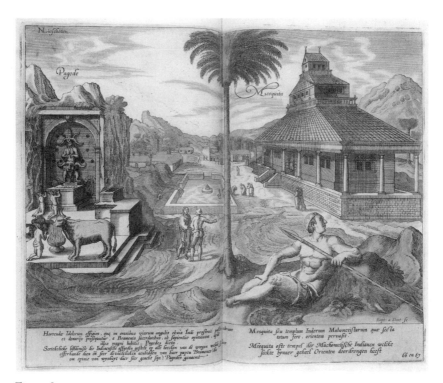

Figure 2

Figure 3. Elephant on the Hunt

Europeans were fascinated by elephants wherever they encountered them—in Africa, India, or the menagerie at the Vatican. During his journey to India, Linschoten learned that large numbers of elephants could be found in Asia. The caption here refers to the king of Cochin whose followers he termed "Nairos." The locals "use to hunt them with great troupes of men," he wrote, and could capture up to two thousand at a time but they would "choose out a hundredth or more as they need, and let the other go," so that their populations would not be threatened. "Those they do in time bring up, and learn to travel with them, and to endure hunger and thirst, with other inventions, so long that they begin to understand men when they speak. Then they anoint them with oil, and wash them, and so do them great good, whereby they become as tame and gentle as men, so that they want nothing but speech."

Bramenes cum mortuus est . secundum eorum legem crematur : uxor autem ejus . prae amore , sese vivam in ignem cum illo conjicit .

De Bramene doot wesende wert nae haer wet verbrant . en zyn vrouwe wt liefde haers mans .verbrant haer levendich met hem.

58 en 59

Figure 4. Burning of a Brahmin Widow

Linschoten paid close attention to indigenous mores during his journey to India. Among the practices he thought notable, and thus worth a picture in his book, was the burning of Brahmin widows in the fires consuming the bodies of their husbands. He described the scene in detail: "When the Brahmins die, all their friends assemble together, and make a hole in the ground, wherein they throw much wood and other things: and if the man be of any account, they cast in sweet Sanders, & other Spices, with Rice, Corn, and such like, and much oil, because the fire should burn the stronger. Which done they lay the dead Brahmins in it: there cometh his wife with music & many of her nearest friends all singing certain praises in commendation of her husband's life, putting her in comfort, & encouraging her to follow her husband, & go with him into the other world. Then she takes all her Jewels, and parts them among her friends, & so with a cheerful countenance, she leaps into the fire, and is presently covered with wood and oil: so she is quickly dead, & with her husband's body burned to ashes." Brahmin widows who refused to leap into the fires had their heads shaved, could no longer wear jewelry, and were "despised, and accounted for a dishonest woman." Linschoten added that such customs could also be found among India's nobles and some merchants (Linschoten, Discourse, 70–71).

Figure 5. Coconuts in India

Like many travelers whose accounts survive from the sixteenth century, Linschoten believed that the flora and fauna of new places demanded explanation. India was no exception. In addition to describing what South Asian plants looked like, he also described how they obtained them and what they did with them. Perhaps no plant was as fascinating as coconuts. "This is the most profitable tree of all India," he declared. "They have no great roots, so that a man would think it were impossible for them to have any fast hold within the earth, and yet they stand so fast and grow so high, that it makes men fear to see men climb upon them, least they should fall down. The Canarijns climb as nimbly, and as fast upon them, as if they were Apes, for they make small steps in the trees like stairs, whereon they step, and so climb up," a feat that was well beyond the abilities of the Portuguese. The trees grew well near houses, "because commonly there they have good earth, and being well looked unto and husbanded, they yield fruit in few years, which is the Canarijns' livings that dwell here and there among those trees, and have no other occupation but only to dress those trees, which they farm of the Landlords, and by the fruit thereof do get their livings. Those trees are more abundant with them than Olive trees in Spain, or willow trees in the Low Countries." Linschoten noted that the locals used the tree trunks to make ships, the leaves to make sails, and the coconuts' shells to make hats to protect them from the sun and the rain; they also ate the fruit and drank the juice from the coconuts (Linschoten, Discourse, 100–101).

Part III
America

The Letter of Columbus to Luis de Santángel, Announcing His Discovery (1493)

By Christopher Columbus, *The Letter of Columbus to Luis de Santángel, Announcing His Discovery*, trans. Albert Bushnell Hart and Edward Channing, 1892

No early modern travel account had the power of Christopher Columbus's first letter describing what he found after he embarked from Spain in 1492 on his journey to find a quicker route to East Asia. Though later reports, including others from Columbus (1451–1506), offered far more detail about the Americas, it was this account announcing the European discovery of the Western Hemisphere that had an impact probably greater than any other contemporary report of a journey across the Atlantic Ocean.

When Columbus set sail, he believed that he would have little trouble reaching Asia by sailing west across the Atlantic Ocean. By his estimate, Japan was only 2,400 nautical miles from the Canary Islands. His estimate, based on his reading of ancient authorities, was wrong; the real distance was 10,600 miles. But the fact that he could not accurately estimate the size of the world or the breadth of the Atlantic turned out to be far less important than his accidental "discovery" of America.

Columbus claimed that he wrote the letter on February 15, while he was on his caravel near the Canary Islands, though he added a postscript once he had landed in Lisbon a month later. Perhaps the report's most shocking moment occurred in the first paragraph when Columbus announced to his royal sponsors Ferdinand and Isabella that he had claimed possession of the islands he found and at once began the process of renaming them. What followed from that moment of arrogance was the kind of material that can be found in other travel accounts. Specifically, Columbus described the people he encountered and the environment they inhabited. The place was remarkable: its trees reached into the sky; the weather was always pleasant; there were inviting commodities to be harvested. He was so confident of his possession that he matter-of-factly stated that he kidnapped some of the local inhabitants so that they could bear witness to his claims once he reached Spain. Though he felt some disdain for those he met since they were naked and thus (by European standards) primitive, he was pleased that he encountered no monsters, some-

thing he had expected given his understanding of the kinds of creatures that roamed lands along the margins of Europeans' imaginations. Still, news that there were islanders who were cannibals did not sit well with him, even if it confirmed one aspect of the inherited wisdom of antiquity.

After he set sail on his return to Europe, Columbus had an experience that was entirely common: he encountered a storm. The storm delayed him for two weeks, but when he landed in Lisbon he learned that he was not alone in experiencing the ferocity of the Atlantic. Other sailors in port told him that it had been the worst winter they had ever experienced and that many ships had sunk.

Within weeks of his arrival, the Barcelona printer Pedro Posa had produced a printed version of Columbus's letter. Almost immediately, printers across Europe rushed to put out versions of the letter. Twelve editions appeared in three languages within a year; one printer in Basel even included woodcuts providing images of the mariner's ships and the peoples he met. There is only one known copy of Posa's first edition.[1]

The quick distribution of Columbus's report around Europe suggests that printers knew there would be an audience for his news. There were many marvels to be found on the far side of the Atlantic, these European readers quickly learned. But getting there would remain difficult. Only the fortunate could expect to reap the rewards that Columbus's letter told them existed.

The translation here appeared in January 1892, one of the many efforts by Americans (and others) to honor the four hundredth anniversary of Columbus's first voyage. The text and extracts from Columbus's journals made up the contents of the first of a series of small pamphlets, each selling for 10 cents; other documents provided information about the Norse voyages to Vinland, John Cabot's 1497 journey, and selected state papers (such as extracts from the Treaty of Paris in 1783 that ended the American Revolution). Though scholarly efforts to mark the anniversary of the events of 1492 were less dramatic than the creation of the World's Fair in Chicago, Columbus remained a popular figure. One hundred years later the situation was almost entirely the opposite: those who analyzed Columbus on the quincentennial of

---

1. For its initial publishing history, see Mauricio Obregón, *The Columbus Papers: The Barcelona Letter of 1493, the Landfall Controversy, and the Indian Guides* (New York: Macmillan, 1991), 6–8.

his journey tended to vilify him, seeing in his actions the origins of environ-mental degradation and slavery in the Western Hemisphere.²

Sir:

As I know you will be rejoiced at the glorious success that our Lord has given me in my voyage, I write this to tell you how in thirty-three days I sailed to the Indies with the fleet that the illustrious King and Queen, our Sovereigns, gave me, where I discovered a great many islands, inhabited by numberless people; and of all I have taken possession for their Highnesses by proclamation and display of the Royal Standard without opposition. To the first island I discovered I gave the name of San Salvador, in commemoration of His Divine Majesty, who has wonderfully granted all this. The Indians call it Guanaham. The second I named the Island of Santa Maria de Concepcion; the third, Fernandina; the fourth, Isabella; the fifth, Juana; and thus to each one I gave a new name. When I came to Juana, I followed the coast of that isle toward the west, and found it so extensive that I thought it might be the mainland, the province of Cathay; and as I found no towns nor villages on the sea-coast, except a few small settlements, where it was impossible to speak to the people, because they fled at once, I continued the said route, thinking I could not fail to see some great cities or towns; and finding at the end of many leagues that nothing new appeared, and that the coast led northward, contrary to my wish, because the winter had already set in, I decided to make for the south, and as the wind also was against my proceeding, I determined not to wait there longer, and turned back to a certain harbor whence I sent two men to find out whether there was any king or large city. They explored for three days, and found countless small communities and people, without number, but with no kind of government, so they returned.

I heard from other Indians I had already taken that this land was an is-land, and thus followed the eastern coast for one hundred and seven leagues, until I came to the end of it. From that point I saw another isle to the eastward, at eighteen leagues' distance, to which I gave the name of Hispaniola. I went

2. See, for example, Kirkpatrick Sale, *The Conquest of Paradise: Christopher Columbus and the Columbian Legacy* (New York: Alfred Knopf, 1990), esp. 3–216. For a review of the litera-ture of the quincentennial that contrasts modern treatments with earlier assessments, see Peter C. Mancall, "The Age of Discovery," in *The Challenge of American History,* ed. Louis Masur (Baltimore: Johns Hopkins University Press, 1999), 26–53.

thither and followed its northern coast to the east, as I had done in Juana, one hundred and seventy-eight leagues extensive. It has many ports along the sea-coast excelling any in Christendom—and many fine, large, flowing rivers. The land there is elevated, with many mountains and peaks incomparably higher than in the center isle. They are most beautiful, of a thousand varied forms, accessible, and full of trees of endless varieties, so high that they seem to touch the sky, and I have been told that they never lose their foliage. I saw them as green and lovely as trees are in Spain in the month of May. Some of them were covered with blossoms, some with fruit, and some in other conditions, according to their kind. The nightingale and other small birds of a thousand kinds were singing in the month of November when I was there. There were palm trees of six or eight varieties, the graceful peculiarities of each one of them being worthy of admiration as are the other trees, fruits, and grasses. There are wonderful pine woods, and very extensive ranges of meadow land. There is honey, and there are many kinds of birds, and a great variety of fruits. Inland there are numerous mines of metals and innumerable people. Hispaniola is a marvel. Its hills and mountains, fine plains and open country, are rich and fertile for planting and for pasturage, and for building towns and villages. The seaports there are incredibly fine, as also the magnificent rivers, most of which bear gold. The trees, fruits, and grasses differ widely from those in Juana. There are many spices and vast mines of gold and other metals in this island. They have no iron, nor steel, nor weapons, nor are they fit for them, because although they are well-made men of commanding stature, they appear extraordinarily timid. The only arms they have are sticks of cane, cut when in seed, with a sharpened stick at the end, and they are afraid to use these. Often I have sent two of three men ashore to some town to converse with them, and the natives come out in great numbers, and as soon as they saw our men arrive, fled without a moment's delay although I protected them from all injury.

At every point where I landed and succeeded in talking to them, I gave them some of everything I had—cloth and many other things—without receiving anything in return, but they are a hopelessly timid people. It is true that since they have gained more confidence and are losing this fear, they are so unsuspicious and so generous with what they possess, that no one who had not seen it would believe it. They never refuse anything that is asked for. They even offer it themselves, and show so much love that they would give their very hearts. Whether it be anything of great or small value, worthless things being given to them, such as bits of broken bowls, pieces of glass, and old straps, although they were as much pleased to get them as if they were the finest jewels in the world. One sailor was found to have got for a leathern strop, gold of the weight of two and a half castellanos, and others for even more worthless things much more; while for a new *blancas* they would give all they had, were it two or three castellanos or pure gold or an arroba or two of spun cotton. Even bits of the broken hoops of wine casks they accepted, and gave in return what they had, like fools, and it seemed wrong to me. I forbade it, and gave a thousand good and pretty things that I had to win their love, and to induce them to become Christians, and to love and serve their Highnesses and the whole Castilian nation, and help to get for us things they have in abundance, which are necessary to us. They have no religion, nor idolatry, except that they all believe power and goodness to be in heaven. They firmly believed that I, with my ships and men, came from heaven, and with this idea I have been received everywhere, since they lost fear of me. They are, however, far from being ignorant. They are most ingenious men, and navigate these seas in a wonderful way, and describe everything well, but they never before saw people wearing clothes, nor vessels like ours. Directly I reached the Indies in the first isle I discovered, I took by force some of the natives, that from them we might gain some information of what there was in these parts; and so it was that we immediately understood each other, either by words or signs. They are still with me and still believe that I come from heaven. They were the first to declare this wherever I went, and the others ran from house to house, and to the towns around, crying our, "Come! come! and see the men from heaven!" Then all, both men and women, as soon as they were reassured about us, came, both small and great, all bringing something to eat and to drink, which they presented with marvelous kindness. In these isles there are a great many canoes, something like rowing boats, of all sizes, and most of them are larger than an eighteen-oared galley. They are not so broad, as they are made of a single plank, but a galley could not keep up with them in rowing, because they go with incredible speed, and with these they row about among all these islands, which are innumerable, and carry on their commerce. I have seen some of these canoes with seventy and eighty men in them, and each had an oar. In all the islands I observed little difference in the appearance of the people, or in their habits and language, except that they understand each other, which is remarkable. Therefore I hope that their Highnesses will decide upon the conversion of these people to our holy faith, to which they seem much inclined. I have already stated how I sailed on hundred and seven leagues along the sea-coast of Juana, in a straight line from west to east. I can therefore assert that this island is larger than England and Scotland together, since beyond these one hundred and seven leagues there remained at the west point two provinces where I did not go, one of which they call Avan, the home of men with tails. These provinces are computed to be fifty or sixty leagues in length, as far as can be gathered from the Indians with me, who are acquainted with all these islands. This other, Hispaniola, is larger in circumference than all Spain from Catalonia to Fuentarabia in Biscay, since upon one of its four sides I sailed one hundred and eighty-eight leagues from west to east. This is worth having, and must on no account be given up. I have taken possession of all these islands, for their Highnesses, and all may be more extensive than I know, or can say, and I hold them for their Highnesses, who can command them as absolutely as the kingdoms of Castile. In Hispaniola, in the most convenient place, most accessible for the gold mines and all commerce with the mainland on this side or with that of the great Khan, on the other, with which there would be great trade and profit, I have taken possession of a large town, which I have named the City of Navidad. I began fortifications there which should be completed by this time, and I have left in it men enough to hold it, with arms, artillery, and provisions for more than a year; and a boat with a master seaman skilled in the arts necessary to make others; I am so friendly with the king of that country that he was proud to call me his brother and hold me as such. Even should he change his mind and wish to quarrel with my men, neither he nor his subjects know what arms are, nor wear clothes, as I have said. They are the most timid people in the world, so that only the men remaining there could destroy the whole region, and run no risk if they know how to behave themselves properly. In all these islands, the men seem to be satisfied with one wife, except they allow as many as twenty to their chief or king. The women appear to me to work harder than the men, and so far as I can hear they have nothing of their own, for I think I perceived that what one had others shared, especially food. In the islands so far, I have found no monsters, as some expected, but, on the contrary, they are people of very handsome appearance. They are not black as in Guinea, though their hair is straight and coarse, as it does not grow where the sun's rays are too ardent. And in truth the sun has extreme power here, since it is within the twenty-six degrees of the equinoctial line. In these islands there are mountains where the cold this winter was very severe, but the people endure it from habit, and with the aid of the meat they eat with very hot spices.

As for monsters, I have found no trace of them except at the point in the second isle as one enters the Indies, which is inhabited by a people considered in all the isles as most ferocious, who eat human flesh. They possess many canoes, with which they overrun all the isles of India, stealing and seizing all they can. They are not worse looking than the others, except that they wear their long hair like women, and use bows and arrows of the same cane, with a sharp stick at the end for want of iron, of which they have none. They are ferocious compared to these other races, who are extremely cowardly; but I only hear this from the others. They are said to make treaties of marriage with the women in the first isle to be met with coming from Spain to the Indies, where there are no men. These women have no feminine occupation, but use bows and arrows of cane like those before mentioned, and cover and arm themselves with plates of copper, of which they have a great quantity. Another island, I am told, is larger than Hispaniola, where the natives have no hair, and where there is countless gold; and from them all I bring Indians to testify to this. To speak, in conclusion, only of what has been done during this hurried voyage, their Highnesses will see that I can give them as much gold as they desire, if they will give me a little assistance, spices, cotton, as much as their Highnesses may command to be shipped, and mastic as much as their Highnesses choose to send for, which until now has only been found in Greece, in the isle of Chios, and the Signoria can get its own price for it; as much lign-aloe as they command to be shipped, and as many slaves as they choose to send for, all heathens. I think I have found rhubarb and cinnamon. Many other things of value will be discovered by the men I left behind me, as I stayed nowhere when the wind allowed me to pursue my voyage, except in the City of Navidad, which I left fortified and safe. Indeed, I might have accomplished much more, had the crews served me as they ought to have done. The eternal and almighty God, or our Lord, it is Who gives to all who walk in His way, victory over things apparently impossible, and in this case signally so, because although these lands had been imagined and talked of before they were seen, most men listened incredulously to what was thought to be but an idle tale. But our Redeemer has given victory to our most illustrious King and Queen, and to their kingdoms rendered famous by this glorious event, at which all Christendom should rejoice, celebrating it with great festivities and solemn Thanksgivings to the Holy Trinity, with fervent prayers for the high distinction that will accrue to them from turning so many peoples to our holy faith; and also from the temporal benefits that not only Spain but all Christian nations will obtain. Thus I record what has happened in a brief note written on board the *Caravel*, off the Canary Isles, on the 15th of February, 1493.

Since writing the above, being in the Sea of Castile, so much wind arose south southeast, that I was forced to lighten the vessels, to run into this port of Lisbon today which was the most extraordinary thing in the world, from whence I resolved to write to their Highnesses. In all the Indies I always found the temperature like that of May. Where I went in thirty-three days I returned in twenty-eight, except that these gales have detained me fourteen days, knocking about in this sea. Here all seamen say that there has never been so rough a winter, nor so many vessels lost. Done the 14th day of March.

Document 16

Mondus Novus (1504)

By Amerigo Vespucci, *Mondus Novus*, trans. G. Northrup
(Princeton: Princeton University Press, 1916)

The experiences of Amerigo Vespucci (1451–1512) did not mirror those of Columbus. Columbus's initial report has barely a critical word to offer about his journey and is bathed instead in triumphal rhetoric. Vespucci's report, by contrast, is more down to earth. Vespucci first sailed across the Atlantic to Brazil in 1499, following the eastern coast of South America northward and passing the mouths of the Amazon and the Orinoco. He returned in 1501, and wrote the report here to describe what he saw on that journey. Near the beginning he complained about the weather: it rained forty-four of the sixty-seven days he was at sea, with storms full of lightning and thunder and conditions so bleak and "so dark that never did we see sun by day or fair sky by night." Still, despite the problems, he knew the significance of the journey: he had sailed to what "we may rightly call a new world" because no one in antiquity had ever imagined that such a place could exist.

Vespucci filled his account with details about the people he met in Brazil, who were naked from the day of their birth to the day of their death. He found the women, as he put it, "tolerably beautiful and cleanly," and he was impressed too at the "well formed and proportioned" bodies of everyone he encountered. That praise gave way to condemnation when he described the ways that these native Brazilians pierced their bodies, making them appear more monstrous than human. Still, even as he condemned the way they abused their own bodies, Vespucci came to believe (as did Columbus) that the terrestrial paradise must be somewhere close by.

The report that follows takes the form of a letter from Vespucci to his patron Lorenzo Pietro di Medici, one of the famed Florentine bankers of that family.

He wrote it after his third voyage but viewed it as a work in progress, a pre-liminary report while he waited for support for yet another journey. It was not Vespucci's only observation on the Western Hemisphere, and he believed, as he mentions here, that this report was destined to reside with others in his own cabinet, perhaps a place where he kept other physical evidence of the world that existed far from Italy. But the letter and his other descriptions of the "novo mondo retrovati" (new found world) did not remain private for long. After an initial printing in French in 1503, publishers across Europe issued versions of this report. In 1504 it was printed in Venice, Augsburg, and Rome. The next year, publishers in Nuremberg, Strasburg, Augsburg, Rostock, Florence, Cologne, Antwerp, Leipzig, Basel, Munich, and Pilsen (where an abbreviated version was published in Czech) issued editions. Print-ers published versions almost every year until 1510 (including ten separate editions in 1506), and by then it was available in the common languages of Latin, Italian, German, and French. Then the interest in Vespucci's views, or at least new printings of his work, dissipated. Only in 1550, when Giovanni Battista Ramusio included the account in his Navigationi e Viaggi, *did it become available again, though that printing led to a new French translation in 1556. Eventually extracts from Vespucci appeared in* Catalogus scrip-torium florentinarum, *published in Florence in 1589, a sign that what had once been a project supported by the elite of that city-state had now become yet another glimpse of its storied past.*

The printers who arranged for translations of Vespucci's tract no doubt be-lieved that there existed an eager audience for any news about the Western Hemisphere. For that audience, Vespucci's narrative of a journey that began in Lisbon on May 1, 1501, fit the bill. His account of native peoples who lived without well-defined marital customs and who inhabited a world in which women chewed poisonous animals and then transferred their toxic-ity to their male partners to enlarge their erections (even at the risk of their penises becoming so fragile they could break off) would have held anyone's attention. The fact that Vespucci believed that the natives lived to be 150 years old because there were no diseases in that land made Brazil seem even more inviting, though some may have recoiled at his reporting that cannibal-ism was widespread.

Fortunately for posterity, Vespucci was able to avert his gaze from the salted limbs hanging from the rafters. When he did so, he paid attention to the eve-ning skies. His account described what he saw, and printers tried to render

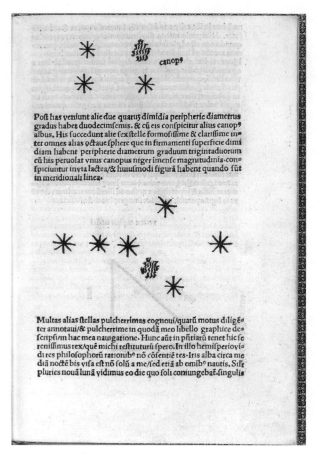

Figure 6. Vespucci's Constellation

"The sky is adorned with the most beautiful constellations and forms among which I noted about twenty stars as bright as we ever saw Venus or Jupiter," Vespucci wrote in Mondus Novus. *He then provided a brief description of what he saw, noting that, among other unusual celestial phenomena, the "Antarctic pole is not figured with a Great and a Little Bear as this Arctic pole of ours is seen to be, nor is any bright star to be seen near it" (Vespucci,* Mondus Novus: Letter to Lorenzo Pietro Di Medici, Paris, 1503?, *9). The picture here represents Vespucci's effort to set into the pages of a book what he saw in the skies above.*

Vespucci's diagram of the stars. The pictures differ from one edition to the next, revealing how difficult it could be to represent accurately even what appeared the simplest kinds of visual information generated abroad.

As the closing paragraph of this letter reveals, Vespucci thought it crucial to have the letter printed in Latin, not in the Italian in which he wrote it, so that it would reach a larger audience and hence let them realize the "vastness of

the earth" that had never been known before. Though his report was eventu-
ally superseded by more elaborate and detailed European accounts of Brazil,
notably those of Hans Stade and Jean de Léry, it remains vivid testimony to
the kinds of information that could be found in European travel accounts at
the dawn of the sixteenth century.

On a former occasion I wrote to you at some length concerning my return from those new regions which we found and explored with the fleet, at the cost, and by the command of this Most Serene King of Portugal. And these we may rightly call a new world. Because our ancestors had no knowledge of them, and it will be a matter wholly new to all those who hear about them. For this transcends the view held by our ancients, inasmuch as most of them hold that there is no continent to the south beyond the equator, but only the sea which they named the Atlantic; and if some of them did aver that a continent there was, they denied with abundant argument that it was a habitable land. But that this their opinion is false and utterly opposed to the truth, this my last voyage has made manifest; for in those southern parts I have found a continent more densely peopled and abounding in animals than our Europe or Asia or Africa, and, in addition, a climate milder and more delightful than in any other region known to us, as you shall learn in the following account wherein we shall set succinctly down only capital matters and the things more worthy of comment and memory seen or heard by me in this new world, as will appear below.

On the fourteenth of the month of May, one thousand five hundred and one we set sail from Lisbon under fair sailing conditions, in compliance with the commands of the aforementioned king, with these ships for the purpose of seeking new regions toward the south; and for twenty months we continuously pursued this southern course. The route of this voyage is as follows: Our course was set for the Fortunate Isles, once so called, but which are now termed the Grand Canary Islands; these are in the third climate and on the border of the inhabited west. Thence by sea we skirted the whole African coast and part of Ethiopia as far as the Ethiopic Promontory, so called by Ptolemy, which we now call Cape Verde and the Ethiopians Beseghice. And that region, Mandingha, lies within the torrid zone fourteen degrees north of the equator; it is inhabited by tribes and nations of blacks. Having there recovered our strength and taken on all that our voyage required, we weighed anchor and made sail. And directing our course over the vast ocean toward the Antarctic we for a time bent westward, owing to the wind called Vulturnus; and from the day when we set sail from the said promontory we cruised for the space of two months and three days before any land appeared to us. But what we suffered on that vast expanse of sea, what perils of shipwreck, what discomforts of the body we endured, with what anxiety of mind we toiled, this I leave to the judgment of those who out of rich experience have well learned what it is to seek the uncertain and to attempt discoveries even though ignorant. And that in a word I may briefly narrate all, you must know that of the sixty-seven days of our sailing we had forty-four of constant rain, thunder and lightning so dark that never did we see sun by day or fair sky by night. By reason of this such fear invaded us that we soon abandoned almost all hope of life. But during these tempests of sea and sky, so numerous and so violent, the Most High was pleased to display before us a continent, new lands, and an unknown world. At sight of these things we were filled with as much joy as anyone can imagine usually falls to the lot of those who have gained refuge from varied calamity and hostile fortune. It was on the seventh day of August, one thousand five hundred and one that we anchored off the shores of those parts, thanking our God with formal ceremonial and with the celebration of a choral mass. We knew that land to be a continent and not an island both because it stretches forth in the form of a very long and unbending coast, and because it is replete with infinite inhabitants. For in it we found innumerable tribes and peoples and species of all manner of wild beasts which are found in our lands and many others never seen by us concerning which it would take long to tell in detail. God's mercy shone upon us much when we landed at that spot, for there had come a shortage of fire-wood and water, and in a few days we might have ended our lives at sea. To Him be honor, glory, and thanksgiving.

We adopted the plan of following the coast of this continent toward the east and never losing sight of it. We sailed along until at length we reached a bend where the shore made a turn to the south; and from that point where we first touched land to that corner it was about three hundred leagues, in which sailing distance we frequently landed and had friendly relations with those people, as you will hear below. I had forgotten to write you that from the promontory of Cape Verde to the nearest part of that continent is about seven hundred leagues, although I should estimate that we sailed more than eighteen hundred, partly through ignorance of the route and the ship-master's want of knowledge, partly owing to tempests and winds which kept us from the proper course and compelled us to put about frequently. Because, if my companions had not heeded me, who had knowledge of cosmography, there would have been no ship-master, nay not the leader of our expedition himself, who would have known where we were within five hundred leagues. For we were wandering and uncertain in our course, and only the instruments for taking the altitudes of the heavenly bodies showed us our true course precisely; and these were the quadrant and the astrolabe, which all men have come to know. For this reason they subsequently made me the object of great honor; for I showed them that though a man without practical experience, yet through the teaching of the marine chart for navigators I was more skilled than all the shipmasters of the whole world. For these have no knowledge except of those waters to which they have often sailed. Now, where the said corner of land showed us a southern trend of the coast we agreed to sail beyond it and inquire what there might be in those parts. So we sailed along the coast about six hundred leagues, and often landed and mingled and associated with the natives of those regions, and by them we were received in brotherly fashion; and we would dwell with them too, for fifteen or twenty days continuously, maintaining amicable and hospitable relations, as you shall learn below. Part of this new continent lies in the torrid zone beyond the equator toward the Antarctic pole, for it begins eight degrees beyond the equator. We sailed along this coast until we passed the tropic of Capricorn and found the Antarctic pole fifty degrees higher than that horizon. We advanced to within seventeen and a half degrees of the Antarctic circle, and what I there have seen and learned concerning the nature of those races, their manners, their tractability and the fertility of the soil, the salubrity of the climate, the position of the heavenly bodies in the sky, and especially concerning the fixed stars of the eighth sphere, never seen or studied by our ancestors, these things I shall relate in order.

First then as to the people. We found in those parts such a multitude of people as nobody could enumerate (as we read in the Apocalypse), a race I say gentle and amenable. All of both sexes go about naked, covering no part of their bodies; and just as they spring from their mothers' wombs so they go until death. They have indeed large square-built bodies, well formed and proportioned, and in color verging upon reddish. This I think has come to them, because, going about naked, they are colored by the sun. They have, too, hair plentiful and black. In their gait and when playing their games they are agile and dignified. They are comely, too, of countenance which they nevertheless themselves destroy; for they bore their cheeks, lips, noses and ears. Nor think those holes small or that they have one only. For some I have seen having in a single face seven borings any one of which was capable of holding a plum. They stop up these holes of theirs with blue stones, bits of marble, very beautiful crystals of alabaster, very white bones, and other things artificially prepared according to their customs. But if you could see a thing so unwonted and monstrous, that is to say a man having in his cheeks and lips alone seven stones some of which are a span and a half in length, you would not be without wonder. For I frequently observed and discovered that seven such stones weighed sixteen ounces, aside from the fact that in their ears, each perforated with three holes, they have other stones dangling on rings; and this usage applies to the men alone. For women do not bore their faces, but their ears only. They have another custom, very shameful and beyond all human belief. For their women, being very lustful, cause the private parts of their husbands to swell up to such a huge size that they appear deformed and disgusting; and this is accomplished by a certain device of theirs, the biting of certain poisonous animals. And in consequence of this many lose their organs which break through lack of attention, and they remain eunuchs. They have no cloth either of wool, linen or cotton, since they need it not; neither do they have goods of their own, but all things are held in common. They live together without king, without government, and each is his own master. They marry as many wives as they please; and son cohabits with mother, brother with sister, male cousin with female, and any man with the first woman he meets. They dissolve their marriages as often as they please, and observe no sort of law with respect to them. Beyond the fact that they have no church, no religion and are not idolaters, what more can I say? They live according to nature, and may be called Epicureans rather than Stoics. There are no merchants among their number, nor is there barter. The nations wage war upon one another without art or order. The elders by means of certain harangues of theirs bend the youths to their will and inflame them to wars in which they cruelly kill one another, and those whom they bring home captives from war they preserve, not to spare their lives, but that they may be slain for food; for they eat one another, the victors the vanquished, and among other kinds of meat human flesh is a common article of diet with them. Nay be the more assured of this fact because the father has already been seen to eat children and wife, and I knew a man whom I also spoke to who was reputed to have eaten more than three hundred human bodies. And I likewise remained twenty-seven days in a certain city where I saw salted human flesh suspended from beams between the houses, just as with us it is the custom to hang bacon and pork. I say further: they themselves wonder why we do not eat our enemies and do not use as food their flesh which they say is most savory. Their weapons are bows and arrows, and when they advance to war they cover no part of their bodies for the sake of protection, so like beasts are they in this matter. We endeavored to the extent of our power to dissuade them and persuade them to desist from these depraved customs, and they did promise us that they would leave off. The women as I have said go about naked and are very libidinous; yet they have bodies which are tolerably beautiful and cleanly. Nor are they so unsightly as one perchance might imagine; for, inasmuch as they are plump, their ugliness is the less apparent, which indeed is for the most part concealed by the excellence of their bodily structure. It was to us a matter of astonishment that none was to be seen among them who had a flabby breast, and those who had borne children were not to be distinguished from virgins by the shape and shrinking of the womb; and in the other parts of the body similar things were seen of which in the interest of modesty I make no mention. When they had the opportunity of copulating with Christians, urged by excessive lust, they defiled and prostituted themselves. They live one hundred and fifty years, and rarely fall ill, and if they do fall victims to any disease, they cure themselves with certain roots and herbs. These are the most noteworthy things I know about them. The climate there was very temperate and good, and as I was able to learn from their accounts, there was never there any pest or epidemic caused by corruption of the air; and unless they die a violent death they live long. This I take to be because the south winds are ever blowing there, and especially that which we call Eurus, which is the same to them as the Aquilo is to us. They are zealous in the art of fishing, and that sea is replete and abounding in every kind of fish. They are not hunters. This I deem to be because there are there many sorts of wild animals, and especially lions and bears and innumerable serpents and other horrid and ugly beasts, and also because forests and trees of huge size there extend far and wide; and they dare not, naked and without covering and arms, expose themselves to such hazards.

The land in those parts is very fertile and pleasing, abounding in numerous hills and mountains, boundless valleys and mighty rivers, watered by refreshing springs, and filled with broad, dense and wellnigh impenetrable forests full of every sort of wild animal. Trees grow to immense size without cultivation. Many of these yield fruits delectable to the taste and beneficial to the human body; some indeed do not, and no fruits there are like those of ours. Innumerable species of herbs and roots grow there too, of which they

222 Travel Narratives from the Age of Discovery

make bread and excellent food. They have, too, many seeds altogether unlike these of ours. They have there no metals of any description except gold, of which those regions have a great plenty, although to be sure we have brought none thence on this our first voyage. This the natives called to our attention, who averred that in the districts remote from the coast there is a great abundance of gold, and by them it is in no respect esteemed or valued. They are rich in pearls as I wrote you before. If I were to seek to recount in detail what things are there and to write concerning the numerous species of animals and the great number of them, it would be a matter all too prolix and vast. And I truly believe that our Pliny did not touch upon a thousandth part of the species of parrots and other birds and the animals, too, which exist in those same regions so diverse as to form and color; because Policletus, the master of painting in all its perfection would have fallen short in depicting them. There all trees are fragrant and they emit each and all gum, oil, or some sort of sap. If the properties of these were known to us, I doubt not but that they would be salutary to the human body. And surely if the terrestrial paradise be in any part of this earth, I esteem that it is not far distant from those parts. Its situation, as I have related, lies toward the south in such a temperate climate that icy winters and fiery summers alike are never there experienced.

The sky and atmosphere are serene during the greater part of the year, and devoid of thick vapors the rains there fall finely, last three or four hours, and vanish like a mist. The sky is adorned with most beautiful constellations and forms among which I noted about twenty stars as bright as we ever saw Venus or Jupiter. I have considered the movements and orbits of these, I have measured their circumferences and diameters by geometric method, and I ascertained that they are of greater magnitude. I saw in that sky three Canopi, two indeed bright, the third dim. The Antarctic pole is not figured with a Great and a Little Bear as this Arctic pole of ours is seen to be, nor is any bright star to be seen near it, and of those which move around it with the shortest circuit there are three which have the form of an orthogonous triangle, the half circumference, the diameter, has nine and a half degrees. . . .

I observed many other very beautiful stars, the movements of which I have diligently noted down and have described beautifully with diagrams in a certain little book of mine treating of this my voyage. But at present this Most Serene King has it, which I hope he will restore to me. In that hemisphere I saw things incompatible with the opinions of philosophers. A white rainbow was twice seen about midnight, not only by me but by all the sailors. Likewise we have frequently seen the new moon on that day when it was in conjunction with the sun. Every night in that part of the sky innumerable vapors and glowing meteors fly about. I said a little while ago respecting that hemisphere that it really cannot properly be spoken of as a complete hemisphere comparing it to ours, yet since it approaches such a form, such may we be permitted to call it. . . .

These have been the more noteworthy things which I have seen in this my last voyage which I call my third chapter. For two other chapters consisted of two other voyages which I made to the west by command of the most Serene King of Spain, during which I noted down the marvelous works wrought by that sublime creator of all things, our God. I kept a diary of noteworthy things that if sometime I am granted leisure I may bring together these singular and wonderful things and write a book of geography or cosmography, that my memory may live with posterity and that the immense work of almighty God, partly unknown to the ancients, but known to us, may be understood. Accordingly I pray the most merciful God to prolong the days of my life that with His good favor and the salvation of my soul I may carry out in the best possible manner this my will. The accounts of the other two journeys I am preserving in my cabinet and when this Most Serene King restores to me the third, I shall endeavor to regain my country and repose. There I shall be able to consult with experts and to receive from friends the aid and comfort necessary for the completion of this work.

Of you I crave pardon for not having transmitted to you this my last voyage, or rather my last chapter, as I had promised you in my last letter. You have learned the reason when I tell you that I have not yet obtained the principal version from this Most Serene King. I am still privately considering the making of a fourth journey, and of this I am treating; and already I have been promised two ships with their equipment, that I may apply myself to the discovery of new regions to the south along the eastern side following the wind-route called Africus. In which journey I think to perform many things to the glory of God, the advantage of this kingdom, and the honor of my old age; and I await nothing but the consent of this Most Serene King. God grant what is for the best. You shall learn what comes of it.

Jocundus, the translator, is turning this epistle from the Italian into the Latin tongue, that Latinists may know how many wonderful things are daily being discovered, and that the audacity of those who seek to scrutinize heaven and sovereignty and to know more than it is licit to know may be held in check. Inasmuch as ever since that remote time when the world began the vastness of the earth and what therein is contained has been unknown.

Document 17

Letters from Mexico

By Hernán Cortés, *Letters from Mexico,* trans. Anthony Pagden
(New Haven, Conn.: Yale University Press, 1916), 102–12

Hernán (Hernando) Cortés (1485–1547) arrived in Mexico on April 22, 1519. By 1521, he had taken control of the Aztec capital of Tenochtitlán (modern-day Mexico City), and his soldiers, their horses, and the diseases that they had unwittingly brought with them had undermined the stability of the Aztec empire, which was then one of the two most powerful polities in the Americas. Indigenous chroniclers described how the Spanish defeated the Aztecs. At one point in the assault, the conquerors came into one temple during a sacred dance and closed the gates behind them. "They ran in among the dancers, forcing their way to the place where the drums were played," one native observer reported. "They attacked the man who was drumming and cut off his arms. Then they cut off his head, and it rolled across the floor." The soldiers proceeded to murder others too, decapitating some and disemboweling others. "The blood of the warriors flowed like water and gathered into pools," the witness recalled. "The pools widened, and the stench of blood and entrails filled the air."[3] Even the Spanish missionary Bartolomé de Las Casas was appalled at what he learned about the conquest of Mexico, including the "barbaric and unprecedented outrage, perpetrated against innocent individuals who had done nothing whatever to deserve such cruelty." Across the mainland he discovered a mirror of the grotesque atrocities he had witnessed in the Caribbean islands.[4]

In the aftermath of Cortés's victory over the Aztecs, Spanish chroniclers offered detailed accounts about what could be found in Mexico and in South America. Among them was Cortés himself, who needed to establish the legitimacy of his venture for the Spanish court. This was no easy task since Cortés had disobeyed orders, and his own superiors believed that his entire enterprise in Mexico was illegitimate. Knowing the stakes were high, Cortés wrote a series of letters that put his achievements in a favorable light. His

3. Miguel Leon-Portilla, ed., *The Broken Spears: The Aztec Account of the Conquest of Mexico* (Boston: Beacon, 1962), 74–76.
4. Bartolomé De Las Casas, *A Short Account of the Destruction of the Indies*, trans. Nigel Griffin (London: Penguin, 1992), esp. 45–56, quotation at 51.

*political agenda influenced his portrayal of what happened, but it also bore
the mark, as the historian J. H. Elliott aptly put it, of Cortés's "masterly capacity for suppression of evidence and ingenious distortion."[5] Yet however
deceptive they may have been, Cortés's letters became an immediate publishing phenomenon. His* Carta de relacion, *the first printed account of his
exploits, appeared in 1522 in a Spanish edition printed in Seville, a French
version printed in Antwerp, and an Italian edition produced in Milan. In
the next few years it appeared time and again, issued by publishers in Sara-
gossa, Nuremberg, Toledo, Valencia, and Cologne within ten years of its first
printing. But then printers mostly lost interest, and only a few offered it or
included it in collections after 1532.*

*The excerpt here provides a description of Temixtitan (Tenochtitlán). Cortés
described the city in some depth, marveling at some of its architecture and
the Aztecs' practice of keeping fish, birds, and even wild animals for their
entertainment. But it is not a description of a city alone: it is also a portrait
of a leader, Mutezuma (also written as Moctezuma or Montezuma) and his
relations with his people. Cortés periodically compared what he saw to what
he knew about Spain and its cities, often noting that the American city was
even more impressive than anything he had seen in his own society.*

This city of Temixtitan is built on the salt lake, and no matter by what
road you travel there are two leagues from the main body of the city to the
mainland. There are four artificial causeways leading to it, and each is as
wide as two cavalry lances. The city itself is as big as Seville or Córdoba. The
main streets are very wide and very straight; some of these are on the land,
but the rest and all the smaller ones are half on land, half canals where they
paddle their canoes. All the streets have openings in places so that the water
may pass from one canal to another. Over all these openings, and some of
them are very wide, there are bridges made of long and wide beams joined
together very firmly and so well made that on some of them ten horsemen
may ride abreast.

Seeing that if the inhabitants of this city wished to betray us they were
very well equipped for it by the design of the city, for once the bridges had

5. J. H. Elliott, "Cortés, Velázquez, and Charles V," in *Hernan Cortes: Letters from Mexico,*
trans. Anthony Pagden (New Haven, Conn.: Yale University Press, 1986), xx.

been removed they could starve us to death without our being able to reach the mainland, as soon as I entered the city I made great haste to build four brigantines, and completed them in a very short time. They were such as could carry three hundred men to the land and transport the horses whenever we might need them.

This city has many squares where trading is done and markets are held continuously. There is also one square twice as big as that of Salamanca, with arcades all around, where more than sixty thousand people come each day to buy and sell, and where every kind of merchandise produced in these lands is found; provisions as well as ornaments of gold and silver, lead, brass, copper, tin, stones, shells, bones, and feathers. They also sell lime, hewn and unhewn stone, adobe bricks, tiles, and cut and uncut woods of various kinds. There is a street where they sell game and birds of every species found in this land: chickens, partridges, cane birds, parrots, eagles and eagle fowls, falcons, sparrow hawks and kestrels, and they sell the skins of some of these birds of prey with their feathers, heads and claws. They sell rabbits and hares, and stags and small gelded dogs which they breed for eating.

There are streets of herbalists where all the medicinal herbs and roots found in the land are sold. There are shops like apothecaries', where they sell ready-made medicines as well as liquid ointments and plasters. There are shops like barbers' where they have their hair washed and shaved, and shops where they sell food and drink. There are also men like porters to carry loads. There is much firewood and charcoal, earthenware braziers and mats of various kinds like mattresses for beds, and other, finer ones, for seats and for covering rooms and hallways. There is every sort of vegetable, especially onions, leeks, garlic, common cress and watercress, borage, sorrel, teasels and artichokes; and there are many sorts of fruit, among which are cherries and plums like those in Spain.

They sell honey, wax, and a syrup made from maize canes, which is as sweet and syrupy as that made from sugar cane. They also make syrup from a plant which in the islands is called *maguey*, which is much better than most syrups, and from this plant they also make sugar and wine, which they likewise sell. There are many sorts of spun cotton, in hanks of every color, and it seems like the silk market at Granada, except here there is a much greater quantity. They sell as many colors for painters as may be found in Spain and all of excellent hues. They sell deerskins, with and without the hair, and some are dyed white or in various colors. They sell both large and small pitchers, jugs, pots, tiles, and many other sorts of vessel, all of good clay and most of them glazed and painted. They sell maize both as grain and as bread and it is better both in appearance and in taste than any found in the islands or on the mainland. They sell chicken and fish pies, and much fresh and salted fish, as well as raw and cooked fish. They sell hen and goose eggs, and eggs of all the other birds I have mentioned, in great number, and they sell *tortillas* made from eggs.

Finally, besides those things which I have already mentioned, they sell in the market everything else to be found in this land, but they are so many and so varied that because of their great number and because I cannot remember many of them nor do I know what they are called I shall not mention them. Each kind of merchandise is sold in its own street without any mixture whatever; they are very particular in this. Everything is sold by number and size, and until now I have seen nothing sold by weight. There is in this great square a very large building like a courthouse, where ten or twelve persons sit as judges. They preside over all that happens in the markets, and sentence criminals. There are in this square other persons who walk among the people to see what they are selling and the measures they are using; and they have been seen to break some that were false.

There are, in all districts of this great city, many temples or houses for their idols. They are all very beautiful buildings, and in the important ones there are priests of their sect who live there permanently; and, in addition to the houses for the idols, they also have very good lodgings. All these priests dress in black and never comb their hair from the time they enter the priesthood until they leave; and all the sons of the persons of high rank, both the lords and honored citizens also, enter the priesthood and wear the habit from the age of seven or eight years until they are taken away to be married; this occurs more among the first-born sons, who are to inherit, than among the others. They abstain from eating things, and more at some times of the year than at others; and no woman is granted entry nor permitted inside these places of worship.

Amongst these temples there is one, the principal one, whose great size and magnificence no human tongue could describe, for it is so large that within the precincts, which are surrounded by a very high wall, a town of some five hundred inhabitants could easily be built. All round inside this wall there are very elegant quarters with very large rooms and corridors where their priests live. There are as many as forty towers, all of which are so high that in the case of the largest there are fifty steps leading to the main part of it; and the most important of these towers is higher than that of the cathedral of Seville. They are so well constructed in both their stone and woodwork that there can be none better in any place, for all the stonework inside the chapels where they keep their idols is in high relief, with figures and little houses, and the woodwork is likewise of relief and painted with monsters and other figures and designs. All these towers are burial places of chiefs, and the chapels therein are each dedicated to the idol which he venerated.

There are three rooms within this great temple for the principal idols, which are of remarkable size and stature and decorated with many designs and sculptures, both in stone and in wood. Within these rooms are other chapels, and the doors to them are very small. Inside there is no light whatsoever; there are only some of the priests may enter, for inside are the sculptured figures of the idols, although, as I have said, there are also many outside.

The most important of these idols, and the ones in whom they have the most faith, I had taken from their places and thrown down the steps; and I had those chapels where they were cleaned, for they were full of the blood of sacrifices; and I had images of Our Lady and of other saints put there, which caused Mutezuma and the other natives some sorrow. First they asked me not to do it, for when the communities learnt of it they would rise against me, for they believed that those idols gave them all their worldly goods, and that if they were allowed to be ill treated, they would become angry and give them nothing and take the fruit from the earth leaving the people to die of hunger. I made them understand through the interpreters how deceived they were in placing their trust in these idols which they had made with their hands from unclean things. They must know that there was only one God, Lord of all things, who had created heaven and earth and all else and who made all of us; and He was without beginning or end, and they must adore and worship only Him, not any other creature things. And I told them all I knew about this to dissuade them from their idolatry and bring them to the knowledge of God our Saviour. All of them, especially Mutezuma, replied that they had already told me how they were not natives of this land, and that as it was many years since their forefathers had come here, they well knew that they might have erred somewhat in what they believed, for they had left their native land so long ago; and as I had only recently arrived from there, I would better know the things they should believe, and should explain to them and make them understand, for they would do as I said was best. Mutezuma and many of the chieftains of the city were with me until the idols were removed, the chapel cleaned and the images set up, and I urged them not to sacrifice living creatures to the idols, as they were accustomed, for, as well as being most abhorrent to God, Your Sacred Majesty's laws forbade it and ordered that he who kills shall be killed. And from then on they ceased to do it, and in all the time I stayed in that city I did not see a living creature killed or sacrificed.

The figures of the idols in which these people believe are very much larger than the body of a big man. They are made of dough from all the seeds and vegetables which they eat, ground and mixed together, and bound with the blood of human hearts which those priests tear out while still beating. And also after they are made they offer them more hearts and anoint their faces with the blood. Everything has an idol dedicated to it, in the same manner as the pagans who in antiquity honored their gods. So they have an idol whose favor they ask in war and another for agriculture; and likewise for each thing they wish to be done well they have an idol which they honor and serve.

There are in the city many large and beautiful houses, and the reason for this is that all the chiefs of the land, who are Mutezuma's vassals, have houses in the city and live there for part of the year; and in addition there are many rich citizens who likewise have very good houses. All these houses have very large and very good rooms and also very pleasant gardens of various sorts of flowers both on the upper and lower floors.

Along one of the causeways to this great city run two aqueducts made of mortar. Each one is two paces wide and some six feet deep, and along one of them a stream of very good fresh water, as wide as a man's body, flows into the heart of the city and from this they all drink. The other, which is empty, is used when they wish to clean the first channel. When the aqueducts cross the bridges, the water passes along some channels which are as wide as an ox; and so they serve the whole city.

Canoes paddle through all the streets selling the water; they take it from the aqueduct by placing the canoes beneath the bridges where those channels are, and on top there are men who fill the canoes and are paid for their work. At all the gateways to the city and at the places where these canoes are unloaded, which is where the greater part of the provisions enter the city, there are guards in huts who receive a *certum quid* of all that enters. I have not yet discovered whether this goes to the chief or to the city, but I think to the chief, because in other markets in other parts I have seen this tax paid to the ruler of the place. Every day, in all the markets and public places there are many workmen and craftsmen of every sort, waiting to be employed by the day. The people of this city are dressed with more elegance and are more courtly in their bearing than those of the other cities and provinces, and because Mutezuma and all those chieftains, his vassals, are always coming to the city, the people have more manners and politeness in all matters. Yet so as not to tire Your Highness with the description of the things of this city (although I would not complete it so briefly), I will say only that these people live almost like those in Spain, and in as much harmony and order as there, and considering that they are barbarous and so far from the knowledge of God and cut off form all civilized nations, it is truly remarkable to see what they have achieved in all things.

Touching Mutezuma's service and all that was remarkable in his magnificence and power, there is so much to describe that I do not know how to begin even to recount some part of it; for, as I have already said, can there be anything more magnificent than that this barbarian lord should have all the things to be found under the heavens in this domain, fashioned in gold and silver and jewels and feathers; and so realistic in gold and silver that no smith in the world could have done better, and in jewels so fine that it is impossible to imagine with what instruments they were cut so perfectly; and those in feathers more wonderful than anything in wax or embroidery.

I have not yet been able to discover the extent of the domain of Mutezuma, but in the two hundred leagues which his messengers traveled to the north and to the south of this city his orders were obeyed, although there were some provinces in the middle of these lands which were at war with him. But from what I have discovered, and what he has told me, I imagine that his kingdom is almost as big as Spain, for he sent messengers from the region of Putunchan, which is the Grijalba River, seventy leagues to a city which is called Cumantan commanding the inhabitants thereof to offer themselves as vassals to Your Majesty, and that city is 230 leagues from the capital; the remaining 150 leagues have been explored by Spaniards on my orders. The greater part of the chiefs of these lands and provinces, especially those from close by, resided, as I have said, for most of the year in this capital city, and all or most of their eldest sons were in the service of Mutezuma. In all these domains he had fortresses garrisoned with his own people, and governors and officials to collect the tributes which each province must pay; and they kept an account of whatever each one was obliged to give in characters and drawings on paper which they make, which is their writing. Each of these provinces paid appropriate tributes in accordance with the nature of the land; thus Mutezuma received every sort of produce from those provinces, and he was so feared by all, both present and absent, that there could be no ruler in the world more so.

He had, both inside the city and outside, many private residences, each one for a particular pastime, and as well made as I can describe—as is befitting so great a ruler. The palace inside the city in which he lived was so marvelous that it seems to me impossible to describe its excellence and grandeur. Therefore, I shall not attempt to describe it at all, save to say that in Spain there is nothing to compare with it.

He also had another house, only a little less magnificent than this, where there was a very beautiful garden with balconies over it; and the facings and flagstones were all of jasper and very well made. In this house there were rooms enough for two great princes with all their household. There were also ten pools in which were kept all the many and varied kinds of water bird found in these parts, all of them domesticated. For the sea birds there were pools of salt water, and for river fowl of fresh water, which was emptied from time to time for cleaning and filled again from the aqueducts. Each species of bird was fed with the food which it eats when wild, so that those which eat fish were given fish, and those which eat worms, worms, and those which eat maize or smaller grain were likewise given those things. And I assure Your Highness that the birds which eat only fish were given 250 pounds each day, which were taken from the salt lake. There were three hundred men in charge of these birds who knew no other trade, as there were others who were skilled only in healing sick birds. Above these pools were corridors and balconies, all very finely made, where Mutezuma came to amuse himself by watching them. There was also in this house a room in which were kept men, women and children who had, from birth, white faces and bodies and white hair, eyebrows and eyelashes.

He had another very beautiful house, with a large patio, laid with pretty tiles in the manner of a chessboard. There were rooms nine feet high and as large as six paces square. The roofs of each of these houses are half covered with tiles while the other half is covered by well-made latticework. In each of these rooms there was kept a bird of prey of every sort that is found in Spain, from the kestrel to the eagle, and many others which have never been seen there. There were large numbers of each of these birds, and in the covered part of each of the rooms was a stick like a perch, and another outside beneath the latticework, and they were on one during the night or when it rained and on the other during the day when the sun was out. All these birds were given chickens to eat each day and no other food. In this house there were several large low rooms filled with big cages, made from heavy timbers and very well joined. In all, or in most of them, were large numbers of lions, tigers, wolves, foxes and cats of various kinds which were given as many chickens to eat as they needed. Another three hundred men looked after these birds and animals. There was yet another house where lived many deformed men and women, among which were dwarfs and hunchbacks and others with other deformities; and each manner of monstrosity had a room to itself; and likewise there were people to look after them. I shall not mention the other entertainments which he has in this city, for they are very many and of many different kinds.

He was served in this manner: Each day at dawn there arrived at his house six hundred chiefs and principal persons, some of whom sat down while others wandered about the rooms and corridors of the house; there they passed the time talking but without ever entering his presence. The servants of these persons and those who accompanied them filled two or three large courtyards and the street, which was very big. And they remained all day until nightfall. When they brought food to Mutezuma they also provided for all those chiefs each according to his rank; and their servants and followers were also given to eat. The pantry and the wine stores were left open each day for those who wished to eat and drink. Three or four hundred boys came bringing the dishes, which were without number, for each time he lunched or dined, he was brought a brazier with hot coals so that the food should not go cold. They placed all these dishes together in a great room where he ate, which was almost always full. The floors were well covered and clean and he sat on a finely made, small leather cushion. While he ate, there were five or six old men, who sat apart from him; and to them he gave a portion of all he was eating. One of the servants set down and removed the plates of food and called to others who were farther away for all that was required. Before and after the meal they gave him water for his hands and a towel which once used was never used again, and likewise with the plates and bowls, for when they brought more food they always used new ones, and the same with the braziers.

He dressed each day in four different garments and never dressed again in the same ones. All the chiefs who entered his house went barefoot, and those he called before him came with their heads bowed and their bodies in a humble posture, and when they spoke to him they did not look him in the face; this was because they held him in great respect and reverence. I know that they did it for this reason because certain of those chiefs reproved the Spaniards, saying that when they spoke to me they did so openly without hiding their faces, which seemed to them disrespectful and lacking in modesty.

When Mutezuma left the palace, which was not often, all those who went with him and those whom he met in the streets turned away their faces so that in no manner should they look on him; and all the others prostrated themselves until he had passed. One of those chiefs always walked before him carrying three long thin rods, which I think was done so that all should know he was coming. When he descended from the litter he took one of these in his hand and carried it to wherever he was going. The forms and ceremonies with which this lord was attended are so many and so varied that I would need more space than that which I have at present to recount them, and a better memory with which to recall them, for I do not think that the sultans nor any of the infidel lords of whom we have heard until now are attended with such ceremony.

Document 18

A Short and Briefe Narration of the Two Navigations and Discourses (1580)

By Jacques Cartier, trans. John Florio (London, 1580), 56–60, 64–66

In the generation following the Iberian conquest of the West Indies and much of Central and South America, other Europeans set their sights on the Americas. Among them was Jacques Cartier (1491–1557), a ship captain from the town of St. Malo, France. From 1534 to 1540, Cartier led three expeditions to territory in modern-day Canada. Though the French themselves never proved to be particularly avid colonizers—even poor men and women usually refused to take a chance on a journey across the Atlantic—his account provided details about what the indigenous peoples of Canada were like. And it was Cartier who gave to the French a vision of Canada that made its way quickly into one of the classic texts of the sixteenth century: L'Heptameron by Marguérite d'Angoulême, queen of Navarre, first published in Paris in 1558.

The account here is from Cartier's second "relation" of 1536, which was first published in Paris in 1545. (The journal of Cartier's first expedition of 1534 was not published for thirty-one years.) The second relation is considerably longer than the first, and it is richer too than the alleged report of his third version, which appeared only in English when Hakluyt included it in his col-

lection of 1600 (along with editions of the first two relations). So the account of the journey of 1534 was both the first published and the most detailed of the three extant reports. It was also the best known in the sixteenth century, since it appeared not only in French but also in Italian when the brilliant Venetian geographer Giovanni Battista Ramusio, who was also a business partner of Gonzalo Fernández de Oviedo y Valdés, included a translation in the third volume of his Navigationi et Viaggi, *published in Venice in 1556. Almost twenty-five years later, that volume of Italian-language accounts fell into the hands of Hakluyt, who was then living in Oxford and in the process of becoming one of Europe's most learned geographical authorities of the age. Hakluyt lent the book to an Italian linguist named John Florio, who was also living in Oxford, who made a translation of it.*

The selection here provides details about Cartier's visit to Stadacona and his interactions with the St. Lawrence Iroquois living there. The first part concentrates on the settlement itself and what he saw there. His concerns reflected those of many European travelers to the Americas. He condemned their religious practices, their apparent licentiousness and loose sexual values, and the laziness of the men. He was not the only observer to fall into the trap of being unable to recognize the well-developed spiritual cosmos that these natives inhabited. Nor was he alone in his assumptions about gender practices and patterns common in many American societies. The second part contains Cartier's writings on a dual epidemic: an unknown illness afflicting the natives and scurvy among the French. Since the ailment had arisen first among the Indians, Cartier—who believed there was only one epidemic in the region at the time—assumed that they passed it on to the visitors. But he was wrong. While his description of the epidemic in Stadacona does not provide sufficient detail for a modern diagnosis, his detailed account of what happened to the French—including the results of an autopsy on a young sailor—has allowed for positive identification of a nutritional deficiency long known to Europeans but which Native Americans rarely suffered.[6]

---

6. For publication details, the identification of scurvy, and other points of clarification, see Ramsay Cook, ed., *The Voyages of Jacques Cartier* (Toronto: University of Toronto Press, 1993).

How we came to the Port of the Holy Crosse, and in what state we found our ships: and how the Lord of the Country came to visit our Captain, and our Captain him: and of certain particular customs of the people

Upon Monday being the eleventh of October we came to the Port of the Holy Cross, where our ships were, & found that the masters and Mariners we had left there, had made and reared a Trench before the ships, altogether closed with great pieces of Timber set upright and very well fastened together: then had they beset the said trench about with pieces of Artillery and other necessary things to shield and defend themselves from the power of all the Country. So soon as the Lord of the Country [Donnacona] heard of our coming, the next day being the twelfth of October, he came to visit us, accompanied with Taignoagny, Domagaia, and many others, faining to be very glad of our coming, making much of our Captain, who as friendly as he could, entertained them, albeit they had not deserved it. Donnacona their Lord desired our Captain the next day to come and see *Canada*, which he promised to do: for the next day being the thirteenth of the month, he with all his gentlemen, and fifty Mariners very well appointed, went to visit Donnacona and his people, about a league from our ships. The place where they make their abode, is called *Stadagona*. When we were about a stone's cast from their houses, many of the inhibitors [inhabitants] came to meet us, being all set in a rank, and (as their custom is) the men all on one side, and the women on the other, still dancing & singing without any ceasing: and after we had saluted and received one another, our Captain gave them knives and such other slight things: then he caused all the women and children to pass along before him, giving each one a ring of Tin, for which they gave him hearty thanks: that done, our Captain was by Donnacona and Taignoagny, brought to their houses (the qualities considered) were very well provided, and stored with such victuals as the Country yeeldeth, to pass away the Winter withal. Then they showed us the skins of five men's heads spread upon boards as we do use parchment, Donnacona told us that they were skins of *Toudamani*, a people dwelling toward the South, who continually do war against them. Moreover they told us, that it was two years past that those *Toudamans* came to assault them, yea even into the said river, in an Island that lyeth over against *Saguenay*, where they had been the night before, as they were going a warfaring in *Honguedo*, with two hundred persons, men, women, and children, who being all asleep in a fort that they had made, they were assaulted by the said *Toudamans*, who put fire round about the fort, and as they would have come out of it to save themselves, they were all slain, only five excepted, who escaped. For which loss they yet sorrowed, showing with signs, that one day they would be revenged: that done, we came to our ships again.

The manner how the people of that Country live: and of certain conditions: of their Faith, manners, and customs.

This people believe no whit in God, but in one whom they call Cudruaigni: they say that often he speaketh with them and telleth them what weather shall follow, whether good or bad. Moreover they say, that when he is angry with them he casteth dust into their eyes: they believe that when they die they go into the Stars, and thence by little and little descend down into the *Horizon*, even as the Stars do, and ye then they go into certain green fields full of goodly fair & precious trees, flowers, and fruits. After that they had given us these things to understand, we showed them their error, and told that their Cudruaigni did but deceive them for he is but a Devil and an evil spirit: affirming unto them, that there is but one only God, who is in Heaven, and who giveth us all necessaries, being the creator of all himself, and that only we must believe in him: moreover, that it is necessary for us to be baptized, otherwise we are damned into Hell. This and many other things concerning our faith and religion we showed them, all which they did easily believe, calling their Cudruaigni, Agouiada: so that very earnestly they desired and prayed our Captain that he would cause them to be baptized, and their Lord, Taignoagny, Domagaia, and all the people of the town came unto us, hoping to be baptized: but because we did not thoroughly know their mind, and that there was no body could give them our belief and religion to understand, we excused our selves, desiring Taignoagny and Domagaia to tell the rest of their Countrymen, that we would come again another time, and bring Ministers and Priests with us, for without them they could not be baptized: which they did easily believe: for Domagaia and Taignoagny had seen many children baptized in Brytain [Brittany] while they were there. Which promise when they heard, they seemed to be very glad. They live in common together, and of such commodities as their Country yeeldeth they are indifferently well stored, the inhabitours [inhabitants] of the Town of [blank in book] Clothe themselves with the skins of certain wild beasts, but very miserably. In Winter they wear hosen and shoes made of wild beasts' skins, and in Summer they go barefooted. They keep and observe the rites of matrimony, saving that every one weddeth two or three wives, which (their husbands being dead) do never marry again, but for the death of their husbands wear a certain black weed all the days of their life, besmearing all their faces with coal dust and grease mingled together almost half a quarter of an inch thick, and by that they are known to be Widows. They have a filthy and detestable use in marrying of their maidens, and that is this, they put them all (after they are of lawful age to marry) in a common place, as harlots free for every man that will have to do with them, until such time as they find a match. This I say, because I have seen by experience many houses full of those Damsels, even as our schools are full of children in *France* to learn to read. Moreover, the misrule and riot that they keep in those houses is very great, for very wantonly they sport and dally together, showing whatsoever God hath sent them. They are no men of great labor. They plough their grounds with certain pieces of wood, as big as half a sword, on which ground growth their corn. The call if *Offici*: it is as big as our small Peason: there is great quantity of it growing in *Brazil*. They have also great store of musk Milions [Melons], Pompions [Pumpkins], Gourds, Cucumbers, Peason [peas], and Beans of every color, yet differing from ours. There groweth also a certain kind of Herb, whereof in Summer they make great provision for all the year, making great account of it, and only men use of it, and first they cause it to be dried in the Sun, then wear it about their neck wrapped in a little beast's skin made like a little bag, with a hollow piece of stone or wood like a pipe: then when they please they make powder of it, and then put it in one of the ends of the said Cornet or pipe, and laying a coal of fire upon it, at the other end suck so long, that they fill their bodies full of smoke, till that it commeth out of their mouth and nostrils, even as out of the Tunnel of a Chimney. They say that this doth keep them warm and in health: they never go without some of it about them. We ourselves have tried the same smoke, and having put it in our mouths, it seemed that they had filled it with Pepper dust, it is so hot. The women of that Country do labor much more than the men, as well in fishing, (whereto they are greatly given) as in tilling and husbanding their grounds, and other things: as well the men as women, and children, are very much more able to resist cold, than savage beasts, for we with our own eyes have seen some of them, when it was coldest, (which cold was extreme raw, and bitter) come to our ships stark naked going upon Snow and Ice, which thing seemeth incredible to them that have not seen it. When as the Snow and Ice lyeth on the ground, they take great store of wild beasts, as Fawns, Stags, Bears, Martens, Hares, and Foxes, with diverse other sorts, whose flesh they eat raw, having first dried it in the Sun or smoke, and so they do their fish. As far forth as we could perceive and understand by these people, it were a very easy thing to bring them to some familiarity and civility, and make them learn what one would. The Lord GOD for his mercies sake set thereunto his helping hand when he seeth cause. Amen. . . .

Of a strange and cruel disease that came to the people of Stadagona, wherewith because we did haunt their company, we were so infected, that there died 25 of our company

In the month of December, we understood that the Plague or Pestilence was come to the people of *Stadagona*, in such sort, that before we knew of it, according to their confession, there were dead above 50 whereupon we forbade them neither to come near our fort, nor about our Ships, or us. And albeit we had driven them from us, the said unknown sickness began to spread itself amongst us, after the strangest sort that ever was either heard of or seen, in so much, as some did lose all their strength, and could not stand on their feet, then did their legs swell, their sinnows shrink as black as any coal. To others, all their Skins was spotted with spots of blood of a purple color: then did it ascend up aloft to their ankles, knees, thighs, shoulders, arms, and neck: their mouth became stinking, their gums so rotten, that all the flesh did fall off, even to the roots of the Teeth, which did also almost all fall out. With such infection did this Sickness spread itself in our three Ships, that about the middle of February, of a hundred and ten persons that we were, there were not ten whole, so that one could not help the other, a most horrible and pitiful case, considering the place we were in, forsomuch as the people of the Country would daily come before our fort, and saw but few of us. There were already eight dead, and more than fifty sick, and as we thought, past all hope of recovery. Our Captain seeing this our misery, and that the sickness was gone so far, ordained and commanded, that every one should devoutly prepare himself to prayer, and in remembrance of Christ, caused his Image to us set up upon a tree, about a flight shot from the fort, amidst the Ice and Snow, giving all men to understand, that on the Sunday following, service should be said there, and that whosoever could go, sick, or whole, should go thither in Procession, singing the seven Psalms of David, with other Litanies, praying most heartily, that it would please the said our Christ to have compassion upon us. Service being done, and as well celebrated as we could, our Captain there made a vow, that if it would please God to give him leave to return to *France*, he would go on pilgrimage to our Lady of *Rocquemado*. That day Philip Rougemont, born in *Amboisa*, died, being two and twenty years old, and because the sickness was to us unknown, our Captain caused him to be ripped [sliced open], to see if by any means possible we might know what it was, and so seek means to save and preserve the rest of the company: he was found to have his heart white, but rotten & more than a pottle [two quarts] of red water about it: his liver was indifferent fair, but his lungs black and mortified, his blood was altogether shrunk about the heart, so that when he was opened, great quantity of rotten blood issued out from about his heart: his milt [spleen] toward the back was somewhat perished, rough as if it had been rubbed against a stone. Moreover, because one of his thighs was very black without, it was opened, but within it was whole and sound: that done, as well as we could he was buried. In such sort did the sickness continue and increase, that there were not above three sound men in the ships, and none was able to go under hatches to draw drink for himself, nor for his fellows. Sometimes we were constrained to bury some of the dead under the Snow, because we were not able to dig any graves for them, the ground was so hard frozen, and we so weak. Besides this, we did greatly fear, that the people of the Country would perceive our weakness and misery, which to hide, our Captain, whom it pleased God always to keep in health, would go out with two or three of the company, some sick, and some whole, whom when he saw out of the fort, he would throw stones at them and chide them, and then with signs show the people of the Country, that we caused all his men to work and labor in the Ships, some in mending them, some in beating of chalk, some in one thing, and some in another, and that he would not have them come forth, till their work was done. And to make his tale seem true and likely, he would make all his men whole and sound to make a great noise, with knocking sticks, stones, hammers, and other things together, at which time, we were so oppressed, and grieved with that sickness, that we had lost all hope ever to see *France* again, if God of his infinite goodness and mercy had not with his pitiful eye looked upon us, and revealed a singular and excellent remedy against all diseases unto us, the best that ever was found upon earth. . . .

Document 19

Journey to the Country of Cībola Newly Discovered (1540)

By Francisco Vásquez de Coronado, "Journey to the Country of Cibola newly discovered," in Richard Hakluyt, ed., *The Principal Navigations, Voyages, Traffiques, and Discoveries of the English Nation*, 3 vols. (London, 1598–1600), 3: 373–82.

In the aftermath of the conquest of Mexico, Central America, the West Indies, and northern South America, ambitious Spanish conquistadors began to turn their attention northward. From 1539 to 1541, Hernando de Soto (1500?–1542) led an expedition northward from Florida and through the interior of much of the southeast of the modern-day United States. A shipwreck survivor named Álvar Núñez Cabeza da Vaca (1490?–1557?) also wandered through much of the interior, enduring nine years of separation from other Spaniards. Farther west, Francisco Vásquez de Coronado (1510–1554) led an extraordinary journey northward from Mexico. He sought a place called Cībola, rumored to be a city bedecked in gold and jewels. Desperate to find such a treasure, he led his forces on an expedition that stretched from modern-day New Mexico to Kansas. He never found the riches he sought, but in the process he and his party became the earliest Europeans to encounter the Pueblos and other indigenous groups in North America.

Coronado's journey through the American Southwest was not received well by all of the indigenous peoples he encountered. The Zuni residents of Hawi-kuh laid cornmeal at the edges of their community, a sacred sign intended to let the Spanish know that they should not enter. In response, the Spanish read the requirimiento, *promising not to attack the natives if they accepted the king and queen of Spain "as superiors and kings" of "this Terra-firme" and if they allowed Catholic missionaries to preach to them. Anyone who resisted, the Spanish continued, declared themselves enemies who would suffer severe consequences.[7] After the Zunis refused to acquiesce to the Spaniards' wishes, Coronado's forces attacked and defeated the natives. Fortunately for him and his companions, many of the Zunis and other indigenous peoples he later encountered proved less hostile. Some allied themselves with the Spaniard while many, as this account demonstrates, offered goods to the visitors when they arrived.*

7. For the text of the document, see Lewis Hanke, ed., *History of Latin American Civilizations: Sources and Interpretations*, 2nd ed. (Boston: Little and Brown, 1973), 94–95.

Unlike the accounts of other Spanish expeditions, the reports generated by Coronado's adventures in that rugged landscape attracted little attention in the sixteenth century. Unlike Vespucci, who published his report in an effort to get support for further journeys, or Cortés, whose self-serving letters had a specific political goal, Coronado's report circulated in manuscript, until Hakluyt published an English translation. By the time that edition appeared in print, the explorer himself had been dead for almost fifty years.

Of the situation and state of the seven cities called the Kingdom of Cibola, and of the customs and qualities of those people, and of the beasts which are found there

It remaineth now to certify your Honour of the seven cities, and of the kingdoms and provinces whereof the Father provincial made report unto your Lordship. And to be brief, I can assure your honor, he said the truth in nothing that he reported, but all was quite contrary, saving only the names of the cities, and great houses of stone: for although they be not wrought with Turquoises, nor with lime, nor bricks, yet are they very excellent good houses of three or four or five lofts high, wherein are good lodgings and fair chambers with lathers [ladders] instead of stairs, and certain cellars under the ground very good and paved, which are made for winter, they are in manner like stoves; and the lathers [ladders] which they have for their houses are all in a manner moveable and portable, which are taken away and set down when they please, and they are made of two pieces of wood with their steps, as ours be. The seven cities are seven small towns, all made with these kind of houses that I speak of: and they stand all within four leagues together, and they are all called the kingdom of Cibola, and every one of them have their particular name: and none of them is called Cibola, but altogether they are called Cibola. And this town which I call a city, I have named Granada, as well because it is somewhat like unto it, as also in remembrance of your lordship. In this town where I now remain, there may be some two hundred houses, all compassed with walls, and I think that with the rest of the houses which are not so walled, they may be together five hundred. There is another town near this, which is one of the seven, & it is somewhat bigger than this, and another of the same bigness that this is of, and the other four are somewhat less: and I send them all painted unto your lordship with the voyage. And the parchment wherein the picture is, was found here with other parchments. The people of this town seem unto me of a reasonable stature, and witty, yet they seem not be such as they should be, of that judgment and wit to build these houses in such sort as they are. For the most part they go all naked, except their privie parts which are covered: and they have painted mantles like those which I sent unto your lordship. They have no cotton wool growing, because the country is cold, yet they wear mantels thereof as your honor may see by the show thereof: and true it is that there was found in their houses certain yarn made of cotton wool. They wear their hair on their heads like those of Mexico, and they are well nurtured and conditioned: And they have Turquoises I think good quantity, which with the rest of the goods they had, except their corn, they had conveyed away before I came thither: for I found no women there, nor no youth under fifteen years old, nor no old folks above sixty, saving two or three old folks, who stayed behind to govern all the rest of the youth and men of war. There were found in a certain paper two points of Emeralds, and certain small stones broken which are in color somewhat like Granites very bad, and other stones of Crystal, which I gave to one of my servants to lay up to send them to your lordship, and he hath lost them as he telleth me. We found here Guinea cocks, but few. The Indians tell me in all these seven cities, that they eat them not, but that they keep them only for their feathers. I believe them not, for they are excellent good, and greater than those of Mexico. The season which is in this country, and the temperature of the air is like that of Mexico: for sometime it is hot, and sometime it raineth: but hitherto I never saw it rain, but once there fell a little shower with wind, as they are wont to fall in Spain.

The snow and cold are wont to be great, for so say the inhabitants of the Country: and it is very likely so to be, both in respect of the manner of the Country, and by the fashion of their houses, and their furs and other things which this people have to defend them from cold. There is no kind of fruit nor trees of fruit. The Country is all plain, and is on no side mountainous: albeit there are some hilly and bad passages. There are small store of fouls: the cause whereof is the cold, and because the mountains are not near. Here is no great store of wood, because they have wood for their fuel sufficient four leagues off from a wood of small Cedars. There is most excellent grass within a quarter of a league hence, for our horses as well to feed them in pasture, as to mow and make hay, whereof we stood in great need, because our horses came hither so weak and feeble. The victuals which the people of this country have, is Maize, whereof they have great store, and also small white Peas: and Venison, which by all likelihood they feed upon, (though they say no) for we found many skins of Deer, of Hares, and Conies. They eat the best cakes that ever I saw, and every body generally eateth of them. They have the finest order and way to grind that we ever saw in any place. And one Indian woman of this country will grind as much as four women of Mexico. They have most excellent salt in kernel, which they fetch from a certain lake a day's journey from hence. They have no knowledge among them of the North Sea, nor of the Western Sea, neither can I tell your lordship to which we be nearest: But in reason they should seem to be nearest to the Western Sea: and at the least I think I am an hundred and fifty leagues from thence: and the Northern Sea should be much further off. Your Lordship may see how broad the land is here. Here are many sorts of beasts, as Bears, Tigers, Lions, Porkspicks [pigs?], and certain Sheep as big as an horse, with very great horns and little tails, I have seen their horns so big, that it is a wonder to behold their greatness. Here are also wild goats whose heads likewise I have seen, and the paws of Bears, and the skins of wild Boars. There is game of Deer, Ounces, and very great Stags: and all men are of opinion that there are some bigger than that beast which your lordship bestowed upon me, which once belonged to John Melaz. They travel eight days journey into certain plains lying toward the North Sea. In this country there are certain skins well dressed, and they dress them and paint them where they kill their Oxen, for so they say themselves.

Document 20

Of the West Indies

By Gonzalo Fernández de Oviedo y Valdés, "Of the West Indies" in *The History of Travayle in the West and East Indies*, ed. Richard Willes (London, 1577), 191–92

Gonzalo Fernández de Oviedo y Valdés (1478–1557), who became involved in the Spanish governance of Hispaniola, was one of the most active Europeans who went to the Western Hemisphere in the sixteenth century. He crossed the Atlantic for the first time in 1514 and from that point forward the Americas and its resources and peoples became the focal point of his activities. Over the course of his career he served as an inspector of gold mines, governor of Cartagena, and the Spanish king's official chronicler of the Indies, a position he received in 1532 in recognition of his powers of observation and his literary skill. Three years later he began a ten-year term as governor of Santo Domingo.

Oviedo wrote a detailed report providing readers with insights into what he had seen and information he had gathered. Much of what he wrote focused on the West Indies, but he also became an expert on the mainland. His observations on what he saw in the Americas appeared first as De la natural hystoria de las Indias, *published in 1526 in Toledo, 1535 in Seville, and 1547 in Salamanca. He also mentioned the West Indies in a chivalric romance titled* Libro del muy esforçado y invinciple cavallero, *which was published in Valencia in 1519.*

Like some other observers, Oviedo was keen to get rich in the Americas, and he hoped that harvesting pearls, the subject of this excerpt, was one way to wealth. Oviedo's account reveals that he was skeptical that there would always be pearls available. But his informants reassured him: even after harvesting pearls in one area the natives could return later and find more. The supply, against any logic, seemed to be infinite. Yet Oviedo wrote as an authority: "I speak this as a true testimony of sight, having been long in that South sea." Once again, a travel account gained legitimacy because it included eye-witness testimony.

Convinced that America contained great treasures that could be extracted, Oviedo eventually formed a partnership with the Venetian scholar Giovanni Battista Ramusio, the secretary to the Council of Ten, and Antonio Priuli, procurator of Venice's basilica of San Marco. They had hoped to organize shipments of American goods from the Caribbean, via Hispaniola, to Venice. Though the agreement apparently produced little monetary profit, Ramusio's version of Oviedo's account became a central part of his Navigationi e Viaggi *published in Venice in the 1550s.*

The translation that appears here comes from Richard Willes, whose 1577 collection of accounts presented English readers with a vast supply of information relating to the Americas as well as other parts of the world.

Of the manner of fishing for pearls.

The Indians exercise this kind of fishing for the most part in the coasts of the North in *Cubagua* and *Cumana*, and many of them which dwell in the houses of certain particular lords in the Islands of *San Dominico* and *Sancti Johannis*, resort to the Island of *Cubagua*, for this purpose. Their custom is to go five, six, or seven, or more in one of their *Canoas* or barks, early in the morning to some place in the sea thereabout, where it appeareth unto them that there should be great plenty of those shell fishes (which some call Muscles, and some Oysters) wherein pearls are engendered, & there they plunge themselves under the water, even unto the bottom, saving one that remaineth in the *Canoa* or boat, which he keepth still in one place as near as he can, looking for their return out of the water: And when one of them hath been a good while under the water, he riseth up, and commeth swimming to the boat, entering into the same, and leaving there all the Oysters which he hath taken and brought with him (for in these are the pearls found) and when he hath there rested himself a while, and eaten part of the Oysters, he returneth again to the water, where he remaineth as long as he can endure, and then riseth again, and swimmeth to the boat with his prey, where he resteth as before, and thus continueth course by course, as do all the other in like manner, being all most expert swimmers and divers: and when the night draweth near, they return to the Island to their houses, and present all the Oysters to the master or steward of the house of their Lord, who hath the charge of the said Indians, and when he hath given them somewhat to eat, he layeth up the Oysters in safe custody, until he have a great quantity thereof, then he causeth the same fishermen to open them, and they find in every of them pearls, other great or small, two, or three, or four, and sometimes five or six, and many small grains, according to the liberality of nature. They save the pearls both small and great which they have found, and either eat the Oysters if they will, or cast them away, having so great quantity thereof, that they in manner abhor them. These Oysters are of hard flesh, and not so pleasant in eating as are ours of Spain. This Island of *Cubagua* where this manner of fishing is exercised, is in the North coast, and is no bigger then the Island of Zeeland. Oftentimes the sea increaseth greatly, and much more than the fishers for pearls would, because whereas the place is very deep, a man can not naturally rest at the bottom, by reason of the abundance of airy substance which is in him, as I have oftentimes proved. For although he may by violence and force descend to the bottom, yet are his feet lifted up again, so that he can continue no time there: and therefore where the sea is very deep, these Indian fishers use to tie two great stones about them with a cord, one every side one, by the weight whereof they descend to the bottom, and remain there until they listeth [want] to rise again, at which time they unloose the stones, and rise up at their pleasure. But this their aptness and agility in swimming, is not the thing that causeth men most to marvel: but rather to consider how many of them can stand in the bottom of the water for the space of one whole hour, and some more or less, according as one is more apt hereunto than another. Another thing there is which seemeth to me very strange: and this is, that whereas I have oftentimes demanded of some of these Lords of the Indians, if the place where they are accustomed to fish for pearls, being but little and narrow, will not in short time be utterly without Oysters, if they consume them so fast. They all answered me, that although they consumed in one part, yet if they go a fishing in an other part, or another coast of the Island, or at another contrary wind, and continue fishing there also until the Oysters be likewise consumed, and then return again to the first place, or any other place where they fished before, and emptied the same in like manner, they find them again as full of Oysters as though they had never been fished. Whereby we may judge, that these Oysters either remove from one place to another, as do other fishes, or eels that they are engendered and increase in certain ordinary places. These Islands of *Cumana* & *Cubagua*, where they fish for these pearls, is in the twelfth degree of the part of the said coast which inclineth toward the North. Likewise pearls are found and gathered in the South sea, called *Mare del Sur*, & the pearls of this sea are very big, yet not so big as they of the Island of pearls, called *de las perlas*, or *Margaritea*, which the Indians call *Terarequi*, lying in the gulf of Saint Michael, where greater pearls are found, and of greater price, than in any other coast of the North sea, in *Cumana*, or any other part. I speak this as a true testimony of sight, having been long in that South sea, and making curious inquisition to be certainly informed of all that pertaineth to the fishing of pearls. From this Island of *Terarequie*, there was brought a pearl of the fashion of a Pear, weighing thirty and one Carats, which *Petrus Arias* had among a thousand and so many pounds of weight of other pearls, which he had when captain *Gaspar Morales* (before *Petrus Arias*) passed to the said Island in the year 1515 which pearl was of great price. From the said Island also, came a great and very round pearl, which I brought out of the sea, this was as big as a small pellet of a Stonebowe [a stone arch or a crossbow], and of the weight of twenty and six Carats: I bought it in the city of *Panama*, in the sea of *Sur*, and paid for it six hundred and fifty times the weight thereof good gold, and had it three years in my custody, and after my return into Spain, sold it to the Earl of *Nansao* Marquess of *Zenete*, great Chamberlain to your Majesty, who gave it to the Marquesse his wife, the Lady *Mentia* of *Mendozza*. I think verily that this pearl was the greatest, fairest, and soundest that hath been seen in those parts. For your majesty ought to understand, that in the coast of the sea of Sur, there are found a hundred great pearls round after the fashion of a Pear, to one that is perfectly round and great. This Island of *Terarequie*, which the Christians call the Island of pearls, and other call it the Island of Flowers, is found in the eighth degree on the South side of the firm land, in the province of golden Castyle, or *Beragua*, and these are the coasts of the firm land, where pearls are found even unto this day: I understand also that there are pearls found in the province and Islands of *Cartagenia*. And since your majesty appointed me a governor and captain, I have made further search, and am advertised that pearls are found in divers other places, as about the Island of *Codego*, which lyeth against the mouth of that port of the Island of *Cartagenia*, which the Indians call Coro, the which Island and port are on the North side, in the tenth degree of the coasts of the firm land.

Document 21

Chronicles of Peru

By Pedro Cieza de León, *Chronicles of Peru*, trans. Harriet de Onas (Norman: University of Oklahoma Press, 1959)

In the generations following Christopher Columbus's initial expedition, Spanish explorers and colonizers traveled through much of the Americas. Many of them returned to provide accounts of their journeys. Those travel accounts reflect the different patterns of the Spanish conquest: the earliest narratives described the Caribbean basin, followed by accounts of Mexico. By the middle of the sixteenth century, Spanish conquistadores *had pushed farther, and many returned telling tales of lands only dimly understood earlier. As Spanish travelers such as Coronado provided detailed information about the interior of North America, another generation of Spaniards had moved south and into the heartland of the Inkan empire.*

The Spanish conquest of the Inkas remains a subject of deep fascination, in large part because it was so unlikely. Francisco Pizarro (c. 1478–1541) arrived in Peru in 1532; by 1535 he had already captured, ransomed, and then killed the Incan king Atahualpa (after he refused to go along with the terms of the requirimiento*) and founded what became the modern city of Lima. His victory over the 14 million inhabitants of the Inkan empire could be attributed to various phenomena, including a smallpox epidemic and superior weaponry.*[8]

---

8. For one recent explanation, see Jared Diamond, *Guns, Germs, and Steel: The Fates of Human Societies* (New York: Norton, 1997), 67–81.

Over the next generation, Europeans learned more about Peru. Among those who described it was de Pedro Cieza de Léon (1520–1560), who arrived in South America when he was fifteen years old. He began to write his account in 1541; he finished it in 1552, when he was, as he put it, "thirty-two years old, having spent seventeen of them in these Indies." According to one of his modern translators, his book "possesses the greatest objectivity of any history ever written about the Incas."[9]

Cieza de León's book was first printed in Seville in 1553. Over the next two decades it appeared in multiple editions published in Antwerp, Rome, and Venice. The excerpts here focus on two of the notable elements of Inkan society: their magnificent city of Cuzco and their use of quipu.

Chapter 44: Of the manner and fashion in which the city of Cuzco is built, and the four highways that lead from it, and the great buildings it had, and who was the founder.

The city of Cuzco is laid out on rough terrain, surrounded by mountains on all sides, between two small brooks, one of which runs through the middle of it, because it has been settled to both sides. To the east there is a valley which begins at the city itself, so the waters of the brooks that run through the city flow out of it westward. Because of the cold climate of this valley there are no fruit-bearing trees except a few *molles*. To the north of the city, on the hill closes to it, there is a fortress [Sacsahuamán], which by reason of its size and strength was once a mighty building, and it still is, even though the greater part of it is in ruins. But the powerful foundations still stand, and the main pillars. To the east and north lie the provinces of Antisuyu, which are the dense forests and mountains of the Andes, and the largest part of Chinchay-suyu, which includes the regions in the direction of Quito. To the south lie the provinces of the Colla and Cunti-suyu, of which the Colla lies between the east wind and austral, or that which navigators call the south, and Cunti-suyu south-southwest. One part of this city is known as Hanan-Cuzco and the other as Hurin-Cuzco, where the principal nobility and the old families lived. In another section stands Karmenka Hill, where at intervals

---

9. *The Incas of Pedro de Cieza de León*, trans. Harriet de Onis (Norman: University of Oklahoma Press, 1959), quotations at lxxx and vii.

there are small towers which they used to study the movement of the sun, to which they attached great importance. Midway between the hills, where most of the inhabitants resided, there was a good-sized square which they say was a swamp or lake in olden times, and which the founders of the city filed in with stones and mortar and made as it is now. From this square four highways emerge; the one called Chincay-suyu leads to the plains and the highlands as far as the provinces of Quito and Pasto; the second, known as Cunti-suyu, is the highway to the provinces under the jurisdiction of this city and Arequipa. The third, by name Anti-suyu, leads to the provinces on the slopes of the Andes and various settlements beyond the mountains. The last of these highways, called Colla-suyu, is the route to Chile. Thus, just as in Spain the early inhabitants divided it all into provinces, so these Indians, to keep track of their wide-flung possessions, used the method of highways. The [Huatanay] river that flows through this city is spanned by bridges.

Nowhere in this kingdom of Peru was there a city with the air of nobility that Cuzco possessed, which (as I have said repeatedly) was the capital of the empire of the Incas and their royal seat. Compared with it, the other provinces of the Indies are mere settlements. And such towns as there are lack design, order, or polity to commend them, whereas Cuzco had distinction to a degree, so those who founded it must have been people of great worth. There were large streets, except that they were narrow, and the houses made all of stone so skillfully joined that it was evident how old the edifices were, for the huge stones were very well set. The other houses were all of wood, thatch, or adobe, for we saw no trace of tile, brick, or mortar. In many parts of this city there were splendid buildings of the Lord-Incas where the heir to the throne held his festivities. There, too, was the imposing temple to the sun, which they called *Curicancha* [the "golden enclosure"], which was among the richest in gold and silver to be found anywhere in the world.

It is well known among the Indians that this temple [of Curicancha] is as old as the city of Cuzco itself; however, the Inca Yupanqui [Pachacuti], son of Viracocha Inca, added to its riches and left it as it was when the Spaniards entered Peru. Most of its treasures were taken to Cajamarca for the ransom of Atahualpa, as we shall tell when the time comes. And the *Orejones* relate that after the conclusion of the dubious war between the inhabitants of Cuzco and the Chancas, who are now the lords of the province of Andahuaylas, in the victory he won over them Pachacuti achieved such widespread renown and esteem that from all sides chieftains came to render him fealty, and the provinces brought him great tribute of gold and silver, for in those days there were great mines and richest lodes. Seeing himself so opulent and powerful, he decided to ennoble the house of the sun, which in their language they call Indehuaxi and to which they gave the name of Curicancha, as well—which means "fenced with gold"—and endow it with riches. And that all who see or read this may know how rich the temple of Cuzco was, and the prowess of those who built it and did such great things in it, I shall give an account of it as I saw it and what I heard from many of the first Spaniards, who had it from the three who went to Cajamarca and saw it, although what the Indians tell is so complete and so true that no other proof is needed.

This temple had a circumference of over four hundred feet, and was all surrounded by a strong wall. The whole building was of fine quarried stone, all matched and joined, and some of the stones were very large and beautiful. No mortar or earth or lime was employed in it, only the pitch which they used in their buildings, and the stones are so well cut that there is no sign of cement or joinings. In all Spain I have seen nothing that can compare with these walls and the laying of the stones except the tower known as the Calahorra, the bridge of Córdoba, and a building I saw in Toledo when I went to present the First Part of my Chronicle to the Prince, Don Philip, which is the hospital built at the orders of the Archbishop of Toledo, Tavera. Although these buildings somewhat resemble those I have mentioned, they are finer, that is to say, as regards the walls and the cutting and laying of the stones, and the fence was plumb and very well laid. The stone seems to me blackish and rough and of excellent quality. It had many gates, and the gateways finely carved; halfway up the wall ran a stripe of gold two handspans wide and four fingers thick. The gateway and doors were covered with sheets of this metal. Inside there were four buildings, not very large, fashioned in the same way, and the walls inside and out were covered with gold, and the beams, too, and the roof was of thatch. There were two benches against that wall, which the rising sun fell upon, and the stones were very skillfully perforated, and the openings set with precious stones and emeralds. These benches were for the Lord-Incas, and if anyone else sat there, he was sentenced to death.

There were guards at the doors of these houses whose duty it was to watch over the virgins, many of whom were daughters of the leading nobles, the most beautiful and comely that could be found. They remained in the temples until they were old, and if any of them knew a man, she was killed or buried alive, and he suffered the same fate. These women were called *mama-conas*; they did nothing but weave and dye woolen garments for the service of the temple and make chichi, which is the wine they drink, of which they always had great vessels.

In one of these houses, which was the richest, there was an image of the sun, of great size, made of gold, beautifully wrought and set with many precious stones. It also held some of the statues of the Incas who had reigned in Cuzco, with a vast store of treasure.

Around this temple there were many small dwellings of Indians who were assigned to its service, and there was a fence inside which they put the white lambs and the children and men to be sacrificed. There was a garden in which the earth was lumps of fine gold, and it was cunningly planted with stalks of corn that were of gold—stalk, leaves, and ears. These were so well planted that no matter how hard the wind blew it could not uproot them. Aside from this, there were more than twenty sheep of gold with their lambs, and the shepherds who guarded them, with their slings and staffs, all of this metal. There were many tubs of gold and silver and emeralds, and goblets, pots, and every kind of vessel all of fine gold. On the other walls there were carved and painted other still greater things. In a word, it was one of the richest temples in the whole world.

The high priest, called Vilaoma [Villac-umu], dwelt in the temple, and aided by the priests, performed the ordinary sacrifices with great ceremony, in keeping with their custom. The general feasts were attended by the Inca to witness the sacrifices, and these were carried out with great celebration. Within the house and temple there were more than thirty bins [made] of silver in which they stored the corn, and the contributions of many provinces were assigned to this temple. On certain days the devil appeared to the priests, and made them vain answers of the sort that he gave.

Many other things could be told of this temple which I omit because it seems to me that what has been said suffices for an understanding of what a great thing it was. For I make no mention of the silverwork, beads, golden feathers, and other things which, if I were to describe them, would not be believed. And, as I have said, there are Spaniards still alive who saw most of this, which was taken to Cajamarca for the ransom of Atahualpa, but the Indians hid much, and it is buried and lost. Although all the Incas had contributed to the aggrandizement of this temple, in the days of Pachacuti he so enhanced it that when he died and Topa Inca, his son, ruled the kingdom, it was in this state of perfection.

Most of the city was settled by *mitimaes*, and the great laws and statutes had been enacted, after the Inca custom, which were obeyed by all, both as refers to their vain observances and temples as well as their government. It was the richest city in all the Indies, as far as we can gather, for the treasures assembled for the glory of the Incas had been collected there for many years, and none of the gold and silver brought into it could be removed, under penalty of death. Sons of all the provincial chieftains came to live at this court with their pomp and service. There were numbers of silversmiths and goldsmiths who worked for the Incas. In the main temple there lived a high priest called Vilaoma. Today there are very good, turreted houses, covered with tiles. Although this city is cold, it is very healthy, and the best provisioned in the whole kingdom, and the largest, where the most Spaniards hold an encomienda of Indians. It was founded and settled by Manco Capac, the first of the Inca lords. And after ten Incas had succeeded him in the rule, it was rebuilt and refounded by Francisco Pizarro, governor and captain-general of these kingdoms, in the name of Emperor Charles V . . . in the month of October of 1534.

As this was the main and most important city of this kingdom, at certain times of the year the Indians of the provinces came there, some to construct buildings, others to clean the streets and districts, and [to do] anything else they were ordered. Near to it, on either hand, there are many buildings which were lodgings and storehouses, all of the design and structure of the others throughout the kingdom, although some are larger, some smaller, some stouter, than others.

As these Incas were so rich and powerful, some of these buildings were gilded, and others were adorned with plates of gold. Their forbears considered a hill near this city, which they called Huana-cauri, sacred, and there, it is said, they made sacrifice of human blood and of many llamas. And as this city was full of strange and foreign peoples, for there were Indians from Chile, Pasto, and Cañari, Chachapoyas, Huancas, Collas, and all the other tribes to be found in the provinces we have described, each of them was established in the place and district set aside for them by the governors of the city. They observed the customs of their own people and dressed after the fashion of their own land, so that if there were a hundred thousand men, they could be easily recognized by the insignia they wore about their heads. Some of these outlanders buried their dead on high hills, others in their houses, and others in their fields, with living women and the things they had prized most, as had been told before, and much food. And the Incas (as I can gather) did not prohibit any of these things, provided they all worshiped the sun, which they called Mocha, and did it homage. In many parts of this city there are large buildings under the ground, and in the bowels of it even today paving stones and pipes are found, and an occasional jewel and piece of gold of that which they buried. Without doubt there must be great treasures buried in the area of this city, of which those now living have no knowledge. As so many people lived there, and the devil held such sway over them, with the permission of God, that there were many wizards, augurs, and idolators. Nor is the city wholly free of such relics, especially as refers to witchcraft. Near this city there are many temperate valleys where there are orchards and gardens, both of which flourish, and much of the produce is brought to the city to be sold. Abundant wheat is now harvested, from which bread is made. In these places to which I refer many oranges and other fruit trees of Spain are raised, as well as the native ones. In the river which runs through the city there are mills, and four leagues away one can see the quarries from which they dug the stone for their buildings, an impressive sight. Aside from the foregoing, many fowl and capons are raised in Cuzco, as good and fat as those of Granada, and in the plains and valleys there are herds of cows and goats and other livestock, both that of Spain and the native. Although there are no orchards in this city, the vegetables of Spain do very well.

Chapter 53: Of how they had chroniclers to keep record of their deeds, and the use of the quipus, and what we see of them now.

We have written how it was ordered by the Incas that the statues be brought out at their feasts, and how they selected from the wisest among their men those who should tell what the life of their kings had been and how they had conducted themselves in the rule of their kingdoms, for the purpose I have stated. It should also be known that, aside from this, it was the custom among them, and a rule carefully observed, for each of them to choose during his reign three or four old men of their nation, skilled and gifted for that purpose, whom they ordered to recall all that had happened in the province during the time of their reign, whether prosperous or adverse, and to make and arrange songs so that thereby it might be known in the future what had taken place in the past. Such songs could not be sung or proclaimed outside the presence of the Inca, and those who were to carry out this behest were ordered to say nothing referring to the Inca during his lifetime, but after he was dead, they said to his successor almost in these words: "Oh, mighty and powerful Inca, may the Sun and Moon, the Earth, the hills and trees, the stones and your forefathers guard you from misfortune and make you prosperous, happy, and blessed among all who have been born. Know that the things that happened to your predecessor were these." And saying this, with their eyes on the ground and heads hanging, with great humility they gave an account and report of all they knew, which they could do very well, for there were many among them of great memory, subtle wit, and lively intelligence, and abounding in knowledge, as those of us who are here and hear them can bear witness. After they said this, when the Inca had heard them, he sent for other of his old Indians whom he ordered to learn the songs the others bore in their memory, and to prepare new ones of what took place during the time of his reign, what was spent, what the provinces contributed, and put all this down in the quipus, so that after his death, when his successor reigned, what had been given and contributed would be known. And except on days of great celebration, or on the occasion of mourning and lament for the death of a brother or son of the Inca, for on such days it was permitted to relate their grandeur and their origin and birth, at no other time was it permitted to deal with this, for it had been forbidden by their lords, and if they did so, they were severely punished.

[The Indians] had a method of knowing how the tributes of food supplies should be levied on the provinces when the Lord-Inca came through with his army, or was visiting the kingdom; or, when nothing of this sort was taking place, what came into the storehouses and what was issued to the subjects, so nobody could be unduly burdened, that was so good and clever that it surpasses the *carastes* used by the Mexicans for their accounts and dealings. This involved the quipus, which are long strands of knotted strings, and those who were the accountants and understood the meaning of these knots could reckon by them expenditures or other things that had taken place many years before. By these knots they counted from one to ten and from ten to a hundred, and from a hundred to a thousand. On one of these strands there is the account of one thing, and on the other of another, in such a way that what to us is a strange, meaningless account is clear to them. In the capital of each province there were accountants whom they called *quipu-camaocs*, and by these knots they keep the account of the tribute to be paid by the natives of that district in silver, gold, clothing, flocks, down to wood and other more insignificant things, and by these same quipus at the end of a year, or ten, or twenty years, they gave a report to the one whose duty it was to check the account so exact that not even a pair of sandals was missing.

I was dubious about this accounting, and even though I was assured that it was so done, I considered it for the most part a fable. But when I was in the province of Jauja, in what they call Marcavillca, I asked the cacique Huacara-pora to explain the system to me in such a way that I could understand it and make sure that it was exact and dependable. Whereupon he sent his servants to fetch the quipus, and as this man is of goodly understanding and reason, for all he is an Indian, he readily satisfied my request. He told me, so that I would better understand, that I should observe that all he had given to the Spaniards from the time of the entry of the Governor Francisco Pizarro in the valley [1533] was recorded there without a single omission; and in this I saw the account of the gold, silver, and clothing that had been given, the llamas and other things, and I was amazed thereby. And there is another thing which I firmly believe: the wars, cruelties, pillaging, and tyranny of the Spaniards have been such that if these Indians had not been so accustomed to order and providence they would all have perished and been wiped out. But being very prudent and sensible, and trained by such wise princes, they all decided that if an army of Spaniards passed through any of the provinces, unless the harm was irreparable, such as destroying the cops and robbing the houses and doing other still greater damage, as all the regions along the highway by which our men passed had their accountants, these would give out all the supplies the people could furnish so as to avoid the destruction of everything, and thus they were provided. And after they had passed through, the chieftains came together with the keepers of the quipus, and if one had expended more than another, those who had given less made up the difference, so they were all on an equal footing.

In each valley there is still this system of accounting, and there are always in the storehouses as many accountants as there are lords, and every four months they cast up their accounts in the manner described. Thanks to this system, they have been able to survive such cruel strife, and if God were pleased to bring it completely to an end, with the good treatment they have lately received and the order and justice that exists, they would revive and multiply, and in some fashion this kingdom might become again what it once was, though I fear this will be late or never. The fact is that I have seen villages, and large ones, which with a single time that the Christian Spaniards had passed through, looked as though they had been razed by fire. And as the people were not so reasonable, they did not aid one another, and fell victims to hunger and disease, for there is little charity among them, and it's each for himself, and that is the end of it.

This orderly system in Peru is the work of the Lord-Incas who ruled it and in every way brought it so high, as those of us here see from this and other greater things. . . .

Document 22

The Captivity of Hans Stade of Hesse Among the Wild Tribes of Eastern Brazil (1547–1555)

By Hans Stade, *The Captivity of Hans Stade of Hesse, in A.D. 1547–1555, Among the Wild Tribes of Eastern Brazil,* trans. Albert Tootal (London: Hakluyt Society, 1874), 51–53, 56–69

Most individuals who left travel accounts went places by choice. But some found themselves in circumstances well beyond their control. This was the case for Hans Stade (fl. 1547–1557?), a German who agreed to join a Portuguese mission to Brazil in the mid-1540s and then was taken captive by the Tupinambas of eastern Brazil. Stade's captivity testified to the one great fear in his life: that someone would not only kill him but would then eat his body. The terror of such a fate permeated the account of his years in captivity in Brazil.

Stade's tale was first published in German in Marpurg in 1557 with the title Warhaftig historia und beschreibung eyner landschafte der Wilden/ Nacketen/ Grimmigen Menschstresser Leuten in der Newenwelt America gelegen—Truthful History and Description of a Landscape of Wild, Naked, Cruel Man-Eating People in the New World of America. *Over the years the book was translated and published in Dutch (1558) and Latin (1592). The Flemish engraver Theodor de Bry, aware of the power of the sensational, chose to embellish the title page to one volume of his* America *series with depictions of what Europeans termed anthropophagi: consumers of human flesh. Here a naked Tupinamba man chews on a human leg and a naked Tupinamba woman nibbles on an arm, while an infant on her back, perhaps wanting a snack, reaches toward the hand. De Bry's book, published in Frankfurt-Am-Main in 1592, included a series of illustrations based on the writings of both authors, with the details of local cannibalism drawn directly from Stade's account. (See the chapter "Pictures of Brazil.")*

As the selection here reveals, Stade learned much about the society of his captors. Yet as a German in Brazil who had come there with the Portuguese, he was not necessarily an ally of every European in the vicinity. As his hopes for rescue dimmed, Stade believed that he would ultimately be redeemed by the kind word of any Christian from Europe. But when he encountered a Frenchman who spoke to Stade in French, a language he did not know, the other European told the Tupinambas to kill the German. Far from home, danger could come even from those who seemed most familiar.

How I was captured by the savages, and the way in which this happened.

I had a savage man, of a tribe called Carios; he was my slave, who caught game for me, and with him I also went occasionally into the forest.

Now it happened once upon a time, that a Spaniard from the island of Sancte Vincente came to me in the island of Sancte Maro, which is five miles (leagues) therefrom, and remained in the fort wherein I lived, and also a German by name Heliodorus, from Hesse, son of the late Eoban of Hesse, the same who was in the island of Sanect Vincente at an ingenio, where sugar is made, and the ingenio belonged to a Genoese named Josepe Ornio [Adorno]. This Heliodorus was the clerk and manager of the merchants to whom the ingenio belonged. (Ingenio, are called houses in which sugar is made.) With the said Heliodorus I had before had some acquaintance, for when I was ship-wrecked with the Spaniards in that country, I found him in the island of Sancte Vincente, and he showed me friendship. He came again to me, wanting to see how I got on, for he had perhaps heard that I was sick.

Having sent my slave the day before into the wood to catch game, I purposed going the next day to fetch it, so that we might have something to eat. For in that country one has little else beyond what comes from the forests.

Now as I with this purpose walked through the woods, there arose on both sides of the path loud yells such as the savages are accustomed to make, and they came running towards me; I knew them, and found that they had all surrounded me, and levelling their bows with arrows, they shot in upon me. Then I cried, "Now God help my soul." I had scarcely finished saying these words when they struck me to the ground and shot (arrows) and stabbed at me. So far they had not (thank God!) wounded me further than in one leg, and torn my clothes off my body; one the jerkin, the other the hat, the third the shirt and so forth. Then they began to quarrel about me, one said he was the first who came up to me, the other said that he had captured me. Meanwhile the others struck me with their bows. But at last two of them raised me from the ground where I lay naked, one took me by one arm, another by the other, and some went behind me, and others before. They ran in this manner quickly with me through the wood towards the sea, where they had their canoes. When they had taken me to the shore, I sighted their canoes which they had drawn up from the sea on to the land under a hedge, at the distance of a stone's throw or two, and also a great number more of them who had remained with their canoes. When they, ornamented with feathers according to their custom, saw me being led along they ran towards me, and pretended to bite into their arms, and threatened as though they would eat me. And a king paraded before me with a club wherewith they despatched the prisoners. He harrangued and said how they had captured me their slave from the Perot (so they call the Portuguese), and they would now thoroughly revenge on me the death of their friends. And when they brought me to the canoes, several of them struck me with their fists. Then they made haste among one another, to shove their canoes back into the water, for they feared that an alarm would be made at Brikioka, as also happened.

Now before they launched the canoes, they tied my hands together, and not being all from the same dwelling-place, those of each village were loath to go home empty-handed, and disputed with those who held me. Some said that they been just as near as the others, and that they would also have their share of me, and they wanted to kill me at once on that very spot.

Then I stood and prayed, looking round for the blow. But at last the king, who desired to keep me, began and said they would take me living homewards, so that their wives might also see me alive, and make their feast upon me. For they purposed killing me "*Kawei Pepicke*," that is, they would brew drinks and assemble together, to make a feast, and then they would eat me among them. At these words they left off disputing, and tied four ropes round my neck, and I had to get into a canoe, whilst they still stood on the shore, and bound the ends of the ropes to the boats and pushed them off into the sea, in order to sail home again. . . .

How they behaved to me on the day when they brought me to their habitations

On that day about vesper time, reckoning by the sun, we beheld their habitations, having therefore been three days on the return voyage. For the place I was let to was thirty miles (leagues) distant from Brikioka.

Now when we arrived close to their dwellings, these proved to be a village which had seven huts, and they called it Uwattibi. We ran up on a beach which borders the sea, and close to it were their women in the plantations of the root which they call Mandioka. In this said plantation walked many of their women pulling up the roots: to these I as made to call out in their language: "*A junesche been ermi vramme,*" that is: "I, your food, have come."

Now when we landed, all young and old ran out of their huts (which lay on a hill), to look at me. And the men with their bows and arrows entered their huts, and left me in the custody of their women, who took me between them and went along, some before me and others behind, singing and dancing in unison, with the songs which they are accustomed to sing to their own people when they are about to eat them.

Now they brought me before the *Iwara* huts, that is the fort which they make round about their huts with great long rails, like the fence of a garden. This they do on account of their enemies.

As I entered, the women ran to me, and struck me with their fists, and pulled my beard, and spoke in their language: "*Sche innamme pepicke a e.*" That is as much as to say: "with this blow I revenge my friend, him whom those among thou hast been, have killed."

Thereupon they led me into the huts, where I had to lie in a hammock, whilst the women came and struck and pulled me before and behind, and threatened me how they would eat me.

And the men were together in a hut, and drank the beverage which they call Kawi, and had with them their gods, called Tammerka, and they sang in praise of them, for their having so prophesied that I should be captured by them.

This song I heard, and for half an hour none of the men came near me, but only women and children. . . .

How my two masters came to me and told me that they had presented me to one of their friends, who was to keep me and kill me, when I was to be eaten

I knew not then their customs so well as I have since learned them, and I thought "Now they prepare to kill thee." After a little while those who had captured me, named Jeppipo (Yeppipo) Wasu, and his brother Alkindar Miri, came to me and told me how they had, from friendship, presented me to their father's brother Ipperu Wasu, who was to keep me, and also to kill me, when I was to be eaten, and thus to gain a new name with me.

For this same Ipperu Wasu had a year before also captured a slave, and had as a sign of friendship presented him to Alkindar Miri. Him he had killed and thereby he had gained a name; so that Alkindar Miri had in return promised to present Ipperu Wasu with the first whom he might capture. And I was the first.

Further the two above-mentioned who had taken me said, "Now will the women lead thee out to the *Aprasst*." This word I understood not then, but it means dancing. Thus they dragged me along with the ropes, which were round my neck, from out of the huts on to an open place. Then came all the women who were in the seven huts, and seized hold of me, and the men went away. Several of the women led me along by the arms, and several by the ropes which were bound round my neck, so roughly and tightly that I could hardly breathe. In this manner they went along with me, and I knew not what they intended doing to me, upon which I remembered the sufferings of our Lord Jesus Christ, and how he suffered innocently at the hands of the vile Jews, whereby I consoled myself and became the more resigned. Then they brought me before the huts of the king, who was called Vratinge Wasu, which means in German, the Great White Bird. Before his huts lay a heap of freshly dug earth, whither they led me and sat me down thereon, and some held me, when I thought nothing else but that they would dispatch me at once. I looked round for the *Iwara Pemme*, wherewith they club men, and asked whether they were going to kill me then, when they answered, "not yet." Upon which a woman came from out of the crowd towards me, holding a fragment of a crystal, set in a thing like a bent ring, and with this same piece of crystal shaved off my eyebrows, and would also have cut the beard from my chin, but this I would not suffer, and said, that they should kill me with my beard. Then they replied, that for the present they would not kill me, and left me my beard. But after some days they cut it off with a pair of scissors, which the Frenchmen had given them.

How they danced with me before the huts, wherein they keep their idols the Tamerka

Then they led me from the place where they had shaved off my eyebrows, to before the huts wherein the Tamerka their idols were, and I made round about me a circle in the middle of which I stood. Two women were with me, and they tied to one of my legs strings of object, which rattled and they also tied an ornament made of birds' tails, and of square shape, behind my neck, so that it projected above my head; it is called in their language *Arasoya*. Thereupon the womenkind all began together to sing, and to their time I was obliged to stamp with the leg to which they had tied the rattles, so that they rattled in harmony. But the leg in which I was wounded pained me so badly that I could hardly stand, for I had not yet been bandaged.

How, after the dance, they took me home to Ipperu Wasu, who was to kill me

Now when the dance came to an end, I was handed over to Ipperu Wasu, who kept me in careful custody. Then he told me that I still had some time to live. And they brought all their gods that were in the huts, and placed them round about me and said, that these had prophesied, that they would capture a Portuguese. Then said I, These things have no power, and also cannot speak. And they lie (in asserting) that I am Portuguese, for I am one of the Frenchmen's allies and friends, and the country where I am at home (to which I belong), is called Allemanien. Then they said that I must lie, for if I was the Frenchmen's friend, what was I doing among the Portuguese? They knew full well that the Frenchmen were just as much the enemies of the Portuguese as they. For the Frenchmen came every year with ships, and brought them knives, axes, looking-glasses, combs, and scissors, and for these they gave them Brazilwood, cotton and other goods, such as featherwork and (red) pepper. Therefore they were their good friends, which the Portuguese had not been. For these had in former years come into the country, and had, in the parts where they were still settled, contracted friendship with their enemies. After that time, they (i.e., the Portuguese) had also come to them, and they had in good faith gone to their ships and entered them, in the same manner in which they to the present day did with the French ships. They said moreover that when the Portuguese had collected enough of them in the ship, they had then attacked them and bound them, and delivered them up to their enemies who had killed and eaten them. Some of them also they had shot dead with their guns, and much more had the Portuguese in their haughty presumption done to them, having also joined with their enemies for the purpose of capturing them in war.

How those who had captured me bewailed in angry mood, how the Portuguese had shot their father; this they would revenge on me

And they further said that the Portuguese had shot the father of the two brothers who had captured me, in such manner that he died, and that they would now revenge their father's death on me. Thereupon I asked why they would revenge this upon me? I was not a Portuguese; (adding that) I had lately arrived there with the Castilians: I had suffered shipwreck, and I had from this cause remained among them.

It happened that there was a young fellow of their tribe, who had been a slave of the Portuguese; and the savages among whom the Portuguese live had gone into the Tuppin Imba's country to make war, and had taken a whole village, and had eaten the elder inhabitants, and had sold those who were young to the Portuguese for goods. So that this young fellow had also been bartered by the Portuguese, and had lived in the neighborhood of Brikioka with his master who was called Anthonio Agudin, a Gallician.

Those who had captured me had retaken the same slave about three months before.

Now as he was of their tribe, they had not killed him. The said slave knew me well and they asked him who I was. He said it was true, that a vessel had been lost on the shore, and the people who had come therein were called Castilians, and they were friends of the Portuguese. With these I had been, further he knew nothing of me.

Now when I heard, and having also understood that there were Frenchmen among them, and that these were accustomed to arrive there in ships, I always persisted in the same story, and said that I belonged to the allies of the French, that they were to let me remain unkilled, until such time as the Frenchmen came and recognized me. And they kept me in very careful confinement, as there were several Frenchmen among them who had been left by the ships to collect pepper.

How one of the Frenchmen who had been left by the ships among the savages came thither to see me, and advised them to eat me, as I was a Portuguese

There was a Frenchman living four miles distant from the huts where I was. Now when he heard the news he proceeded thither, and went into another hut opposite to that wherein I was. Then the savages came running towards me, and said, "Now a Frenchman has arrived here, and we shall soon see if you also are a Frenchman or not." I felt glad of this, and I thought, at all events he is a Christian, and he will say anything for the best.

Then they took me in to him naked as I was, and I saw that he was a young fellow, the savages called him Karwattu ware. He addressed me in French, and I of course understood him not. The savages stood round about us and listened. Now when I could not answer him, he said to the savages in their language, "Kill and eat him, the villain, he is a true Portuguese, my enemy and yours." And this I understood well. I begged him therefore for God's sake, that he would tell them not to eat me. Then he said: "They want to eat you," upon which I remembered the words of Jeremiah (chapter xvii) who says: "Cursed is he who putteth his trust in man." And herewith I again went away from them very sorrowful at heart; and I had at the time a piece of linen tied around my shoulders (where could they have obtained it?). This I tore off and threw it before the Frenchman's feet, and then the sun had scorched me severely, and I said to myself, "If I am to die, why should I preserve my flesh for another?" Then they conducted me back to the huts where they confined me. I then went to lie down in my hammock. God knows the misery I endured, and thus I tearfully began to sing the hymn,

> Now beg we of the Holy Ghost
> The true belief we wish for most.
> That he may save us at our end
> When from this vale of tears we wend. . . .

The above-mentioned Frenchman remained two days there in the huts: on the third day he went on his way. And they had agreed that they would prepare everything, and kill me on the first day after they had collected all things together, and they watched me very carefully, and both young and old mocked and derided me.

Document 23

History of a Voyage to the Land of Brazil (1578)

By Jean de Léry, *History of a Voyage to the Land of Brazil*, trans. Janet Whatley (Berkeley: University of California Press 1992), 15–19, 64–68

Hans Stade was no fan of Tupinamba society, and his constant fear of being eaten shaped his writings about these Brazilian people. By contrast, the French Huguenot missionary Jean de Léry (1534–1613) offered readers a much more complete assessment of the Tupinambas. Though both witnessed many of the same customs and local behaviors, Léry was a far more sympathetic observer. Of course, he did not spend his entire time in Brazil wondering if he was about to be eaten.[10]

10. Jean de Léry, *History of a Voyage to the Land of Brazil*, trans. Janet Whatley (Berkeley: University of California Press, 1990), 142.

In the excerpts here, Léry described his experiences at sea, including his astonishment at some of the creatures he observed, and his views of Tupinamba women. He contrasted crucial aspects of the natives' society, notably the nakedness of women and girls, with what he deemed proper female modes of dress in France at the time. His views may have shocked some of his readers, but they reveal Léry to be both an able (if amateur) ethnographer as well as a cleric able to use his experiences abroad to make a pointed critique about social organization at home.

The extraordinary precision of Léry's text identifies it as one of the most important printed works of European ethnography of the sixteenth century. Its only real rivals are Linschoten's description of India and Thomas Harriot's account of the Carolina Algonquians. Each of these reports suggests that it was possible—though not common—for Europeans to offer detailed accounts of very different kinds of peoples. This is not to suggest that the visitors shared a modern anthropologist's desire to observe a society without introducing changes to it. Harriot wrote quite clearly that he believed the natives he met would eventually come to live and behave like Europeans once they fell under the control of colonists, and Linschoten and Léry (himself a missionary) aimed to alter indigenous peoples' religious beliefs. It would be a mistake to assume that any of these observers could put aside such powerful agendas or sets of beliefs. It would be perhaps more accurate to state that Léry was something of an ethnographic pioneer whose works, which were available in print by the late 1570s, the others may or may not have read; and that all three of them left published accounts crucial for understanding the peoples of disparate parts of the world before many of their traditions disappeared.

Léry's account of his time crossing the Atlantic is invaluable, particularly on two crucial points. First, while voyages across the open ocean always involved risk, many crews also knew how to keep themselves alive and well fed by harvesting the abundant riches of the sea. (See the section "Pictures of Brazil" for one memorable image of flying fish.) His description of the way that the sailors tortured a shark is an example, if not an explanation, of an earlier sense of humor that is as distant to modern readers as the societies that talented travelers described. Second, he paid careful attention to different gender roles and behaviors, as can be seen here in his depiction of Tupinamba girls and women.

Léry's Histoire d'un voyage faict en la terre du Bresil autrement dite Amerique *was first published in French in Geneva in 1578, and it was sufficiently popular for subsequent editions to appear there in 1580, 1585, 1594, 1599, and 1600; a Dutch edition was printed in Amsterdam in 1597. But his ideas reached a much greater audience when the Flemish engraver Theodor de Bry used the text, along with Stade's, as the basis for one of the volumes of his America series in 1592. It is in that volume that the pictures of Tupinamba society reproduced here can be found.*

Of the bonitos, albacore, gilt-fish, porpoises, flying fish, and others of various kinds that we saw and took in the torrid zone.

From that time on we had a frothy sea and so fair a wind that we were pushed to three or four degrees this side of the Equator. There we caught a great many porpoises, dorado, albacore, bonitos, and a large quantity of several other kinds of fish. I had always thought that the sailors who spoke of flying fish were telling us tall tales; however, experience showed me that they really did exist.

We began to see big schools of them jump out of the water and soar into the air (just as larks and starlings do on land), flying almost as high as a pike's length, and sometimes to a distance of more than a hundred paces. Since often it even happened that some would hit against the masts and fall into our ships, we could easily catch them in our hands. Now to describe this fish (and I have seen and held any number of them going and coming from Brazil): it is something like a herring in form, but a little longer and rounder, with little barbells under the throat, and wings like those of a bat, almost as long as the whole body; it is very flavorful and good to eat. Since I have not seen any of them this side of the tropic of Cancer, I am of the Opinion (although I am not completely sure) that, liking a warm climate, they remain in the Torrid Zone, and do not venture out of it in the direction of either of the poles. There is still another thing that I have observed: these poor flying fish, whether they are in the water or in the air, are never at rest. For when they are in the sea, the albacore and other big fish, pursuing them to eat them, wage continual war; and if they try to escape by flight, there are certain sea-birds that seize and feed on them.

These sea-birds, which live as predators, are so tame that often, when they light on the coamings, rigging and spars of our ships, they let themselves be caught by hand. Since I have eaten some—and therefore seen both the inside and the outside—here is a description. They are of gray plumage, like sparrow-hawks; although they seem from the outside to be as big as crows, when they are plucked, you see that they have hardly more flesh than a sparrow, so it is a wonder that, being so small of body, they can still seize and eat fish bigger than they are. They have only one bowel, and their feet are flat like those of ducks.

To get back to the other fish that I have mentioned just now: the bonito, who is one of the best to eat that can be found, is very much like our common carp; however, it has no scales. I have seen a great many of them, for during the whole six weeks of our voyage they hardly left our ships, which they apparently followed because of the pitch and tar that the ships were rubbed with.

As for the albacore, they resemble the bonitos, but in size, there is no comparison between the two kinds, for I have seen and eaten my share of albacore that were almost five feet long and as big as a man's body. The albacore is not at all viscous; its flesh is as flaky as a trout's. With only one bone in its whole body and very little in the way of entrails, it must rank as one of the best seafish. Indeed, since we didn't have on hand everything necessary to prepare it well (nor do any passengers who make these long voyages), we did nothing but salt it and put big round slices of it on the coals, and we found it wonderfully good and flavorful even cooked in this fashion.

Those gentlemen who are so fond of delicacies, who refuse to venture onto the sea, and yet want fish to eat (as one says of cats who want the same without getting their feet wet)—if they could obtain this fish on land as easily as they do other seafood, and could have it prepared with a German sauce or in some other way, do you doubt that they would lick their fingers? I say expressly, if they could have it at their disposal on land: for as I have said of the flying fish, I don't think that these albacore, whose habitat is mainly in the deep ocean between the two tropics, come close enough to the shore for the fishermen to be able to get them home before they spoil. However, this holds only for us who live in this climate; as for the Africans to the east, and those of Peru and the regions on the west, it may well be that they have plenty.

The dorado—which I think bears that name because in the water it appears yellow, and shines like gold—has a shape something like that of a salmon; nonetheless, it is different in that it has a sort of hollow place in the back. But from having tasted it, I maintain that this fish is better than all those I have just mentioned; neither in salt water nor in fresh water is there a more delicate one.

Concerning porpoises, there are two kinds. While some have a face almost as pointed as a goosebeak, in others it is so rounded and blunt that when they lift their nose out of the water it looks like a ball. Because of the resemblance between these and hooded monks, when we were on the sea we called them "monks'-heads." I have seen some of both kinds that were five to six feet long, with a wide, forked tail; they all had an opening on the head, through which they not only took in wind and breathed, but also sometimes sprayed out water. But especially when the sea begins to stir itself up, these porpoises, appearing suddenly on the water in the midst of the waves and billows that toss them about, even at night turn the sea green, and indeed seem themselves to be all green. It is a great amusement to hear them blow and snort; you would think that they really were ordinary pigs, such as we have on land. When the mariners see them swim about and bestir themselves in this way, they take it as a sure sign of an approaching storm, which I have often seen borne out. In moderate weather, when the sea was only frothy, we sometimes saw them in such great abundance that all around us, as far as our view could extend, it seemed that the sea was all porpoises; however, since they did not let themselves be caught as easily as did many other kinds of fish, we didn't have them as often as we wished.

Since we are on the subject, to better satisfy the reader, I want to describe the means I saw the sailors use to catch them. The one among them who is most expert and experienced in this kind of fishing lies in wait along the bowsprit, holding an iron harpoon hefted with a pole of the thickness and about half of the length of a pike, tied to four or five fathoms of line. When he sees a school of porpoises approach, he picks out one to aim for, and throws this weapon with such force that if it reaches its target it does not fail to pierce it. Once he has struck it, he lets out the rope, still firmly holding on to the end. The porpoise, in struggling, works the harpoon deeper into himself, and loses blood in the water. When he has lost a little strength, the other mariners, to help their companion, come with an iron hook called a "gaff" (also hafted with a long wooden pole), and by the strength of their arms they haul the porpoise into the ship. On the voyage over we caught about twenty-five of them in this fashion.

As for the insides of a porpoise: its four flippers are lifted off, just as you would remove the four hams from a pig; it is split, and the tripes (the backbone too if so desired) and the ribs are removed; open and hung in that fashion you would say that it is an ordinary pig—indeed, his liver has the same taste, although it is true that the fresh meat is too sweetish in smell and is not good. As for the lard, all those that I have seen had only an inch of it, and I think there are none that have more than two inches. Therefore no longer be duped when those merchants and fishwives, both in Paris and elsewhere, say that their Lenten bacon, which is four fingers thick, is porpoise: for it is certainly whale fat. There were little ones in the bellies of some that we caught (which we roasted like sucking pigs), and therefore, whatever others may have written to the contrary, I think that porpoises, like cows, carry their litters in their bellies instead of multiplying by eggs, as almost all the other fishes do. Even though I would not make any decision here, lest anyone would argue the point by citing to me those who have firsthand experience—rather than those who have only read books—, no one will meanwhile prevent my believing what I have seen.

We also caught many sharks; found in the sea even when it is calm and quiet, they seem all green. Some are more than four feet long, and proportionately thick. Still, since their flesh is not very good, the mariners don't eat it unless they are forced to it by lack of better fish. They have a skin almost as coarse and rough as a file, and a flat, wide head with the mouth as deeply cleft as that of a wolf or an English mastiff. These sharks, moreover, are not only monstrous in appearance but also, since they have very sharp and cutting teeth, are so dangerous that if they grab a man by the leg or some other part of the body, they either carry that member off, or drag him to the bottom. When the sailors, in time of calm, bathe in the sea, they are much afraid of them; when we fished for them (as we often did with fishhooks as thick as a finger) and got them on to the deck of the ship, we had to be as careful as you would have to be on land with ill-tempered and dangerous dogs. Not only are these sharks no good for eating, but whether they are caught or whether they are in the water, they do only harm. So, just as you do with dangerous beasts, after we had stabbed and tormented those that we could catch, as if they were mad dogs, either we beat them with great blows of iron clubs, or else, having first cut their flippers and tied a barrel ring to their tails, we threw them back into the sea. Since they floated and struggled a long time on the surface of the water before sinking, we had much good sport watching them.

Although the sea tortoises in this Torrid Zone are far from being so huge and monstrous that you could roof a whole house or make a navigable ship from a single shell (as Pliny claimed for the ones from the Indies and the islands of the Red Sea), nevertheless, because you see some that are so long, wide, and thick as to be scarcely believable for those who haven't seen them, I will mention them here in passing. And without making a longer discourse on the subject, I will let the reader judge what they can be like by the following sample. One that was caught by the ship of our Vice-Admiral was so big that eighty people in the ship had a good meal off it (at least by the standards of shipboard life). The oval upper shell, which was given to our captain the Sieur de Sainte-Marie, was more than two and a half feet wide, and proportionately strong and thick. Moreover, the flesh is so much like veal that, especially when it is larded and roasted, it has almost the same taste.

This is how I saw them caught on the sea. During fair and calm weather (you rarely see them otherwise), when they come up out of the water, the sun warms their backs and their shells until they can no longer stand it, and to cool off they flip over and lie belly up. The mariners who see them in that state approach in their boat as quietly as they can; when they are near they hook them between two shells with the iron gaffs I have mentioned. Then it is as much as four or five men can do with the strength of their arms to haul them into the boat. This, in brief, is what I wanted to say about the tortoises and fish that we caught at that time; for I will speak later about dolphins, as well as whales and other sea monsters. . . .

Of the natural qualities, strength, stature, nudity, disposition and ornamentation of the body of the Brazilian savages, both men and women, who live in America, and whom I frequented for about a year

[F]or now let us leave a little to one side our Tupinamba in all their magnificence, frolicking and enjoying the good times that they know so well how to have, and see whether their wives and daughters, whom they call *quoniam* (and in some parts, since the arrival of the Portuguese, *Maria*) are better adorned and decked out.

First, besides what I said at the beginning of this chapter—that they ordinarily go naked as well as the men—they also share with them the practice of pulling out all body hair, as well as the eyelashes and eyebrows. They do not follow the men's custom regarding the hair of the head: for while the latter, as I have said above, shave their hair in front and clip it in the back, the women not only let it grow long, but also (like the women over here), comb and wash it very carefully; in fact, they tie it up sometimes with a red-dyed cotton string. However, they more often let it hang on their shoulders, and go about wearing it loose.

They differ also from the men in that they do not slit their lips or cheeks, and so they wear no stones in their faces. But as for their ears, they have them pierced in so extreme a fashion for wearing pendants that when they are removed, you could easily pass a finger through the holes; what is more, when they wear pendants made of that big scallop shell called *vignol*, which are white, round, and as long as a medium-sized tallow candle, their ears swing on their shoulders, even over their breasts; if you see them from a little distance, it looks like the ears of a bloodhound hanging down on each side.

As for their faces, this is how they paint them. A neighbor woman or companion, with a little brush in hand, begins a small circle right in the middle of the cheek of the one who is having her face painted; turning the brush all around to trace a scroll or the shape of a snail-shell, she will continue until she has adorned and bedizened the face with various hues of blue, yellow, and red; also (as some shameless women in France likewise do), where the eyelashes and eyebrows have been plucked, she will not neglect to apply a stroke of the brush.

Moreover, they make big bracelets, composed of several pieces of white bone, cut and notched like big fish-scales, which they know how so closely to match and so nicely to join—with wax and a kind of gum mixed together into a glue—that it could not be better done. When the work is finished, it is about a foot and a half long; it could be best compared to the cuff used in playing ball over here. Likewise, they wear the white necklaces (called *boüre* in their language) that I have described above, but they do not wear them hung around the neck, as you have heard that the men do; they simply twist them around their arms. That is why, for the same use, they find so pretty the little beads of glass that they call *mauroubi*, in yellow, blue, green, and other colors, strung like a rosary, which we brought over there in great number for barter. Indeed, whether we went into their villages or they came into our fort, they would offer us fruits or some other commodity from their country in exchange for them, and with their customary flattering speech, they would be after us incessantly, pestering us and saying "*Mair, deagatorem, amabé mauroubi*": that is, "Frenchman, you are good; give me some of your bracelets of glass beads." They would do the same thing to get combs from us, which they call *guap* or *kuap*, mirrors, which they call *aroua*, and all the other goods and merchandise we had that they desired.

But among the things doubly strange and truly marvelous that I observed in these Brazilian women, there is this: although they do not paint their bodies, arms, thighs, and legs as often as the men do, and do not cover themselves with feathers or with anything else that grows in their land, still, although we tried several times to give them dresses and shifts (as I have said we did for the men, who sometimes put them on), it has never been in our power to make them wear clothes: to such a point were they resolved (and I think they have not changed their minds) not to allow anything at all on their bodies. As a pretext to exempt themselves from wearing clothes and to remain always naked, they would cite their custom, which is this: whenever they come upon springs and clear rivers, crouching on the edge or else getting in, they throw water on their heads with both hands, and wash themselves and plunge in with their whole bodies like ducks—on some days more than a dozen times; and they said that it was too much trouble to get undressed so often. Is that not a fine and pertinent excuse? But whatever it may be, you have to accept it, for to contest it further with them would be in vain, and you would gain nothing by it.

This creature delights so much in her nakedness that it was not only the Tupinamba women of the mainland, living in full liberty with their husbands, fathers, and kinsmen, who were so obstinate in refusing to dress themselves in any way at all; even our women prisoners of war, whom we had bought and whom we held as slaves to work in our fort—even they, although we forced clothing on them, would secretly strip off the shifts and other rags, as soon as night had fallen, and would not be content unless, before going to bed, they could promenade naked all around our island. In short, if it had been up to these poor wretches, and if they had not been compelled by great strokes of the whip to dress themselves, they would choose to bear the heat and burning of the sun, even the continual skinning of their arms and shoulders carrying earth and stones, rather than to endure having any clothes on.

And there you have a summary of the customary ornaments, rings, and jewelry of the American women and girls. So, without any other epilogue here, let the reader, by this narration, contemplate them as he will.

When I treat the marriage of the savages, I will recount how their children are equipped from birth. As for the children above the age of three or four years, I especially took great pleasure in watching the little boys, whom they call *conomi-miri*; plump and chubby (much more so than those over here), with their bodkins of white bone in their split lips, the hair shaved in their style, and sometimes with their bodies painted, they never failed to come dancing out in a troop to meet us when they saw us arrive in their villages. They would tag behind us and play up to us, repeating continually in their babble, "*Contoüassat, amabé pinda*": that is, "My friend and my ally, give me some fishhooks." If thereupon we yielded (which I have often done), and tossed ten or twelve of the smallest hooks into the sand and dust, they would rush to pick them up; it was great sport to see this swarm of naked little rascals stamping on the earth and scratching it like rabbits.

During that year or so when I lived in that country, I took such care in observing all of them, great and small, that even now it seems to me that I have them before my eyes, and I will forever have the idea and image of them in my mind. But their gestures and expressions are so completely different from ours, that it is difficult, I confess, to represent them well by writing or by pictures. To have the pleasure of it, then, you will have to go see and visit them in their own country. "Yes," you will say, "but the plank is very long." That is true, and so if you do not have a sure foot and a steady eye, and are afraid of stumbling, do not venture down that path.

We have yet to see more fully, as the matters that I treat present themselves, what their houses are like, and to see their household utensils, their ways of sleeping, and other ways of doing things.

Before closing this chapter, however, I must respond both to those who have written and to those who think that the frequenting of these naked savages, and especially of the women, arouses wanton desire and lust. Here, briefly, is what I have to say on this point. While there is ample cause to judge that, beyond the immodesty of it, seeing these women naked would serve as a predictable enticement to concupiscence; yet, to report what was commonly perceived at the time, this crude nakedness in such a woman is much less alluring than one might expect. And I maintain that the elaborate attire, paint, wigs, curled hair, great ruffs, farthingales, robes upon robes, and all the infinity of trifles with which the women and girls over here disguise themselves and of which they never have enough, are beyond comparison the cause of more ills than the ordinary nakedness of the savage women—whose natural beauty is by no means inferior to that of the others. If decorum allowed me to say more, I make bold to say that I could resolve all the objections to the contrary, and I would give reasons so evident that no one could deny them. Without going into it further, I defer concerning the little that I have said about this to those who have made the voyage to the land of Brazil, and who, like me, have seen both their women and ours.

I do not mean, however, to contradict what the Holy Scripture says about Adam and Eve, who, after their sin, were ashamed when they recognized that they were naked, nor do I wish in any way that this nakedness be approved; indeed, I detest the heretics who have tried in the past to introduce it over here, against the law of nature (which on this particular point is by no means observed among our poor Americans).

But what I have said about these savages is to show that, while we condemn them so austerely for going about shamelessly with their bodies entirely uncovered, we ourselves, in the sumptuous display, superfluity, and excess of our own costume, are hardly more laudable. And, to conclude this point, I would to God that each of us dressed modestly, and more for decency and necessity than for glory and worldliness.

Pictures of Brazil

From the time that Vespucci arrived in Brazil, images of that land began to circulate in Europe. Those pictures included a 1505 broadside that purported to show a Tupinamba settlement, with individuals dressed in feathers in the foreground engaging in a variety of activities (including a mother nursing an infant) while European sailing vessels arrive in the background. The Tupinambas are gathered under what appears to be a hut with a thatched roof, with beams holding various human body parts, apparently drying before being consumed. Images that appeared in Sebastian Münster's Cosmographia Univeralis, *published in 1552, also demonstrate cannibalism: in one memorable image two Tupinambas stand alongside a table happily chopping up some unfortunate victim.*

The pictures that appear here illustrated the accounts of Hans Stade and Jean de Léry. Each corresponds to particular segments of their travel accounts. The artist who created the first image is unknown; the rest were engraved by Theodor de Bry, who was also responsible for the images that appeared in other illustrated books in the late sixteenth century. The images from his America series, including these pictures of Brazil, are among the most well-known visual images of any sixteenth-century population.

The pictures depict memorable scenes in the narratives: Stade witnessing cannibal acts; the title page of de Bry's book, in which cannibalism can be found in three distinct scenes; the flying fish that Léry described; a Tupinamba ritual; Brazilian mourning customs; and a vivid depiction of the roasting and eating of human body parts.

Figure 7. Stade and the Cannibals

Hans Stade was obsessed with the fear that he was going to be killed and eaten. The picture here represents a composite of scenes described in his text. Stade, the bearded figure, can be seen being held on his knees as one Tupinamba prepares to hit him, and gesticulating toward a decapitated corpse; limbs roast over open fires. This image can be found in the earliest published version of Stade's account: Warhaftig historia und beschreibung eyner landschafte der Wilden/ Nacketen/ Grimmigen Menschstresser Leuten in der Newenwelt America gelegen *(Marpurg, 1557).*

Figure 8. Tupinamba Cannibals

Figure 9. Tupinamba Cannibals

Almost forty years after the first publication of Stade's account, the Flemish engraver Theodor de Bry offered another version. He coupled the account with the narrative of Jean de Léry in Americae Tertia Pars, *published in Frankfurt am Main in 1592. The title page for that volume was among the most notable of the sixteenth century, featuring three Tupinamba cannibals: a man chewing on a human leg, a woman gnawing on a forearm, and a toddler perched on her shoulder apparently waiting for a piece of flesh. At the bottom of the title page and on the picture from the inside of the book, the viewer can see such behavior in its own setting, with Tupinamba men and women alike consuming human body parts roasting over an open fire. The child from the cover can be seen in the lower right corner, eating a human finger.*

Léry offered his readers a detailed account of how the Tupinambas prepared the body. They sliced the body open and "in order to incite their children to share their vengefulness, take them one at a time and rub their bodies, arms, thighs, and legs with the blood of their enemies." Once they had cut the body into pieces—"no butcher" in France "could more quickly dismember a sheep"—the "old women (who, as I have said, have an amazing appetite for human flesh) are all assembled beside it to receive the fat that drips off along the posts of the big, high wooden grills, and exhort the men to do what it takes to provide them always with such meat. Licking their fingers, they say 'Yguatou': that is, 'It is good'" [(image) De Bry, Americae Tertia Pars, *Frankfurt, 1592; (text) Léry,* History of a Voyage, *126].*

Figure 10. Flying Fish in the Atlantic

The missionary Jean de Léry's account included fantastic scenes of flying fish leaping out of the sea while his ship crossed the Atlantic. Some of those fish landed on the decks of the Europeans' vessels, providing welcome sustenance to the travelers. These "poor flying fish, whether they are in the water or in the air, are never at rest," Léry wrote. "For when they are in the sea, the albacore and other big fish, pursuing them to eat them, wage continual war; and if they try to escape by flight, there are certain sea-birds that seize and feed on them" (Léry, History of a Voyage, *15). De Bry captured the essence of the text in this illustration. The image did more than provide visual evidence to support the travel account. By representing at least some of the Atlantic's denizens in this way, his vision contradicted the many images of the Atlantic which emphasized the dangers to be found in its waters, including the sea monsters awaiting the unwary who crossed their paths (de Bry,* Americae Tertia Pars, *Frankfurt, 1592).*

Figure 11. Tupinamba Dance

Europeans who traveled to the Western Hemisphere often wrote about native tobacco uses. For much of the sixteenth century, the plant seemed to be a panacea to Europeans, who read accounts of the ways that it could be used to cure an astonishing variety of human ailments. Yet at the same time that travelers offered reports testifying to the plant's medicinal potential, images such as this scene from de Bry's illustration of Léry's account also suggested the close links between the plant and what Europeans believed were savage customs or worship of the devil. In this picture a small group of European men, evident in the top right corner, survey the scene but do not participate in it, despite the temptations of tobacco. In describing the use of tobacco in an indigenous ritual, Léry wrote that those in the middle of the circle blow "the smoke in all directions on the other savages" and "say to them, 'So that you may overcome your enemies, receive all of you the spirit of strength'"(Léry, History of a Voyage, *142). By the early seventeenth century, when Europeans began to enjoy the sensations of smoking and used tobacco for enjoyment instead of only as a cure, some critics made the link between the weed and its use by Native Americans (de Bry,* Americae Tertia Pars, *Frankfurt, 1592).*

Figure 12. Tupinambas Crying

According to Jean de Léry, Tupinamba Indians cried on two occasions: when greeting a traveler and in mourning. In the first instance, the missionary noted that "as soon as the visitor has arrived in the house" of the host, "he is seated on a cotton bed suspended in the air, and remains there for a short while without saying a word. Then the women come and surround the bed, crouching with their buttocks against the ground and with both hands over their eyes; in this manner, weeping their welcome to the visitor, they will say a thousand things in his praise."

But crying also took place in more familiar circumstances to the Europeans. When a member of a Tupinamba community died, especially if the person was a household head, the singing of a village "is suddenly turned to tears," as Léry reported, "and they lament so loudly that if we were in a village where someone had recently died, either we didn't try to find a bed there, or we didn't expect to sleep that night." He watched the preparations of the corpse for burial, noting that their graves were round instead of rectangular and the deceased's limbs bound together and then the dead placed almost in a sitting position in the hole. "If it is some worthy elder who has died," he added, "he will be entombed in his house, enveloped in his cotton bed; buried with him will be some necklaces, feathers and other objects that he used to wear when he was alive" [(image) De Bry, America Tertia Pars, *Frankfurt, 1592; (text) Léry,* History of a Voyage to the Land of Brazil, *164, 173–175].*

Document 24

The New Found Worlde, or Antarctike (1568)

By André Thevet, *The New Found Worlde, or Antarctike*
(London, 1568)

André Thevet (1516?–1592) was no neophyte when he crossed the Atlantic Ocean on a voyage that took him to Brazil in 1555. He had by that point been traveling since the 1540s and had already produced an important travel account, titled Cosmographie de Levant, *which had been published in Lyons in 1554 after he returned from a four-year journey to the East. That book described his travels in Venice, Jerusalem, Alexandria, Athens, and Constantinople*

His Brazilian journey was briefer than he had intended. Only ten weeks after he arrived, Thevet became ill and decided to return to France, which he reached in January 1556. He later claimed that he had seen parts of North America, including Florida and possibly even Canada, but there is no proof that he ever made such a journey. As a result, his accounts have always been suspect, especially in the minds of a rival such as Jean de Léry, who was skeptical about all of Thevet's claims. Still, despite the hostility that he received—which was based at least in part on the fact that Thevet was a Catholic and his critics tended to be Protestants—Thevet managed to find printers eager to publish his account. Les Singularitez de la France antarctique, *published in Paris in 1557, contained his first substantial writings about the Western Hemisphere. An Italian version was published in Venice in 1561. Nine years after the first printing in Paris, an English-language edition appeared and found at least one well-known reader: Sir Walter Ralegh, who later referred to Thevet's writings in his own work.*[11]

The parts of Thevet's account here focus on particular aspects of the society of the Tupinambas, particularly the ways that they understood their dreams, the importance of visions in their society, and their belief in the immortality of the soul. Given his brief time in Brazil, it is certainly possible that Thevet

---

11. For details on Thevet's life and writings, see Roger Schlesinger and Arthur P. Stabler, eds., *André Thevet's North America: A Sixteenth-Century View* (Kingston, Canada: McGill-Queen's University Press, 1986), xvii–xli; and Frank Lestrigant, *Mapping the Renaissance World: The Geographical Imagination in the Age of Discovery*, trans. David Fausett (Berkeley: University of California Press, 1994; orig. pub. Paris, 1991).

had little grasp of the complex interior lives of the Tupinambas. Nonetheless, given his prominence and the wide circulation of his ideas, the fact that he published this report provides crucial insight into European views of Native Americans.

After he returned, Thevet achieved widespread acclaim in France. He be-came the royal cosmographer to four French kings and the personal chaplain (aumônier) to Catherine de' Medici, King Henri II's wife. Over time he also came to supervise the royal cabinet of curiosities, kept at Fontainebleau, and he had control of precious manuscripts that told of distant places. Such ac-cess to prominent patrons and valuable information enabled Thevet to create his masterwork, La Cosmographie Universelle, *a massive two-volume geography of the entire world known to Europeans in 1575. In his later years he produced a substantial compendium of brief biographies of notable figures titled* Les Vrais pourtraits vies des hommes illustres, *published in Paris in 1584, and an unpublished work of geography.*

Of visions, dreams and illusions, that these Americans have, and of the persecution that they receive of wicked spirits

It is a wonderful thing, that these poor men although they be not rea-sonable, for ye they are deprived from the right use of reason, and from the knowledge of God, are subject to many fantastical illusions & persecutions of wicked spirits. We have said that before the coming of our saviour Jesus Christ, we were in like manner vexed: for the devil studieth only to seduce that creature that hath no knowledge of God. Even so these poor *Americans* do oftentimes in an other, the which they name in their language *Agnan*, the which spirit persecuteth them day and night, not only their soul, but also their body, beating them, and doing them much injury, so that you shall hear them make a pitiful cry, saying in their language, (if there be any christian by or near) seest thou not *Agnan* ye beateth me, defend me if thou wilt that I shall serve thee, and cut thy wood: for many times they will travel to the Brazil wood for a small reward. Therefore in the night they will not go out of their cabins or houses, without bearing fire with them, the which they say, is a sovereign defense and remedy against their enemy. And I thought that it had been a Fable when it was showed me first, but I have seen by experience this wicked spirit to be driven out by a christian, in invocating & naming

Jesus Christ. Also the people of *Ginney* [Guinea], & of *Canada* are likewise tormented, chiefly in the woods, wheras they have many visions, and they call this sprite in their language *Grigri*. Furthemore these wild men of *America* being this disprovided of reason, and of the knowledge of verity, are easy to fall into many foolish errors. They note & observe their dreams diligently, thinking that all that they have dreamed, should suddenly come to pass. If they have dreamed that they shall have victory of their enemies, or to be van-quished and overcome, you shall not persuade them the contrary, but they believe it assuredly, as we do the Gospel. Of a truth there be Philosophers which hold opinion, that some dreams will naturally come to pass, according to the humors that reign, or other dispositions of the body, as to dream of fire, water, black things & such like. But to believe and affirm the other dreams, as those of these *Americans*, it is a thing impertinent, & contrary to the true religion of Jesus Christ: and to my judgement so are all other. Macrobius in the dream of Scipion, saith that some dreams come to pass, & happen because of the vanity of ye dreamers. Other dreams come of things that we have too much apprehended. Others beside our *Americans*, do give credit to dreams, as the *Lacedemonians*, the *Persians* & certain others. These wild men have another strange opinion which is an abuse, they esteem some among them to be very Prophets, whom they name in their language *Pages*, to whom they declare their dreams, & the others do interpret them, & they hold opinion that they tell truth. These may be compared to Philon the first interpreter of dreams, & to Trogus Pompeius, that therein was very excellent. I might here bring in many things of dreams & divinations, and what dreams are true or no. Like-wise of their kinds & the causes thereof, as we have been instructed of our elders. But for that it is repugnant to our religion, and for that defense is made to give thereto any credit, we will leave it, and leave only to the holy scrip-ture, and to that which is commanded us, & therefore I will speak thereof no more: but sure I am that for one that hitteth right, there are a number contrary. Let us return to our wild men of *America*, they bear great reverence to these Prophets, otherwise named *Pages* or *Charaibes*, which is to say, half Gods, and they are truly idolators, even as were the ancient Gentiles.

Of false Prophets and Magicians, that are in this country of America, the which invoke and call upon wicked spirits, and of a tree named Ahouai

This people being so far from the truth, beside the persecution that they receive of wicked spirits, their errors and dreams, yet are they so far out of reason that they worship the devil, by the mean of some of his ministers named *Pages*, of the which sort we have spoken already. These *Pages* or *Charaibes*, are men of a wicked life, the which are given to serve the devil for to deceive their neighbors. Such deceivers for to color their wickedness, and to be esteemed honorable among others, remain not continually in one place, but they are vagabonds, wandering here and there, through the woods and other places, and returning with others, at certain hours, making them believe that they have conferred and counseled with the sprits, for public affairs, and that they must do so and so, or that this or that shall happen, and then they are received and entertained honorably, being nourished and entertained for this their doing: and they esteem themselves happy, that may remain in their favor and good grace, and give or offer to them some present. Likewise if it happen, that any of them have indignation or quarrel against his neighbor, they come to these *Pages*, to the end that they [murder] with poison him or them to whom they will evil. Among other things they help themselves with a tree named in their language *Ahouai*, bearing fruit venomous and mortal, the which is of the greatness of a little chestnut, and it is very poison, especially the nut. The men for a light and little cause will give thereof to their wives, being angered, and the women likewise to the men: likewise these wicked women when they are with child, if their husbands have displeased them, they will take instead of this fruit a certain herb, for to make their fruit of their womb to come before their time, this fruit being white with this nut, is made like this greek letter Δ Delta, and of this fruit the wild men when the nut or kernel is out, they make bells, and hang them on their legs, the which maketh as a great noise as the Morris dancers in our country. The wild men will in no wise give of this fruit to strangers being fresh gathered, likewise they forbid their children in no wise to touch thereof before that the kernel be fallen away. This tree in height is like to our pear trees, the leave of two or three fingers long, and two fingers broad, being green or springing all the year long, the bark is whitish. When there is a branch cut thereof, it rendreth a white juice or liquor almost like milk, the tree being cut it casteth a marvelous stinking smell, therefore the wild men will put it to no use, not to make therewith fire wood. I will forbear here to set forth the properties of many trees, bearing fruits marvelous fair, nevertheless as much and rather more venemous than this tree of which we speak. Furthermore ye must note that the wild men have these *Pages* in such honor and reverence, that they worship them or rather do Idolatry to them, especially when they return from any place: ye shall see this people go before them prostrating themselves, and praying them, saying, Make that I be not sick, that I die not, neither I nor my children, and such like things. And they will answer, it thou shalt not die, thou shalt not be sick and such like. If it chance that these *Pages* speak not truth, and that things happen otherwise than they have predestinated, they make no difficulty to kill him or them, as unworthy of that title and dignity of *Pages*, ever Village nourisheth of them, some one, some two or three, according to their greatness, and when it behooveth to know any great thing, they use certain ceremonies and devilish invocations, the which are made after this manner. First is made a new lodging, in the which never man before hath dwelled, and there within they will rear [raise] or make a new white bed and clean according to their manner. Then they will carry into the said lodging great quantity of victuals, as *Cahouin*, which is their ordinary drink made by a virgin of ten or twelve years of age, likewise of their food made of roots, the which they use instead of bread. So all things being thus prepared the people being assembled do guide this their gentle Prophet to this new lodging, whereas he shall remain alone, after that a maid hath given him water to wash withal, but ye must note, before this mystery he must abstain from his wife the space of nine days, being in the house alone: and the people gone a little back, he lieth flat down on the bed, and beginneth to invocate and call the wicked spirit for the space of an hour, and furthermore making his accustomed ceremonies, in such sort that in the end of his invocations, the spirit commeth to him hissing, and whistling, as they say. Others have showed me, that this wicked spirit commeth sometimes in the presence of all the people, though they see him not, but they here a fearful noise, then they cry all with one voice in their language, saying: we pray the to tell the truth to our Prophet, that tarieth for thee there within: their intorrogations is of their enemies, to know who shall have the victory, with the like answers, that say, who shall be taken and eaten of their enemies? Who shall be hurt or offended with any wild beast or such like. Some of them among other things, showed me that their Prophet had forshowed our coming. They call this spirit *Houioulsira*: this & many other things have Christians affirmed me of, that had dwelled there a long time. And they never take any great enterprise in hand, before they know the answer of their Prophet. When this mystery is accomplished, the Prophet commeth out, who being compassed about with people, maketh a long narration unto them, wherein he reherseth all that he hath heard of this spirit: and God knoweth the greetings, rewards and presents that are made unto him. The *Americans* have not been the first that have practiced magic, but before them it hath been common in many nations, until the coming of our Saviour Jesus Christ, whose presence did efface and overthrow the power of Satan, by the which means the devil fought to beguile and deceive ye world: it is not therefore without a cause, that it is forbidden by the holy Scripture, yea by God's own mouth. Of this *Magic*, we find two chief & principal kinds, one is in having familiar and secret talk with wicked spirits, who openeth & showeth the most secretest things of nature in deed, the one is more wickeder than the other, but they are both naught & full of curiosity. Why should we, seeing that by the providence of God we have all things that to us is necessary and needful, go about to seek out the secrets of nature and other things, which our Saviour Jesus Christ both observed to himself: such curiousness in us, showeth an unperfect Judgement, want of faith and true Religion, and yet the simple people that believeth such things is most abused: Surely I cannot but marvel, especially in a country (where good and politic laws are used) why such filthy and wicked abuses be left unpunished, with a company of old witches, which put herbs to arms, writings about necks, with other mysteries and ceremonies, as to heal fevers and other things, which are very Idolatry, and worthy of grievous punishment. But at this day such wickedness may be found among those that are in Authority, of which sort we should have good counsel and judgment, but they themselves are first blind. . . .

How these Americans believe the soul to be immortal

This poor people although they be ignorant & err, yet their error and ignorance is more to be born with all, than the *Arians* of our time which being not content to have been created to the image and likeness of the eternal God, perfit [perfect?] above all creatures, against all scripture and miracles, they will show themselves like brute beasts without law or reason, and therefore because of their obstinate error, they should be handled like beasts, for there is no beast be he never so wild and brutish, but will obey and serve man, as the very image of God, the which we daily see. But it will one day come to pass, that these wicked Imps shall well know that there resteth somewhat after the death of this world that at the later day shall appear before the majesty of God, there to give account of their wicked and damnable error. Now therefore these poor people do think ye soul to be immortal, the which they name in their language *Cherepicouare*, the which I knew in asking of them what became of their soul when they were dead. The souls said they of them that have valiantly fought with their enemies, goeth with many other souls to places of pleasure, goodly woods, gardens, and orchards, but to the contrary those that have not well defended their country nor resisted their enemies shall go with *Agnan*, that is, to the wicked spirit that tormented them. In a time I boldened my self to ask or inquire of a great king of that country as touching the immortality of the soul, who was come above thirty leagues of[f?], to see us, but he answered me fiercely in his language these words, knowest thou not said he that after we be dead, our souls to into a far country whereas they be found altogether in fair & goodly places, as our Prophets do say that visit them oftentimes & speak unto them, the which opinion they believe and hold of a truth. Another time we went to visit another great king of that country named *Pindahouson*, whom we found sick in his bed of an Ague, who among other things demanded of me what became of the souls of our friends, and others when they died, and I made answer that they went with *Toupan*, the which he did easily believe, upon the which he answered me these words: come hither said he, I have heard of the[e?] speak much of *Toupan*, that can do all things, speak to him for me that I be healed, and if I can be made whole, I will give the[e] many fair gifts, yea I will be clad, and arrayed as thou art, bear such a great beard, and honor *Toupan*, as thou dost. And indeed when that he was whole, the Lord of *Villegagnon* was determined to have him baptized, and therefore he kept him always with him. They have another foolish opinion, the which is, that being on the water, be it sea or River, for to go against their enemies, if that in the mean time there arise a tempest or rage on the water, as many times there doth, they think that it commeth of the souls of their parents or friends, but wherefore they cannot tell, and for to appease the tempest they cast some thing into the water, in token of a present or offering, thinking by this means to appease the winds.

Document 25

A True Reporte of the Laste Voyage into the West and Northwest (1577)

By Dionyse Settle, *A True reporte of the laste voyage into the West and Northwest regions, & c. 1577, worthily atchieved by Capteine Frobisher* (London, 1577)

Martin Frobisher (1535?–1594) was convinced that the Northwest Passage existed and that he would find it. In 1576, 1577, and 1578 he led English expeditions across the frigid waters of the North Atlantic and toward the Western Hemisphere. He and his crew met and learned how to trade with the indigenous Inuit of that region. But the visitors also discovered that these native peoples could pose a threat to them, and so they often approached them warily. The Inuit, for their part, welcomed the possibility of trading with the newcomers, though they learned that Europeans were often dangerous. Opportunism and suspicion mingled uneasily in this world strewn with icebergs.

Frobisher wanted to find the quick water route to East Asia that had eluded many Europeans before him. But the journals from these voyages suggest that he became preoccupied with two unrelated phenomena. First, he became convinced that there was gold to be found on the islands. The signs of it were obvious: the rock glittered as if it contained precious metal, and his men found dead spiders on those rocks—a sure sign, according to the inherited wisdom, that gold lay within. After Frobisher brought back a small number of rocks on his first voyage, an assayer in England offered the opinion that there was gold to be found. By the time Frobisher went back for his third voyage, he brought with him enough miners to carve away two hundred tons of ore, which they loaded onto the ships for the return. The news this time was less promising: there was no gold there.

Frobisher and his crew also became obsessed with another local phenomenon: icebergs. The journals that survive from these three expeditions contain countless references to the ice, the cold, and the raging winter storms that at any moment threatened to kill the unlucky or the unwary. Though Frobisher lost only five men during these years—they were left behind on one voyage and apparently fashioned their own small boat and tried to sail back on their own before winter's blast had subsided—the "mountains of icebergs" mentioned by Dionyse Settle made a permanent impression on those who survived.

Dionyse Settle, one of the chroniclers of these voyages, left a particularly riveting account of the day-to-day struggles that beset the travelers. His book, small and light enough to slip into a jacket pocket, included incidents that seem almost incredible now. The English doubted the intellectual capacity of the individuals they met, who seemed locked in an earlier stage of development (evident by their consumption of raw food); they even pulled off the buskins of one elderly woman to see if she had cloven feet. Yet when Frobisher wanted to gather information about the five missing men, he left a pen, ink, and paper for the natives to use, assuming that they would know how to employ these tools to make some kind of effective communication. The Inuit did know what happened, but Frobisher's inability to carry on sustained conversations with them left him, not them, ignorant on the subject.

Frobisher managed to survive the three perilous crossings, and his feats were celebrated in England. Publishers issued various reports from those who went with him, and the records of the Stationers' Company of London suggests that there were even more titles about his journeys that no longer survive. Although Settle and others who sailed on those journeys feared that the ice and the cold would kill them all, Frobisher died in an English assault on the Spanish fortress of Crodon in 1594, a victim not of a journey to a distant part of the world but instead to the tragic hostilities of his age.[12]

The excerpt from Settle's account of Frobisher's second voyage picks up the journey as the crew nears Jackman's Sound. The narrative moves back and forth between notable incidents, such as the English sailors' battle with some Inuit, to observations of the ways that the natives utilized the resources of the environment to survive. Much of the time Settle seems skeptical, especially when he doubted that anyone could live for long in this region. Yet despite his sense that the Inuit were uncivilized, Settle's detailed remarks about the region's fauna and the ways that the local people prepared their weapons suggests something approaching appreciation for the skill with which these natives managed to find ways to master their environment.

At our first coming, the straights seemed to be shut up with a long mure [wall] of ice, which gave no little cause of discomfort unto us all: but our General, (to whose diligence, imminent dangers, and difficult attempts seemed nothing, in respect of his willing mind, for the commodity of his Prince and country,) with two little Pinnaces prepared of purpose, passed twice through them to the East shore, and the islands thereunto adjacent: and the ship, with the two barks, lay off and on something further into the sea, from the danger of the ice.

---

12. For material on Frobisher and his journeys, see two excellent works by James McDermott: *Martin Frobisher: Elizabethan Privateer* (New Haven, Conn.: Yale University Press, 2001), and his edition of *The Third Voyage of Martin Frobisher to Baffin Island, 1578* (Hakluyt Society, 3rd ser., 6 [London, 2001]).

Whilst he was searching the country near the shore, some of the people of the country showed themselves, leaping and dancing, with strange shrieks and cries, which gave no little admiration to our men. Our General desirous to allure them unto him by fair means, caused knives, & other things, to be proffered unto them, which they would not take at our hands: but being laid on the ground, & the party going away, they came and took up, leaving something of theirs to countervail the same. At the length, two of them leaving their weapons, came down to our General and Master, who did the like to them, commanding the company to stay, and went unto them: who, after certain dumb signs and mute congratulations, began to lay hands upon them, but they deliverly [quickly] escaped, and ran to their bows and arrows, and came fiercely upon them (not respecting the rest of our company, which were ready for their defense) but with their arrows hurt diverse of them: we took the one, and the other escaped.

Whilst our General was busied in searching the country and those Islands adjacent on the East shore, the ship and barks having great care, not to put far into the sea from him, for that he had small store of victuals, were forded to abide in a cruel tempest, chancing in the night, amongst and in the thickest of the ice, which was so monstrous, that even the least of a thousand had been of force sufficient, to have shivered our ship and barks into small portions, if God (who in all necessities, hath care upon the infirmity of man) had not provided for this our extremity a sufficient remedy, through the light of the night, whereby we might well discern to flee from such imminent dangers, which we avoided with 14 Bourdes [?] in one watch the space of 4 hours. If we had not incurred this danger amongst these monstrous Islands of ice, we should have lost our General and Master, and the most of our best sailors, which were on the shore destitute of victuals: but by the valor of our Master Gunner, being expert both in Navigation and other good qualities, we were all content to incur the dangers afore rehearsed, before we would, with our own safety, run into the Seas, to the destruction of our said General and his company.

The day following, being the 19 of July, our Captain returned to the ship, with good news of great riches, which showed itself in the bowels of those barren mountains, wherewith we were all satisfied. A sudden mutation. The one part of us being almost swallowed up the night before, with cruel Neptune's force, and the rest on shore, taking thought for their greedy paunches, how to find the way to New found land: at one moment we were all rapt with joy, forgetting, both where we were, and what we had suffered. Behold the glory of man, tonight contemning riches, and rather looking for death than otherwise: and tomorrow devising how to satisfy his greedy appetite with Gold.

Within four days after we had been at the entrance of the Straights, the Northwest and West winds dispersed the ice into the Sea, and made us a large entrance into the Straights, that without any impediment, on the 19 of July, we entered them, and the 20 thereof our General and Master, with great diligence, sought out and found the West Shore, and found out a fair Harbor for the ship and barks to ride in, and named it after our Master's mate, Jackman's sound, and brought the ship, barks, and all their company to safe anchor, except one man, which died by God's visitation.

Who so maketh Navigations to these countries, hath not only extreme winds, and furious Seas, to encounter withal, but also many monstrous and great Islands of ice: a thing both rare, wonderful, and greatly to be regarded.

We were forced, sundry times, while the ship did ride here at anchor, to have continual watch, with boats and men ready with Halsers, to knit fast unto such ice, which with the ebb and flood were tossed to and fro in the Harbor, and with force of oars to hale [haul?] them away, for endangering the ship.

Our General, certain days searched this supposed continent with America, and not finding the commodity to answer his expectation, after he had made trial thereof, he departed thence with two little barks, and men sufficient, to the East shore, being the supposed continent of Asia, & left the ship with most of the Gentlemen, Soldiers, and Sailors, until such time as he, either thought good to send, or come for them.

The stones of this supposed continent with America, be altogether sparkled, and glister in the Sun like Gold: so likewise doth the sand in the bright water, yet they verify the old Proverb: All is not gold that glistereth.

On this West shore we found a dead fish floating, which had in his nose a horn straight & torquet, of length two yards lacking two inches, being broken in the top, where we might perceive it hollow, into which some of our Sailors putting Spiders, they presently died. I saw not the trial hereof, but it was reported unto me of a truth: by the virtue whereof, we supposed it to be the sea Unicorn.

After our General had found out good harbor for the Ship and Barks to anchor in: and also such store of Gold oar as he thought himself satisfied withal, he sent back our Master with one of the Barks, to conduct the great Ship unto him, who coasting along the West shore, perceived a fair harbor, and willing to sound the same, at the entrance thereof they espied two tents of Seal skins.

At the sight of our men, the people fled into the mountains: nevertheless, our said Master went to their tents, and left some of our trifles, as Knives, Bells, and Glasses, and departed, not taking any thing of theirs, except one Dog to our Ship.

On the same day, after consultation had, we determined to see, if by fair means we could either allure them to familiarity, or otherwise take some of them, and so attain to some knowlege of those men, whom our General lost the year before.

At our coming back again, to the place where their tents were before, they had removed their tents further into the said Bay or Sound, where they might, if they were driven from the land, flee with their boats into the sea. We parting ourselves into two companies, and compassing a mountain, came suddenly upon them by land, who espying us, without any tarying fled to their boats, leaving the most part of their oars behind them for haste, and rowed down the Bay, where our two Pinnaces met them, & drove them to shore: but, if they had had all their oars, so swift are they in rowing, it had been lost time to have chased them.

When they were landed, they fiercely assaulted our men with their bows and arrows, who wounded three of them with our arrows: and perceiving themselves thus hurt, they desperately leapt off the Rocks into the Sea, and drowned themselves: which if they had not done, but had submitted themselves: or if by any means we could have taken them alive, (being their enemies as they judged) we would both have saved them, and also have sought remedy to cure their wounds received at our hands. But they, altogether void of humanity, and ignorant what mercy meaneth, in extremities look for no other than death: and perceiving they should fall into our hands, thus miserably by drowning rather desired death, than otherwise to be saved by us: the rest, perceiving their fellows in this distress, fled in to the high mountains. Two women, not being so apt to escape as the men were, the one for her age, and the other being encumbered with a young child, we took. The old wretch, whom divers of our Sailors supposed to be either a Devil, or a Witch, plucked off her buskins, to see, if she were cloven footed, and for her ugly hew and deformity, we let her go: the young woman and the child, we brought away. We named the place where they were slain, Bloody point: and the Bay or Harbor, York's sound, after the name of one of the Captains of the two Barks.

Having this knowledge, both of their fierceness and cruelty, and perceiving that fair means, as yet, is not able to allure them to familiarity, we disposed ourselves, contrary to our inclination, something to be cruel, returned to their tents, and made a spoil of the same. Their riches are neither Gold, Silver, or precious Drapery, but their said tents and boats, made of the skins of red Dear and Seal skins: also, Dogs like unto Wolves, but for the most part black, with other trifles, more to be wondered at for their strangeness, than for any other commodity needful for our use. . . .

In the time of our abode here, some of the country people came to show themselves unto us, sundry times on the main shore, near adjacent to the said Isle. Our General, desirous to have some news of his men, whom he lost the year before, with some company with him repaired with the Ship boat, to common, or sign with them for familiarity, whereunto he is persuaded to bring them. They, at the first show, made tokens, that three of his five men were alive, and desired pen, ink, and paper, and that within three or four days, they would return, and (as we judged) bring those of our men, which were living, with them.

They also made signs or tokens of their King, whom they called Cacough, and how he was carried on men's shoulders, and a man far surmounting any of our company, in bigness and stature.

With these tokens and signs of writing, pen, ink, and paper was delivered them, which they would not take at our hands: but being laid upon the shore, and the party gone away, they took up: which likewise they do, when they desire any thing for change of theirs, laying for that which is left, so much as they think will countervail the same, and not coming near together. It seemeth they have been used to this trade or traffic, with some other people adjoining, or not far distant from their Country.

After 4 days, some of them showed themselves upon the firm land, but not where they were before. Our General, very glad thereof, supposing to here of our men, went from the Island, with the boat, and sufficient company with him. They seemed very glad, and allured him, about a certain point of the land: behind which they might perceive a company of the crafty villains to lie lurking, whom our General would not deal withal, for that he knew not what company they were, and so with few signs dismissed them, and returned to his company.

Another time, as our said General was coasting the country, with two little Pinnaces, whereby at our return he might make the better relation thereof, three of the crafty villains, with a white skin allured us to them. Once again, our General, for yet he hoped to hear of his men, went towards them: at our coming near the shore, whereon they were we might perceive a number of them lie hidden behind great stones, & those three in sight laboring by all means possible, that some would come on land: & perceiving we made no haste by words nor friendly signs, which they used by clapping of their hands, and being without weapon, and but three in sight, they sought further means to provoke us thereunto. One alone laid flesh on the shore, which he tooke up with the Boat hook, as necessary victuals for the relieving of the man, woman, & child, whom we had taken: for as yet, they could not digest our meat: whereby they perceived themselves deceived of their expectation, for all their crafty allurements. Yet once again, to make (as it were) a full show of their crafty natures, and subtle sleights, to the intent thereby to have entrapped and taken some of our men, one of them counterfeited himself impotent and lame of his legs, who seemed to descend to the water side, with great difficulty: and to cover his craft the more, one of his fellows came down with him, and in such places, where he seemed unable to pass, he took him on his shoulders, set him by the water side, and departed from him, leaving him (as it should seem) all alone, who playing his counterfeit pageant very well, thought thereby to provoke some of us to come on shore, not fearing, but that any one of us might make our party good with a lame man.

Our General, having compassion of his impotency, thought good (if it were possible) to cure him therof: wherefore, he caused a souldier to shoot at him with his Caleever [Caliver, a light harquebus], which grazed before his face. The counterfeit villain deliverly [quickly] fled, without any impediment at all, and got him to his bow and arrows, and the rest from their lurking holes, with their weapons, bows, arrows, slings, and darts. Our General caused some Caleevers to be shot off at them, whereby some being hurt, they might hereafter stand in more fear of us.

This was all the answer, for this time, we could have of our men, or of our General's letter. Their crafty dealing, at these three several times, being thus manifest unto us, may plainly show, their disposition in other things to be correspondent. We judged that they used these stratagems, thereby to have caught some of us, for the delivering of the man, woman, & child whom we have taken.

They are men of a large corporature, and good proportion: their color is not much unlike the Sun burnt Country man, who laboreth daily in the Sun for his living.

They wear their hair something long, and cut before, either with stone or knife, very disorderly. Their women wear their hair long, and knit up with two loops, showing forth on either side of their faces, and the rest foltred [?] up on a knot. Also, some of their women race [slash or cut] their faces proportionally, as chin, cheeks, and forehead, and the wrists of their hands, wherupon they lay a color, which continueth dark azurine.

They eat their meat all raw, both flesh, fish, and foul, or something par-boiled with blood & a little water, which they drink. For lack of water, they will eat ice, that is hard frozen, as pleasantly as we will do Sugar Candy, or other Sugar.

If they, for necessity's sake, stand in need of the premises, such grass as the country yieldeth they pluck up, and eat, not daintily, or salletwice [like a salad], to allure their stomachs to appetite: but for necessity's sake, without either salt, oils, or washing, like brutish beasts devour the same. They nei-ther use table, stool, or table cloth for comeliness: but when they are imbrued [stained] with blood, knuckle deep, and their knives in like sort, they use their tongues as apt instruments to lick them clean: in doing whereof, they are as-sured to lose none of their victuals.

They frank [enclose and feed] or keep certain dogs, not much unlike Wolves, which they yoke together, as we do oxen and horses, to a sled or trail: and so carry their necessaries over the ice and snow, from place to place: as the captive, whom we have, made perfect signs. And when those Dogs are not apt for the same use: or when with hunger they are constrained, for lack of other victuals, they eat them: so that they are as needful for them, in respect of their bigness, as our oxen are for us.

They apparel themselves in the skins of such beasts as they kill, sewed together with the sinews of them. All the fowl which they kill, they skin, and make thereof one kind of garment or other, to defend them from the cold.

They make their apparel with hoods and tails, which tails they give, when they think to gratify any friendship showed unto them: a great sign of friendship with them. The men have them not so side [long] as the women.

The men and women wear their hose close to their legs, from the waist to the knee, without any open before, as well the one kind as the other. Upon their legs, they wear hose of leather, with the fur side inward, two or three pair on at once, and especially the women. In those hose, they put their knives, needles, and other things needful to bear about. They put a bone within their hose, which reacheth from the foot to the knee, whereupon they draw their said hose, and so in place of garters, they are holden from falling down about their feet.

They dress their skins very soft and supple with the hair on. In cold weather or Winter, they wear the fur side inward: and in Summer outward. Other apparel they have none, but the said skins.

Those beasts, flesh, fishes, and fowls, which they kill, they are both meat, drink, apparel, houses, bedding, hose, shoes, thread, sail for their boats, with many other necessaries, whereof they stand in need, and almost all their riches.

Their houses are tents, made of Seal skins, pitched with four for quarters, four square, meeting at the top, and the skins sewed together with sinews, and laid thereupon: so pitched they are, that the entrance into them, is always South, or against the Sun.

They have other sorts of houses, which we found, not to be inhabited, which are raised with stones and Whale bones, and a skin laid over them, to withstand the rain, or other weather: the entrance of them being not much unlike an Oven's mouth, whereto, I think, they resort for a time, to fish, hunt, and fowl, and so leave them for the next time they come thither again.

Their weapons are Bows, Arrows, Darts, and Slings. Their Bows are of a yard long of wood, sinewed on the back with strong veins, not glued too, but fast girded and trye [tied?] on. Their Bow strings are likewise sinews. Their arrows are three pieces, nocked with bone, and ended with bone, with those two ends, and the wood in the midst, they pass not in length half a yard or little more. They are feathered with two feathers, the pen end being cut away, and the feathers laid upon the arrow with the broad side to the wood: in somuch that they seem, when they are tied on, to have four feathers. They have likewise three sorts of heads to those arrows: one sort of stone or iron, proportioned like to a heart: the second sort of bone, much like unto a stopt [blocked up] head, with a hook on the same: the third sort of bone likewise, made sharp at both sides, and sharp pointed. They are not made very fast, but lightly tied to, or else set in a nock, that upon small occasion, the arrow leaveth these heads behind them: and they are of small force, except they be very near, when they shoot.

Their Darts are made of two sorts: the one with many forks of bone in the fore end, and likewise in the middest: their proportions are not much unlike our toasting irons, but longer: these they cast out of an instrument of wood, very readily. The other sort is greater than the first aforesaid, with a long bone made sharp on both sides, not much unlike a Rapier, which I take to be their most hurtful weapon.

They have two sorts of boats, made of Leather, set out on the inner side with quarters of wood, artificially tied together with thongs of the same: the greater sort are not much unlike our Wherries, wherein sixteen or twenty men may sit: they have for a sail, dressed the guts of such beasts as they kill, very fine and thin, which they sew together: the other boat is but for one man to sit and row in, with one oar.

Their order of fishing, hunting, and fowling, are with these said weapons: but in what sort, or how they use them, we have no perfect knowledge as yet.

I can not suppose their abode or habitation to be here, for that neither their houses, or apparel, are of no such force to withstand the extremity of cold, that the country seemeth to be infected with all: neither do I see any sign likely to perform the same.

Those houses, or rather dens, which stand there, have no sign of footway, or any thing else trod, which is one of the chiefest tokens of habitation. And those tents, which they bring with them, when they have sufficiently hunted and fished, they remove to other places: and when they have sufficiently stored them of such victuals, as the country yieldeth, or bringeth forth, they return to their Winter stations or habitations. This conjecture I do make, for the infertility, which I perceive to be in that country.

They have some iron, whereof they make arrow heads, knives, and other little instruments, to work their boats, bows, arrows, and darts withal, which are very unapt to do any thing withal, but with great labor.

It seemeth that they have conversation with some other people, of whom, for exchange, they should receive the same. They are greatly delighted with any image that is bright, or giveth a sound.

What knowledge they have of God or what Idol they adore, we have no perfect intelligence. I think them rather Anthropophagi, or devourers of man's flesh, than otherwise: for that there is no flesh or fish, which they find dead, (smell it never so filthily) but they will eat it, as they find it, without any other dressing. A loathsome spectacle, either to the beholders, or hearers.

There is no manner of creeping beast hurtful, except some Spiders (which, as many affirm, are signs of great store of Gold) and also certain stinging Gnats; which bite so fiercely, that the place where they bite, shortly after swelleth, and itcheth very sore.

They make signs of certain people, that wear bright plates of Gold in their foreheads, and other places of their bodies.

The Countries, on both sides the straights, lie very high with rough stony mountains, and great quantity of snow thereon. There is very little plain ground, and no grass, except a little, which is much like unto moss that groweth on soft-ground, such as we get Turfs in. There is no wood at all. To be brief, there is nothing fit or being able for the use of man, which that Country with root yieldeth or bringeth forth: Howbeit, there is great quantity of Deer, whose skins are like unto Asses, their heads or horns do far exceed, as well in length as also in breadth, any in these our parts or Country: their feet likewise, are as great as our oxens, which we measured to be seven or eight inches in breadth. There are also Hares, Wolves, fishing Bears, and Sea foul of sundry sorts.

As the Country is barren and unfertile, so are they rude and of no capacity to culture the same, to any perfection: but are contented by their hunting, fishing, and fowling, with raw flesh and warm blood, to satisfy their greedy panches, which is their only glory.

There is great likelihood of Earthquakes, or thunder: for that huge and monstrous mountains, whose greatest substance are stones, and those stones to shaken with some extraordinary means, that one is separated from another, which is discordant from all other Quarries.

There are no rivers, or running springs, but such, as through the heat of the Sun, with such water as descendeth from the mountains and hills, whereon great drifts of snow do lie, are engendred.

It argueth also, that there should be none: for that the earth, which with the extremity of the Winter, is so frozen within, that that water, which should have recourse within the same, to maintain Springs, hath not his motion, whereof great waters have their original, as by experience is seen otherwhere. Such vallies, as are capable to receive the water, that in the Summer time, by the operation of the Sun, descendeth from great abundance of snow, which continually lyeth on the mountains, and hath no passage, sinketh into the earth, and so vanisheth away, without any runnel [stream] above the earth, by which occasion, or continual standing of the said water, the earth is opened, and the great frost yieldeth to the source thereof, which in other places, four or five fathoms within the ground, for lack of the said moisture, (the earth, even in the very Summer time) is frozen, and so combineth the stones together, that scarcely instruments with great force can unknit them.

Also, where the water in those vallies can have no such passage away, by the continuance of time, in such order as is before rehearsed, the yearly descent from the mountains, filleth them full, that at the lowest bank of the same, they fall into the next valley, and so continue, as fishing Ponds or Stagnant in the Summer time full of water, and in the Winter hard frozen: as by scars that remain thereof in Summer, may easily be perceived: so that, the heat of Summer, is nothing comparable, or of force, to dissolve the extremity of cold, that commeth in Winter.

Nevertheless, I am assured, that below the force of the frost, within the earth, the waters have recourse, and empty themselves out of sight into the sea, which through the extremity of the frost, are constrained to do the same, by which occasion, the earth within is kept the warmer, and springs have their recourse, which is the only nutriment of Gold and Minerals within the same.

There is much to be said of the commodities of these Countries, which are couched within the bowels of the earth, which I let pass till more perfect trial be made thereof.

Document 26

The Famous Voyage of Sir Francis Drake into the South Sea (1577–1580)

"The famous voyage of Sir Francis Drake into the South Sea" in Richard Hakluyt, ed., *The Principal Navigations, Voyages, Traffiques, and Discoveries of the English Nation*, 3 vols. (London, 1598–1600), 3: 736–38

Sir Francis Drake (1540?–1596) was not the first person to lead an expedition around the world. But Drake, unlike his Portuguese predecessor Ferdinand Magellan, had the privilege of surviving his circumnavigation. A veteran of three journeys to the West Indies in the early 1570s, Drake's experience at sea was no guarantee of a successful voyage when he departed in 1577. Upon his return three years later, he was hailed as a hero whose feat remains one of the grandest achievements of the age of discovery. Among the tributes he received was the grounding of his flagship, the Golden Hind, *so that it would become a permanent monument to his greatness. So many English men, women, and children flocked to see it that the gangplanks leading to its deck occasionally cracked under their weight.*

During his journey Drake encountered resistance from Spaniards whom he met along the shores of South America. Though he managed to prevail in his encounters, and also managed to enrich himself by robbing their treasure ships, he never forgot the experience. Six years after he returned to England he was back again in American waters, eager to punish every Spanish ship he met.

During his circumnavigation, Drake headed north along the west coast of the Americas in search of the winds that would propel him across the vast Pacific Ocean and toward the Spice Islands. Before he sailed westward, his expedition reached the shores of modern-day California, territory which Drake claimed for the queen of England. The account here, whose author is not known, suggests that he had only peaceful relations with California's indigenous peoples.[13] If that was the case, the natives he met were lucky: in subsequent generations they suffered under a Spanish regime that some modern scholars have deemed lethal.

Drake purportedly left behind a plaque to declare that California was now English territory, though it has never been found. What has survived is the account of his voyage, part of which appears here, along what Richard Hak-luyt memorably referred to the "backside of America."

By the early seventeenth century, the Golden Hind, *still land bound, had become so rotted that it was falling apart. But it still attracted visitors, who came to see the ship that had survived a trip around the world. Some of those visitors broke off pieces of the ship to take home with them, souvenirs from a legendary vessel that epitomized an age of long-distance travel.*

The Pilot brought us to the haven of Guatulco, the town whereof, as he told us, had but 17 Spaniards in it. As soon as we were entered this haven, we landed, and went presently to the town, and to the Town-house, where we found a Judge sitting in judgment, being associate with three other officers, upon three Negros that had conspired the burning of the Town: both which Judges & prisoners we took, and brought them a shipboard, and caused the chief Judge to write his letter to the Town, to command all the Townsmen to avoid, that we might safely water there. Which being done, and they departed, we ransacked the Town, and in one house we found a pot of the quantity of a bushell, full of reals of plate, which we brought to our ship.

And here one Thomas Moone one of our company, took a Spanish Gentle-man as he was flying out of the town, and searching him, he found a chain of gold about him, and other jewels, which he took, and so let him go.

13. For a year-to-year detailed account of Drake's mission, see Harry Kelsey's excellent *Sir Francis Drake: The Queen's Pirate* (New Haven, Conn.: Yale University Press, 1998); for this account and the issue of its authorship see 177–79.

At this place our General among other Spaniards, set ashore his Portuguese Pilot, which he took at the Islands of Cape Verde, out of a ship of S. Mary port of Portugal: and having set them ashore, we departed hence, and sailed to the Island of Canno, where our General landed, and brought to shore his own ship, and discharged her, mended, and graved [cleaned the bottom] her, and furnished our ship with water and wood sufficiently.

And while we were here, we espied a ship, and set sail after her, and took her, and found in her two Pilots, and a Spanish Governor, going for the Islands of the Philippines: we searched the ship, and took some of her merchandise, and so let her go. Our general at this place and time, thinking himself both in respect of his private injuries received from the Spaniards, as also of their contempts and indignities offered to our country, and Prince in general, sufficiently satisfied, and revenged: and supposing that her Majesty at his return would rest contented with this service, purposed to continue no longer upon the Spanish coasts, but began to consider and to consult of the best way for this Country.

He thought it not good to return it by the Straits, for two special causes: the one, lest the Spaniards should there wait, and attend for him in great number and strength, whose hands, he being left but one ship, could not possibly escape. The other cause was the dangerous situation of the mouth of the straits in the South sea, where continual storms reigning [raining?] and blustering, as he found by experience, besides the shoals and sands upon the coast, he thought it not a good course to adventure that way: he resolved therefore to avoid these hazards, to go forward to the Islands of the Malucos, and therehence to sail the course of the Portuguese by the Cape of Buena Esperança.

Upon this resolution, he began to think of his best way to the Malucos, and finding himself where he now was becalmed, he saw that of necessity he must be forced to take a Spanish course, namely to sail somewhat Northerly to get a wind. We therefore set sail, and sailed 600 leagues at the least for a good wind, and thus much we sailed from the 16 of April til the 3 of June.

The 5 day of June, being in 43 degrees towards the pole Arctic, we found the air so cold, that our men being grievously pinched with the same, complained of the extremity thereof, and the futher we went, the more the cold increased upon us. Whereupon we thought it best for that time to seek the land, and did so, finding it not mountainous, but low plain land, till we came within 38 degrees towards the line. In which height it pleased God to send us into a fair and good Bay, with a good wind to enter the same.

In this Bay we anchored, and the people of the Country having their houses close by the water's side, showed themselves unto us, and sent a present to our General.

When they came unto us, they greatly wondered at the things that we brought, but our General (according to his natural and accustomed humanity) courtously entreated them, and liberally bestowed on them necessary things to cover their nakedness, whereupon they supposed us to be gods, and would not be persuaded to the contrary: the presents which they sent to our General, were feathers, and calles [challices] of net-work.

Their houses are digged round about with earth, and have from the uttermost brims of the circle, cliffs of wood set upon them, joining close together at the top like a spire steeple, which by reason of that closeness are very warm.

Their beds [are] the ground with rushes strewed on it, and lying about the house, have the fire in the midst. The men go naked, the women take bullrushes, and comb them after the manner of hemp, and thereof make their loose garments, which being knit about their middles, hang down about their hips, having also about their shoulders a skin of Deer, with the hair upon it. These women are very obedient and serviceable to their husbands.

After they were departed from us, they came and visited us the second time, and brought with them feathers and bags of Tobacco for presents: And when they came to the top of the hill (at the bottom whereof we had pitched our tents) they stayed themselves: where one appointed for speaker wearied himself with making a long oration, which done, they left their bows upon the hill, and came down with their presents.

In the meantime the women remaining on the hill, tormented themselves lamentably, tearing their flesh from their cheeks, whereby we perceived that they were about a sacrifice. In the meantime our General with his company went to prayer, and to reading of the Scriptures, at which exercise they were attentive, & seemed greatly to be affected with it: but when they were come unto us, they restored again unto us those things which before we bestowed upon them.

The news of our being there being spread throughout the Country, the people that inhabited round about came down, and amongst them the King himself, a man of goodly stature, & comely personage, with many other tall and warlike men: before whose coming were sent two Ambassadors to our General, to signify that their King was coming, in doing of which message, their speech was continued about half an hour. This ended, they by signs requested our General to send some thing by their hand to their king, as a token that this coming might in peace: wherein our General having satisfied them, they returned with glad tidings to their King, who marched to us with a princely majesty, the people crying continually after their manner, and as they drew near unto us, so did they strive to behave themselves in their actions with comeliness.

In the fore-front was a man of goodly personage, who bear the scepter or mace before the King, whereupon hanged two crowns, a lesser and a bigger, with three chains of a marvelous length: the crowns were made of knit work wrought artificially with feathers of divers colors: the chains were made of a bony substance, and few be the persons among them that are admitted to wear them: and of that number also the persons are stinted [fixed by authority], as some ten, some 12 &c. Next unto him which bear the scepter, was the King himself, with his Guard about his person, clad with Cony skins, & other skins: after them followed the naked common sort of people, every one having his face painted, some with white, some with black, and other colors, & having in their hands on thing or another for a present, not so much as their children, but they also brought their presents.

In the meantime our General gathered his men together, and marched within his fenced place, making against their approaching, a very war-like show. They being trooped together in their order, and a general salutation being made, there was presently a general silence. Then he that bear the scepter before the King, being informed by another, whom they assigned to that office, with a manly and lofty voice proclaimed that which the other spoke to him in secret, continuing half an hour: which ended, and a general Amen as it were given, the King with the whole number of men and women (the children excepted) came down without any weapon, who descending to the foot of the hill, set themselves in order.

In coming towards our bulwarks and tents, the scepter-bearer began a song, observing his measures in a dance, and that with a stately countenance, whom the King with his Guard, and every degree of persons allowing, did in like manner sing and dance, saving only the women, which danced & kept silence. The General permitted them to enter within our bulwark, where they continued their song and dance a reasonable time. When they had satisfied themselves, they made signs to our General to sit down, to whom the King, and divers others made several orations, or rather supplications, that he would take their province and kingdom into his hand, and become their King, making signs that they would resign unto him their right and title of the whole land, and become his subjects. In which, to persuade us the better, the King and the rest, with one consent, and with great reverence, joyfully singing a song, did set the crown upon his head, enriched his neck with all their chains, and offered unto him many other things, honoring him by the name of Hioh, adding thereunto as it seemed, a sign of triumph: which thing our General thought not meet to reject, because he knew not what honor and being it might be to our Country. Wherefore in the name, and to the use of her Majesty, he took the scepter, crown, and dignity of the said Country into his hands, wishing that the riches & treasure thereof might so conveniently be transported to the enriching of her kingdom at home, as it aboundeth in the same.

The common sort of people leaving the King and his Guard with our General, scattered themselves together with their sacrifices among our people, taking a diligent view of every person: and such as pleased their fancy, (which were the youngest) they enclosing them about offered their sacrifices unto them with lamentable weeping, scratching, and tearing the flesh from their faces with their nails, whereof issued abundance of blood. But we used signs to them of disliking this, and stayed their hands from force, and directed them upwards to the living God, whom only they ought to worship. They showed unto us their wounds, and craved help of them at our hands, whereupon we gave them lotions, plaisters, and ointments agreeing to the state of their griefs, beseeching God to cure their diseases. Every third day they brought their sacrifices unto us, until they understood our meaning, that we had no pleasure in them: yet they could not be long absent from us, but daily frequented our company to the hour of our departure, which departure seemed so grievous unto them that their joy was turned into sorow. They entreated us, that being absent we would remember them, and by stealth provided a sacrifice, which we misliked.

Our necessary business being ended, our General with his company traveled up into the Country to their villages, where we found herds of Deer by 1000 in a company, being most large, and fat of body.

We found the whole Country to be a warren of strange kind of Conies, their bodies in bigness as be the Barbary Conies, their heads as the heads of ours, the feet of a Want [mole], and the tail of a Rat being of great length: under her chin is on either side a bag, into the which she gathereth her meat, when she hath filled her belly abroad. The people eat their bodies, and make great account of their skins, for their King's coat was made of them.

Our General called this Country Nova Albion, and that for two causes: the one in respect of the white banks and cliffs, which lie towards the sea: and the other, because it might have some affinity with our Country in name, which sometime was so called.

There is no part of earth here to be taken up, wherein there is not some being able show of gold or silver.

At our departure hence our General set up a monument of our being there, as also of her Majesty's right and title to the same, namely a plate, nailed upon a fair great post, whereupon was engraved her Majesty's name, the day and year of our arrival there, with there, with the free giving up of the province and people into her Majesty's hands, together with her highness's picture and arms, in a piece of six pence of current English money under the plate, whereunder was also written the name of our General.

It seemeth that the Spaniards hitherto had never been in this part of the Country, neither did ever discover the land by many degrees, to the South-wards of this place. . . .

Document 27

The Naturall and Morall Historie of the East and West Indies (1604)

By José de Acosta, *The Naturall and Morall Historie of the East and West Indies*, trans. E. G[rimstone] (London, 1604), 101–102, 219–23, 333–35

José de Acosta (1540–1600) left Spain to spread the gospel to the native peoples of Peru in 1571. He stayed there for fourteen years. That was a tumultuous period in this corner of Spain's vast empire. While Acosta was there, the Spanish viceroy Don Francisco de Toledo undertook a campaign to bring the former Inkan empire even further under Iberian control. His campaign included executions of Inka leaders and the forced confinement of indigenous people into designated pieces of land where they had to pay tribute to their new overlords. Acosta protested such treatment, but to little avail.

When Acosta returned to Spain in 1588 he prepared his account of what he had seen. His book, published as Historia natural y moral de las Indias *in Seville in 1590, described the climate, topography, and local resources (including the discovery of silver at Potosí). This was not a simple work of description but instead an attempt, as the historian Anthony Pagden has noted, to produce "the first moral history—[a] history that is of mores, 'customs'—of the New World."[14] To answer some questions he drew on classi-*

---

14. Anthony Pagden, *European Encounters with the New World: From Renaissance to Romanticism* (New Haven, Conn.: Yale University Press, 1993), 54.

cal authorities such as Aristotle and Plato, but he recognized that what the Spanish had found in America could not always be answered by ancient authorities who had no idea that the Western Hemisphere existed. Most of his book thus concentrates on what could be observed in South America, such as the natives' religious practice, which he described in detail for his readers. He provided information about Mexico as well as Peru.

Acosta's book quickly attracted attention across Europe. After a second Spanish edition appeared in Barcelona in 1591, the volume was translated into Italian (published in Venice in 1596), Dutch (printed in Haarlem in 1598), German (published in Cologne in 1598 and 1600), and French (printed in Paris in 1598 and 1600). The first English edition, which included this excerpt, appeared in 1604.

Acosta believed that the Peruvians' preexisting belief in supernatural powers would make it easier for later missionaries to spread Christianity among them. In that hope he was not alone: other travelers in the Western Hemisphere, most notably Thomas Harriot, also believed that the indigenous peoples of the Americas were likely to convert to European ways because Christianity would take hold naturally among individuals who already grasped the existence of the divine.

That the Burning Zone is not violently hot, but moderate

Hitherto we have treated of the humidity of the Burning Zone, now it shall be fit to discourse of the other two qualities, Hot and Cold. We have showed in the beginning of this Discourse, how the Ancients held that the burning Zone was hot and exceeding dry, the which is not so; for it is hot and moist, and in the greatest part, the heat is not excessive, but rather moderate, which some would hold incredible, if we had not tried it. When I passed to the *Indies,* I will tell what chanced unto me: having read what Poets and Philosophers write of the burning Zone, I persuaded myself, that coming to the Equinoctial, I should not endure the violent heat, but it fell out otherwise; for when I passed, which was when the sun was there for Zenith, being entered into *Aries,* in the month of March, I felt so great cold, as I was forced to go in to the Sun to warm me, what could I else do then, but laugh at *Aristotle's* Meteors and his Philosophy, seeing that in that place, and at that season, when as all should be scorched with heat, according to his rules, I, and all my companions were a cold? In truth there is no region in the world more pleasant and temperate, than under the Equinoctial, although it be not in all parts of an equal temperature, but have great diversities. The burning Zone in some parts is very temperate, as in *Quitto,* and on the plains of *Peru,* in some parts very cold, as at *Potozi,* and in some very hot, as in *Ethiopia, Bresill,* and the *Molucques.* This diversity being known and certain unto us, we must of force, seek out another cause of cold and heat than the Sun beams, seeing that in one season of the year, and in places of one height and distance, from the Pole and Equinoctial we find so great diversity, that some are environed [surrounded] with heat, some with cold, and others tempered with a moderate heat. *Plato* placeth his most renowned *Atlantike* Island under the burning Zone; then he sayeth, that at certain seasons of the year, it hath the Sun for Zenith, and yet it was very temperate, fruitful, and rich. *Pliny* sayth that *Taprobana* (which at this day they call *Sumatra,*) is under the Equinoctial, as in effect it is, writing, that it is not only happy and rich, but also peopled with men and beasts: whereby we may easily judge, that although the Ancients held the heat of the burning Zone to be insupportable, yet might they well understand, that it was not so great as they had spoken. The most excellent Astrologer and Cosmographer *Ptolome,* and the worthy Philosopher and Physician *Avicen,* were of a better resolution, being both of opinion, that under the Equinoctial, there were very commodious habitations. . . .

Of the mountain or hill of Potosi, and the discovery thereof

The mountain or hill of *Potosi* so famous, situate in the Province of *Charcas,* in the kingdom of *Peru,* distant from the Equinoctial towards the South, or Pole Antartic, 21 degrees and two thirds: so as it falls under the Tropic, bordering upon the burning Zone, and yet this region is extremely cold, yea, more then old *Castille* in the kingdom of *Spain,* and more than *Flanders* itself, although by reason it should be hot or temperate, in regard of the height and elevation of the Pole where it is seated. The reason of this so cold a temperature, is the height of the mountain, whereas cold and intemperate winds continually blow, especially that which they call *Thomahavi,* which is boistrous and most cold. It rains most commonly in June, July, and August. The ground and soil of this mountain is dry, cold, and very unpleasant, yea altogether barren, which neither engenders nor brings forth any fruit, grass, nor grain; it is naturally inhabitable, for the intemperature of the heaven, and the barrenness of the earth. But the force of silver, which draws unto it the desire of all things, hath peopled this mountain more than any other place in all these Kingdoms, making it so fruitful of all kinds of meats, as there wants nothing that can be desired, yea, in great abundance; and although there be nothing but what is brought by carriage, yet every place abounds so with fruit, conserves exquisite wines, silks, & all other delicates, as it is not inferior to any other part. This mountain is of color dark red, and is in form pleasing at the first sight, resembling perfectly the fashion of a pavilion, or of a sugar loaf. It exceeds all other hills and mountains about it in height. The way whereby they ascend, is very rough and uneven, and yet they go upon horse-back. It is round at the top, & at the foot it hath a league in circuit. It contains from the top to the bottom 1680 common yards, the which reduced to the measure of Spanish leagues, makes a quarter of a league. At the foot of this mountain there is another small hill that riseth out of it, in the which there hath been sometimes mines of metal dispersed, which were found as it were in purses, and not in fixed or continued veins; yet were they very rich, though few in number. This small rock was called by the Indians *Guayna Potosi*, which is young *Potosi*; at the foot whereof begins the dwellings of the Spaniards and Indians, which are come to the riches and work of *Potosi*, which dwelling may contain some two leagues in circuit, and the greatest traffic and commerce of all *Peru* is in this place. The mines of this mountain were not digged nor discovered in the time of their *Inguas*, which were the Lords of *Peru*, before the Spaniards entered, although they had digged and opened the mines of *Porco*, near to *Potosi*, distant only six leagues. The reason might be the want of knowledge thereof, although some do report I know now what fable, that having sometimes labored to open those mines, a voice was heard, commanding them not to touch it, being reserved for others. In truth they had no knowledge of *Potosi*, nor of the wealth thereof, till after twelve years that the Spaniards were entered into *Peru*, the discovery whereof was made in this manner.

An Indian called *Gualpa*, of the Nation of *Chumbibilca*, which is a Province of *Cusco*, going one day to hunt for venison, passing towards the west whither the beast was fled, he began to run up against the rock, which at that time was covered and planted with certain trees, they call *Quinua*, and with thick bushes, and as he strived to get up a way which was somewhat rough and uneasy, he was forced to lay hold upon a branch, which issued from a vein of a silver mine (which since they have called *Rich*) which he pulled up, perceiving in the hole or root thereof, metal, the which he knew to be very good, by the experience he had of the mines of *Porco*: and after finding upon the ground, certain pieces of metal, which lay broken and dispersed near to this vein, being scarce well able to judge thereof, for that the color was spoiled and changed by the Sun and rain. He carried it to *Porco* to try by the *Guayras* (which is the trial of metal by fire), and having thereby found the great riches and his happy fortune, he secretly digged and drew metal out of this vein, not imparting it to any man, until that an Indian called *Guanca*, of the valley of *Xaura*, which is upon the borders of the City of *Kings*, who remaining at *Porco*, near unto *Gualpa* of *Chumbibilca*, perceived one day that he made a refining, and that his wedges and bricks were greater than such as were usually made in those places: and also increasing in his expense of apparrel, having till then lived but basely. For this reason, and for that the metal his neighbor refined was different from that of *Porco*, he thought to discover this secret, and wrought so, that although the other kept it as secret as he could, yet through importunity he was forced to carry him unto the rock of *Potosi*, having enjoyed this rich treasure full two months. And then *Gualpa* the Indian willed *Guanca* for his part to take a vein, which he had discovered near to the rich vein, which at this day is called the vein of *Diego Centeno*, that was not less rich, but more hard to dig and to draw forth; and so by agreement they divided between them the richest rock in the world. It chanced after, the Indian *Guanca* finding some difficulty to dig and draw forth his metal, being most hard, and the other *Gualpa* refusing to impart [share] any of his mine unto him, they fell at debate; so as *Guanca* of *Xaura* grieved therewith, and with some other discontents, discovered this secret unto his master called *Villaroel* a Spaniard, who then remained at *Porco*. This *Villaroel* desirous to understand the truth, went to *Potosi*, & finding the riches his *Yanacona* or servant had discovered unto him, caused the Indian *Guanca* to be enrolled, undertaking with him the said vein, which was called *Centeno*, they call it undertaking, that is as much as to note and mark the mine, and so much ground in circuit for him, which the Law grants unto those that discover any mine, or unto those that dig them: by means whereof, having discovered them to the Justice, they remained Lords of the mine, to dig and draw forth the silver, as being their own, paying only their duties unto the King, which is a fifth part. So as the first discovery and inregistering of the mines of *Potosi* was the 21 of April, in the year of our Lord, one thousand five hundred forty five in the territory of *Porco*, by the said *Villaroel* a Spaniard, and *Guanca* an Indian. Presently after they discovered another vein, which they called the vein of Tin, the which is very rich, although it be rough and very painful to work in, the metal being as hard as flint. Since the thirt[ieth] day of August in the same year of a thousand five hundred forty and five the vein called *Mendieta* was enrolled, and these are the four principal veins of *Potosi*. They say of the rich vein, the first that was discovered that the metal lay above the ground the height of a lance, like unto rocks, raising the superficies of the earth, like unto a crest of three hundred foot long, and thirteen foot broad, and that this remained bare & uncovered by the deluge. This vein having resisted the violence and force of the water, as the hardest part. The metal was so rich as it was half silver, and this vein continued in his bounty fifty or three score stades, which is the height of a man, and then it failed. In this manner the mines of *Potosi* were discovered by the Divine Providence, who (for the felicity of *Spain*) would have the greatest treasure that ever was in this world, discovered, at such time whenas the Emperour *Charles* the fifth of famous memory held the Empire, the kingdoms of *Spaine*, and the Seigniory of the *Indies*. Presently after that, the discovery of *Potosi* was known in *Peru*; many Spaniards, and the most part of the Bourgeois of the silver City, which is eighteen leagues from *Potosi*, came thither to take mines: yea there came many Indians from divers provinces, especially the *Guayzadores* of *Porco,* so as within a short space it was the best peopled habitation of all the kingdom. . . .

That the Indians have some knowledge of God

First, although the darkness of infidelity holdeth these Nations in blindness, yet in many things the light of truth and reason works somewhat in them. And they commonly acknowledge a supreme Lord and Author of all things, which they of *Peru* called *Unachocha,* and gave him names of great excellence, as *Pachacamac,* or *Pachayachachic,* which is, the Creator of heaven and earth: and *Usapu,* which is admirable, and other like names. Him they did worship, as the chiefest of all, whom they did honor in beholding the heaven. The like we see amongst them of *Mexico,* and *China,* and all other infidels. Which accordeth well with that which is said of Saint *Paul,* in the Acts of the Apostles, where he did see the Inscription of an Altar; *Ignoto Deo*: To the unknown God. Whereupon the Apostle took occasion to preach unto them, saying, *He whom you worship without knowing, him do I preach unto you* [Acts 17]. In like sort, those which at this day do preach the Gospel to the *Indians,* find no great difficulty to persuade them that there is a high God and Lord over all, and that this is the Christians' God, and the true God. And yet it hath caused great admiration in me, that although they had this knowledge, yet had they no proper name for God. If we shall seek into the Indian tongue for a word to answer to this name of God, as in Latin, *Deus*, in Greek, *Theos*, in Hebrew, *El*, in Arabike, *Alla*; but we shall not find any in the *Cuscan* or *Mexicaine* tongues. So as such as preach or write to the *Indians*, use our Spanish name Dios, fitting it to the accent or pronounciation of the *Indian* tongues, the which differ much, whereby appears the small knowledge they had of God, seeing they cannot so much as name him, if it be not by our very name: yet in truth they had some little knowledge, and therefore in *Peru* they made him a rich temple, which they called *Pachacamac*, which was the principal Sanctuary of the realm. And as it hath been said, this word of *Pachacamac*, is as much to say, as the Creator, yet in this temple they used their idolatries, worshipping the Devil and figures. They likewise made sacrifices and offerings to *Viracocha*, which held the chief place amongst the worships which the King's Inguas made. Hereof they called the Spaniards *Virocochas*, for that they hold opinion they are the sons of heaven, and divine; even as others did attribute to a deity to *Paul* and *Barnabas*, calling the one *Jupiter*, and the other *Mercury*, so would they offer sacrifices unto them, as unto gods: and as the Barbarians of *Melite* (which is *Malté*) seeing that the viper did not hurt the Apostle, they called him God [Acts 18].

As it is therefore a truth, comformable to reason, that there is a sovereign Lord and King of heaven, whome the Gentiles (with all their infidelities and idolatries) have not denied, as we see in the Philosophy of *Timee* in *Plato*, in the Metaphisics of *Aristotle*, and in the Æsculape of *Tresmigister*, as also in the Poesies of *Homer* & *Virgil*. Therefore the Preachers of the Gospel have no great difficulty to plant & persuade this truth of a supreme God, be they Nations of whom they preach never so barbarous and brutish. But it is hard to root out of their minds, that there is no other God, nor any other deity than one: and that all other things of themselves have no power, being, nor working proper to themselves, but what the great and only God and Lord doth give and impart unto them. To conclude, it is necessary to persuade them by all means, in reproving their errors, as well in that wherein they generally fail, in worshiping more than one God, as in particular, (which is much more) to hold for Gods, and to demand favour and help of those things which are not God's, nor have any power, but what the true God their Lord and Creator hath given them. . . .

Document 28

A Briefe and True Report of the New Found Land of Virginia (1590)

By Thomas Harriot, *A Briefe and True Report of the New Found Land of Virginia* (London, 1590), 24–30

Thomas Harriot (1560–1621) was, along with the Dutch traveler Jan Huygen van Linschoten and the Huguenot missionary Jean de Léry, one of the most astute European observers of the sixteenth century. Though others who traveled to the Western Hemisphere also demonstrated keen literary and analytical abilities, none had the ability to evoke an entire indigenous population with the sensitivity of Harriot's often spare prose. Of course, it helped that Harriot had along with him the talented painter John White, and that once the two of them returned to London in 1586 after their stint in Roanoke they made contact with the younger Richard Hakluyt, who then arranged for the publication not only of Harriot's words (in 1588 and again in 1589) but also for an illustrated edition of his work. By the time the Flemish engraver Theodor de Bry and his sons had completed their work in Frankfurt-am-Main in 1590, Europeans who could read English, French, German, or Latin had an opportunity to see for themselves what the eastern shore of North America looked like. It is no exaggeration to suggest that the four-language edition of Harriot's Briefe and True Reporte of the New Found Land of Virginia *was the most significant travel account published in the entire sixteenth century. (See the section "Pictures of Roanoke" for the product of this international collaboration.)*

Harriot's report had a dual purpose. On the one hand, he (and Hakluyt) intended it to serve as a rallying point for English colonization in the Americas. Up to that point, the English had been extraordinarily slow to organize any overseas settlements, despite the fact that their historic enemy Spain had enriched itself through the transportation of American wealth (especially silver) to Europe since the early decades of the century. Hakluyt, a trained minister who feared the continuous rise of Catholic Europe, had been working for several years to convince his fellow English Protestants that the time had come to launch colonies and, in the process, to finally follow up the late fifteenth-century expeditions of the Cabots. He believed that the Briefe and True Report *could help advance that political agenda.*

Although Harriot's text can be read as a piece of nationalistic propaganda, it is also without question a genuine work of ethnography. Its opening chapters (not included here) provide a detailed account of the local environment. Harriot paid close attention to plants that grew naturally in the region, as well as the Carolina Algonquians' agriculture. He followed with details about the area's fauna, and then described the dense local forests and their variety of trees, many of them no longer growing in England. Then Harriot set out to describe the Algonquians themselves; this crucial part of his Report *follows.*

Harriot tried to paint an objective portrait of the people he met. Though he could not escape his biases, especially his sense that these people needed to be converted to Christianity, his description of their religious practices, clothing, economy, and settlements display an eagerness to tell about the Carolina Algonquians as accurately as possible. There are no monsters to be found roaming around Roanoke. There were, instead, human beings who Harriot believed did not possess the intellectual abilities of the English but who nonetheless seemed worthy potential neighbors. Perhaps he found it amusing that some of the Algonquians thought that the English were gods when they stood amazed at the compasses, guns, and books that they brought along on their venture. But he had no better explanation than they did for why the natives succumbed to diseases that did not afflict the newcomers. Tensions sometimes arose between the Algonquians and the English, especially when the visitors perhaps overstayed their welcome. Yet Harriot's double agenda—his desire to promote English colonization and his efforts to describe this indigenous population—led him away from condemning all of the native Carolinians. Instead, he believed that his travel account would provide potential immigrants with sufficient information to coexist with the natives they encountered.

Harriot's report is famous in American history for telling much about the nascent English settlement at Roanoke, the fabled "lost colony" of the English. Yet while the fate of those early colonists may never be known, the True Report *also has become an epitaph for the Carolina Algonquians, a people obliterated by the forces of European colonization.*

Of the nature and manners of the people

It resteth I speak a word or two of the natural inhabitants, their natures and manners, leaving large discourse thereof until time more convenient hereafter: now only so far forth, as that you may know, how that they in respect of troubling our inhabiting and planting, are not to be feared, but that they shall have cause both to fear and love us, that shall inhabit with them.

They are a people clothed with loose mantles made of deer skins, and aprons of the same round about their middles, all else naked; of such a difference of statures only as we in England; having no edge tools or weapons of iron or steel to offend us withal, neither know they how to make any: those weapons that they have, are only bows made of Witch-hazle, and arrows of reeds, flat edged truncheons also of wood about a yard long, neither have they any thing to defend themselves but targets made of barks, and some armors made of sticks wickered together with thread.

Their towns are but small, and near the Sea coast but few, some containing but ten or twelve houses; some 20 the greatest that we have seen hath been but of 30 houses: if they be walled, it is only done with barks of trees made fast to stakes, or else with poles only fixed upright, and close one by another.

Their houses are made of small poles, made fast at the tops in round form after the manner as is used in many arbories in our gardens of England, in most towns covered with barks, and in some with artificial mats made of long rushes, from the tops of the houses down to the ground. The length of them is commonly double to the breadth, in some places they are but 12 and 16 yards long, and in other some we have seen of four and twenty.

In some places of the Country, one only town belongeth to the government of a Wiroans or chief Lord, in other some two or three, in some six, eight, and more: the greatest Wiroans that yet we had dealing with, had but eighteen towns in his government, and able to make not above seven or eight hundreth fighting men at the most. The language of every government is different from any other, and the further they are distant, the greater is the difference.

Their manner of wars amongst themselves is either by sudden surprising one another most commonly about the dawning of the day, or moonlight, or else by ambushes, or some subtle devices. Set battles are very rare, except it fall out where there are many trees, where either part may have some hope of defense, after the delivery of every arrow, in leaping behind some or other.

If there fall out any wars between us and them, what their fight is likely to be, we having advantages against them so many manner of ways, as by our discipline, our strange weapons and devices else, especially Ordinance great and small, it may easily be imagined: by the experience we have had in some places, the turning up of their heels against us in running away was their best defense.

In respect of us they are a people poor, and for want of skill and judgment in the knowledge and use of our things, do esteem our trifles before things of greater value: Notwithstanding, in their proper manner (considering the want of such means as we have), they seeme very ingenious. For although they have no such tools, nor any such crafts, Sciences and Arts as we, yet in those things they do, they show excellence of wit. And by how much they upon due consideration shall find our manner of knowledges and crafts to exceed theirs in perfection, and speed for doing or execution, by so much the more is it probable that they should desire our friendship and love, and have the greater respect for pleasing and obeying us. Whereby may be hoped, if means of good government be used, that they may in short time be brought to civility, and the embracing of true Religion.

Some religion they have already, which although it be far from the truth, yet being as it is, there is hope it may be the easier and sooner reformed.

They believe that there are many gods, which they call *Mantoac*, but of different sorts & degrees, one only chief and great God, which hath been from all eternity. Who, as they affirm, when he purposed to make the world, made first other gods of a principal order, to be as means and instruments to be used in the creation and government to follow, and after the Sun, moon, and stars as petty gods, and the instruments of the other order more principal. First (they say) were made waters, out of which by the gods was made all diversity of creatures that are visible or invisible.

For mankind they say a woman was made first, which by the working of one of the gods, conceived and brought forth children: And in such sort they say they had their beginning. But how many years or ages have passed since, they say they can make no relation, having no letters nor other such means as we to keep Records of the particularities of times past, but only tradition from father to son.

They think that all the gods are of human shape, and therefore they represent them by images in the forms of men, which they call *Kewasowok*, one alone is called *Kewas*: them they place in houses appropriate or temples, which they call *Machicomuck*, where they worship, pray, sing, and make many times offering unto them. In some *Machicomuck* we have seen but one *Kewas*, in some two, and in other some three. The common sort think them to be also gods.

They believe also the immortality of the soul, that after this life as soon as the soul is departed from the body, according to the works it hath done, it is either caried to heaven the habitacle [dwelling place] of gods, there to enjoy perpetual bliss and happiness, or else to a great pit or hole, which they think to be in the furthest parts of their part of the world toward the Sun set, there to burn continually: the place they call *Popogusso.*

For the confirmation of this opinion, they told me two stories of two men that had been lately dead and revived again, the one happened but few years before our coming into the Country of a wicked man, which having been dead and buried, the next day the earth of the grave being seen to move, was taken up again, who made declaration where his soul had been, that is to say, very near entering into *Popogusso,* had not one of the gods saved him, and gave him leave to return again, and teach his friends what they should do to avoid that terrible place of torment.

The other happened in the same year we were there, but in a town that was three score miles from us, and it was told me for strange news, that one being dead, buried, and taken up again as the first, showed that although his body had lien dead in the grave, yet his soul was alive, & had traveled far in a long broad way, on both sides whereof grew most delicate and pleasant trees, bearing more rare and excellent fruits, than ever he had seen before, or was able to express, and at length came to most brave and fair houses, near which he met his father that had been dead before, who gave him great charge to go back again, and show his friends what good they were to do to enjoy the pleasures of that place, which when he had done he should after come again.

What subtlety soever be in the *Wiroances* and Priests, this opinion worketh so much in many of the common and simple sort of people, that it maketh them have great respect to their Governors, and also great care what they do, to avoid torment after death, and to enjoy bliss, although notwithstanding there is punishment ordained for malefactors, as stealers, whoremongers, and other sorts of wicked doers, some punished with death, some with forfeitures, some with beating, according to the greatness of the facts.

And this is the sum of their Religion, which I learned by having special familiarity with some of their priests. Wherein they were not so sure grounded, nor gave such credit to their traditions and stories, but through conversing with us they were brought into great doubts of their own, and no small admiration of ours, with earnest desire in many, to learn more than we had means for want of perfect utterance in their language to express.

Most things they saw with us, as Mathematical instruments, sea Compasses, the virtue of the load-stone in drawing iron, a perspective glass whereby was showed many strange sights, burning glasses, wild fireworks, guns, hooks, writing and reading, spring clocks that seem to go of themselves and many other things that we had were so strange unto them, and so far exceeded their capacities to comprehend the reason and means how they should be made and done, that they thought they were rather the works of gods than of men, or at the leastwise they had been given and taught us of the gods. Which made many of them to have such opinion of us, as that if they knew not the truth of God and Religion already, it was rather to be had from us whom God so specially loved, than from a people that were so simple, as they found themselves to be in comparison of us. Whereupon greater credit was given unto that we spoke of, concerning such matters.

Many times and in every town where I came, according as I was able, I made declaration of the contents of the Bible, that therein was set forth the true and only God, and his mighty works, that therein was contained the true doctrine of salvation through Christ, with many particularities of Miracles and chief points of Religion, as I was able then to utter, and thought fit for the time. And although I told them the book materially and of itself was not of any such virtue, as I thought they did conceive, but only the doctrine therein contained: yet would many be glad to touch it, to embrace it, to kiss it, to hold it to their breasts and heads, and stroke over all their body with it, to show their hungry desire of that knowledge which was spoken of.

The *Wiroans* with whom we dwelt called *Wingina*, and many of his people would be glad many times to be with us at our Prayers, and many times call upon us both in his own town, as also in others whither he sometimes accompanied us, to pray and sing Psalms, hoping thereby to be partaker of the same effects which we by that means also expected.

Twice this *Wiroans* was so grievously sick that he was like to die, and as he lay languishing, doubting of any help by his own priests, and thinking he was in such danger for offending us and thereby our God, sent for some of us to pray and be a means to our God that it would please him either that he might live, or after death dwell with him in bliss, so likewise were the requests of many others in the like case.

On a time also when their corn began to wither by reason of a drought which happened extraordinarily, fearing that it had come to pass by reason that in some thing they had displeased us, many would come to us and desire us to pray to our God of England, that he would preserve their Corn, promising that when it was ripe we also should be partakers of the fruit.

There could at no time happen any strange sickness, losses, hurts, or any other cross unto them, but that they would impute to us the cause or means thereof, for offending or not pleasing us. One other rare and strange accident, leaving others, will I mention before I end, which moved the whole Country that either knew or heard of us, to have us in wonderful admiration.

There was no town where we had any subtle device practiced against us, we leaving it unpunished or not revenged (because we sought by all means possible to win them by gentleness) but that within a few days after our departure from every such Town, the people began to die very fast, and many in short space, in some Towns about twenty, in some forty, and in one six score, which in truth was very many in respect of their numbers. This happened in no place that we could learn, but where we had been, where they used some practice against us, & after such time. The disease also was so strange, that they neither knew what it was, nor how to cure it, the like by report of the oldest men in the Country never happened before, time out of mind. A thing specially observed by us, as also by the natural inhabitants themselves.

Insomuch that when some of the inhabitants which were our friends, and especially the *Wiroans Wingina* had observed such effects in four or five Towns to follow their wicked practices, they were persuaded that it was the work of our God through our means, and that we by him might kill and slay whom we would without weapons, and not come near them.

And thereupon when it had happened that they had understanding that any of their enemies had abused us in our journeys, hearing that we had wrought no revenge with our weapons, and fearing upon some cause the matter should so rest: did come and entreat us that we would be a means to our God that they as others that had dealt ill with us might in like sort die, alleging how much it would be for our credit and profit, as also theirs, and hoping furthermore that we would do so much at their requests in respect of the friendship we professed them.

Whose entreaties although we showed that they were ungodly, affirming that our God would not subject himself to any such prayers and requests of men: that indeed all things have been and were to be done according to his good pleasure as he had ordained: and that we to show ourselves his true servants ought rather to make petition for the contrary, that they with them might live together with us, be made partakers of his truth, and serve him in righteousness, but notwithstanding in such sort, that we refer that, as all other things, to be done according to his divine will and pleasure, and as by his wisdom he had ordained to be best.

Yet because the effect fell out so suddenly and shortly after according to their desires, they thought nevertheless it came to pass by our means, & that we in using such speeches unto them, did but dissemble the matter, and therefore came unto us to give us thanks in their manner, that although we satisfied them not in promise, yet in deeds and effect we had fulfilled their desires.

This marvelous accident in all the Country wrought so strange opinions of us, that some people could not tell whether to think us gods or men, and the rather because that all the space of their sickness, there was no man of ours known to die, or that was specially sick: they noted also that we had no women amongst us, neither that we did care for any of theirs.

Some therefore were of opinion that we were not borne of women, and therefore not mortal, but that we were men of an old generation many years past, then risen again to immortality.

Some would likewise seem to prophesy that there were more of our generation yet to come to kill theirs and take their places, as some thought the purpose was, by that which was already done. Those that were immediately to come after us they imagined to be in the air, yet invisible and without bodies, and that they by our entreaty and for the love of us, did make the people to die in that sort as they did, by shooting invisible bullets into them.

To confirm this opinion, their Physicians (to excuse their ignorance in curing the disease) would not be ashamed to say, but earnestly make the simple people believe, that the strings of blood that they sucked out of the sick bodies, were the strings wherewithal the invisible bullets were tied and cast.

Some also thought that we shot them ourselves out of our pieces, from the place where we dwelt, and killed the people in any town that had offended us, as we listed, how far distant from us soever it were.

And other some said, that it was the special work of God for our sakes, as we ourselves have cause in some sort to think no less, whatsoever some do, or may imagine to the contrary, specially some Astrologers, knowing of the Eclipse of the Sun which we saw the same year before in our voyage thitherward, which unto them appeared very terrible. And also of a Comet which began to appear but a few days before the beginning of the said sickness. But to exclude them from being the special causes of so special an accident, there are further reasons than I think fit at this present to be alleged.

These their opinions I have set down the more at large, that it may appear unto you that there is good hope they may be brought through discreet dealing and government to the embracing of the truth, and consequently to honor, obey, fear and love us.

And although some of our company towards the end of the year, showed themselves too fierce in slaying some of the people in some Towns, upon causes that on our part might easily enough have been borne withal: yet notwithstanding, because it was on their part justly deserved, the alteration of their opinions generally and for the most part concerning us is the less to be doubted. And whatsoever else they may be, by carefulness of ourselves need nothing at all to be feared. . . .

Now I have (as I hope) made relation not of so few and small things, but that the Country (of men that are indifferent and well disposed) may be sufficiently liked: If there were no more known than I have mentioned, which doubtless and in great reason is nothing to that which remaineth to be discovered, neither the soil, nor commodities. As we have reason so to gather by the difference we found in our travels, for although all which I have before spoken of, have been discovered and experimented not far from the Sea coast, where was our abode and most of our traveling: yet sometimes as we made our journeys further into the main and Country; we found the soil to be fatter, the trees greater and to grow thinner, the ground more firm and deeper mould, more and larger champions, finer grass, and as good as ever we saw any in England; in some places rocky and far more high and hilly ground, more plenty of their fruits, more abundance of beasts, the more inhabited with people, and of greater policy and larger dominions, with greater towns and houses.

Why may we not then look for in good hope from the inner parts of more and greater plenty, as well of other things, as of those which we have already discovered? Unto the Spaniards happened the like in discovering the main of the West Indies. The main also of this Country of Virginia, extending some ways so many hundreds of leagues, as otherwise than by the relation of the inhabitants we have most certain knowledge of, where yet no Christian prince hath any possession or dealing, cannot but yield many kinds of excellent commodities, which we in our discovery have not yet seen.

What hope there is else to be gathered of the nature of the Climate, being answerable to the Island of Japan, the land of China, Persia, Jury, the Islands of Cyprus and Candy, the South parts of Greece, Italy and Spain, and of many other notable and famous Countries, because I mean not to be tedious, I leave to your own consideration.

Whereby also the excellent temperature of the air there at all seasons, much warmer than in England, and never so vehemently hot, as sometimes is under and between the Tropics, or near them, cannot be known unto you without further relation.

For the wholesomeness thereof I need to say but thus much: that for all the want of provision, as first of English victual, excepting for twenty days, we lived only by drinking water, and by the victual of the Country, of which some sorts were very strange unto us, and might have been thought to have altered our temperatures in such sort, as to have brought us into some grievous and dangerous diseases. Secondly the want of English means, for the taking of beasts, fish and foul, which by the help only of the inhabitants and their means could not be so suddenly and easily provided for us, nor in so great number and quantities, nor of that choice as otherwise might have been to our better satisfaction and contentment. Some want also we had of clothes. Furthermore in all our travels, which were most specially and often in the time of Winter, our lodging was in the open air upon the ground. And yet I say for all this, there were but four of our whole company (being one hundreth and eight) that died all the year, and that but at the latter end thereof, and upon none of the aforesaid causes. For all four, especially three, were feeble, weak, and sickly persons before ever they came thither, and those that knew them, much marveled that they lived so long being in that case, or had adventured to travel.

Seeing therefore the air there is so temperate and wholesome, the soil so fertile, and yielding such commodities, as I have before mentioned, the voyage also thither to and fro being sufficiently experimented to be performed twice a year with ease, and at any season thereof: And the dealing of *Sir Walter Ralegh* so liberal in large giving and granting land there, as is already known, with many helps and furtherances else. (The least that he hath granted hath been five hundred acres to a man only for the adventure of his person.) I hope there remains no cause whereby the action should be misliked.

If that those which shall thither travel to inhabit and plant be but reasonably provided for the first year, as those are which were transported the last, and being there, do use but that diligence and care, that is requisite, and as they may with ease. There is no doubt, but for the time following, they may have victuals that are excellent good and plenty enough, some more English sorts of cattle also hereafter, as some have been before, and are there yet remaining, may, and shall be God willing thither transported. So likewise, our kind of fruits, roots, and herbs, may be there planted and sowed, as some have been already, and prove well. And in short time also they may raise so much of those sorts of commodities which I have spoken of, as shall both enrich themselves, as also others that shall deal with them. . . .

Pictures of Roanoke

The images that appear here are engraved versions of watercolor paintings done in Roanoke by John White. They are the best known visual depictions of any indigenous population of North America in the early modern age. They remain, along with George Catlin's paintings of Plains Indians in the nineteenth century, the most important series of images of Native Americans before the advent of photography. The pictures' significance lies in their precision and in the texts that accompanied them when they appeared in the illustrated edition of Thomas Harriot's Briefe and True Report of the New Found Land of Virginia. *The Carolina Algonquians in these pictures were destroyed by the forces of conquest and colonization; though individuals no doubt survived and joined other native communities, the culture evident in these engravings vanished sometime in the seventeenth century.*

Harriot's book included twenty-three plates depicting America and Americans, in addition to five images of the ancient inhabitants of Britain. He included these last images, of which one is included here, noting that John White painted five pictures based on an old English chronicle and told Harriot to add them at the end "for to showe how that the Inhabitants of the great Britannie have bin in times past as savage as those of Virginia."

Harriot recognized that visual images provided information beyond what his text could demonstrate. The child holding an armillary sphere and a doll, for example, could be described in the text, but the image is more compelling. The text contained descriptions of the Algonquians' economy, but Harriot could do much more by using White's paintings showing how they fished, an image that demonstrated their inventiveness, or how they organized the economy and society of the town of Secota. The image of the tomb of the weroans (principle chiefs) provides details about elite mortuary practices bodies and the constant care that the bodies received from an idol seated on the side of the chamber and the man who perpetually tended to the shrine. Painted on the spot from life and then later engraved, these pictures of various activities stand in contrast to the final images of the ancient inhabitants of Britain. The picture of the Pict, which was a confabulation, gained strength because of its juxtaposition with the images of the more benign Algonquians. Picts were not only savage in the past, as the text declares, but far more bloodthirsty than the Native Americans. None of the indigenous people of Carolina come off as menacing as this man, who has decapitated his victim so recently that the head is still dripping blood while the head of another victim lies at his feet.

The captions under each picture are those used in the 1590 English language edition of Harriot's Briefe and True Report.

Figure 13. Carolina Algonquian Woman and Child

"About 20 miles from that Island, near the lake of Paquippe, there is another town called Pomioock hard by the sea. The apparel of the chief ladies of [that] town differ but little from the attire of those which live in Roanaak [Roanoke]. For they wear their hair trussed up in a knot, as the maiden do which we spoke of before, and have their skins pownced [perforated?] in the same manner, yet they wear a chain of great pearls, or beads of copper, or smooth bones 5 or 6 fold about their necks, bearing one arm in the same, in the other hand they carry a gourd full of some kind of pleasant liquor. They tie deer skin doubled about them [hooking] higher about their breasts, which hang down before almost to their knees, and are almost altogether naked behind. Commonly their young daughters or 7 or 8 years old to wait upon them wearing about them a girdle of skin, which hangs down behind, and is drawn underneath between their twist, and bound above their navel with moss of trees between that and their skins to cover their [privates] withal. After they be once past 10 years of age, they wear deer skins as the older sort do. They are greatly Delighted with puppets, and babes [dolls] which were brought out of England."

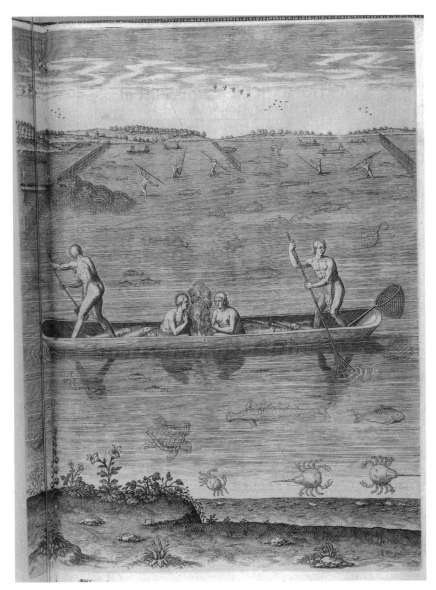

Figure 14. Their Manner of Fishing in Virginia

"*They have likewise a notable way to catch fish in their Rivers, for whereas they lack both iron, and steel, they fast unto their Reeds or long Rods, the hollow tail of a certain fish like to a sea crab instead of a point, wherewith by night or day they strike fishes, and take them up into their boats. They also know how to use the prickles, and pricks of other fishes. They also make weirs, with setting up reeds or twigs in the water, which they so plant one within another, that they grow still narrower, and narrower, as appeareth by this figure. There was never seen among us so cunning a way to take fish withal, whereof sundry sorts as they found in their Rivers unlike unto ours which are also of a very good taste. Doubtless it is a pleasant to see the people, sometimes wading, and going sometimes failing in those Rivers, which are shallow and not deep, free from all care of heaping up Riches for their posterity, content with their state, and living friendly together of those things which god of his bounty hath given unto them, yet without giving him any thanks according to his desert. So savage is this people, and deprived of the true knowledge of God. For they have none other then is mentioned before in this work.*"

Figure 15. The Town of Secota

"Their towns that are not enclosed with poles are commonly fairer. Then such as are enclosed, as appeareth in this figure which lively expresseth the town of Secota. For the houses are Scattered here and there, and they have gardens expressed by the letter E wherein growth Tobacco which the inhabitants call Uppowoc. They have also groves wherein they take deer, and fields wherein they sow their corn. In their corn fields they build as it were a scaffold whereon they set a cottage like to a round chair, signified by F wherein they place one to watch for there are such number of foul, and beasts, that unless they keep the better watch, they would soon devour all their corn. For which cause the watchman maketh continual cries and noise. They sow their corn with a certain distance noted by H otherwise one stalk would choke the growth of another and the corn would not come unto his ripeurs [become ripe] G For the leaves thereof are large, like unto the leaves of great reeds. They have also several broad plots C, where they meet with their neighbors, to celebrate their chief solemn feasts as the . . . picture doth declare: and a place D where after they have ended their feast they make merry together. Over against this place they have a round plot B where they assemble themselves to make their solemn prayers. Not far from which place there is a large building A wherein are the tombs of their kings and princes . . . likewise they have garden noted by the letter I wherein they use to sow pompions [pumpkins]. Also a place marked K wherein they make a fire at their solemn feasts, and hard without the town a river L from whence they fetch their water. This people therefore void of all covetousnouss live cheerfully and at their hearts' ease. But they solemnize their feasts in the night, and therefore they keep very great fires to avoid darkness, and to testify their joy."

Figure 15

Figure 16. The Tomb of Their Weroans or Chief Lords

"*They build a Scaffold 9 or 10 feet high as is expressed in this figure under the tombs of their Wero-ans, or chief lords which they cover with mats, and lay the dead corpses of their weroans thereupon in manner following. First the bowels are taken forth. Then laying down the skin, they cut all the flesh clean from the bones, which they dry in the sun, and well dried they inclose in Mats, and place at their feet. Then their bones (remaining still fastened together with the ligaments whole and uncorrupted) are covered again with leather, and their carcass fashioned as if their flesh were not taken away. They lap each corpse in his own skin after the same is thus handled, and lay it in his order by the corpses of the other chief lords. By the dead bodies they set their Idol Kiwasa. . . . For they are persuaded that the same doth keep the dead bodies of their chief lords that nothing may hurt them. Moreover under the aforesaid scaffold some one of their priests hath his lodging, which Mumbleth his prayers night and day, and hath charge of the corpses. For his bed he hath two deerskins spread on the ground, if the weather be cold he maketh a fire to warm by withal. These poor souls are thus instructed by nature to reverence their princes even after their death.*"

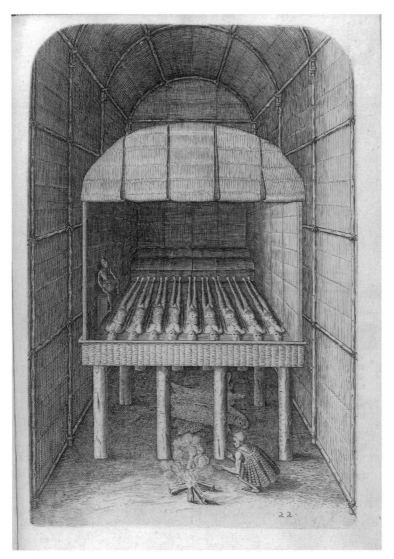

Figure 16

Figure 17. The True Picture of One Pict

"In times past the Picts, inhabitants of one part of Great Britain, which is now named England, were savages, and did paint all their body after the manner following. They did let their hair grow as far as their Shoulders, saving those which hang upon their forehead, the which they did cut. They shave all their beard except the mustaches, upon their breast were painted the head of some bird, and about the paps as it were beams of the sun, upon the belly some fearful and monstrous face, spreading the beams very far upon the thighs. Upon the two knees some faces of lion, and upon their legs as it hath been shells of fish. Upon their Shoulders griffons' heads, and then they hath serpents about their arms. They carried about their necks one ayerne [iron?] ring, and another about the mids of their body, about the belly, and the said hang on a chain, a scimitar or turkey sword, they did carry in one arm a target made of wood, and in the other hand a pick, of which the ayerne was after the manner of a Lick, with tassels on, and the other end with a round ball. And when they hath overcome some of their enemies, they did never fail to carry away their heads with them."

Figure 17

Document 29

The Discovery of the Large, Rich, and Bewtiful Empyre of Guiana (1596)

By Walter Ralegh, *The Discovery of the Large, Rich, and Bewtiful Empyre of Guiana* (London, 1596), 41–43, 54–56, 59–60, 69–71

Sir Walter Ralegh (1552?–1618), one of the patrons of Thomas Harriot, was a talented poet, favorite of Queen Elizabeth I of England, and among the military despoilers of Ireland. By the 1580s, he had become obsessed with the Americas. The Queen rewarded his Irish service with patents to sizable parcels in North America, including the "Virginia" that Harriot described. Eventually she supported his expedition to Guiana. In 1595 he went on his first exploratory voyage into the Orinoco delta.

Guiana was to sixteenth-century Europeans a place of mystery and marvel. Besides containing native peoples who Europeans believed needed their souls saved through conversion to Christianity, explorers from across the Atlantic thought that following the meandering branches of the Orinoco would eventually take them to a land of spectacular wealth—the same dream that had prompted Coronado to go searching for Cíbolla's riches on the great plains of what is now the United States. Ralegh had a particularly English vision of what he could do: he knew that Guiana lay in the middle of Spain's American territory, and he hoped that an English colony there would enable his realm to raid Spanish treasure ships hauling silver back to the Iberian peninsula. To advance his goals he wrote a brief promotional tract titled The Discovery of the Large, Rich, and Bewtiful Empyre of Guiana, with a relation of the great and Golden City of Manoa (which the Spanyards call El Dorado) and of the Provinces of Emeria, Arromaia, Amapaia, and other Countries, with their rivers adjoining. *The book was published in London in 1596, shortly before Ralegh led military assaults against the Spanish at Cádiz. By the end of the century, a Dutch edition had been published in Antwerp, and Latin and German editions appeared in Nuremberg.*

Ralegh longed to get back to the Orinoco after his first venture there. But Elizabeth's death in 1603 deprived him of the royal patronage he needed to mount another expedition. He also lost his freedom: from 1603 to 1616 he was confined to the Tower of London, accused of plotting to assassinate King James. When he was finally released, he did manage to organize another mis-

sion to Guiana, this time with his own son along. But the expedition proved to be a disaster, with his son among the many English who perished in South America. He arrived back in London in 1618 to face charges raised by the Spanish ambassador that he had led an assault on San Tomás. King James ordered him arrested, and then finally executed.

The excerpts from Ralegh's 1596 book here reveal some of the marvels that he found, including natives living in trees in the shallow waters of the Orinoco delta and the ways that the indigenous peoples of the region used poisoned arrows to kill their enemies. He also revealed his belief that deep in the interior lived creatures he called Ewaipanoma—*men and women with their faces in their chests. Ralegh never saw them with his own eyes, but he knew that they existed because Mandeville had written about them and various individuals whom Ralegh trusted had actually seen them. Besides, as he wrote here, it was inconceivable that there could be so many reports about them if they were imaginary. The fact that Ralegh, one of the last sixteenth-century European travelers to the Western Hemisphere, believed that such monsters existed reveals much about the persistence of certain ideas. Ralegh was not alone in keeping the tales of these mythic creatures alive. William Shakespeare, a reader of Ralegh's account, inserted a creature with its head on its chest into the dialog in* Othello. *In Shakespeare's version, the monsters were also cannibals, thus demonstrating the perpetual allure to Europeans of that purportedly common act among Americans. Perhaps he was inspired by the pictures in Ralegh's report, some of which appear after the excerpts from the text.*

On the Natives who lived in islands in the estuary of the Orinoco

The great river of *Orenoque [Orinoco]* or *Baraquan* hath nine branches which fall out on the north side of his own main mouth: on the south side it hath seven other fallings into the sea, so it disembogueth [discharges] by 16 arms in all, between Islands and broken ground, but the Islands are very great, many of them as big as the Isle of *Wight* and bigger, and many less: from the first branch on the north to the last of the south it is at least 100 leagues, so as the river's mouth is no less than 300 miles wide at his entrance into the sea, which I take to be far bigger than that of *Amazons*: all those that inhabit in the mouth of this river upon the several north branches are these *Tivitivas,* of where there are two chief Lords which have continual wars one with the other: the Islands which lie on the right hand are called *Pallamos*, and the land on the left *Hororotomaka*, and the river by which *John Dowglas* returned within the land from *Amana* to *Capuri*, they call *Macuri*.

These *Tivitivas* are a very goodly people and very valiant, and have the most manly speech and most deliberate that ever I heard of what nation so-ever. In the summer they have houses on the ground as in other places. In the winter they dwell upon the trees, where they build very artificial towns and villages, as it is written in the Spanish story of the *West Indies*, that those people do in the low lands near the gulf of Uraba: for between *May* and *September* the river of *Orenoke* riseth thirty foot upright, and then are those Islands over-flown twenty foot high above the level of the ground, saving some few raised grounds in the middle of them: and for this cause they are enforced to live in this manner. They never eat any thing that is set or sown, and as at home they use neither planting nor other manurance, so when they come abroad they refuse to feed of ought, but of that which nature without labor bringeth forth. They use the tops of *Palmitos* for bread, and kill Deer, fish and porks for the rest of their sustenance, they have also many sorts of fruits that grow in the woods, and great variety of birds and foul.

And if to speak of them were not tedious and vulgar, surely we saw in those passage of very rare colors & forms, not elsewhere to be found, for as much as I have either seen or read. Of these people those that dwell upon the branches of *Orenoque* called *Capuri* and *Macureo*, are for the most part Carpen-ters of *Canoas* [Canoes], for they make the most and fairest houses, and sell them into *Guiana* for gold, and into *Trinedado* for *Tobacco*, in the excessive tak-ing whereof, they exceed all nations, and notwithstanding the moistness of the air in which they live, the hardness of their diet, and the great labors they suffer to hunt, fish, and foul for their living, in all my life either in the Indies or in Europe did I ever behold a more goodly or better favoured people, or a more manly. They were wont to make war upon all nations, and especially on the *Canibals*, so as none durst without a good strength trade by those rivers, but of late they are at peace with their neighbors, all holding the Spaniards for a common enemy. When their commanders die, they use great lamentation, and when they think the flesh of their bodies is putrified, and fallen from the bones, then they take up the carcass again, and hang it in the *Casiquies* [cacique's] house that dies, and deck his skull with feathers of all colors, and hang all his gold plates about the bones of his arms, thighs, and legs. Those nations which are called *Arwacas* [Arawaks] which dwell on the south side of

Orenoque, (of which place and nation our Indian Piolot was) are dispersed in many other places, and do use to beat the bones of their Lords into powder, and their wives and friends drink it all in their several sorts of drinks. . . .

At the mouth of the Orinoco

That night we came to anchor at the parting of three goodly rivers (the one was the river of *Amana* by which we came from the north, and ran athwart towards the south, the other two were of *Orenoque* which crossed from the west and ran to the sea towards the east) and land upon a fair land, where we found thousands of *Tortugas'* eggs, which are very wholesome meat, and greatly restoring, so as our men were now filled and highly contented both with the fare, and nearness of the land of *Guiana* which appeared in sight. In the morning there came down according to promise the Lord of that border called *Toparimaca,* with some thirty or forty followers, and brought us divers sorts of fruits, & of his wine, bread, fish, and flesh, whom we also feasted as we could, at least he drank good Spanish wine (whereof we had a small quantity in bottles) which above all things they love. I conferred with this *Toparimaca* of the next way to *Guiana,* who conducted our galley and boats to his own port, and carried us from thence some mile and a half to his town, where some of our Captains garoused [caroused] of his wine till they were reasonable pleasant, for it is very strong with pepper, & the juice of divers herbs, and fruits digested and purged, they keep it in great earthen pots of ten or twelve gallons very clean and sweet, and are themselves at their meetings and feasts the greatest garousers [carousers] and drunkards of the world: when we came to his town we found two *Cassiques* [caciques], whereof one of them was a stranger that had been up the river in trade, and his boats, people, and wife encamped at the port where we anchored, and the other was of that country a follower of *Toparimaca:* they lay each of them in a cotton *Hamaca,* which we call brazil beds, & two women attending them fix cups and a little ladle to fill them, out of an earthen pitcher of wine, and so they drank each of them three of those cups at a time, one to the other, and in this sort they drink drunk at their feasts and meetings.

That *Cassique* that was a stranger had his wife staying at the port where we anchored, and in all my life I have seldom seen a better favored woman. She was of good stature, with black eyes, fat of body, of an excellent countenance, her hair almost as long as her self, tied up again in pretty knots, and it seemed she stood not in that awe of her husband, as the rest, for she spoke and discoursed, and drank among the gentlemen and Captains, and was very pleasant, knowing her own comliens [beauty], and taking great pride therein. I have seen a Lady in England so like her, as but for the difference of color I would have sworn might have been the same. . . .

On the Aroras of Guiana and their poisoned arrows

There was nothing whereof I was more curious, than to find out the true remedies of these poisoned arrows, for besides the mortality of the wound they make, the party shot endureth the most insufferable torment in the world, and abideth a most ugly and lamentable death, sometimes dying stark mad, sometimes their bowels breaking out of their bellies, and are presently discolored, as black as pitch, and so unsavory, as no man can endure to cure, or to attend them. And it is more strange to know, that in all this time there was never Spaniard, either by gift or torment that could attain to the true knowledge of the cure, although they have martyred and put to invented torture I know not how many of them. But every one of these Indians know it not, no not one among thousands, but their soothsayers and priests, who do conceal it, and only teach it but from the father to the son.

Those medicines which are vulgar, and serve for the ordinary poison, are made of the juice of a root called *Tupara*: the same also quencheth marvellously the heat of burning fevers, and health inward wounds, and broken veins, that bleed within the body. But I was more beholding to the *Guianans* than any other, for Anthonio de Berreo told me that he could never attain to the knowledge thereof, & yet they taught me the best way of healing as well thereof, as of all other poisons. Some of the Spaniards have been cured in ordinary wounds, of the common poisoned arrows with the juice of garlic: but this is a general rule for all men that shall herafter travel the Indies where poisoned arrows are used, that they must abstain from drink, for if they take any liquor into their body as they shall be marvellously provoked thereunto by drought, I say, if they drink before the wound be dressed, or soon upon it, there is no way with them but present death. . . .

Monsters

Next unto *Arvi* there are two rivers *Atoica* and *Caora*, and on that branch which is called *Caora* are a nation of people, whose heads appear not above their shoulders, which though it may be thought a mere fable, yet for mine own part I am resolved it is true, because every child in the provinces of *Arromaia* and *Canuri* affirm the same: they are called *Ewaipanoma*: they are reported to have their eyes in their shoulders, and their mouths in the middle of their breasts, & that a long train of hair growth backward between their shoulders. The son of *Topiawari*, which I brought with me into England told me that they are the most mighty men of all the land, and use bows, arrows, and clubs thrice as big as any of *Guiana*, or of the *Orenoqueponi*, and that one of the *Iwarawakeri* took a prisoner of them the year before our arrival there, and brought him into the borders of *Arromaia* his father's Country. And farther when I seemed to doubt of it, he told me that it was no wonder among them, but that they were as great a nation, and as common, as any other in all the provinces, and had of late years slain many hundreds of his father's people, and of other nations their neighbors, but it was not my chance to hear of them til I was come away, and if I had but spoken one word of it while I was there, I might have brought one of them with me to put the matter out of doubt. Such a nation was written of by *Mandevile*, whose reports were held for fables many years, and yet since the East *Indies* were discovered, we find his relations true of such things as heretofore were held incredible: whether it be true or no the matter is not great, neither can there by any being in the imagination, for mine own part I saw them not, but I am resolved that so many people did not all combine, or forethink to make the report.

When I came to *Cumana* in the west Indies afterwards, by chance I spoke with a Spaniard dwelling not far from thence, a man of great travel, and after he knew that I had been in *Guiana*, and so far directly west as *Caroli*, the first question he asked me was whether I had seen any of the *Ewaipanoma*, which are those without heads: who being esteemed a most honest man of his word, and in all things else, told me that he had seen many of them: I may not name him because it may be fore his disadvantage, but he is well known to *Monsier Muchron's* son of London, and to *Peter Muchron* merchant of the *Flemish* ship that was there in trade, who also heard what he avowed to be true of those people.

Figures 18 and 19. Ralegh's Monsters in Guiana and Amazons

Europeans always feared that monsters inhabited their world. The fact of their existence in distant climes did not come as a surprise, especially when such learned authorities as the French anatomist Ambroise Paré and such mid-century encyclopedists as Conrad Gesner included depictions of European monsters in their pages. When travelers went abroad, they believed that demonic creatures lurked just out of reach. Such thoughts were firm in Sir Walter Ralegh's mind when he journeyed to Guiana. These two images from a 1599 printed edition of his account depict the kinds of beings he was convinced could be found in South America: Amazons who laid down their arms to mate once a year with nearby men, knowing full well that they would keep any girls who were born but give up the boys; and Ewaipanoma, whose heads were not on their shoulders but on their chests. (An armadillo, a species indigenous only to the Americas, can be seen walking near the lower right corner of the picture of the Ewaipanoma.) [Brevis and Admiranda descritio regni Guianae, avri abundantissimi, in America, (Noribergae, 1599).]

Figure 18

Figure 19

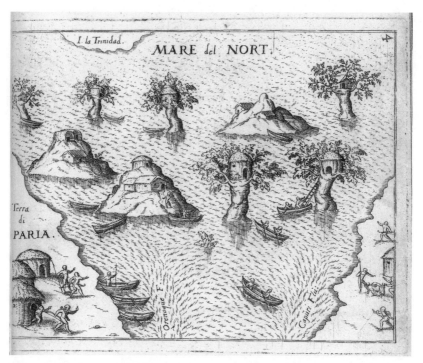

Figure 20. People Living in Trees

Among the people Ralegh described were those he termed Tivitivas, who lived near the mouth of the Orinoco. Because of annual flooding of the river, they lived in houses built high up in trees. "They never eat any thing that is set or sown, and as at home they use neither planting nor other manurance, so when they come abroad they refuse to feed of ought, but of that which nature without labor bringeth forth," Ralegh wrote. "They use the tops of Palmitos for bread, and kill Deer, fish and porks for the rest of their sustenance, they have also many sorts of fruits that grow in the woods, and great variety of birds and foul." Ralegh praised these natives' (and others') abilities as carpenters, and the picture showed how they moved back and forth between their tree lodges and the higher ground. The lower right corner of the image depicts a scene of cannibalism, a familiar trope which appeared frequently in European depictions of Native Americans. [Brevis and Admiranda descritio regni Guianae, avri abundantissimi, in America (Noribergae, 1599).]

Document 30

El primer nueva corónica y buen gobierno (1615–1616)

By Felipe Guaman Poma de Ayala, *El primer nueva corónica y buen gobierno*, [1615/1616], Copenhagen, Royal Library, Gks 2232 4to, tran. Rolena Adorno and José Cárdenas Bunsen

Felipe Guaman Poma de Ayala (1535?–1616?), a native of Santiago de Chipao in the southern Peruvian Andes, wrote to King Philip III of Spain in February 1615, presenting him with what he called a "chronicle or general history." It was a long and extraordinary document, including his 399 illustrations. Born after the fall of the Inkan state, the world he saw was already irrevocably changed by the arrival of Europeans. His family had been mitmaqkuna, *individuals whom the Inka had given special privileges as their emissaries to peoples they conquered. But the Spanish conquest had altered their status. "To put it succinctly," as the literary scholar Rolena Adorno has written, "the pre-Columbian ambassadorial settlers who represented the Inka's power and prestige and carried out his imperial mission became the viceroyalty's migrants and outsiders." It was from this status that he wrote his report—a man aware of a legacy of special privilege now undermined but not yet obliterated, at least not to him. He thus took it upon himself to inform Philip III of what was taking place in this part of the Spanish empire. He did so as a man from an elite family who considered himself a Christian who had learned Spanish ways despite his indigenous origin. But even this assimilation could not free him from verbal abuse at the hands of Europeans. He was destined to remain one of the* forasteros—*outsiders—in the colonial order.[15]*

Yet despite such recognition, Guaman Poma felt compelled to write to the King to tell him "all that I have seen as well as that which I have learned from very old lords of this kingdom, who had full accounts and reports of everything about their ancestors, so that their memory might endure throughout the ages of their world and so that things so great and memorable might not be lost on account of the lack of writing, and so that Your Majesty's historians may have fuller understanding than that which I understand them

---

15. Rolena Adorno, *Guaman Poma and His Illustrated Chronicle from Colonial Peru: From a Century of Scholarship to a New Era of Reading* (Copenhagen: Museum Tusculanum Press, 2001), 15, 19–20, 27–29.

to have been able to have until now." *Compiling this account came at great personal cost to Guaman Poma and his family: "I, my wife and children have suffered great necessity, poverty, and nakedness on account of not being able to have access to my herds and fields, enduring everything with great patience, with the goal of doing a great service to God our Lord and to Your Majesty."[16] Those personal costs were necessary for Guaman Poma to produce an account of Inka rituals, history, and customs, much of it based on interviews he conducted during the thirty years that he claims to have spent on the road. He also wrote with a sense of urgency to let the king know of the misery suffered by the Peruvians at the hands of local Spanish authorities.*

Guaman Poma was among a small group of Native Americans whose testimony about the changes in their societies during the first century of European colonization has survived. Though much of Guaman Poma's account details the ways that the Spanish had altered daily life in the Andes of South America, the section here contains his reflections on his return to his home after a long absence. It is a testimony that is riveting in its attention to detail and heart rending at the anguish that he suffered encountering what was for him a new world, a place transformed by the encounter with Europeans and the subsequent colonization of his homeland. This is a testimony of a specific kind of travel: a journey back home to a world almost as unrecognizable as the many places Guaman Poma had seen during his time away.

Guaman Poma's Nueva corónica *survived in a manuscript that has been in the Royal Library of Denmark in Copenhagen at least since the mid-seventeenth century.[17] Though it resembles many of the narratives in this volume, it is also a very different kind of text. As Adorno has effectively argued, Guaman Poma's account was part of a "counteroffensive" in which some American authors, who had "lived through the first, critical moments of Spanish American cultural and political history," began to engage "in a process of decolonization in which the territories to be recovered were not only geographical but also spiritual and historical."[18] Guaman Poma hoped that his account would lead*

16. Guaman Poma's letter of 15 February 1615, in Adorno, *Guaman Poma and His Illustrated Chronicle*, 84–86.
17. Rolena Adorno and Ivan Boserup, *New Studies of the Autograph Manuscript of Felipe Guaman Poma de Ayala's* Nueva corónica y buen gobierno (Copenhagen:Museum Tusculanum Press, 2002), 19–20.
18. For the context of Guaman Poma's account see Rolena Adorno, *Guáman Poma: Writing and Resistance in Colonial Peru*, 2nd ed. (Austin: Institute of Latin American Studies and University of Texas Press, 2000), quotation at 3.

the monarch to halt practices that had become so obviously destructive to the native peoples of South America. In that sense, his intent echoed that of the Dominican Bartolomé de Las Casas, who believed that if the Iberian monarchs understood the abuses being conducted in their name they would order their subordinates to behave responsibly toward the natives.

Guaman Poma claimed that he traveled over the entire viceroyalty of Peru in order to investigate the evils of Spanish colonial governance. Although he journeyed to the ancient Inka capital of Cuzco, and from Huamanga and Santiago de Chipao to Lima, the main travel account that he presents is his journey, excerpted here, from his homeland in southern Peru to Lima to present his manuscript to the viceroy for dispatch to the king in Spain. Along the way he witnessed a range of social pathologies. Referring to himself in the third person, he wrote that "he saw half the Indians of the province turned into servants and rogues who wear European clothes and make deals, being scoundrels and thieves who seek the favor of the priests and the Spaniards." He wrote too of the decline of native families, the conversion of local women into prostitutes, and population collapse. Not everyone he met treated him badly, but the tone of his account reveals Guaman Poma's sadness as he gazed out upon a land that his people had once dominated.

Judging from Guaman Poma's own testimony, it is clear that he wanted to have his work published by the king in Spain.[19] The translation here is part of a major work-in-progress by Adorno, José Cárdenas Bunsen, Jan Szeminski, and John Charles. When complete, it will bring to an English-speaking audience a powerful testament to the transforming power of the European colonization of the Americas. Parts of this copyrighted translation can be found alongside the original text and its pen-and-ink illustrations at the Guaman Poma website of the Royal Library of Denmark (www.kb.dk/elib/mss/poma/). This authoritative text will be the standard English-language edition and should be consulted by anyone interested in either Guaman Poma or an indigenous perspective on the Spanish conquest and colonization of the Andes.

19. *Felipe Guaman Poma de Ayala, El* primer nueva corónica y buen gobierno, Copenhagen, Royal Library, GkS 2232, 4 to, 11: "And the aforementioned favor he requests and beseeches forever of His Majesty for the previously mentioned printing of the aforementioned book, composed by the previously mentioned author, don Felipe Guaman Poma de Ayala, lord and powerful *apu*, which means prince, because he merits it for his aforesaid abilities and labors."

1094 [1104]

The author returns from the world. He entered his home, in the middle of this kingdom, in the province of the Andamarcas, Soras, and Lucanas, and the towns in its center and its head, San Cristóbal de Suntunto, New Castile, and Santiago Chipao, eagle and royal lion of this kingdom. First he visited the poor sick people and the elderly and the orphans, and he visited the church and performed good deeds in it. And then he saw the town and the province in ruins and taken over [by outsiders] and destroyed.

Thirty years he had been serving His Majesty, and he found everything tumbled to the ground and his houses and cultivated fields and pastures invaded. And he found his sons and daughters destitute, serving poor, tribute-paying Indians. His children and nephews and nieces and relatives did not recognize him because he came so old; he would be eighty years of age, all white hair and thin and naked and barefoot.

Because he used to go about dressed all in silk and finely woven woolens, and he customarily accoutered himself as a lord and prince, being the grandson of the tenth king. He made himself poor and destitute only in order to observe and apprehend the world with the blessing and permission of His Majesty and as an eyewitness on his behalf. What Christian will do this, leave family and estate valued at twenty thousand, and become destitute, in order to live among the poor for thirty years?

1096 [1106]

The author don Felipe Guaman Poma de Ayala completed his journey through the world, being eighty years of age.

And he decided to return to his home, where he had houses and cultivated fields and pastures, and where he was a high-ranking native lord, and chief head and administrator, protector [of the Indians], and lieutenant of the Spanish civil administrator (*corregidor*) of the aforementioned province of the Andamarcas, Soras, and Lucanas Indians, on behalf of His Majesty and as a prince of this kingdom.

And thus as he went to the aforementioned towns of San Cristóbal de Suntunto and Santiago de Chipao, where an Indian with authority over ten Indians had been made a high-ranking official. And he called himself "powerful lord," don Diego Suyca, a tributary Indian who had been punished with his sister for being a witch. The corregidor Martín de Mendoza burned two of his snakes which were called *soliman, matacallo* and other dirty things. This

Indian, having placed himself at the disposal of the said corregidor Juan de León Flores and father Peralta, was well liked by them because he wove for them five hundred pieces of clothing made of common cloth, and he gave them Indians to be used for trafficking and goods for barter, and he made bothersome demands of the Indians.

And in San Cristóbal de Suntunto don Gabriel Cacyamarca was acting as the highest-ranking native official and

1097 [1107]

don Francisco Usco, a legitimate lord, served as his second-in-command. And so it was that he [the author] found everything destroyed because of the schemes of the aforementioned corregidores and priests of the said province. And he found there that all the Indians—men and women—had fled because they had so much hard labor. And in addition to this, he found Pedro Colla Quispe and Esteban Ata Pillo installed in his house and on his ancestral land as well as in his cultivated field at Chinchay Cocha, and with them other Indians, all by order of this said tributary Indian, don Diego Suyca.

Why did the aforementioned author not turn back, having seen all that has been described? The said author and the others started to weep, as did the other poor Indians, men and women, seeing themselves with so much hardship and misfortune in the aforementioned, their town and province. And the arrival of the said author weighed heavily upon don Diego Suyca and don Cristóbal de León and the other high-ranking Indian officials who made themselves such when they were actually tributary Indians, as well as upon the aforementioned corregidor, notary, and their adjuncts and the Spaniards who rob the Indians. And, by the same token, it [displeased] all the priests of the said parishes, all of whom flayed the skin of the poor Indians.

The said author was very tired and very poor, and he had not a single kernel of maize or anything else because of having journeyed so many years in the world, serving God and His Majesty and His Holiness and the lord viceroys, grandees, dukes and counts, marquises, and the

1098 [1108]

royal council of His Majesty of Castile and of this kingdom, for the service of the royal crown and the well-being, benefit, increase, and growth of the poor Indians of His Majesty. Being in this situation, the said author sought

346 Travel Narratives from the Age of Discovery

to go to present himself to His Majesty so that [the recommendations stem-
ming from] his service and labors of so many years might be put into effect.

[. . . . . .]

1100 [1110]

And so it was that he departed for the City of Kings of Lima to present
himself to His Majesty on behalf of his poor, and [this] happened to the said
author on the way: Two of his mules died in the snow because of the cold,
and he went along on the road in all his poverty with [only] a horse. He came
upon two Christian men, friends of the poor, named Pedro Mosquera and
Francisco Juárez. They carried the said author forward and favored him, and
arrived at the establishment of Choclo Cocha, where the silver mines of Asto
Uaraca were located, as well as the chapel of Our Lady of the Peña de Francia,
to which he was devoted. And a Christian man named Miguel Machado and
his wife were at their mines, where they treated him well and favored him.

And from there he left for the city of Castrovirreina of Coyca Pallca where
he had been earlier. The said author went along very poor, and he presented
himself to a very Christian lordly gentleman named don Fernando de Castro,
governor, who gave him money for his sustenance. And Juan de la Cruz Orel-
lana and Antonio de Mendieta, miners, paid him great honor and treated him
well. And the father and priest and vicar of the mountain, a creole from Ica,
and very Christian, gave him silver coins and favored and honored him.

1101 [1111]

Being in this situation, the Indians' advocate named Juan de Mora y Car-
vajal ordered that a white horse that cost fifty pesos be stolen from him [the
author]. And he protested it but justice was not done. And thus the author
gave up and spoke about it and gave thanks to God: "Look, Lord, God of
heaven, an Indians' advocate does this harm to the said author. What will he
do to my poor Indians of Jesus Christ?"

Being in this situation, there was a disturbance and harm done to the
poor because the priests of the parishes of San Cristóbal calumniated the
Yauyos and Uachos Indians. It is said that the aforementioned priest had demanded that they give him Indians for trafficking and many single women
to weave clothing and [to perform] other tasks and labors. Don Pedro [López
de Toledo] responded. And in order to do ill and harm to the Indians because
of this, he [the priest] accuses them falsely, calling them witches who worship
stones.

And to that effect, he began to hang the old men and women and children one by one and torment them until they gave false confessions; because of the agony, they said that they possessed objects of devotion (*huacas*) and idols, and they showed him stones of different types.

And thus they took one hundred Indians and whipped them very cruelly on the authority of the judge of Castrovirreina. And in the jail, being deprived of food and clothing, eighty tributary Indians and old men and women, died.

With the high-ranking authority don Pedro [Colla Quispe], the said priest took from them all their finery and silver service and jewelry and clothes, such as silver bowls and brooches and garments, all of silver, and clothing of fine cloth and of common cloth, animal horns, feathers, and red-dyed wool, with which in their feasts they sing and dance and frolic. He gathered up goods from all the houses, and out of them he made new sets of silver service and out of the wool, [new] sets of bed covers.

1102 [1112]

Oh great God of mine, Lady Saint Mary, oh most high lord, our Catholic king, have compassion because of this for the creatures who cost Him so much suffering and punishment and torment and death, and bought with His precious blood! Have compassion, Jesus Christ, for your poor! Oh lord, our king, [consider] how from your estate eighty souls have been lost! Neither the priest nor the corregidor suffer on account of it because they strip and take away everything that the poor have. The corregidor flays [the poor], and he takes twelve thousand [pesos] and other things. Afterward this said corregidor carries out the punishment; he hangs this poor Indian because he stole or because he lived in concubinage. He exiles his Indian women to other cities, and he ignores the theft of twenty thousand from the [community's] strong box; the said corregidor and the priest take the same amount, the Spanish trustee of Indians (*encomendero*), again as much. And thus in this kingdom he flays and makes use of the poor of Jesus Christ for his own benefit.

[. . . . . .]

1105 [1115]

And he [the author] went throughout the world to bear witness and to bring his [Majesty's] justice and remedy to the poor.

And thus the said author turned back to his journey to offer the advice and provide the means for His Majesty to impose the redress of grievances.

And thus he resumed his travel; he left very poor. God was served, and by the mercy of the Mother of God, His Mother, Saint Mary of the Peña de Francia, he received comfort and nourishment. And in this way a miracle was performed [by Saint Mary] for the poor and lordly author. And thus he journeyed to the city of Castrovirreina, where he undertook his trip once more.

There once again he found complete misery. An Aymara Indian from the town of Uaquirca had been the victim of theft of a saddle and other small items. This said Indian was called don Pedro de León Cautillo. And besides this, his [the author's] eldest son abandoned him, and don Francisco de Ayala left him since he found himself poor and without means of support, he who was so poor and afflicted, and there was no one to loan or help him with a single *real*. See here all the poverty that he endured in order to serve God our Lord and favor the poor of Jesus Christ and give an account of this kingdom to His Majesty for the succor and salvation of souls!

[. . . . . .]

1108 [1118]

As has been said, the author left from the town of San Cristóbal and arrived at the city of Castrovirreina and spent a night there. From there he went forward alone, very poor, and wherever he went, he encountered many Spaniards and Indians on the road.

And they asked him in whose company he went and whom he served. Spaniards and Indians asked him this. He responded that he came serving a solemn man named Cristó-bal; as a way of saying Christ, he added the "bal", although he said "Cristóbal [Christopher] of the Cross." The men asked who this said Christopher of the Cross was, whether he was a miner or a rich man. He responded that his master had been a great miner and that he was now rich and a powerful lord. They asked: "Will we be seeing this man?" The author answers,

1109 [1119]

"He'll be catching up with me. Your mercy can find him if you look for him." With these aforementioned words, the author always went through the world in search of the poor of Jesus Christ and in His holy service and the service of His Majesty. And in this manner the said poor lordly author went about his business. And he again arrived at his friend, the Christian Miguel Machado, who was on his property at the chapel of Our Lady of la Peña de Francia of Chocllo Cocha. And there he had in his service twenty Indians from the town of the said author, during the second week of Lent. On Sunday they met with his Indians, and the Indians, men, women and children, received him [the author], where all wept because of the misery and hardship that they were suffering.

First, weeping with tears, he [one of the Indians] spoke to his lord, the author, and asked him if he was truly alive, because the poor of Jesus Christ of the entire province had wept for him: "And our town alone spins and weaves eighty pieces of clothing of common cloth, and the said corregidor and the said priests and lieutenants and Spaniards of the wayside inns (*tambos*) demand a hundred Indians for trafficking and a great quantity of items for barter that we are required to produce. Sir, the rest of the high-ranking officials who are appointed are tributary and low born Indians: don Carlos, don Cristóbal de León, don Diego Suyca. All they want to do is take bribes. Likewise we suffer very great harm in these said mines because a majordomo, a Guanca Indian, Juan Puxare, from the Lurin Guanca community, who pays no tribute nor performs any service, cruelly punishes us, stripping us and underpaying our labors. And in a similar manner, this same harm is done by the miner named Juan Tomás de Contrerias at the mines of Guancabilca."

[. . . . . .]

1113 [1123]

He [the author] entered the prosperous town of Oropesa of Guancabilca. He went into the church and out onto the plaza. The said author remarks that he was shocked and astonished to see in that plaza so many poor native lords slapped about and beaten around the head. Some of these lords were called "horses", "dogs", and in many ways they [themselves] mistreat the rest of the poor Indians. The author says that it seemed to him that all the demons of hell had come forth in order to trouble the poor of Jesus Christ and that he writes these words as a summary of all that he saw in the said plaza. And the said author found himself among poor people who did not know him, although his vassals knew him and embraced him and told him about all the misery and hardships that they suffered in their said province and in the said mines. And thus the aforementioned, his poor Indian subjects, took the said author to their dwellings.

And they said: Sir, look carefully at these aforementioned torments and martyrdoms that we suffer in these said mines in the labors assigned to the Indians: The corregidor Juan de León Flores and his notary Andrés Ualliente sent a formal report that tallied the number of missing Indians and claimed that twenty-six Andamarcas Indians, whom the said captain had contracted and paid for, did not appear. And of the Lucanas Indians, thirty were missing, and of the Soras Indians, none showed up; only ten Indians came forth in all. Upon being asked how it was that so many Indians failed to appear for their assigned turns at labor (*mita*), the said Indians and their captains replied that a hundred Indians,

1114 [1124]

including the aforementioned Indian leaders of highest rank and seconds- in-command and other Indian officials, had been pulled out in order to transport the corregidor's wine and other goods for barter, and that he had sent them all to the place at Uata Cocha to dispatch the wine for transport.

And from there the said author departed for the valley of Xauxa. On the road at the place called Llallas, while [he was] sleeping in a cave, it is said that two Lurin Uanca Indians came to assault him, whereby God was served. Inside the cave there were six Indians, of these said Indians who, from the time of Chalco Chima, were known as great thieves and robbers who performed assaults all over the kingdom. And so they ply their trade to the present day. This is written as a summary of the entire subject.

And thus, hastening out of love for the solemnities of Holy Thursday and Easter, the said author came upon many Spanish muleteers and barterers who were traveling along without attending either the vesper service or the mass or the sermon. Look, Christian, if you do this being an Old Christian, what would you expect my Indians to do? You pull the Indians out of their devotion by force. And if an Indian were to do that, the corregidor, the lieutenant, and the priest would arraign and accuse him. And thus the author says that it is a holy thing to observe [the rites from] the vespers of Palm Sunday through the four days of Easter and Sundays and the feasts of the entire year, and, during these times, that it be considered unlawful to travel in this kingdom, under pain of punishment by the Holy Mother Church. With that there will be Christianity and order in this kingdom.

The said author arrived very poor to the town of Huancayo. And he was very ill, and thus he went to the vespers service and procession, and he heard a very good sermon by the commissary priest. And the day of the solemnity

1115 [1125]

of Holy Friday, he heard a much better sermon by the prior. It turned out that the said author, because of being so poor, did not find lodging in the whole town of Huancayo. And he found neither Christians nor Christian charity in them, although they all go about carrying rosaries.

And from there he was given lodging in the house of an Indian named Pedro Carua Rinri. And he was a cantor and he had [ecclesiastical] duties and he collected the alms of the holy bull of the Crusades for six years. And he was an alms collector and majordomo of the church of the said town of Huancayo, where he gave charity and alms [to the author].

The said author was in the middle of the town and plaza and of the world, witnessing everything. Because he was so poor and in tatters, there was no one who called him for Easter. He says that he fasted. The second day the aforementioned owner of the house gave hospitality to him and other very poor people.

From there he went to the town of Concepción de Lurin Guanca and to Xauxa. The author says that in the said towns he saw half the Indians of the province turned into servants and rogues who wear European clothes and make deals, being scoundrels and thieves who seek the favor of the priests and the Spaniards. And he observed more: another half province of Indian women turned into prostitutes. They wear European skirts, sleeves, footwear, and bodices, each of them bearing a half dozen [little] mestizos and mulattos, cholos, and other children of mixed blood. Because of being such great whores, they no longer want to marry their Indian peers. These aforementioned ones carry with them the other poor Indians. And thus the said Indians flee and fail to multiply, and the towns become depopulated, and they come to an end. This is occurring because the highest-ranking native lord ends up marrying his daughters and his sisters to mestizos and mulattos. Since they see their leader and the others doing so, they are happy to give birth to mestizos. They [the Indian women] no longer want to marry Indian men, and the kingdom is being lost.

And so the author said that he well remembered the ordinances of don Francisco de Toledo, in which he commanded that the Indians go about dressed in their natural garb and that Spanish dress be taken away from

1116 [1126]

the Indians, men and women, and that no Spaniard or mestizo or mulatto be allowed to reside in the said towns among the Indians in the entire kingdom. And thus from one year to the next he [Toledo] ordered that mestizos and mulattos and Spaniards be drafted for the defense of the city of Chile and the cordillera, the tropical forest, and the North Sea, where there are many nations of warring, infidel Indians. Spaniards and mestizos and mulattos and freed blacks should serve God and His Majesty, observe the law of Castile and not be exempted: The tributary Indian should pay his tribute, the gentlemen pay his taxes, and both be held accountable. As I have said, all the provinces of this kingdom are half depopulated; the said Spaniards and the said corregidores and priests and missionary priests and encomenderos are destroying it. On account of all of them, the kingdom is being lost, and His Majesty is losing his estate and the riches of the world.

In order that the truth be known, and because there is no justice for the poor Indians in this kingdom, be it noted that don Juan Apo Alanya, the highest-ranking lord of the district of Hanan Uanca, was married to doña María Manco Carua. And his aforementioned cunning mother, doña María Alta, the mother of don Juan Apo Alanya, was married to a mestizo named Francisco Zerrano, the stepfather of the said don Juan Apo Alanya. While this said don Juan Apo Alanya was serving His Majesty in the mines of Guancabilca, it occurred that Francisco Zerrano, the said mestizo and his stepfather, raped Apo Alanya's wife. And since the said Apo Alanya found out about it, he caught them one night, and he killed both him and her. And because of this, the said corregidor punished the said don Juan Apo Alanya and confiscated his entire estate. Another result was that Francisco Serrano's brothers, Juan Zerrón and Miguel Campusano, who were the sons of Juan Serrano, and Diego López, the son of Villegas, and another Diego López, sought revenge. They were four persons armed with weapons. Like traitors and enemies of the poor Indians, they murdered poor don Juan Apo Alanya when he was alone in the countryside.

Look here, unfeeling officer of justice, [consider] who is at fault, don Juan or the said four Spaniards or his aforementioned stepfather? Their sins killed the aforementioned [Serrano y doña María] and the said don Juan should have been set free without punishment, and the four traitors should be punished and quartered and their properties confiscated and they should be made to compensate the said son of don Juan Apo Alanya, the young boy, don Juan Guayna Alanaya. The responsibility for all that goes to the lord viceroy and the high court of criminal and civil justice and to those who consent that such a roguish caste of Spaniards and mestizos and mulattos and blacks live among the Indians.

For this reason and also because of the laws and ordinances of this kingdom, it should be mandated that the said Spaniards, mestizos, blacks and mulattos, and other people of mixed blood be expelled from the provinces and towns of the Indians of this kingdom and go to the aforementioned cities. Although they be married to Indian women, the said Spaniards and mestizos and mulattos should take their wives with them. And the aforementioned judges and law officers of His Majesty should expel the said Indians, men and women, from the cities and towns and send them to their own provinces and towns.

1118 [1128]

And thus the said Indians of this kingdom will increase, and there will not be so many underhanded dealings and delays in the payment of the aforementioned tribute or so many absences of the Indians from their labor obligations in the said mines. And these aforementioned ones should get time off every year, and this time should be paid for by the same aforementioned delinquent Indians and delinquent Spaniards and vagabonds who refuse to live in the cities, preferring to rob and commit outrages among the Indians. And thus there will be remedy and justice, as His Majesty orders in his royal decrees and provisions and laws. And so I say that there is no justice when it concerns complaints by Indians, but when it comes to Spaniards, there will be justice. Look here how there is no justice in this said [case] of the death of don Juan Apo Alanya. In the same manner, there is none in the entire kingdom for the poor Indians.

Now I will tell you the truth about how the said author called to mind the Yauyos Indians from near the town of Córdoua: On the road a Spaniard assaulted ten Indians, taking away their possessions and sustenance. While the Indians were defending themselves, he unsheathed his sword and wounded three Indians. And thus, defending themselves from the said Spaniard, the aforementioned Indians killed the aforementioned Spaniard. And so it was that without any investigation or judicial inquiry, the law officers hanged the said ten Yauyos Indians, without investigating.

See here how the said Spaniards receive justice and the said Indians get none in this kingdom, nor is there anyone who advocates for them. The said author went forward by way of the great river of Uanbo on a raft to the towns of Chongo, Chupaca, Cicaya, Urcotonan, Mito Hincos and Uari Pampa. And there the said author bore witness; there he saw how the Uancas Indians, falsely assimilated, insincere Christians, robbed the poor women of as much as they could

1119 [1129]

and how the dishonest Indian cantors remained in the town. And those who did not know about it were thrown out of their towns and houses and lands. And these said ones [the cantors] sought the favor of the parish friars, as did the said Indian women who wore European dress. And thus [the town] was half depopulated, of which the said Indian women made themselves the greatest trouble-makers, for the reasons that they are the concubines of the said priests and missionary priests and of the said Spaniards and mestizos and mulattos. And thus they are given force and free reign, and in this way the said Indian women turn the world upside down, and they know how to falsely accuse their husbands, while they [themselves] are fornicating with Spaniards. Just as false accusations were made [by his wife] against don Diego Chuqui Llanqui, the lord of Cochangara, saying that he had raped his daughter and fornicated with his sisters, and that he was a sorcerer. And other perverse things were said [by his wife] only for the purpose of wanting to send him to the gallows and become herself a thorough cheating whore.

Likewise an Indian cantor named Sancho told the said author about something similar. He said that he had beaten his wife and that the said woman shouted and screamed, saying: "Be witness to the fact that this my husband has raped and abused my daughter!"

See here, Christians, how you see the said Indians, men and women, carrying rosaries and receiving the sacrament and always being drunk and spending all day in the church as the twenty-fourth member of the confraternity. God help us! For all this His Lordship [the bishop] is responsible, as well as the parish priests who give them the sacrament without knowing any more about them than that they behave in an ostentatious, apparently reverent manner when they habitually do harm rather than act kindly or do good. And thus the sacrament should not be given nor should anyone be allowed to join a confraternity without first being repentant, and they should never drink chicha or wine in their whole life, and they should come forth contrite of spirit and heart, and they should not be trouble-makers or make false accusations against anyone. And thus the said witnesses, if they be lying, deceiving Indians, men and women, they should be punished and should not be taken as witnesses nor be given any office in law enforcement.

1120 [1130]

The author sets out from Santo Domingo de Cicaya and a very Christian Indian, the cantor of the said town, named don Juan Bautista Guamalli

Chuqui Llanquis, the legitimate son of Santiago Achicac Chuqui Llanqui, accompanies him to Lima. This said person was a very Christian man, a great servant of God and His Majesty, who served six months as chief courier. And he has been chief civil officer and magistrate, and he was the son and grandson of the highest-ranking Chuqui Llanquis.

And thus as a Christian, he ordered his son, as a service to God and His Majesty, to serve the said author until arriving in Lima. The father of this said Chuqui Llanqui, in service to God and His Majesty, had captured the traitor Francisco Hernández Girón. And thus they went along the road and sites of Uachac, Angascaca, and Pucara and at the site of Nina Pampa and Paria Caca they arrived directly onto the royal road. There there was a petty merchant who does very great harm in the lands and pastures and cultivated fields of the Indians of San Felipe.

On the Paria Caca road, the said author came upon the said Spaniards and pack animals and wayfarers and women who brought along half a dozen prostituted Indian women,

1121 [1131]

and some [were] from Uadachiri and others from Xauxa and from Uancallo, to which [places] they take Indian guides burdened like horses, animals, driving them before their steeds. The author says that it is a very great injury, even though it is permitted by law that Indians be used as guides only. The author says that thus it is very just and right that no Indian be assigned as guide or at turns of forced labor in this kingdom, in conformity with the law in force in Castile and for the service of God and His Majesty. That in this way there will be remedy.

The said author arrived at the town of San Felipe. And having arrived, the aforementioned Indians and don Pedro Puypa Caxa, of one hundred and twenty years of age, very old, spoke to him. They all wept and showed him their church, the asylum for the ill, the priest's home, and the town hall, all of which had been pulled down, and the said church had been defaced. The author says that in his opinion the said poor Indians had suffered five thousand pesos' worth of damage in the church and public buildings, and that they lost again as much in the destruction of their private homes.

And they had been forced to go two leagues away from their cultivated fields to the town of San Pedro. And on the road the aforementioned Spaniards and mestizos and blacks raped their wives and daughters. And in addition to that, they robbed them of their means of sustenance.

And besides all this, they told him that an inspector of the holy church named doctor Ávila and the corregidor, under the guise of calling them idolaters, confiscated from them great quantities of gold and silver and clothing and plumes and other fine things, clothes of fine cloth and of common cloth, brooches, garments, urns and vessels, all of gold and silver, all of which they used to dance and frolic in their feasts and festivals, the annual Corpus Christi. And all this has been taken away from the poor Indians. And beyond this, in the town of San Lorenzo he [the inspector] has left two more inspectors, his disciples. And in addition to this, what price will be exacted of all of them and their servants for the foodstuffs and labor obligations and damages and other things? Because he [the doctor] is favored by the bishop, he skins alive the poor of Jesus Christ and there is no remedy and he is not accountable.

1122 [1132]

Look here, Christian, the opposite should be occurring: Send inspectors to examine the aforementioned priests and missionary priests and punish them. He [the doctor] skins and punishes the said poor Indians. He forgave the priest because he bribes him and has [his] support. And thus the author says that it is very just that His Majesty send an inspector from Spain to investigate the said priests and missionary priests of the said parishes of this kingdom and to favor the aforementioned Indians of this said kingdom. In this way there will be justice.

The said author says that, although the aforementioned Yauyos Indians and the others, since they are from the highlands and from near the South Sea, are cunning people who have neither charity nor the love of humankind nor Christianity, that they are therefore fools given over to roguishness and evil doings, that they are good only for eating and drinking and have neither rosaries nor religious images, that's the way the aforementioned priests of the said parishes want it. And they instruct them thus, and they do not preach the Holy Gospel to them nor [instruct] them in the holy works of mercy but rather [urge them] to seek gain and goods for barter in the city of Lima. [Saying] "give me silver, take the silver," they let their souls go to hell for the sake of becoming rich from the sweat of the poor Indians.

The said author passed from the town of Uadachiri, and at the summit he met some men and ladies who were coming from the wayside inn of Chorrillo. And the said author asked them why they were not coming with Indians. They responded that they preferred to go burdened themselves rather than to burden the poor Indians, because in Christian law and in that of Castile, Christians were not used as carriers; horses and other animals were. For that, God created the animals, and for that reason in Castile no person was assigned as guide or made to perform forced labor. And this is the way we fear God.

These aforementioned words they replied to the said author,

1123 [1133]

and he says that since they saw him old and poor, they gave him half a dozen loaves of bread and half a container of preserved quince from that which they brought from Lima. He said that no Spaniard nor any lady on the road or in the cities had given him alms. And the said author acknowledges that these said men and ladies were neither creoles nor mestizos, but rather that, in his opinion, they had been born in Castile. And thus the said author asked them, and they said they were from Castile and that for ten years they had been going about in this kingdom of Peru.

The said author arrived at the wayside inn of Chorrillo. There some poor Indians, old men and women, served him. There some Indians had spoken to the said author and told him that all the Indians of the valley of Xauxa were carrying a great quantity of clothing, that they sold it at two *patagones*, and at one *patagón*, per piece, and that they brought it stolen from the whole kingdom, that they had bartered for the clothing, even though it was new, in exchange for small amounts of toasted maize, and that they did the same in San Pedro, San Felipe, San Lorenzo, and at the wayside inn of Uadachiri.

To this the said author says that of the said poor petitioners from the provinces who go to seek justice, some of these aforementioned ones go being ill, others carry nothing to eat or the means to pay for anything, and that thus they are deceived and their meager possessions taken from them, that the Yauyos Indians have no charity or merciful works or Christianity, nor do their priests teach them [to give] holy alms; so he [the author] declares it.

From there the said author went

1124 [1134]

to the town and wayside inn of Cicicaya and upon arriving [learned] that the highest-ranking lord, a Christian named don Martín, the son of don Diego, was not there but at the chapel of the lord San Martín de Chuntay, where his Indians were cleaning the irrigation canal for the aforesaid community, and where they received him [the author] with love and charity and were generous to him and showed him favor and gave him alms. And they nourished him for the love of God and that of the lord San Martín and because he was poor and old, infirm. And he went along the marsh and he climbed the steep hill of Aysauilca, where the said author met a poor man named Diego de Aguayo, a native of the city of Chuquisaca. He was a very poor man. The said author and the aforementioned man met in the sandy terrain en route to the city of Lima.

On the said road, they met another man, a muleteer who was stiff and proper; God save us! He presented himself as a law enforcement officer and he threatened the poor man for the purpose of wanting to take from him a mule that the aforementioned poor man was bringing with him. And he asked him

1125 [1135]

where he came from, and where the said mule was from, and why he was not bringing it already slain and butchered, and that it looked like one of his own mules for, after all, one egg looked like another. He said to him these aforementioned reasons only for the purpose of wanting to take the aforementioned mule away from the said poor man on the road.

And thus the said author and the aforementioned poor man went on and entered the said City of Kings of Lima very late. And they found no lodging nor any one to help them. Because of being so poor, they slept in a doorway without eating a single bite, and their mounts went without grass because they came so impoverished. And from there he arrived beyond the enclosed street of El Cercado, and he went into another house in front of the monastery of the discalced ladies. Once installed there, they threw him out onto the street because they saw him so poor and in tatters. Although he begged them in the name of the love of God and His Mother Saint Mary, there was no pity for the said poor author.

The said author sold the meager things that he had in order to obtain some silver coins so that he could sustain his poverty. Then he went to the church of Our Lady of the Peña de Francia of Santa Clara

1126 [1136]

because of the devotion of the said author to the Mother of God. And then he went to the chapel of the Souls in Purgatory because of his devotion to acts of charity and the love of humankind. Because of loving the poor of Jesus Christ our Lord, he exercised patience. And in the said city he rented a house and paid twenty *reales* a month for himself as a poor man as well as for the other poor people whom he brought with him for the love of God.

Look here, Christians, how you make yourselves greater than you are! If you are a poor Jew or a tribute payer or a poor laborer, why do you pretend to be officers of the law, wanting to know about the lives of others when you are ignorant of your own? You interrogate the poor man more for your greed of the said mule than for inquiring of him in order to give him any alms at all, of eight *reales* or of four. I see all of you making yourselves judges. You do everything only for the purpose of taking away the aforementioned mule; the world is upside down. It is a sign that there is no God and there is no king. They are in Rome and Castile. For the poor and in order to punish them, there is a system of retribution, and for the rich, there is none. May God remedy what he can, Amen. Here you see for what cause, and for its remedy, the poor author, making himself poor, labored.

1127 [1137]

As is evident, the said author endured so much travail, leaving behind all that he had, estate and children, alone in the service of God and His Majesty, although according to the order of the Indians of this kingdom he was a very great lord and gentleman. How it was necessary to defend his kingdom and speak and communicate with so great and high a lord, king and monarch of the world over all the kings and emperors of Christendom and over all the infidels, Moors and Turks, Englishmen, and those of other nations of the world as God created them, all that which the sun revolves around, day and night, throughout the world.

Who will be able to write or speak to or approach so great a personage, a Christian Catholic lord, Holy Catholic Royal Majesty?

1128 [1138]

And thus he [the author] dared to do so as a vassal of his royal crown and his knight of this kingdom of the Indies of the New World, who is a prince, which means *auqui*, of this kingdom, the grandson of the tenth king, Topa Ynga Yupanqui, the legitimate son of doña Juana Curi Ocllo Coya, which means *coya*, queen of Peru.

And thus it was necessary to investigate and to write the said *Nueva corónica y buen gobierno* of this kingdom in service to God and His Majesty and for the well-being and increase and preservation and growth of the said Indians of this kingdom. In the service of God and of the royal crown of His

Majesty, the said author, having entered the said City of Kings of Lima, found it full of Indians who had abandoned their communities and African slaves who had escaped from their masters and become servants, even officials, although they were laborers, low born and tribute-paying Indians, who put on fine clothing, and dressed like Spaniards and donned swords. And others cut their hair in order to avoid paying tribute or serving in the mines. See here the world upside down!

And thus, since they see these runaway Indians, other Indians abandon their communities and there is no one to pay tribute nor is there anyone to serve in the said mines. And in the same manner the said author saw very many Indian women, prostitutes, loaded down with mestizo and mulatto children, all of them wearing European skirts and short boots and coifs. Although they are married, they go about with Spaniards and black men. And thus, in order to keep on with their whorish ways, others do not want to marry Indians or leave the said city. And the aforementioned poor districts of the said city are full of Indians, and there is no remedy for it. And they do harm to the service of God our Lord and His Majesty. And thus the said Indians in this kingdom do not multiply.

Part IV
Europe

Turkish Letters (1554–1562)

By Ogier Ghiselin de Busbecq, *The Turkish Letters of Ogier Ghiselin de Busbecq, Imperial Ambassador at Constantinople, 1554–1562,* trans. Seymor Forster (Oxford, 1927), 34–39

Ogier Ghiselin de Busbecq was born in Comines in western Flanders, near the village of Busbecq. He received a sound classical education and in 1554 served as part of an embassy sent to England by the Hapsburg emperor Ferdinand. There he attended the wedding of Philip II of Spain and Queen Mary of England, one of the most important dynastic couplings of the sixteenth century. Soon after his return he became Hapsburg ambassador to the Ottoman Empire. He traveled from Vienna to Constantinople in 1554. While there he wrote a series of letters to one of his old schoolmates named Nicholas Michault. Though not initially intended for publication, these texts formed the basis of Busbecq's Turkish Letters, *which enjoyed wide circulation; published first in Latin in 1581 in Antwerp, the book appeared in three other Latin editions by the end of the century, in addition to editions in German (published in Frankfurt in 1596) and Bohemian (published in Prague in 1594). By the middle of the seventeenth century, editions had appeared in English, French, Flemish, and Spanish.[1]*

Busbecq arrived in Constantinople near the height of the power of the Ottoman Empire. The Ottomans' ascendancy had begun with the accession and reign of Mehmet II from 1451 to 1481 and reached its highest point under the reign of Süleyman I (the Magnificent), who ruled from 1520 to 1566. It was into Süleyman's Constantinople that Busbecq arrived in 1554 after a journey that had taken him through much of central and southern Europe. In Buda he met with the Janissaries, an army he estimated at 12,000 across the sultan's empire. In that city he described his meeting with "many Turks"

---

1. For details on Busbecq's life, see translator Edward Seymour Forster's introduction to Ogier Ghiselin De Busbecq, *The Turkish Letters of Ogier Ghiselin De Busbecq, Imperial Ambassador at Constantinople, 1554-1562* (Oxford: Oxford University Press, 1927; rpt. 1968), ix–xvi; and Charles T. Forster and F. H. B. Daniell, *The Life and Letters of Ogier Ghiselin De Busbecq,* 2 vols. (London, 1881). For the editions of *The Turkish Letters,* see Forster and Daniell, *Life and Letters,* II: 288–291. For a history of the Ottoman Empire during this period, see Stanford Shaw, *Empire of the Gazis: The Rise and Decline of the Ottoman Empire, 1280–1808,* Vol. 1 of *History of the Ottoman Empire and Modern Turkey* (Cambridge: Cambridge University Press, 1976), 55–111.

who were, he wrote, "attracted to my table by the lure of my wine, a luxury which they appreciate all the more because they have little opportunity of enjoying it, and which therefore they consume with all the greater avidity whenever they have the chance." From there he boarded a ship to descend the Danube to Belgrade, a journey that lasted only five days—a full week less than the more dangerous overland route. From Belgrade he made his way to Jagodina, a Serbian village where he arrived during a funeral and decided to take notes about local burial practices. As he continued on his way he stayed at various inns which, as he put it, "inspired me with particular disgust." These lodgings provided no privacy, which meant that "everything must be done in public, and the darkness of night alone shields one from the sight of it all." He eventually made it to Sofiya, where he stood in amazement at the local women's "towering head-dresses and bonnets (if they can be so called)." These Bulgarian headpieces made the women even more impressive; they carried themselves, he wrote, "as you would imagine that Clytemnestra would take the stage, or Hecuba while Troy still flourished."[2]

Eventually Busbecq made it to Constantinople. As his traveling party approached the capital, he noted, "we crossed by bridges over two lovely arms of the sea. It is a district the like of which for beauty could not, I think, be found anywhere, if only it were cultivated and art gave a little assistance to nature." Yet even his first impression, or at least the first impression he committed to paper, demonstrated his ambivalence about the Ottomans. "As it is, the land seems to lament its fate and the neglect and scorn of its barbarian lords." Despite his initial misgivings, Busbecq was still keen to explore the city. Upon his arrival a messenger raced to Süleyman to tell the sultan that Busbecq was available. "While we were awaiting a reply," Busbecq later wrote, "I had an opportunity to see the sights of Constantinople at my leisure."[3] The excerpt that follows constitutes the Hapsburg ambassador's views of what he saw when he went out into the metropolis.

Busbecq eventually left public service to the Hapsburgs and hoped to retire to his estate near the banks of the Lys. But in 1592, as he made his way through war-torn Normandy, his health failed him. He died on October 28, 1592, at a castle near St. Germain. He was buried there, but not before his

---

2. Busbecq, *Turkish Letters*, 8–9 (Buda), 12 (Danube), 15–16 (Jagodina), 17 (inns), 22 (Sofiya).
3. Busbecq, *Turkish Letters*, 26, 34.

heart could be removed. Placed in its own casket, Busbecq's heart was taken to the family tomb.[4]

My first desire was to visit the church of St. Sophia, admission to which was only granted as a special favour; for the Turks hold that the entrance of a Christian profanes their places of worship. It is indeed a magnificent mass of buildings and well worth a visit, with its huge vault or dome in the middle and lighted only by an open space at the top. Almost all the Turkish mosques are modeled upon St. Sophia. They say that formerly it was much larger and that its subsidiary buildings spread over a large area but have now been done away with, and that only the central shrine of the church remains.

As for the site of the city itself, it seems to have been created by nature for the capital of the world. It stands in Europe but looks out over Asia, and has Egypt and Africa on its right. Although these latter are not near, yet they are linked to the city owing to ease of communication by sea. On the left lie the Black Sea and the Sea of Azof, round which many nations dwell and into which many rivers flow on all sides, so that nothing useful to man is produced through the length and breadth of these countries which cannot be transported by sea to Constantinople with the utmost ease. On one side the city is washed by the Sea of Marmora; on another side a harbour is formed by a river which Strabo calls, from its shape, the Golden Horn. On the third side it is joined to the mainland, and thus resembles a peninsula or promontory running out with the sea on one side, on the other the bay formed by the sea and the above-mentioned river. From the center of Constantinople there is a charming view over the sea and the Asiatic Olympus, white with eternal snow.

The sea is everywhere full of fish, either making their way down, as is their habit, from the Sea of Azof and the Black Sea through the Bosporus and the Sea of Marmora to the Aegean and Mediterranean, or else on their journey up thence to the Black Sea. They travel in such large and densely packed shoals that they can sometimes even be captured by hand. Mackeral, tunny, mullet, bream, and sword-fish are caught in great abundance. The fishermen are usually Greeks rather than Turks. The latter, however, do not despise fish when they are placed before them, provided they are of the kind which they regard as clean; they would sooner take deadly poison than eat

4. Busbecq, *Turkish Letters*, xv–xvi.

the other kinds. I may mention in passing that a Turk would rather have his tongue cut out or his teeth drawn than taste any food which he looks upon as unclean—frogs, for example, and snails and tortoises. The Greeks entertain similar scruples. I had engaged a boy of the Greek religion to serve as a caterer in my household. The other servants had never been able to induce him to eat shell-fish, until one day they placed before him a plate of them so cooked and seasoned that, thinking that they were some other kind of fish, he ate most heartily of them. But when he learned from their laughter and derision and from the shells which were afterwards shown to him that he had been deceived, you cannot imagine how upset he was. He retired to his chamber and indulged in endless vomiting and tears and misery. It would take fully two months' pay, he said, to atone for his sin; for the Greek priests are in the habit of charging those who have confessed to them a greater or a less sum for absolution according to the nature and gravity of the offence, and will only grant absolution to those who pay them the price they ask.

At the end of the promontory, which I have mentioned, is the Palace of the Sultans, which, as far as I can judge (for I have not yet myself entered it), is not remarkable for the splendour of its architecture or decoration. Beneath the Palace, on the lower ground, stretching right down to the sea, lie the Imperial Gardens. It is usually held that the ancient Byzantium lay in this quarter. You must not expect me to tell you why the people of Chalcedon, the site of which was opposite Byzantium and scarcely shows a trace at the present day, were called blind; nor about the perpetual and tideless current which flows down the Straits; nor about the pickled delicacies which are brought to Constantinople from the Sea of Azof and are called by the Italians *moronella, botarga,* and *caviare.* All these details are unsuited to a letter, the limits of which I have already exceeded; besides, they can be learnt from authors, both ancient and modern.

But to return to Constantinople. No place could be more beautiful or more conveniently situated. As I have already said, you will look in vain for elegant buildings in Turkish cities, nor are the streets fine, being so narrow as to preclude any pleasing appearance.

In many places there are remarkable remains of ancient monuments, though one cannot help wondering why so few have survived, when one considers the number which were brought by Constantine from Rome. It is beside my present purpose to describe them in detail; but I will mention a few of them. In the space occupied by the ancient Hippodrome two serpents of bronze are to be seen, also a fine obelisk. Two remarkable columns are also to be seen in the city. One of them stands in the neighborhood of the caravanserai where we lodged, the other in the market which the Turks call Avret-Bazar, that is, the Women's Market. This column is covered with reliefs from top to bottom representing some expedition of Arcadius, who set it up and whose statue long surmounted it. It would be more accurate to describe it as a spiral than as a column, on account of the interior staircase which gives access to the summit. The column which stands opposite the apartments usually occupied by the imperial representatives is composed, except for the base and capital, of eight solid blocks of porphyry so fitted together that they appear to form a monolith; and indeed this is the popular belief. Where the blocks fit into one another there are laurel-wreaths surrounding the whole column, so that the joints are hidden from those who look up from below. This column, having been shaken by frequent earthquakes and burnt by a neighboring fire, is splitting in many places, and is bound together by numerous iron rings to prevent it from falling to pieces. It is said to have been crowned by statues, first of Apollo, then of Constantine, and finally of Theodosius the elder, all of which were dislodged by gales or earthquakes.

The following story is told by the Greeks about the obelisk in the Hippodrome, which I have mentioned above. It was torn from its base and for many centuries lay upon the ground, until in the days of the later Emperors an architect was discovered who undertook to re-erect it on its base. When the price had been agreed upon, he set up an elaborate apparatus consisting chiefly of wheels and ropes, whereby he raised an immense stone and lifted it into the air, so that it was only a finger's length from the top of the base on which it had to rest. The spectators imagined that he had wasted his time and trouble on such vast preparations and would have to make a fresh start with great labor and expense. However, he was not in the least discouraged, and, profiting by his knowledge of natural science, ordered an immense quantity of water to be fetched. With this he drenched his machine for many hours, with the result that ropes which held the obelisk in position gradually became soaked and naturally tightened and contracted, so that they lifted the obelisk higher and set it upon the base, amid the admiration and applause of the multitude.

At Constantinople I saw wild beasts of various kinds—lynxes, wild cats, panthers, leopards, and lions. One of these was so well broken in and tamed that it allowed the keeper before my eyes to pull out of its mouth a sheep, which had just been given to it to eat, and remained quite calm, though its jaws had barely tasted blood. I also saw a quite young elephant which greatly amused me, because it could dance and play ball. I imagine that you will be unable to suppress a smile and will exclaim: "What! an elephant playing ball and dancing!" But why not, when Seneca tells us of one which walked the tight rope, and Pliny is our evidence for another which knew the Greek alphabet? Now listen to my account, so that you may not think I am inventing or misunderstand what I say. When the elephant was ordered to dance it advanced on alternate feet, swaying to and for with its whole body, so that it obviously meant to dance a jig. It played with a ball by cleverly catching it, when it was thrown, with its trunk and hurling it back, as we do with the hand. If you are not satisfied from my account that it danced and played ball, you must find some one to give a clearer and more learned description.

There had been a camelopard [giraffe] among the animals at Constantinople, but it had died just before my arrival. But I had its bones, which had been buried, dug up for my inspection. This animal is much taller in front than behind; it is, therefore, called a camelopard because it has a head and neck like a camel's and a skin covered with spots like a leopard's.

If I had not visited the Black Sea when I had an opportunity of sailing thither I should deserve to be regarded as very lazy; for to have seen the Black Sea was regarded as not less difficult than to have sailed to Corinth. I had a delightful excursion, and was allowed to enter several of the Sultan's country-houses, places of pleasure and delight. On the folding doors of one of them I saw a vivid representation in mosaic of the famous battle of Selim against Ismael, King of Persia. I also saw numerous parks belonging to the Sultan situated in charming valleys. What homes for the Nymphs! What abodes of the Muses! What places for studious retirement! The very earth, as I have said, seemed to mourn and to long for Christian care and culture. And even more so Constantinople itself; nay, the whole of Greece. The land which discovered all the arts and all liberal learning seems to demand back the civilization whish she has transmitted to us and to implore our aid, in the name of our common faith, against savage barbarism. But all in vain; for the lords of Christendom have their minds set on other objects. The grievous bonds wherewith the Turks oppress the Greeks are no worse than the vices which hold us in thrall—luxury, gluttony, pride, ambition, avarice, hatred, envy, and jealousy. By these our hearts are so weighed down and stifled that they cannot look up to heaven, or harbor any noble thought or aspire to any great achievement. Our religion and our sense of duty ought to have urged us to help our afflicted brethren; nay, even if fair glory and honor fail to illumine our dull minds, yet at any rate self-interest, the ruling principle of these days, ought to stir us to rescue from the barbarians regions so fair and so full of resources and advantages, and possess them in their stead. As it is, we seek the Indies and the Antipodes over vast fields of ocean, because there the booty and spoil is richer and can be wrung from the ignorant and guileless natives without the expenditure of a drop of blood. Religion is the pretext, gold the real object.

Document 32

Discoverie of Vaigatz and Nova Zembla (1556)

By Richard Johnson, "Discoverie of Vaigatz and Nova Zembla " in *Principal Navigations, Voyages, Traffiques and Discoveries of the English Nation*, Richard Hakluyt, ed., 3 vols. (London, 1598–1600), 1: 283–85

Richard Chancelour (fl. 1550–1556; or Chancellor as it is often written) was no novice seaman when he agreed to captain the Edward Bonaventure *on an expedition seeking the Northeast Passage in 1555. His success on an earlier adventure had prompted Sir Hugh Willoughby to lead a journey "for the search and discovery of the northern part of the world." Their goal was to reach India by crossing through the Arctic to the Pacific and then around Southeast Asia to their destination. They never made it. Instead, Chancelour found his way deep into Russia. On his return to England, he produced goods that he had obtained there, and helped to convince the English that trade with Russia could be profitable. His efforts thus contributed to the formation of the Muscovy Company, which aimed to promote English commerce to the east.*

When he returned to England, Chancelour told a Cambridge-educated schoolmaster named Clement Adams (1519?–1587) about the voyage. Adams, who was also an expert on Sebastian Cabot's voyage and had provided a map of that expedition for London's mercantile community, wrote up Chancelour's findings. His report eventually appeared in both editions of Richard Hakluyt's Principal Navigations.

But Adams was not on the voyage, and his account thus lacked the immediacy of that which a participant might give. Richard Johnson, by contrast, provided a firsthand account of the expedition. His report was less thorough than that of Adams, but through Hakluyt it too brought attention to a region that until that time was little known to the wider world. Johnson's account of Chancelour's experiences dwells little on the experiences at sea and more directly with what the English found on land. He paid particular attention, as so many travelers did, to religious practice, from the striking architecture of wooden steeples to the chants uttered in a language he obviously never understood.

Though he never found the Northeast Passage, Chancelour did agree to lead another expedition to Russia. The crew departed in May 1555, but on its return to England the ship foundered in waters off Aberdeenshire and sank. Chancelour, like too many others, became a victim of an expedition that never brought its members all the way home.

First, after we departed out of England we fell with Norway, and on that coast lieth Northbern or Northbergen, and thus people are under the King of Denmark: But they differ in their speech from the Danes, for they speak North [Norse]. And North of Northbern lie the Isles of Rose and Lofoot, and these Islands pertain unto Finmarke, and they keep the laws and speak the language of the Islanders. And at the Easternmost part of that land is a castle which is called the Ward house, and the King of Denmark doth fortify it with men of war: and the Russians may not go to the Westward of that castle. And East Southeast from that castle is a land called Lappia: in which land be two manner of people, that is to say, the Lappians, and the Scrickfinnes, which Scrickfinnes are a wild people which neither know God, nor yet good order: and these people live in tents made of Deerskins: and they have no certain habitations, but continue in herds and companies by one hundred and two hundreds. And they are a people of small stature, and are clothed in Deerskins, and drink nothing but water, and eat no bread but flesh all raw. And the Lappians be a people adjoining to them & be much like to them in all conditions: but the Emperor of Russia hath of late overcome many of them, and they are in subjection to him. And this people will say that they believe in the Russes's God. And they live in tents as the other do. And Southeast and by South from Lappia lyeth a province called Corelia, and these people are called Kerilli. And South southeast from Coerlia lyeth a country called Novogardia. And these three nations are under the Emperor of Russia, and the Russes keep the Law of the Greeks in their Churches, and write somewhat like as the Greeks write, and they speak their own language, and they abhor the Latin tongue, neither have they to do with the Pope of Rome, and they hold it not good to worship any carved Image, yet they will worship painted Images on tables or boards. And in Russia their Churches, steeples and houses are all of wood: and their ships that they have are sowed with withes [twigs or branches] and have no nails. The Kerilles, Russians, and Moscovians be much alike in all conditions. And South from the Moscovians lyeth Tartarians, which be Mahumetans, and live in tents and wagons, and keep in herds and companies: and they hold it not good to abide long in one place, for they will say, when they will curse any of their children, I would though mightest tarry so long in a place that thou mightest smell their own dung, as the Christians do: and this is the greatest curse that they have. And East Northeast of Russia lieth Lampas, which is a place where the Russes, Tartars and Samoeds be in subjection to the Emperor of Russia, and they lie in tents made of Deer skins, and they use much witchcraft, and shoot well in bows. And Northeast from the river Pechere lieth Vaygatz, and there are the wild Samoeds which will not suffer the Russes to land out of the Sea, but they will kill them and eat them, as we are told by the Russes: and they live in herds, and have all their carriages with deer, for they have no horses. Beyond Vaygatz lyeth a land called Nova Zembla, which is a great land, about we saw no people, and there we had foul enough, and there we saw white Foxes and white Bears. And the said Samoeds which are about the banks of Pechere, which are in subjection to the Emperor of Russia, when they will remove from one place to another, then they will make sacrifices in manner following. Every kinred doth sacrifice in their own tent, and he that is most ancient is their Priest. And first the Priest doth begin to play upon a thing like to a great sieve [?], with a skin on the one end like a drum: and the stick that he playeth with is a piece of a shirt of mail, with many small ribs, and teeth of fishes, and wild beasts hanging on the same mail. Then he signeth as we use here in England to hallow, whoop, or shout at hounds, and the rest of the company answer him with this *Owtis, Igha, Igha, Igha*, and then the Priest replieth again with his voices. And they answer him with the selfsame words so many times, that in the end he becommeth as it were mad, and falling down as he were dead, having nothing on him but a shirt, lying upon his back I might perceive him to breathe. I asked them why he lay so, and they answered me, Now doth our God tell him what we shall do, and whither we shall go. And when he had loyen [lain] still a little while, they cried thus three times together, *Oghao, Oghao, Oghao*, and as they use these three calls, he riseth with his head and lieth down again, and then he rose up and sang with like voices as he did before. Then he took a sword of a cubit and a span long, (I did mette [measure] it myself) and put it into his belly halfway and sometime less, but no wound was to be seen (they continuing in their sweet song still). Then he put the sword into the fire till it was warm, and so thrust it into the slit of his shirt and thrust it through his body, as I thought, in at his navel and out at his fundament: the point being out of shirt behind, I laid my finger upon it, then he pulled out the sword and sat down. This being done, they set a kettle of water over the fire to heat, and when the water doth seeth, the Priest beginneth to sing again they answering him, for so long as the water was in heating, they sat and sang not. Then they made a thing being four square, and in height and squareness of a chair, and covered with a gown very close the forepart thereof, for the hinder part stood to the tent's side. Their tents are round and are called *Chome* in their language. The water still seething on the fire, and this square seat being ready, the Priest put off his shirt, and the thing like a garland which was on his head, with those things which covered his face, & he had on yet all this while a pair of hose of deers' skins with the hair on, which came up to his buttocks. So he went into the square seat, and sat down like a tailor and sang with a strong voice or hallowing. Then they took a small line made of deers' skins of four fathoms long, and with a small knot the Priest made it fast about his neck, and under his left arm, and gave it unto two men standing on both sides of him, which held the ends together. Then the kettle of hot water was set before him in the square seat, all this time the square set was not covered, and then it was covered with a gown of broad cloth without lining, such as the Russes do wear. Then the 2 men which did hold the ends of the line still standing there, began to draw, & drew till they had drawn the ends of the line stiff and together, and then I heard a thing fall into the kettle of water which was before him in the tent. Thereupon I asked them that sat by me what it was that fell in to the water that stood before him. And they answered me, that it was his head, his shoulder and left arm, the line had cut off, I mean they know which I saw afterward drawn hard together. Then I rose up and would have looked whether it were so or not, but they laid hold on me, and said, that if they should see him with their bodily eyes, they should live no longer. And the most part of them can speak the Russe tongue to be understood: and they took me to be a Russian. Then they began to hallow with these words, *Oghaoo, Oghaoo, Oghaoo*, many times together. And as they were thus singing & outcalling, I saw a thing like a finger of a man two times together thrust through the gown from the Priest. I asked them that sat next to me what it was that I saw, and they said, not his finger: for he was yet dead: and that which I saw appear through the gown was a beast, but what beast they knew not nor would not tell. And I looked upon the gown, and there was no hole to be seen: and then at the last the Priest lifted up his head with his shoulder and arm, and all his body, and came forth to the fire. Thus far of their service which I saw during the space of certain hours; but how they do worship their Idols that I saw not: for they put up their stuff for to remove from that place where they lay. And I went to him that served the Priest, and asked him what their God said to him when he lay as dead. He answered, that his own people doth not know, neither is it for them to know: for they must do as he commanded. This I saw the fifth day of January in the year of our Lord 1556, after the English account.

Document 33

En-Nafhat El-Miskiya, Fi-S-Sifarat Et-Tourkiya: Relation d'une ambassade Marocaine en Turque (1589–1591)

By Abu '1-Hasan 'Ali al-Tamgruti, *En-Nafhat El-Miskiya, Fi-S-Sifarat Et-Tourkiya: Relation d'une ambassade Marocaine en Turque, 1589–1591,* French trans., Henry De Castries, 1929; English trans., Lisa Bitel and Peter C. Mancall

In the sixteenth century, as in other eras, Muslims traveled frequently. Many made the hajj to Mecca; others made visits (ziyaras) to shrines or expeditions in search of knowledge (rihla and talab al-'ilm); and still others sought places where they could practice their religion freely (hijra). These journeys invariably produced accounts, but relatively few of them for the sixteenth century have made it into print.

There is little known about Abu'l-Hasan 'Ali al-Tamgruti (Abou-L Hasan Ali Ben Mohammed Et-Tamgrouti) beyond what can be inferred from comments embedded in the narrative of his journey from Morocco to Turkey in 1589.[5] He was probably born in 1560 in Tamgrut. In 1589 he traveled as an ambassador from Sa'di Sultan Amhad al-Mansur to the Istanbul court of the Ottoman Sultan Murad III.

---

5. The biographical details about his life can be found in Abderrahmane El Moudden, "The ambivalence of *rihla*: Community integration and self-definition in Moroccan travel accounts, 1300–1800," in *Muslim Travellers: Pilgrimage, Migration, and the Religious Imagination,* ed. Dale F. Eickelman and James Piscatori (Berkeley: University of California Press, 1990), 69–84, esp. 79–82.

As the excerpt from his travel narrative here reveals, Al-Tamgruti was awed by much of what he saw in Istanbul. He found the city's architecture amazing, and also the number of people there. The entry here contains his description of Hagia Sofia, one of the most famous religious buildings in the world. Al-Tamgruti reveled in the sheer size of the structure and was careful to provide details about what a traveler would see there. It was, in some sense, representative of the greatness of Istanbul. Even a fire that would have destroyed another metropolis had limited impact on the entire city, no doubt because so many people and buildings survived it. Though he did not leave a complete record of all that he saw—one modern observer, for example, has noted that he did not write down the name of any scholar he met even though he acknowledged that he had visited their seminars and learned from them[6]—he paid close attention to things beyond buildings. His text enumerated the kinds of ships to be found in the city's docks and elements of Turkish grammar.

Yet though he was fascinated by what he saw in Istanbul, al-Tamgruti offered a mixed assessment of the Ottoman Turks. They had, he wrote, "oppressed the inhabitants of Tripolitania very much. They had devastated the country with cruelty, depriving people of part of their lands and houses and ransacking their wealth." He claimed that they forced young Muslim women to marry them, which ended their chances of marrying anyone else. He believed that such tactics had begun to persuade Arabs from Tunisia (Ifriqia) to Egypt to establish better ties to Morocco. "They want to share peace, equity, mercy and benefits that the Moroccans (Magribis) enjoy" because of the sharifs. Though such declarations fit his political agenda, al-Tamgrouti also relied on the notion that the Moroccan sharifs were the descendants of the Prophet Mohammed.[7]

Al-Tamgruti died in Marrakesh in either 1594 or 1595. His travel account survived to the present day in the form of one known manuscript, which was copied in 1716. According to Henri de Castries, who translated that text into French (the same year that it was published in Arabic as Kitab al-Nafha al-Miskiyya fi'l-Sifara al-Turkiyya—The Book of the Musky Breeze of the Embassy to Turkey [Lith, 1929]), that manuscript contained a number of errors and lacunae. De Castries used other texts to fill the gaps. Shortly

6. El Moudden, "Ambivalence of *rihla*," 81.
7. Ibid.

after completing the introduction, de Castries died, leaving it to other editors to complete the annotation. This is the first known translation of this part of the text into English, though there are brief translations in Abderrahmane El Moudden's study of rihla.

Constantinople is a city of immense size. It is one of the largest in the world. It is also one of the most celebrated. The number of *hadiths* (traditions) of the Prophet—May God bless him and grant him peace—are alone enough to make it famous. Here is one, collected from the mouth of the Prophet—May God bless him and grant him peace—"The first troops of my nation who conquer the city of Caesar will obtain the pardon of God." By the city of Caesar, the Prophet meant Constantinople. . . .

This city is very vast and surrounded by walls. Its gates are numerous, its population huge. Numerous also are its mosques, both great and small, numerous its markets, its *hammams* [Turkish baths], its *fonduqs* [inns]. It was the capital of the Greeks' country and the seat of the Empire, the city of Caesar.

The Muslims who live in this city today too call themselves Greeks and prefer this historical origin to their own. Even this script they refer to as Greek script.

The houses that abut [the water's edge] all around the harbor are immense and sunk deeply into the ground. All kinds of ships and of vessels come there to anchor: galleys, galleons, treasure ships, flat-bottomed boats, barks, small galleys, frigates, and dinghies.

Barks swarm this port. They function as beasts of burden for the people of Constantinople. The Turks use them to transport trade goods and staples to Galata, in the vicinity of the city and elsewhere. They rely on them for all kinds of articles, even herbs, straw, and wood.

The principal city, which is found to the right of the port, is called Istanbul, the other, which is found to the left, is called Galata. This last is a small city, surrounded by walls like Istanbul.

On the outside of the walls of these two cities, one sees neighborhoods, houses, and other buildings which continue without interruption. There are buildings right in the sea, raised on stone blocks which have been sunk underwater or set on wooden pilings driven into the water, whose heads hold up the building. These constructions serve as houses; they extend the whole length of the shore without break with additional stories built on top.

There is almost no port in the entire world as grand, as deep, as well sheltered against all the winds, as Constantinople. When the sea is high and its waves strongest, one rarely sees rough water. The largest ships drop anchor close to houses and draw up so close to shore that one has only to take a step and one is on a boat. At the far end of the port, a freshwater river runs into the sea.

The markets of this city are countless. All of the known products of the world can be found there. If the inhabitants of the whole earth would come there for provisioning, they would find all they require and more.

There are in Istanbul large and small mosques where the name of God constantly echoes. The largest is situated at the gate of the Imperial Palace. It is called Hagia Sofia [Saint Sophie]. With its ancient architecture, it is one of the most admirable and grandest buildings in the world. No writer could produce a description to match its beauty. It must be seen to understand its value. The imagination of those who only know it from hearsay cannot gain an accurate idea. A report is nothing compared to [what is seen with] the eyes.

This was, before Islam, a grand cathedral which—God knows the truth—was already constructed [like the great mosque] of Jerusalem.[8] It is said in a history book that it was built by a king called Constantine. This prince, after having embraced Christianity with his people, was installed [?] in Constantinople. It was he who built this city, along with the cathedrals and the churches found there, including Hagia Sophia, where a statue of the emperor seated was erected.

According to another version, Constantinople had been founded by Asaf, son of Barakhia and one the maternal aunts of the prophet Solomon—upon whom fortune! This history is by Ibn Battuta and God knows that it must be the truth, because the architecture of this cathedral more closely resembles that of the Djinn. Men are in general unable to build anything to match such buildings.

In the middle of the cathedral, there rises a magnificent cupola of such breadth and rising to such height that a pigeon that flies to the summit of the vault (arch) seems no larger than a sparrow to a man sitting on the floor. This was the first monument of Constantinople that appeared to us at sea, so tall and golden.

The circumference of this cupola at its height measures more than one

8. The Dome of the Rock.

hundred steps. It is built on foundations of massive construction, made of enormous stone blocks, colossal and marvelously sculptured (they say that the rocks are cut high in the mountains), and the very tall and thick multicolored marble columns are of such diameter that two men could not put their arms around them.

Around this magnificent central cupola, behind their foundations and columns, are found other small and lesser heights, whose roofs are distinctive and under which the faithful make their prayers.

One hanging gallery, from which one can view the space covered by the central cupola, rules the periphery there; it is supported by the bands of iron thrust into the wall. At the top of this gallery, I myself one day viewed people seated under the cupola. They appeared to me as small as children, so highly situated is the gallery. Even higher are two other galleries which are also [in] the tower of the central cupola. There are two narrow corridors, which serve as the dormitories for the men attached to service in this mosque. The smaller gallery is furnished with three rows of glass lamps forming three circles around the cupola, which are lit during the nights of Ramadan. The floor of this mosque is entirely finished with paving stones of marble; their walls are all similarly covered.

The entire interior of this mosque is adorned with decorations of different multicolored patterns. Everything is admirably beautiful, curiously elaborated, enhanced by gold leaf and affecting many forms, octagons, hexagons, squares. These gilded designs represent trees and leaves in regular rows, of marvelous execution, excellent and accomplished by sustained talent. What a splendid spectacle, what beautiful brilliance! Who would know this if time had not a little tarnished this splendor?

The lamps of gold and glass suspended in this mosque are innumerable. The *minbar* (pulpit) is of grand height. It is put in a single block of pure white marble and surmounted by a golden dome. The *mihrab* [slab indicating the direction to Mecca] is similarly of marble and surrounded by verses of the Koran arranged in tiers. To the right and to the left of the *mihrab,* some candles are placed in golden chandeliers. All around the *mihrab* and up to the mid-height of the cupola hang tapestries of great value.

In this mosque one finds many chairs reserved for scholars, the *muezzins* [those who proclaimed the hours of prayer], and readers of the Koran, all supported by white marble columns, of which the top portion is covered in gold. On the outside, a number of minarets stand, circling the exterior with lanterns lit during Ramadan, like those on the inside of the mosque.

Moreover, all the minarets of the city, indeed, all of those of the Orient, are lit during Ramadan.

In the interior of Hagia Sofia, one can see a great number of painted images, of which one represents the Cross. The others represent the angels Gabriel, Michael, Azrael, Israfil, etc. The images of the prophets appear at the top of the walls, also those of John, Zacharias, and Mary, carrying in her arms the baby Jesus, of Jesus in the cradle, and of the other childish things the Infidels are fond of. When the Muslims took Constantinople, they removed all the representations of the Cross, and with them a certain number of other pictures, leaving only a part.

In Constantinople, they have tried to imitate the architecture of this grand mosque, but in vain:

> What distance separates the Pleiades from the earth!
> You have some likeness to her, but you can not have the whiteness
>   of her teeth.

The mosque called Suleimaniya most closely approaches Hagia Sofia. It was constructed by the emperor Suleiman, who is buried there. It is like Hagia Sofia in architecture and layout. Suleiman transported to Alexandria four columns of marble on two boats, one of which was shipwrecked with the two columns loaded on it and the other arrived at the port with its cargo. Suleiman put these latter in his mosque. I encountered one day a man from Monastir. He told me that he had been in Alexandria when these four columns were removed, and that, before they could be brought trough the gates of the city, they had to cut a gap in the ancient wall.

The architecture of Hagia Sofia is sturdier, it is of a grander character, and a more massive appearance: that of Suleimaniya is more elegant, more agreeable and more spacious. Do we not see there—and God knows how true this is—a striking analogy with the character of the two founders' edifices? One belongs to Islam and the other to the Infidels. Each of them takes on the essential character of its founder.

Water flows abundantly in Constantinople, particularly in the mosques.

What will surprise the traveler to Constantinople, is the considerable quantity of men and of merchandise that one meets there: workers, artisans, valuable precious objects, merchants, commodities, boutiques, books, everything there is incalculable and only God—Exalted is He—can tell the number: one can find there also a number of markets for the shabbiest merchandise.

The winter before our visit to Constantinople there had been a fire in this city. This was Saturday [April 7, 1588]. There was an inventory of the damage: twenty-eight mosques, both large and small, were destroyed, also twenty-two thousand houses, hostels, and bazaars, which the Turks call *bedestan*, fifteen thousand shops and nine bath houses. Yet the fire ravaged only a relatively small part of the city, considering its immense size and its multiple quarters (districts). Those who suffered the most in the fire were the Jews, even though Jews, Christians and Muslims live mixed together

Document 34

An Itinerary . . . Containing His Ten Years Travell (1617)

By Fynes Moryson, *An Itinerary . . . Containing His Ten Years Travell* (London, 1617), 209–211, 217–19

Fynes Moryson (1566–1617?), the son of a member of the English Parliament from Cadeby, Lincolnshire, lived near the highest levels of British society. One of his brothers became a chief colonial administrator in Ireland, and Moryson himself, who studied law at Peterhouse, Cambridge, enjoyed the kinds of financial and political privileges that marked him as a member of the elite. He is known to posterity as the author of one of the most thorough travel accounts of the sixteenth century.

On May 1, 1591, Moryson and his brother Henry boarded a ship in Leigh (near Southend) and set off on a voyage that eventually took six years. His journey was not a single expedition but instead a grand tour broken in two substantial parts. The first stretched from his departure until his return to England in May 1595. During these years he saw much of northern Europe, including Germany, Poland, Denmark, and Austria, and he eventually made it to Italy, where he remained from October 1593 until early 1595. The second part of his itinerary, which began in December 1595, took him much farther, including visits to ports along the fringes of the Mediterranean and the Adriatic. After a sojourn that began in Venice and took him through Jerusalem, Tripoli, Aleppo, Antioch, and Constantinople, Moryson returned to London in July 1597.

Although Moryson had the kinds of connections that gave him access to rare treasures, he could not dodge the tragedies that so often afflicted early modern people. While in Prague in 1591, he had a dream that his father died, and

subsequent news informed him that the death had occurred that night. Henry died on July 4, 1596, near Antioch. A year later, Moryson traveled on the last leg of his journey, which took him from Venice to London. Soon after, he left for Ireland and various positions in the colonial administration. He was back in London in February 1612, where he participated in the funeral of his sister at St. Botolph's church in Aldersgate.

Moryson's personal history was shared by few individuals. Few Europeans possessed the resources to take such an extended journey. (Moryson himself estimated that his trips cost him £480, a substantial sum in the late sixteenth century.) But it was not his wealth that has made him famous, but instead the survival of his writings. Sometime after his travels, Moryson wrote until his manuscript was so lengthy that even he believed it served no purpose. He destroyed it. Fortunately, he then began again, purportedly on a more modest scale (something hard to believe, given how much he wrote in the surviving Itinerary and another extant manuscript). In early April 1617, he registered the title with the Stationers' Company of London, thereby protecting his copyright. Apparently, he died soon after the book appeared in print.

The Interary is without question a remarkable document, though it has not held the attention of all its readers. His biographer for the Dictionary of National Biography called Moryson "a sober and truthful writer, without imagination or much literary skill." But if his prose lacks pizzazz, he nonetheless kept careful track of what he saw. By the time he finished his journey, Moryson had traveled through much of Europe and offered comments on such diverse topics as local architecture, governing customs, and the ways that people drank alcohol. He provided details about the day-to-day burdens of travel itself: what things cost, how long a traveler might have to wait for a captain to decide a boat was ready to sail, how to protect one's belongings on a journey. He also offered opinions about the nature of travel itself, as well as a detailed account of Irish history and politics at the dawn of the seventeenth century. Near the end he added a section of "Precepts for Travellers, which may instruct the unexperienced." That part of his narrative contained 27 suggestions. He recommended that travelers pray daily, make wills before leaving, stay in the best hotels and lock their doors at night, learn the language that the locals speak, be humble, avoid arguments (which could turn into fights), and renew old friendships after returning home. It was not necessary to learn how to swim.

What follows here are segments of his journey from Venice, through the Adriatic to Jerusalem. In the space of a few weeks he traveled to two of the most important cities in the Old World (and shortly after journeyed to Constantinople). His writings reflect how he as an outsider came to understand each of these ancient crossroads. As the text here reveals, Moryson was not a fan of all that he surveyed. He insulted Jerusalem's residents, for example. Fortunately, he followed one of his own precepts by observing "the underwritten things."

It is the Mariners' fashion that being to go to Sea, they will affirm they set sail presently, that the Merchants and passengers may bring their goods on board, which done, they will not easily take them out again, though that ship after long delays should go last out of the Haven. Therefore we kept our goods in our lodging, still inquiring after the *Scrivano*, who dwelt hard by us; and when he professed seriously that he would take the ship the next day, then we presently shipped our provisions. So on Friday the 19 of *April* (after the new style) in the year 1596, we together with the Patron (our Master) went aboard. And the Patron returned that night to *Venice*, but we lodged in the ship. The Patron had some month past promised me and my brother, that we should set our chests (upon which we were to rest) above the hatches, hard by the stern, where (the ship being great) we had commodity to set them in a place covered over the head, but open on the side towards the prow, and this place was close at the other end, lying at the very door of the Patron's cabin, where he slept, and laid his private goods. And this place seemed to me very pleasant, and fit to rest in, since we were covered from rain; and the winds blew commonly upon the stern, while we were at sea, (for we sailed commonly with a fore wind, the winds being more constant in that sea; at set seasons of the year, than in our seas), and for the time of our abiding in Havens, and otherwise in that calm sea, if the winds were contrary, yet in summer time, and in a clime so near the Æquinoctial line, we could receive no hurt, but rather pleasure by their coolness. Besides, being thus parted from the Mariners, we were free from lice, and all filthiness, wherewith the French-men our consorts were much annoyed; who slept under the hatches, and that the rather, because they wore woollen stockings, we silk, (drawn over with linnen); and they slept in their apparell, we only in our doublets, and linen breeches and stockings;

which doublets of ours were lined with taffeta, wherein lice cannot breed or harbor: so as howsoever I wore one and the same doublet till my return into *England*, yet I found not the least uncleanliness therein. And give me leave to joy in my good fortune, (as the common sort speak). Namely that the taffeta lining of my doublet, being of green color, which color none may wear upon great danger, but only they who are of the line and stock of *Mahomet*, (of whom I could challenge no kindred), yet it happened that by sleeping in my doublet aswell by land as by sea, no Turk ever perceived this my error. Neither did I understand by any Christian, no not by our English Merchants at *Haleppo*, in what danger I was for the same, till I came to *Constantinople*, where our English Ambassadour told me of the strict Law forbidding the use of this color; and that a poor Christian some few days before had been beaten with cudgels at *Constantinople*, and was hardly kept from being killed, because ignorantly he wore a pair of green shoestrings. Whereupon I was yet in fear when all danger was almost past, yet would I not cast off my doublet, but only more warily kept the lining from sight, till I entered the Greek ship wherein I passed thence to *Venice*, and so was free from all danger.

I return to my purpose. The Patron of our ship (as I said) returned to *Venice*; but we stayed in the ship, to dispose all our provisions fitly for the journey. The next day, being the twentieth of April (after the new style), the Patron, Scrivano, and all the Merchants came aboard, and the following night being clear, our ship was drawn out of *Malamocco* the Venetian Haven, by little boats fastened to the ship by ropes, and making their way with oars, (for great ships use no sails to go out of this Haven.)

Upon Sunday the 21 of April, in the year of 1596, being thus put to sea, we set sail with a fair wind. Then all falling on our knees, we prayed unto God for a happy Voyage, kneeling above the hatches, but praying every man privately and silently to himself. Some write, that in the Ships of *Venice*, they use to pray publicly in Latin every day after the Roman fashion, and some days to celebrate Masses: but in this our ship the Patron and most of the Mariners were Greeks, and only the Scrivano (that is, Scribe) with some Merchants were Italians, and of the Roman Religion. Therefore every day a Bell was rung at prayer time, but each man prayed privately after his own manner. There were besides in the ship many Eastern Christians, of diverse Sects and Nations, and Turks, and Persians, yea, very Indians worshipping the Sun, all which, at the ringing of this bell to prayer, went under the hatches. My self and my brother willingly prayed with them above the hatches, after the foresaid manner, whereof we thought no scruple of conscience to be made, since Greeks prayed with us, as well as Italians and French, whose difference in Religion was well known to themselves, so as this our private prayer was void of all dissimulation. And we were glad that no profession of our Religion was imposed upon us, in regard of our consorts, with whom we were to go to *Jerusalem*, and of the Italians, who after our return might perhaps meet us in *Italy*.

Prayers being ended, they used a ceremony, which I liked well: for the sub-Patron giving the sign with his silver whistle, all the Mariners bareheaded, and turning their faces to the East, cried with a loud voyce *Buon´ viaggio, Buon´ viaggio*, (that is, a good voyage), and the same sign given, did cease, and again cried so three times. Upon Tuesday, the Patron with the Scrivano standing by him, stood upon the Castle of the ship, and made a solemn Oration to the sub-Patron and the Mariners, standing upon the lower hatches, whom he admonished how they should behave themselves, and especially to refrain from swearing, blasphemy, and sodomy, under great penalty. Then he wrote the names of the Mariners, and gave every man his charge. And lastly turning himself to the passengers, exhorted them to behave themselves modestly. And I must truly witness, that the Patron, the Scrivano, and the sub-patron, used all passengers courteously, yet so kept their gravity, as they had due respect at all times, particularly at the Table, where they did first set down, others expecting till they came, then the Friars did sit down, and lastly the Lay-men in due order. Neither do any sit or walk upon the highest hatches, save only they who did eat at the Table of the Patron, but the rest and all the Eastern people (whom he never admits to his Table) were on the middle Hatch, or at the Prow.

Upon Wednesday in the morning, we did see upon the shore of *Italy*, the Mountains of *Ancona*, which are two hundred Italian miles distant from *Venice*. Upon Thursday, the five and twenty of April, we sailed by the Island or Mountain *Poma* (or *Pamo*), seated in the middest of the Gulf of *Venice*, which was a high Rock, rising sharp at the top, and uninhabited, where in the Autumn they take Falcons: and we sailed by the Island Saint *Andrea*, (distant one hundred miles from *Ancona*) on the North side, and the shore of *Italy* on the South side. And the same night we sailed by the Island *Ischa*, and the next morning being Friday, by the Islands *Buso, Aulto, Catsa*, and towards the evening, by the Islands *Cazola, Augusta*, and *Palaosa*: for in this Gulf of *Venice* be many Islands, whereof the most are subject to *Venice*, and the rest to *Raguza*, and other Lords, and some towards the North-shore to the great Turk.

Here great store of Dolphins followed our ship; and the voice of the Mariners (as they use to do), and they playing about us, did swim as fast as if they had flown. Then we did see the Island *Liozena*, being all of Mountains, subject to *Venice*, and inhabited by Gentlemen, where the Venetians had built a strong Fort upon the Haven for the Gallies. And after five miles we did see the Island *Curzola*, subject to *Venice*, and having a Bishop. And the wind being high, we cast anchor near *Curzola*, but the wind soon falling, we set sail again. . . .

On Jerusalem

I am unskilful in Geography, and much more in the making of Maps: but according to the faithful view of my eyes, I will first draw the situation of *Jerusalem*, and after explain it, as well as I can. And first I think good to profess that by my journey to this City, I had no thought to expiate any least sin of mine; much less did I hope to merit any grace from God; but when I had once begun to visit foreign parts, I was so stirred up by emulation, and curiosity, as I did never behold any without a kind of sweet envy, who in this kind had dared more than myself. Thus affected, I thought no place more worthy to be viewed in the whole world, than this City, where howsoever I gave all divine worship to God, and thought none to be given to the places, yet I confess that (through the grace of God) the very places struck me with a religious horror, and filled my mind prepared to devotion, with holy motions. In like sort I profess that I will faithfully relate the situation of the City, and the description of the monuments made to me by the Friars, making conscience not to add or detract, but as near as I can to use their own words. Yet do I not myself believe all the particulars I write upon their report, neither do I persuade any man to believe them. But for many monuments, the scripture gives credit to them, and it is not probable in so great difference and emulation, (whereof I shall after speak) of Sects of Christians there abiding. And being most apt to note errors one in another, that any apparent fictions could be admitted on the contrary, it is most certain, that some superstitious invention (wherewith all the sects are more or less infected) have in time obtained, to be reputed true, and religiously to be believed. Howsoever he that confers the situation of the City and of the monuments, with the holy Scriptures, and with the old ruins of *Rome*, and other Cities, shall easily discern what things are necessarily true or false, and what are more or less probable. . . .

The houses here, and in all parts of Asia that I have seen, are built of Flint stone, very low, only one story high, the top whereof is plain, and plastered, and hath battlements almost a yard high, and in the day time they hide themselves within the chamber under this plastered floor from the Sun, and after Sun-set, walk, eat, and sleep, upon the said plastered floor, where as they walk, each one may see their neighbors sleeping in bed, or eating at table. But as in the heat of the day, they can scarce endure to wear linen hose, so when the Syren [Siren?] or dew falls at night, they keep themselves within doors till it be dried up, or else fling some garment over their heads. And with this dew of the night all the fields are moistened, the falling of rain being very rare in these parts towards the Equinoctiall line, and in this place particularly happening only about the month of October, about which time it falls sometimes with great force by whole pails full. The houses near the Temple of *Salomon*, are built with arches into the street, under which they walk dry, and covered from the Sun, as likewise the houses are built in that sort, in that part of the City, where they show the house of *Herod*, in both which places the way on both sides the street is raised for those that walk on foot, lying low in the middest for the passage of laded Asses. In other parts the City lies uninhabited, there being only Monasteries of divers Christian Sects, with their Gardens. And by reason of these waste places, and heaps of Flint lying at the doors of the houses, and the low building of them, some streets seem rather ruins then dwelling houses, to him that looks on them near hand. But to them who behold the City from eminent places, and especially from the most pleasant Mount *Olivet* (abounding with Olives, and the highest of all the Mountains), the prospect of the City, and more specially of the Churches and Monasteries (which are built with elevated Globes covered with brass, or such glistering metal) promiseth much more beauty of the whole City to the beholders' eyes, then indeed it hath. The circuit of the walls containeth some two or three Italian miles.

All the Citizens are either Tailors, Shoemakers, Cooks, or Smiths (which Smiths make their keys and locks not of Iron, but of wood), and in general poor rascal people, mingled of the scum of divers Nations, partly Arabians, partly Moors, partly the basest inhabitants of neighbor Countries, by which kind of people all the adjoining Territory is likewise inhabited. The Jews in *Turkey* are distinguished from others by red hats, and being practical, do live for the most part upon the seacoasts, and few or none of them come to this City, inhabited by Christians that hate them, and which should have no traffic, if the Christian Monasteries were taken away. Finally, the Inhabitants of *Jerusalem* at this day are as wicked, as they were when they crucified our Lord, gladly taking all occasions to use Christians despitefully. They esteemed us Princes, because we wore gloves, and brought with us shirts, and like necessaries, though otherwise we were mostly poorly appareled, yet when we went to see the monuments, they sent out their boys to scorn us, who leaped upon our backs from the higher parts of the street, we passing in the lower part, and snatched from us our hats and other things, while their fathers were no less ready to do us all injuries, which we were forced to bear silently and with incredible patience. Hence it was that *Robert* Duke of *Normandy*, being sick, and carried into Jerusalem upon the backs of like rascals, when he met by the way a friend, who then was returning into Europe, desiring to know what he would command him to his friends, he earnestly intreated him to tell them, that he saw Duke *Robert* carried into heaven upon the backs of Devils.

Document 35

Travels in England (1598)

By Paul Hentzner, "Travels in England, 1598," in *England As Seen By Foreigners in the days of Elizabeth and James the First,* William Brenchley Rye, ed. (London, 1865), 103–13

Paul Hentzner (?–1623), a lawyer from Brandenberg, arrived in England in August 1598 as an associate of Duke Charles of Münsterberg and Oels. He remained there until the end of September. While there, he managed to see a remarkable cross-section of English society, ranging from farmers bringing corn to market to the queen's visitors at the royal court. He praised the fertility of the soil and especially the luxurious quality of the fleece of English sheep, and he noted certain public buildings. At the castle at Woodstock he even saw some graffiti left by Elizabeth when she was imprisoned there. He took passing note of Puritans, though he did not go into much depth about what set those dissenters apart from the Church of England.

Hentzner's account of his travels across Europe was first published in Nuremberg in 1612. The first English translation appeared in 1747 when Horace Walpole privately printed an edition by Richard Bentley. Hentzner noted in his account that he, like other travelers, was not permitted to remove much currency from the nation. Fortunately, no one prevented him from taking away memories of what he had seen, thus enabling him to provide insight into the domestic lives of people who by the late sixteenth century were perhaps more obsessed with the lives of others than with their own lives. The selection here focuses primarily on his assessment of Elizabeth and her court, which he describes in the kind of ethnographic language that can be found in European accounts of places from East Asia to North America.

Elizabeth, the reigning Queen of England, was born at the Royal Place of Greenwich, and here she generally resides, particularly in summer, for the delightfulness of its situation. We were admitted by an order, which Mr. Rogers (Daniel Rogerius) had procured from the Lord Chamberlain, into the Presence-Chamber hung with rich tapestry, and the floor, after the English fashion, strewed with hay, through which the Queen commonly passes in her way to chapel. At the door stood a gentleman dressed in velvet, with a gold chain, whose office was to introduce to the Queen any person of distinction that came to wait on her. It was Sunday [September 6], when there is usually the greatest attendance of nobility. In the same hall were the Archbishop of Canterbury, the Bishop of London, a great number of Counsellors of State, Officers of the Crown, and Gentlemen, who waited the Queen's coming out, which she did from her own apartment when it was time to go to prayers, attended in the following manner:—

First went Gentlemen, Barons, Earls, Knights of the Garter, all richly dressed and bareheaded; next came the Lord High Chancellor of England, bearing the seals in a red silk purse, between two, one of whom carried the royal sceptre, the other the sword of state in a red scabbard, studded with golden fleur-de-lis, the point upwards; next came the Queen, in the 65th year of her age (as we were told), very majestic; her face oblong, fair but wrinkled; her eyes small, yet black and pleasant; her nose a little hooked, her lips narrow, and her teeth black, (a defect the English seem subject to, from their too great use of sugar); she had in her ears two pearls with very rich drops; her hair was of an auburn colour, but false; upon her head she had a small crown, reported to be made of some of the gold of the celebrated Luneburg table; her bosom was uncovered, as all the English ladies have it till they marry; and she had on a necklace of exceeding fine jewels; her hands were slender, her fingers rather long, and her stature neither tall nor low; her air was stately, her manner of speaking mild and obliging. That day she was dressed in white silk, bordered with pearls of the size of beans, and over it a mantle of black silk shot with silver threads; her train was very long, the end of it borne by a marchioness; instead of a chain, she had an oblong collar of gold and jewels. As she went along in all this state and magnificence, she spoke very graciously, first to one, then to another (whether foreign ministers, or those who attend for different reasons), in English, French, and Italian; for besides being well skilled in Greek, Latin, and the languages I have mentioned, she is mistress of Spanish, Scotch, and Dutch. Whoever speaks to her, it is kneeling; now and then she raises some with her hand. While we were there, William Slawata, a Bohemian baron, had letters to present to her; and she, after pulling off her glove, gave him her right hand to kiss, sparkling with rings and jewels—a mark of particular favour. Wherever she turned her face as she was going along, everybody fell down on their knees. The ladies of the court followed next to her, very handsome and well-shaped, and for the most part dressed in white. She was guarded on each side by the gentlemen pensioners, fifty in number, with gilt halberds. In the ante-chapel, next the hall where we were, petitions were presented to her, and she received them most graciously, which occasioned the acclamation of *God save the Queene Elizabeth!* She answered it with *I thancke you myn good peupel*. In the chapel was excellent music; as soon as it and the service were over, which scarcely exceeded half-an-hour, the Queen returned in the same state and order, and prepared to go to dinner. But while she was still at prayers, we saw her table set out with the following so-lemnity:— A gentleman entered the room bearing a rod, and along with him another who had a table-cloth, which after they had both knelt three times, with the utmost veneration, he spread upon the table, and after kneeling again, they both retired. Then came two others, one with the rod again, the other with a salt-cellar, a plate and bread; when they had knelt as they others had done, and placed what was brought upon the table, they too retired with the same ceremonies performed by the first. At last came an unmarried lady of extraordinary beauty (we were told that she was a countess) and along with her a married one, bearing a tasting-knife; the former was dressed in white silk, who, when she had prostrated herself three times, in the most graceful manner approached the table and rubbed the plats with bread and salt with as much awe as if the Queen had been present. When they had waited there a little while, the yeomen of the guard entered, bareheaded, clothed in scar-let, with a golden rose upon their backs, bringing in at each turn a course of twenty-four dishes, served in silver most of it gilt; these dishes were received by a gentleman in the same order as they were brought and placed upon the table, while the lady-taster gave to each of the guard a mouthful to eat of the particular dish he had brought, for fear of any poison. During the time that this guard, which consists of the tallest and stoutest men that can be found in all England, 100 in number, being carefully selected for this service, were bringing dinner, twelve trumpets and two kettle-drums made the hall ring for half-an-hour together. At the end of all this ceremonial, a number of unmarried ladies appeared, who with particular solemnity lifted the meat off the table, and conveyed it into the Queen's inner and more private chamber, where after she had chosen for herself, the rest goes to the ladies of the Court. The Queen dines and sups alone with very few attendants; and it is very seldom that any body, foreigner or native, is admitted at that time, and then only at the intercession of some distinguished personage.

Near this place is the Queen's park, stocked with various wild animals. Such parks are common throughout England, belonging to those that are distinguished either for their rank or riches. In the middle of this is an old square tower, called *Mirefleur,* supposed to be that mentioned in the Romance of Amadis de Guala; and joining to it a plain, where knights and other gentlemen use to meet at set times and holidays to exercise on horseback.

It is worthy of observation, that every year upon St. Bartholomew's Day, when the Fair is held, it is usual for the Mayor, attended by the twelve principal Aldermen, to walk into a neighbouring field, dressed in his scarlet gown, and about his neck a golden chain, to which is hung a Golden Fleece, and besides, that particular ornament, which distinguishes the most noble Order of the Garter. During the year of his magistracy, he is obliged to live so magnificently that foreigner or native, without any expense, is free, if he can find a chair empty, to dine at his table, where there is always the greatest plenty. When the Mayor goes out of the precincts of the City, a sceptre, a sword, and a cap are borne before him, and he is followed by the principal Aldermen in scarlet gowns, with gold chains; himself and they on horseback. Upon their arrival at a place appointed for that purpose, where a tent is pitched, the mob begin to wrestle before them, two at a time; the conquerors receive rewards from the Mayor. After this is over, a parcel of live rabbits are turned loose among the crowd, which boys chase with great noise. While we were at this show, one of our company, Tobias Salander, Doctor of Physic, had his pocket picked of his purse, with nine crowns, which without doubt was so cleverly taken from him by an Englishman who always kept very close to him, that the Doctor did not in the least perceive it. . . .

The soil is fruitful and abounds with cattle, which inclines the inhabitants rather to feeding than ploughing, so that near a third part of the land is left uncultivated for grazing. The climate is most temperate at all times, and the air never heavy, consequently maladies are scarcer, and less physic is used there than anywhere else. There are but few rivers. Though the soil is productive, it bears no wine; but that want is supplied from abroad by the best kinds, as of Orleans, Gascon, Rhenish, and Spanish. The general drink is ale, which is prepared from barley, and is excellently well tasted, but strong and intoxicating. There are many hills without one tree or any spring, which produce a very short and tender grass, and supply plenty of food to sheep; upon these wander numerous flocks extremely white, and whether from the temperature of the air or goodness of the earth, bearing softer and finer fleeces than those of any other country. This is the true Golden Fleece, in which consist the chief riches of the inhabitants, great sums of money being brought into the island by merchants, chiefly for that article of trade. The dogs here are particularly good. It has mines of gold, silver and tin (or which all manner of table utensils are made, in brightness equal to silver, and used all over Europe), of lead, and of iron, but not much of the latter. The horses are small but swift. Glass-houses are in plenty here.

The English are grave like the Germans, lovers of show; followed wherever they go by whole troops of servants, who wear their masters' arms in silver fastened to their left arms, and are not undeservedly ridiculed for wearing tails hanging down their backs. They excel in dancing and music, for they are active and lively, though of a thicker make than the French; they cut their hair close on the middle of the head, letting it grow on either side; they are good sailors and better pirates, cunning, treacherous, and thievish; above 300 are said to be hanged annually at London; beheading with them is less infamous than hanging; they give the wall as the place of honour; hawking is the common sport with the gentry. They are more polite in eating than the French, consuming less bread but more meat, which they roast in perfection; they put a great deal of sugar in their drink; their beds are covered with tapestry, even those of farmers; they are often molested with the scurvy, said to have first crept into England with the Norman Conquest; their houses are commonly of two stories, except in London, where they are of three and four, though but seldom of four; they are built of wood, those of the richer sort with bricks, their roofs are low, and where the owner has money, covered with lead. They are powerful in the field, successful against their enemies, impatient of anything like slavery; vastly fond of great noises that fill the ear, such as the firing of cannon, drums, and the ringing of bells, so that in London it is common for a number of them that have got a glass in their heads to go up into some belfry, and ring the bells for hours together, for the sake of exercise. If they see a foreigner very well made, or particularly handsome, they will say, "It is pity he is not an Englishman."

September 14th. As we were returning to our inn [at Windsor], we happened to meet some country people celebrating their Harvest-home; their last load of corn, they crown with flowers, having besides an image richly dressed, by which perhaps they would signify Ceres; this they keep moving about, while men and women, men and maid-servants, riding through the streets in the cart, shout as loud as they can till they arrive at the barn. The farmers here do not bind up their corn in sheaves, as they do with us, but directly they have reaped or mowed it, put it into carts and convey it into their barns.

There is a certain sect in England called Puritans. These, according to the doctrine of the Church of Geneva, reject all ceremonies anciently held, and admit of neither organs nor epitaphs in their places of worship, and entirely abhor all difference of rank among ecclesiastics, such as bishops, abbots, &c. They were first named Puritans by the Jesuit Sanders. They do not live separate, but mix with those of the Church of England in the colleges.

We came to Canterbury on foot. Being tired, we refreshed ourselves with a mouthful of bread and some ale, and immediately mounted post-horses, and arrived about two or three hours after nightfall at Dover. In our way to it, which was rough and dangerous enough, the following accident happened to us. Our guide or postillion a youth, was before with two of our company, about the distance of a musket-shot, we by not following quick enough had lost sight of our friends; we came afterwards to where the road divided, on the right it was down hill and marshy, on the left was a small hill; whilst we stopped here in doubt, and consulted which of the roads we should take, we saw all on a sudden on our right-hand some horsemen, their stature, dress, and horses exactly resembling those of our friends; glad of having found them again, we determined to set on after them; but it happened through God's mercy, that though we called to them, they did not answer us, but kept on down the marshy road, at such a rate that their horses' feet struck fire at every stroke, which made us with reason begin to suspect that they were robbers, having had warning of such, or rather that they were nocturnal spectres, which as were afterwards told, are frequently seen in those places; there were likewise a great many Jack-a-lanterns, so that we were quite seized with horror and amazement. But fortunately for us, our guide soon after sounded his horn, and we following the noise, turned down the left-hand road, and arrived safe to our companions; who, when we had asked them if they had not seen the horsemen who had gone by us? answered, not a soul. Our opinions, according to custom, were various upon this matter; but whatever the thing was, we were without doubt in imminent danger, from which that we escaped the glory is to be ascribed to God alone.

We take ship for Calais (Sept. 24). In our company were the noble Lord Wilhelm Slawata, a Bohemian baron, with his servant Corfutius Rudth, a noble Dane, Wilhelm and Adolphus ab Eynatten, brothers, from Juliers, and Henricus Hoen their relation. Before we set sail from hence [Dover], each of us was obliged to give his name, the reason of his visit to England, and the place to which he was going. This having been done, and permission to depart obtained, our valises and trunks were opened by those who are appointed for this object, and most diligently examined for the sake of discovering English money, for no one is allowed to carry out of England more than ten English pounds. Whatever surplus there may be, it is taken away and paid into the royal Exchequer.

Document 36

Shipwreck Suffered by Jorge d'Albuquerque Coelho (1601)

By [Afonso Luís], "Shipwreck Suffered by Jorge d'Albuquerque Coelho, Captain and Governor of Pernambuco," in *Further Selections from the Tragic History of the Sea*, trans. C. R. Boxer (Cambridge: Hakluyt Society, 1968), 126–34, 137–39

"I can truthfully assure all those who may read this account, that I have not written here the half of all that happened to us, because when we were suffering these tribulations I had no intention nor opportunity of writing them down, nor when they were past could I bear to think of them." That was the claim that Afonso Luís made about a disastrous voyage commanded by the Portuguese captain Jorge d'Albuquerque Coelho. The book remains a remarkable narrative of a frightening ocean passage. "This is merely the brief sum of what I can recollect," he continued, "of having suffered in this voyage; but praised be the name of Jesus, whose goodness and mercy brought me to safety."

Jorge d'Albuquerque Coelho (1539–1601) was born to Portuguese parents in the colonial outpost of Olinda, the most important settler town in the captaincy of Pernambuco in Brazil. His father, Duarte Coelho Pereira, had served the Portuguese in Southeast Asia from 1511 to 1530. As a child, Jorge was sent by his parents to Lisbon for an education, but he later returned to Brazil and fought to suppress an indigenous rebellion in Pernambuco in

1560. From then until 1565, he led Portuguese forces against native Brazilians; in the process he suffered repeatedly from the wounds of arrows.[9]

On June 29, 1565, the feast-day of Saint Peter and Saint Paul, Coelho left Olinda on a journey intended to take him back to Portugal once again. But as the travelers neared the Azores, a French ship, with far more men on board, raided the Portuguese vessel. Coelho realized that there were Portuguese, Scots, and Englishmen on that ship too, though such knowledge did him no good.

After the French took command of the ship, they invited Coelho, as the captain, to join them for a meal. They even placed him at the head of the table and asked him to say grace "after the Portuguese manner." He proceeded to make the sign of the cross over the food, a gesture that infuriated his French hosts, who were Protestants. Some of them wanted to throw him overboard, but calmer minds prevailed.

As the journey progressed toward France, Coelho hatched a plan to take control of his ship back from the French, who had stationed seventeen men on board. The Portuguese bided their time, waiting for an opportune moment. It never came. Instead, a "most extraordinary and hellish storm of wind" struck the vessel on September 12, leading to the shipwreck that Coelho's narrative describes.

The Naufrágio *was published soon before Coelho died. It was sufficiently popular that a second edition appeared soon after. Perhaps its appeal lay in the unexpected survival of Coelho. Perhaps some readers became engaged by the Portuguese captain's faith, which had led him at one point to toss a crucifix with a piece of the true cross in it overboard lest it fall into the hands of Protestants. Perhaps the account's appeal could be found in Coelho's recounting of an apparition of the Virgin Mary cradling the infant Jesus in her arms above the ship. Whatever the source of readers' desires then, the story remains an almost incredible tale of human survival against the bleakest odds, and a reminder of the kinds of death that thousands of travelers suffered in the sixteenth century.*

The identity of the author was unclear until the historian C. R. Boxer published a translation in 1968. As Boxer points out, a passage in the first chap-

9. For the context of Coelho's account and his family background, see C. R. Boxer, *The Tragic History of the Sea, 1589–1622* (Hakluyt Society, 2nd ser., 112 [Cambridge, 1959]).

ter ascribes the text to Afonso Luís, a pilot who was on the journey as a passenger.

When both of these ships were in the latitude which I have mentioned, on a Wednesday, 12 September, they were struck by the greatest, the most extraordinary and hellish storm of wind from the southeast that ever yet was seen, as can be judged from what it did to us. For the favourable wind which we had hitherto, suddenly dropped, then veered sharply to the southeast and began to blow so violently that we were all frightened at the threatening storm, seeing the rage and fury with which it was beginning to blow. And in this fear we started to take such precautions as are usual in such a crisis, throwing the cargo overboard in order to save our lives. And thus we threw overboard everything which was on the upper deck and between decks; and as the sea ran higher than ever with the increasing force of the storm, we cut away the topmasts and threw overboard all the sea chests in which everyone kept his kit. And lest anyone should find this difficult, Jorge d'Albuquerque was the first to throw overboard the chest in which he kept his clothes and other valuables. And seeing that all this did not suffice, and that the seas were getting so huge that they threatened to swamp us, we threw overboard our artillery and many chests of sugar and many sacks of cotton.

While we were labouring with these difficulties, a sea struck us by the poop which dismantled our rudder, so that within a very few days it dropped off astern, leaving the ship lying ahull; and although we tried to shape a course and let her drive before the wind, all our attempts proved vain. Seeing ourselves in such deadly peril, without a rudder, and with such huge and heavy seas running, some or rather nearly all of us began to lose heart. And Jorge d'Albuquerque seeing us all so affected, and with such good reason, although he himself felt the same way as each and all of us, yet he began to encourage us with brave words, and gave orders to some people how they should try to find some ways of steering the ship, while the others should kneel and pray to Our Lord and Our Lady for deliverance from such trial and tribulation. By this time (which was about nine o'clock in the morning) there was no sign of the French ship; and those Frenchmen who were on board our ship, seeing the raging storm, the rudder loose, the ship lying ahull, and the great confusion aboard her, became so frightened that they all jumped into the waist and came up to our people in a friendly way and said to them: "We are all lost, none of us can escape, since the ship is rudderless and the seas so high." And being thus numbed by fear they did whatever we ordered them, as if they had been the slaves, prisoners and servants of us all. We then rigged up a jury mast and sail abaft the fore castle, to see if we could steer the ship by this means; but no sooner had we done so than a most extraordinary and unheard of thing happened to us. For at ten o'clock in the morning the weather became so thick that it was as black as night, while the sea with the violent clashing of the waves against each other seemed to give light from the white of the foam. The sea and the wind made such a frightful noise that we could hardly hear each other shouting or make ourselves understood.

At this moment, a tremendous sea, much higher than the previous one, bore down directly on the ship, so black and dark below and so white with foam above, that all those who saw it fully realized that it would bring us all to the end of our lives in a few seconds. This sea, crashing over the bow with a gust of wind, broke over the ship in such a manner that it swept away the foremast and sail, yard and shrouds, as well as the bowsprit, the beak-head, and the forecastle with five men inside it, besides three anchors which were stowed there, two on one side and one on the other. In addition to this, it smashed the half-deck in such a way that it killed a sailor underneath it, and broke the ship's boat into four or five pieces, and stove in all the pipes of water and other provisions which were still left. Moreover, this sea so damaged the ship from the bow to the mainmast that it left it level with the sea and waterlogged for about half an hour, with those people below deck having no idea where they were. And seeing themselves in such mortal peril, they were all terrified and scared out of their wits, fearing and believing that their last hour had come. And with this fear they all crowded round a Father of the Company of Jesus, named Alvaro de Lucena, who was a passenger on board, and they made their respective confessions to him, in the briefest possible terms, as time did not permit of anything more. And after they had all made their confessions, and begged pardon of each other, they all fell on their knees, begging Our Lord for mercy and taking as their mediator Our Lady the Most Holy Virgin, Mother of the Son of God, Lady of Luz and of Guadalupe. The sea and the wind waxed stronger hourly, and everything was so terrifying with the thunder claps and lightning flashes, that it seemed as if the end of the world had come. Jorge d'Albuquerque, seeing the miserable condition of himself and his companions, gathering strength from weakness (into which he had fallen at the unhappiness of seeing his friends and himself in the state which they were) began to encourage them in a loud voice, with these words: "My friends and comrades, we deserve to be afflicted with much worse hardships than those which we are suffering now; because if we were to be punished according to the measure of our sins, then the sea would have already devoured us. But let us all trust in the mercy of that Lord whose compassion is infinite, that He will take pity on us for His own sake and will deliver us out of this tribulation. Let us help ourselves with the arms that are necessary in such a crisis, which are heartfelt repentance of our past sins, and the determination not to sin again, and this in the steadfast faith and hope in the goodness of Him who created us and redeemed us with His precious blood, that He may vouchsafe us His mercy, not regarding our faults, for He is capable of everything, being allwise and all powerful as He is. Let us remember that never yet did anyone implore God for mercy with a pure heart and be refused. Therefore let us all ask Him for it, and meanwhile try to do everything we can to save ourselves, some of us working at the pump, others bailing out the water from the waist and between decks, so long as we have life and hope that Our Lord will supply through His great mercy and goodness what is wanting in our hands. And if it should please Him to dispose of us otherwise, then let each one of us accept this patiently, since He alone knows what is best for us." With these words and many others which he said, some people at once went to man the pumps, while others bailed out the water above and below decks. The French who were left in our ship (for their own had disappeared at the beginning of the storm), seeing themselves in this tribulation, fell on their knees and raised their hands to call on God, which up till then they had not done; and they asked us Portuguese for pardon, saying that this storm had arisen because of their sins, begging us to pray to God for them, since they gave themselves up for lost, as the ship was in the state which we all saw.

While some of us were thus manning the pump, and others bailing out the water, and those who were not otherwise employed were on their knees praying to Our Lord to save them in their great distress, a third most enormous sea struck us with a gust of wind on the stern quarter. This carried away the mainmast, yard, sails, and shrouds, as also part of the poop and the cabins, together with the mizzen-mast and one of the leading Frenchmen. Our men working at the pump were flung all over the waist, some of them breaking their arms and others their legs. Jorge d'Albuquerque received such a blow that his right hand was maimed for nearly a year; and one of his servants named Antonio Moreira broke his arm and died of his injury a few days later. The others who were standing near him in the waist were covered by the sea for such a long time that they all thought they were drowned. So much water poured in from this sea, since the half-deck was already smashed, that the ship was left quite helpless for a considerable time, and there was so much water in the waist and the quarterdeck that it almost came up to our knees. And when Jorge d'Albuquerque told them to find out how much water the ship was making below decks, they found that with another three spans she would have been completely waterlogged. Everyone seeing themselves so overwhelmed with tribulations, which increased with every moment, so likewise did their plaintive cries increase as they implored Our Lord for mercy, with the grief which filled them at the prospect of imminent and certain death. Jorge d' Albuquerque, finding himself and his companions at the last gasp, and so bereft of help, strength and comfort, and seeing that some people were so faint hearted, he went up to them and said: "My friends and brothers, you have every reason to dread greatly the danger and tribulation in which we all are now, for you can see that human help no longer avails us this is just what gives us a much greater motive to trust in the mercy of Our Lord, with which He usually helps those who completely abandon all hope of human remedy. Wherefore I earnestly entreat you all, that trusting in Him like we ought to do as Christians that we are, we should implore Him to extend His helping hand to us, since we have no other recourse whatsoever. As for myself, I assure you that I hope that in His goodness He will save us from the danger in which we are, and that I will yet see myself safe on land, where I will recount this many times, so that the world will learn of the mercy that Our Lord vouchsafed towards us."

As he finished saying this, they all saw a refulgent splendour in the middle of the heavily overcast sky above them, whereupon they all fell on their knees, saying in loud voices: "Good Jesu help us! Good Jesu have mercy on us! Virgin Mother of God pray for us!" And each one with the most devout words of which he was capable commended himself and his comrades to Our Lady the Virgin, advocate of sinners. The sea was raging so terribly and fearfully that I believe it had never looked so awe-inspiring. The seas that broke over the ship were so huge that they opened the seams and threw in such a quantity of sand that it was amazing. And the people who were struck by the waves were so covered in sand that they were nearly blinded and could hardly see each other. For this reason they suspected that they must be over some sandbanks or shallows, for it seemed impossible that the waves could fling such a quantity of sand into the ship unless she was in shallow water. On the other hand, the storm was such, that we could well believe that this mass of sand which was thrown into the ship had been dredged up from the depths of the sea. The wind howled around the ship with such fury that nobody dared to appear on the deck, save only Jorge d'Albuquerque, the master, and two or three men who were making the sign of the cross while awaiting the seas which battered the ship as if they wished to break her open and all this with such thunder and lightning that it seemed as if all the devils in hell were loose.

On top of these tribulations we met with another greater and unexpected one, which caused us much anxiety. This was that the mainmast when it was broken and went by the board in the storm, was caught by the masthead in the shrouds on the leeward side; and being held fast in this way, it drifted under the ship to the windward side, and with each successive wave, it was dashed against the ship like a battering ram, and with such violence that it seemed as if it would smash in the hull. Seeing all these setbacks, we gave ourselves up for lost, feeling each blow that the mast gave against the ship as if it had been inflicted on each one of us. And with each new tribulation that occurred, we all raised our voices imploring God for mercy, and begging Him to deliver us from the deadly danger in which we were placed by our own mast. His infinite goodness was pleased to send some seas which disengaged the mast from the ship and thus freed us from that unexpected tribulation. Let anyone who reads this, judge how people in that state we were in must have felt, overwhelmed by so many trials and tribulations, in which we had no other alleviation than the tears and sighs with which we implored Our Lord to remember us. For there was no question of either eating or drinking, since it was three days that we had done either, for this was as long as the storm raged, although the height of it lasted for about nine hours. But during the whole of these three days, we were almost submerged by the sea, working the pump night and day, seeing death in front of us and expecting to meet it hourly. And we were still more certain of it when at the end of those three days we found ourselves without a rudder, without masts, nor sails, nor yards, nor shrouds, nor cables, nor anchors, nor boat, and without any drinking water and provisions. Including the Frenchmen, we numbered nearly fifty people, and the ship was leaking so badly in many places that it seemed as if she was foundering, and we were 240 leagues from land. This storm was so fierce that it struck us in 43° Northern latitude and left us in 47°, without masts or sails. One thing I can affirm, and that is that what little is written here is as different from what we actually endured as a painting is from real life.

Concerning a miracle that happened to us

On the day that the storm broke, Jorge d'Albuquerque, on the advice of some of his companions, ordered to be thrown into the sea a cross of gold, in which was inserted a fragment of the Holy Wood of the True Cross and many other relics, the said cross being tied with a twist of green silk to a very strong cord, with a large nail as a weight, the end of this cord being tied to the ship's poop. And after the storm was over, Jorge d'Albuquerque bethought him of his reliquary, and he went to the poop to see if the cord with which it was tied was still there. He found that it had got tangled up with some nails so he earnestly begged and entreated Afonso Luís, the pilot who had embarked as a passenger, to allow himself to be lowered at a rope's end so that he could free the cord with which the reliquary was tied, which Afonso Luís accordingly did. And having freed the cord, he told those on the poop to haul it up, and a man named Graviel Damil hauling the whole length of the cord up inside the ship, the cross fell on the quarterdeck quite untied and free, wrapped up in a little piece of cotton. All of us were astounded on seeing this miracle, and we gave many thanks to Our Lord for comforting and encouraging us with so great a miracle, by which it seemed to us that He wished to show us that He would miraculously deliver us from shipwreck, just as He had delivered the Reliquary-Cross from such a storm. This cross besides being tied to the cord with a silken twist was originally held fast by the twist running through the ring of the said cross, and how it had come untied and yet come up on deck with the cord, Our Lord alone knows. Suffice it to say that when we got the cord and the nail up into the ship, the said cross just fell among us standing there, not tied to anything and with its ring broken, though the silken twist was still tied to the cord as it had been when thrown into the sea. While our people were in transports of joy over such a miracle, many of the Frenchmen who were in the ship gathered round to see what we were so pleased about; and although all our people kissed the relics in front of the French with great devotion, it seems that Our Lord did not allow the latter to see what they were actually doing; for I am convinced that if they had seen them they would have taken them, as they were of gold, which they covet so greatly. And not only did they not see them then, but they did not on any other of the days when Jorge d'Albuquerque had them on his person, for whereas they often felt him to see if he was carrying anything concealed, they never found them. For which we must give many thanks to Our Lord for this miracle, and for the others which He wrought on behalf of all of us during this shipwreck. We did not fail to note, those of us who were there, that perchance Our Lord wished to grant us this favour on account of the Wood of the Holy Cross, and because of the sign of the cross that Jorge d'Albuquerque had made when saying grace at the Frenchmen's table, on which account they wanted to kill him or to throw him overboard. It seems that Our Lord permitted that this cross with the Holy Wood and relics which were therein should not be lost but should be returned to the hand of the said Jorge d'Albuquerque, since he had offered to die out of love for this holy sign of the cross, to which he always showed himself devoutly attached throughout the whole voyage. And he told us several times that he had always felt this way since childhood, and that this devotion was inherited by him, because in all the four shields of the arms which he bore by virtue of his descent from two paternal and two maternal grandparents, the cross figured in all of them, which are the arms of the Albuquerques, the Coelhos, from whom he is directly descended, the Pereiras and the Bulhões.

Document 37

Travels in England (1599)

By Thomas Platter, *Travels in England, 1599,* trans. Clare Williams (London, 1937), 171–73

Thomas Platter (fl. 1599), a native of Basel, crossed the English Channel from Calais to Dover on September 16, 1599. After prescribing some remedies for the city's mayor and spending the night at an inn, he rode on a post horse twelve miles to Canterbury, had a drink, and then rode another twelve miles to Sittingbourne. At that point he joined others and rode in a wagon through "many very dangerous localities as report has it," he wrote, arriving near dawn at Rochester, and then proceeding to Gravesend, where he spent his second night in the country. Then he boarded a small craft and sailed twenty-two miles down the Thames to London, a city so much grander than any other settlement that Platter wrote "that London is not said to be in England, but rather England to be in London." He had been in England for only two days, yet he knew that he was seeing something remarkable. "This city of London is so large and splendidly built," he added, "so populous and excellent in crafts and merchant citizens, and so prosperous, that it is not only the first in the whole realm of England, but is esteemed one of the most famous in all Christendom."

Once in the city, Platter took careful note of the hustle and bustle along the Thames and in the crowded blocks of London itself. The ebb and flow of the tide brought 100 large ships into the city, more than he had ever seen in a single port. He stood amazed at London Bridge, with its twenty arches and finely wrought merchant dwellings along it, and recorded that he saw at least thirty skulls of executed criminals impaled on stakes on one of the towers. He marveled at the commerce of merchants whose business took them or their wares across the earth. Platter even visited the Tower of London and saw its collection of royal armor and weaponry, along with the "ropes used to rack malefactors" in the dungeon. On September 20 he visited Whitehall, "where the Queen when in London holds her court." He saw her library which contained "many books written in Latin with her own hand," one notable sign of the intellectual gifts of the monarch.

While Platter was in the city he took in the sights that attracted any visitor. He saw plays and cockfights and went to see a twice-weekly spectacle, held every Sunday and Wednesday, in which English mastiffs battled bears and bulls. He drank in taverns and noted the "particularly curious" fact that women drank along with men. In those same dank inns he watched the English smoke tobacco, which "they regard as a curious medicine for defluctions" but which had also become such a common habit that the English smoked wherever they went. Since he was obviously keen to see anything of note, it is not surprising that he eventually made his way to a well-known cabinet of curiosity, a place where a Mr. Cope displayed the items from around the world that he had collected. Though such cabinets were not an English invention, the details that Platter provides here suggest that the acquisitive desires that had been obvious in Europe for at least a century were well suited to an age of long-distance exploration.

This same Mr. Cope inhabits a fine house in the Snecgas; he led us into an apartment, stuffed with queer foreign objects in every corner, and amongst other things I saw there, the following seemed of interest.

1. An African charm made of teeth.
2. Many weapons, arrows and other things made of fishbone.
3. Beautiful Indian plumes, ornaments and clothes from China.

4. A handsome cap made out of goosefoots from China.

5. A curious Javanese costume.

6. A felt cloak from Arabia.

7. Shoes from many strange lands.

8. An Indian stone axe, like a thunder-bolt.

9. Beautiful coats from Arabia.

10. A string instrument with but one string.

11. Another string instrument from Arabia.

12. The horn and tail of a rhinoceros, is a large animal like an elephant.

13. A fan made out of a single leaf.

14. Curious wooden and stone swords.

15. The twisted horn of a bull seal.

16. A round horn which had grown on an English woman's forehead.

17. An embalmed child (Mumia).

18. Leathern weapons.

19. The bauble and bells of Henry VIII's fool.

20. A unicorn's tail.

21. Inscribed paper made of bark.

22. Indian stone shears.

23. A thunder-bolt dug out of a mast which was hit at sea during a storm; resembles the Judas stone.

24. A stone against spleen disorders.

25. Artful little Chinese box.

26. Earthen pitchers from China.

27. Flying rhinoceros.

28. (Caterpillar) Hairy worm, sidopendra.

29. Flies which glow at night in Virginia instead of lights, since there is often no day there for over a month.

30. A small bone implement used in India for scratching oneself.

31. The Queen of England's seal.

32. Turkish Emperor's golden seal.

33. Porcelain from China.

34. Falcon's head made of fine feathers.

35. Many holy relics from a Spanish ship which he helped to capture.

36. A Madonna made of Indian feathers.

37. A Turkish pitcher and dishes.

38. An Indian chain made of monkey teeth.

39. A sea-halcyon's nest, sign of a calm sea.

40. A pelican's beak, the Egyptian bird that kills its young, and after-
    wards tears open its breast and bathes them in its own blood, until
    they have come to life.
41. A mirror which both reflects and multiplies objects.
42. Crowns made of claws (ungulis).
43. Heathen idols.
44. Saddles from many strange lands; they were placed round the top
    on stands.
45. Two beautifully dyed Indian shepskins with silken shen.
46. Remora. A little fish which holds up or hinders boats from sailing
    when it touches them, likewise another species called "torpedo"
    which petrifies and numbs the crews' hands if it so much as touches
    the oars.
47. A sea mouse (mus marinus).
48. Numerous boned instruments.
49. Reed pipes like those played by Pan.
50. A long narrow Indian canoe, with the oars and sliding planks, hung
    from the ceiling of this room.

He possessed besides many old heathen coins, fine pictures, all kinds of
corals and sea-plants in abundance. There are also other people in London
interested in curios, but this gentleman is superior to them all for strange
objects, because of the Indian voyage he carried out with such zeal. In one
house on the Thames bridge I also beheld a large live camel.

Index